A Certain Magical Index

CHUYA KOGINO
ORIGINAL STORY:
KAZUMA KAMACHI
CHARACTER DESIGN:
KIYOTAKA HAIMURA

20

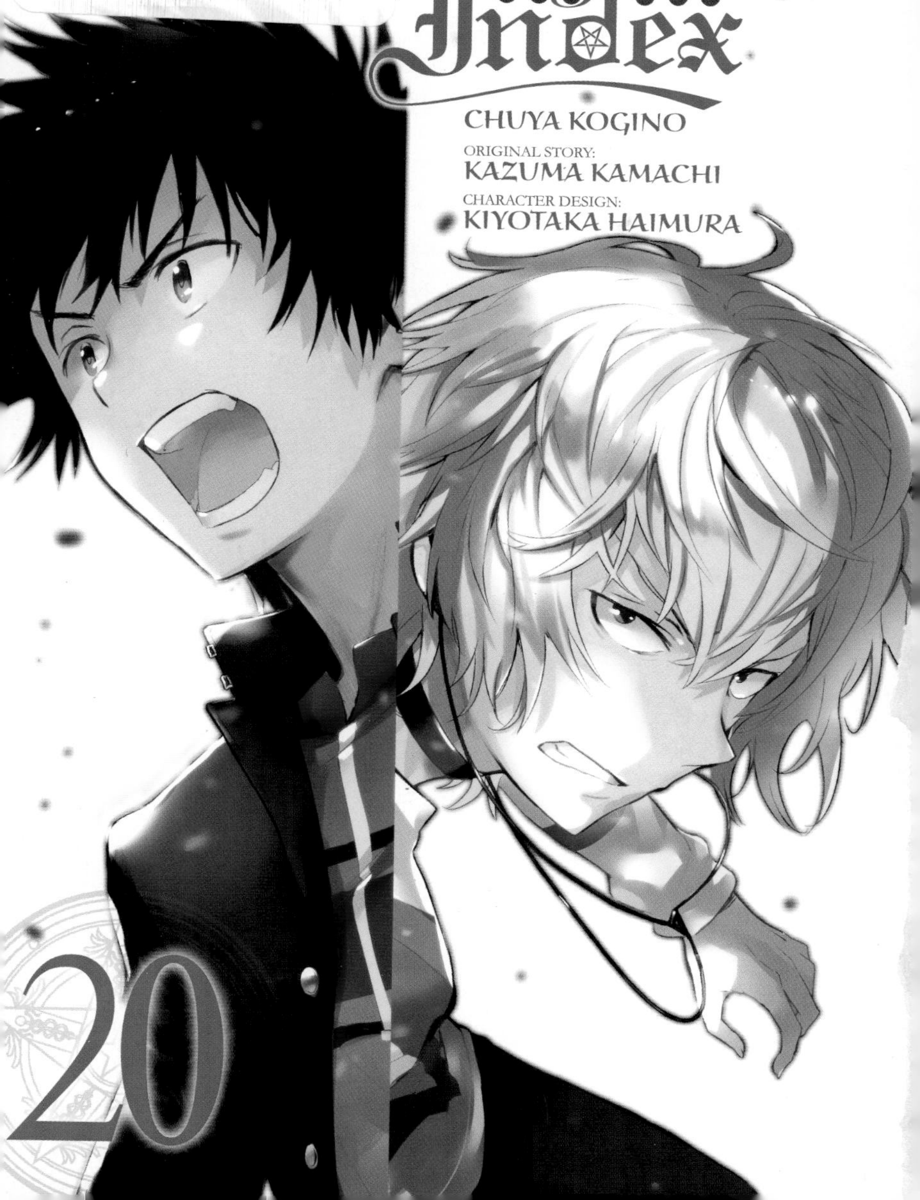

A CERTAIN MAGICAL INDEX ⑳ TABLE OF CONTENTS

Index Librorum Prohibitorum

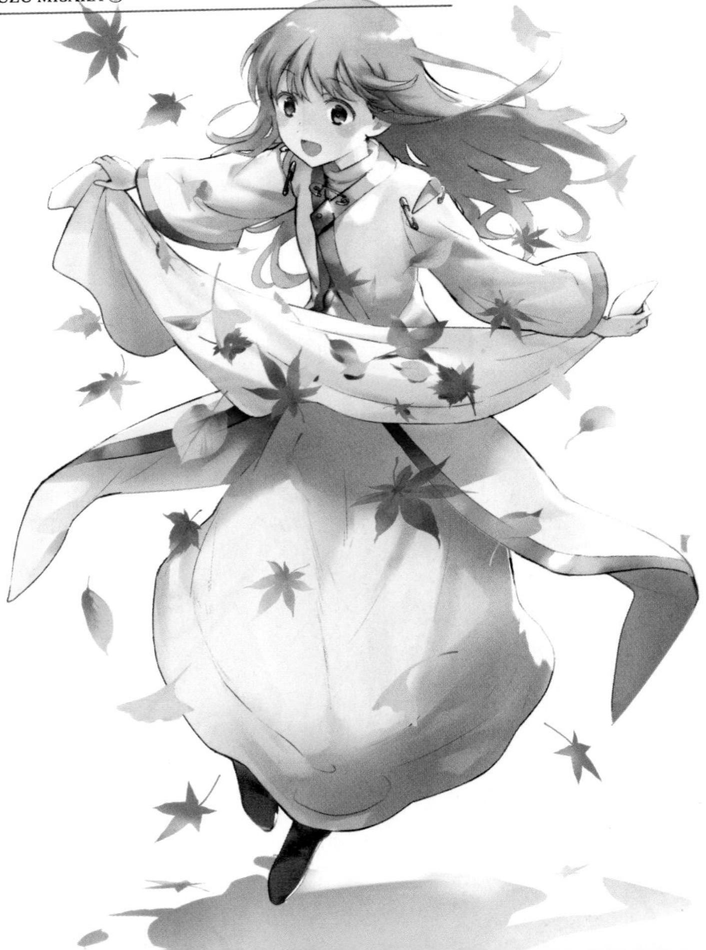

#117 GROUP ①

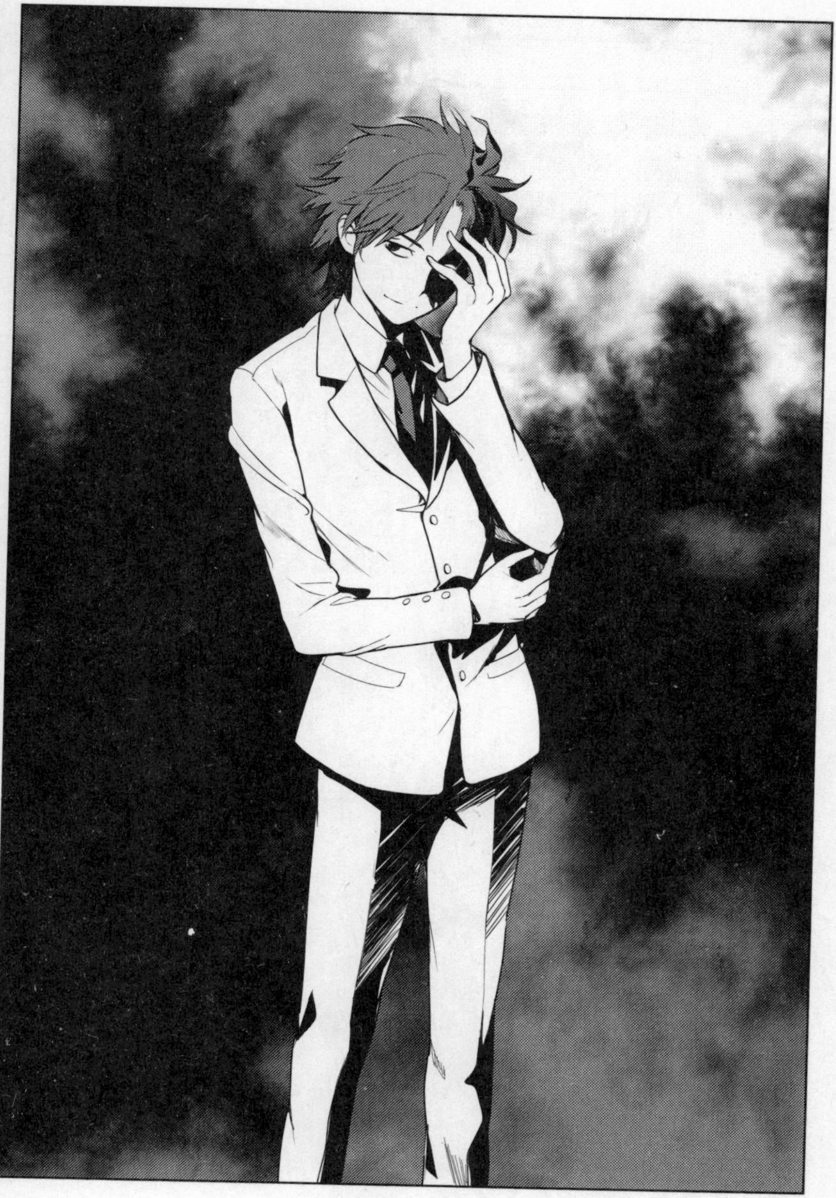

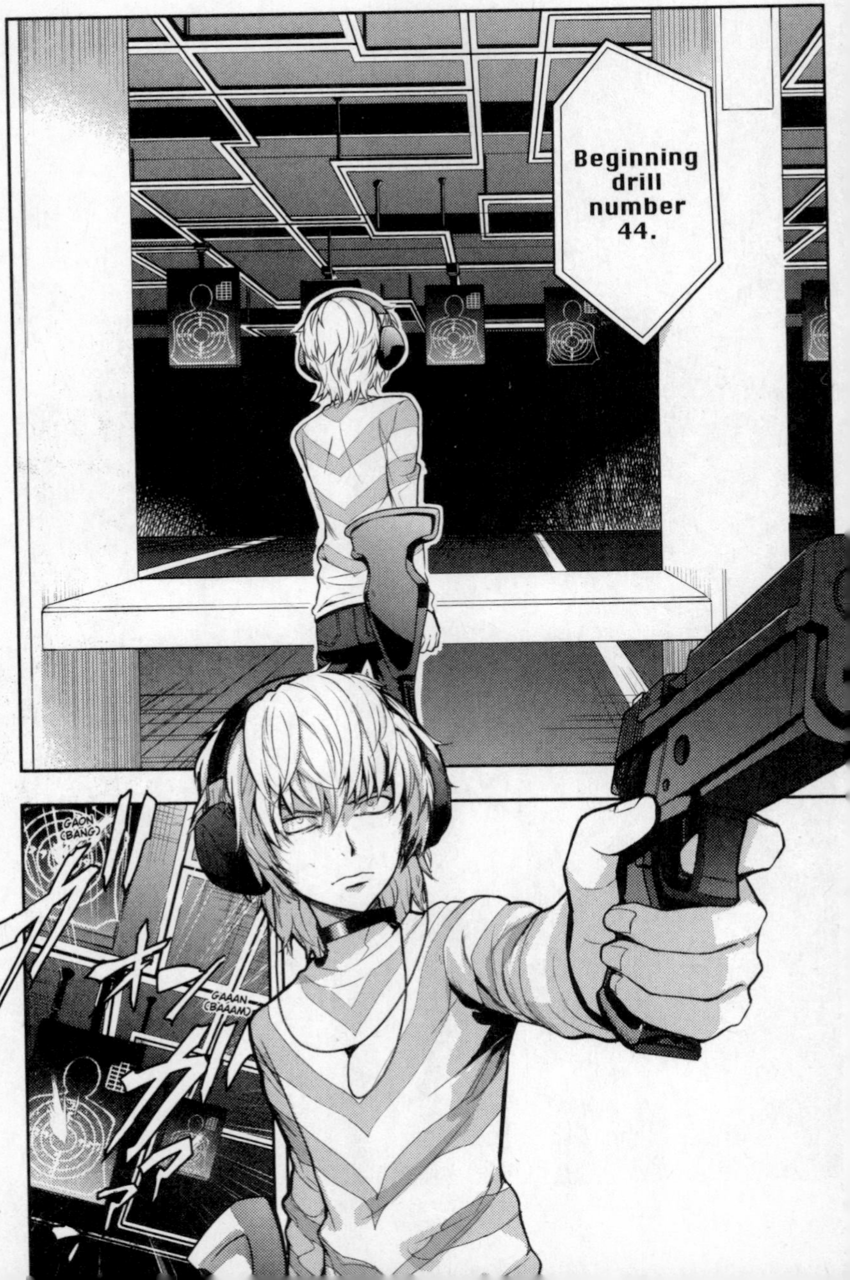
Beginning drill number 44.
GAON (BANG)
GAAAN (BAAAM)

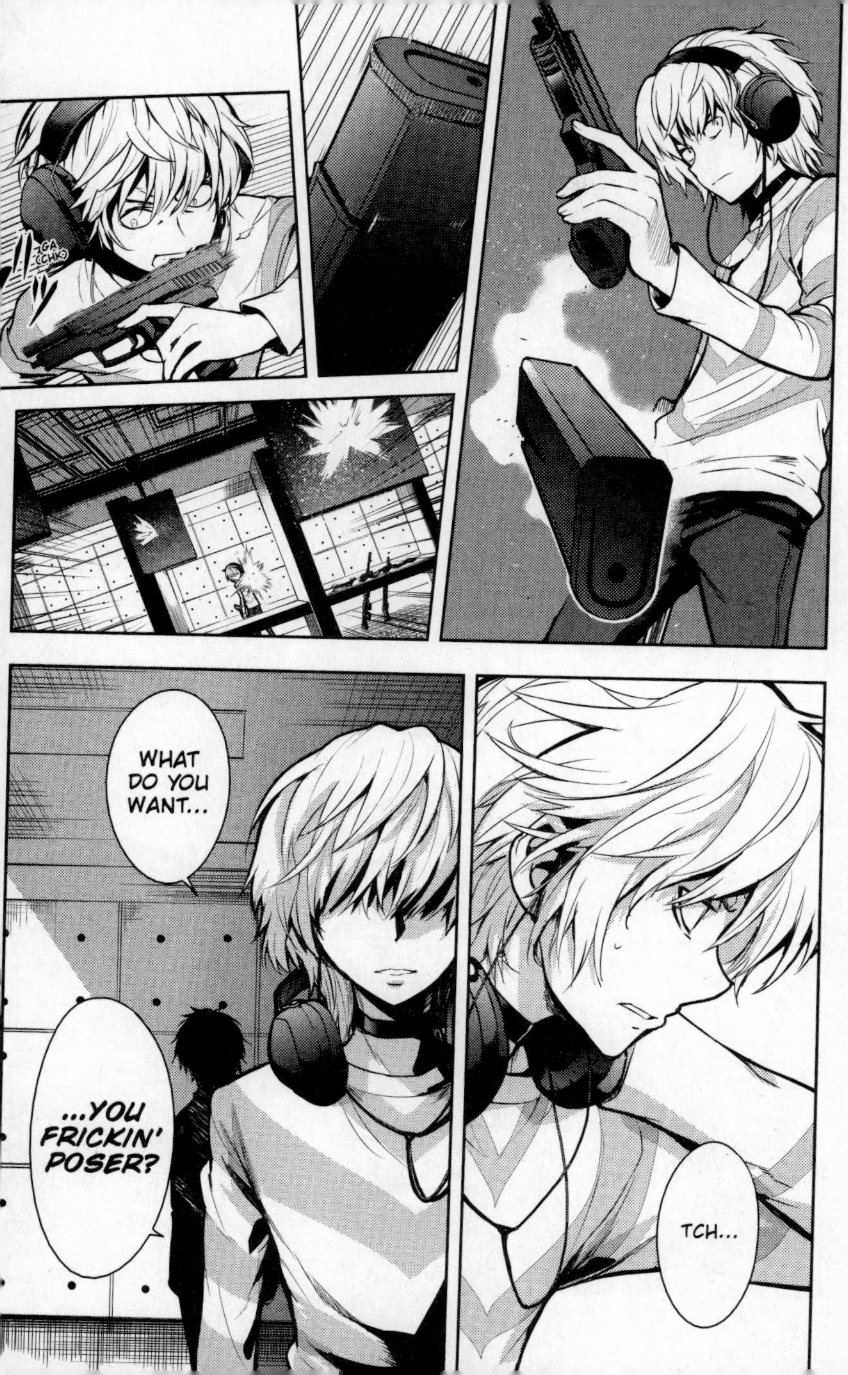
GA CHK
TCH...
WHAT DO YOU WANT...
...YOU FRICKIN' POSER?

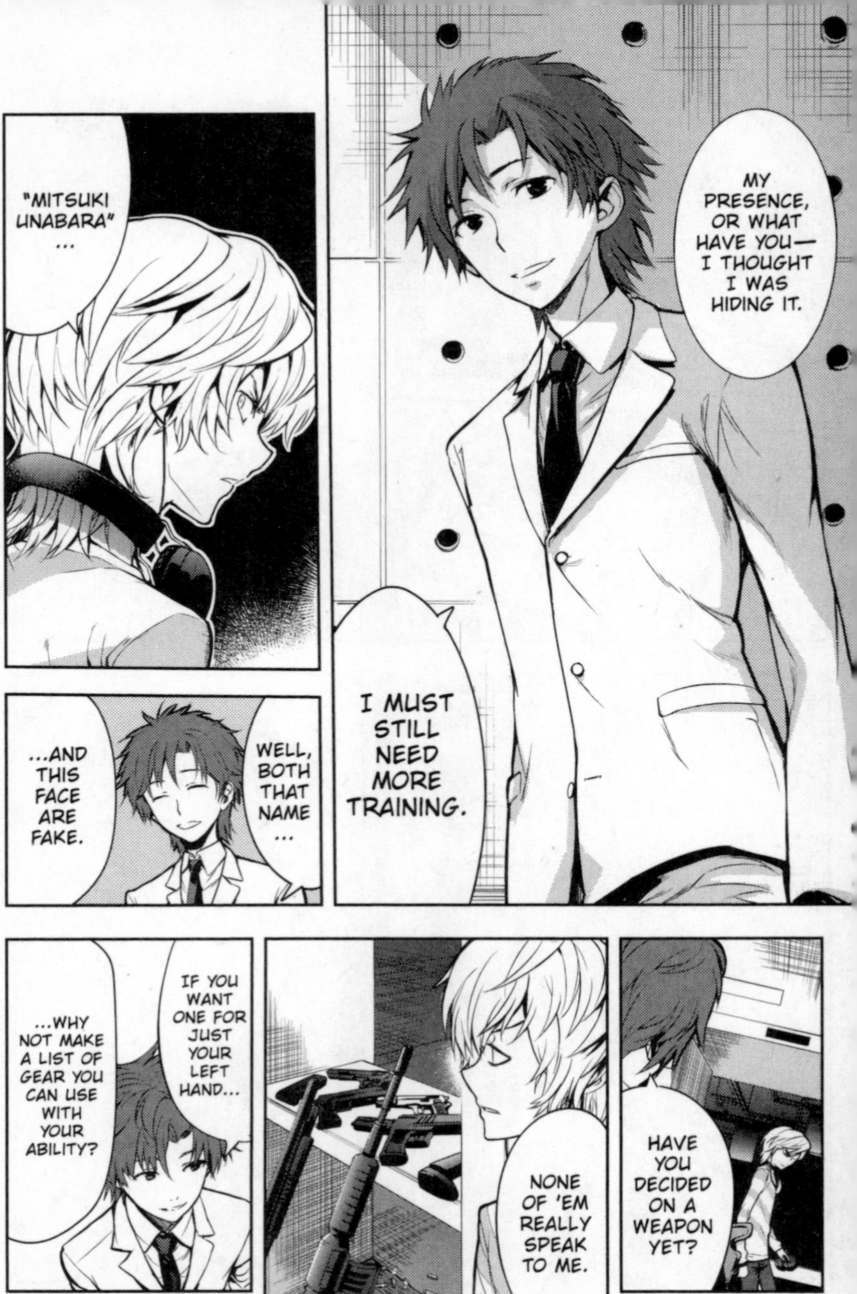
MY PRESENCE, OR WHAT HAVE YOU— I THOUGHT I WAS HIDING IT.
I MUST STILL NEED MORE TRAINING.
"MITSUKI UNABARA" ...
WELL, BOTH THAT NAME ...
...AND THIS FACE ARE FAKE.
HAVE YOU DECIDED ON A WEAPON YET?
NONE OF 'EM REALLY SPEAK TO ME.
IF YOU WANT ONE FOR JUST YOUR LEFT HAND...
...WHY NOT MAKE A LIST OF GEAR YOU CAN USE WITH YOUR ABILITY?

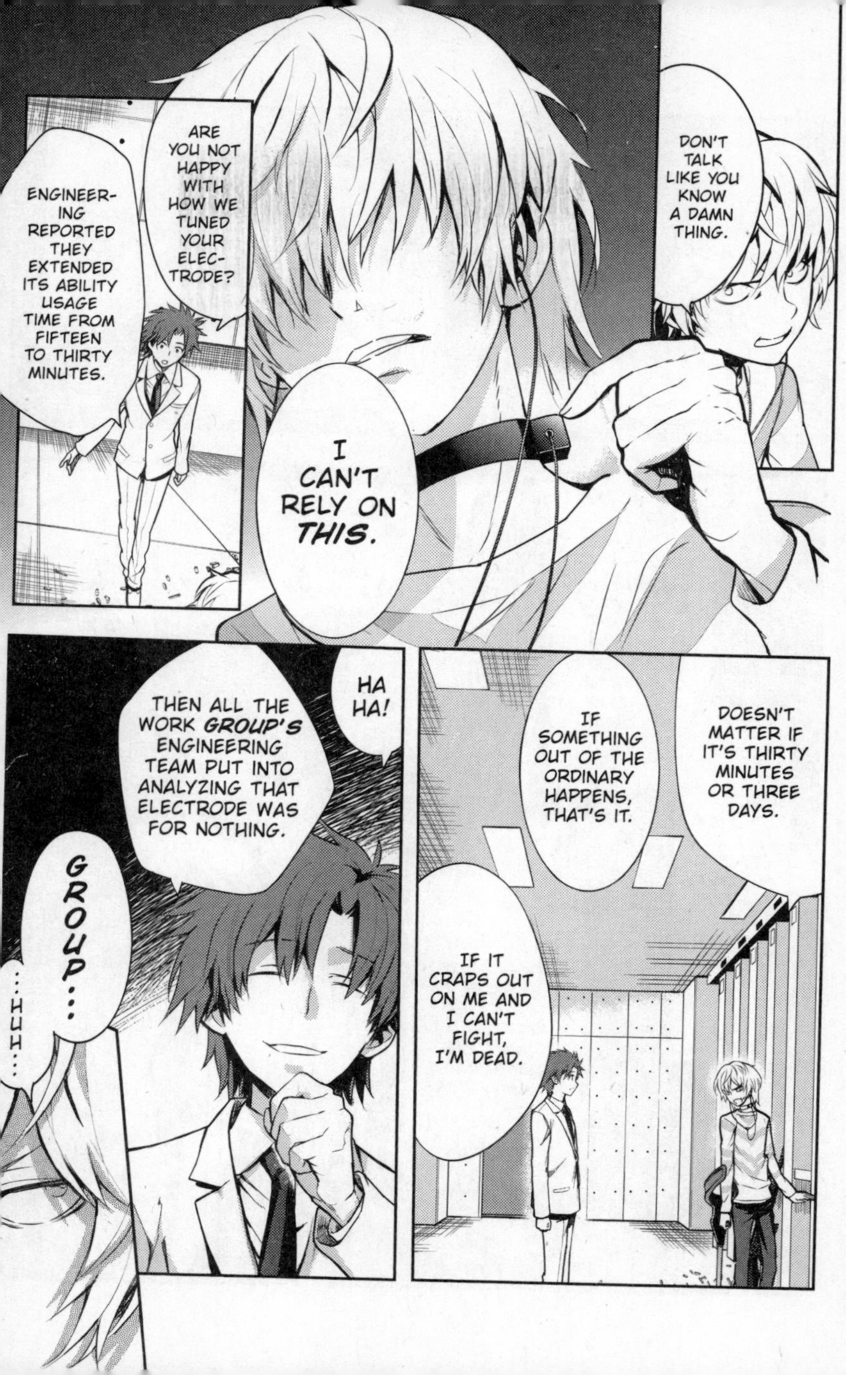
DON'T TALK LIKE YOU KNOW A DAMN THING.
I CAN'T RELY ON *THIS*.
ARE YOU NOT HAPPY WITH HOW WE TUNED YOUR ELECTRODE?
ENGINEERING REPORTED THEY EXTENDED ITS ABILITY USAGE TIME FROM FIFTEEN TO THIRTY MINUTES.
DOESN'T MATTER IF IT'S THIRTY MINUTES OR THREE DAYS.
IF SOMETHING OUT OF THE ORDINARY HAPPENS, THAT'S IT.
IF IT CRAPS OUT ON ME AND I CAN'T FIGHT, I'M DEAD.
HA HA!
THEN ALL THE WORK *GROUP'S* ENGINEERING TEAM PUT INTO ANALYZING THAT ELECTRODE WAS FOR NOTHING.
GROUP...
...HUH...

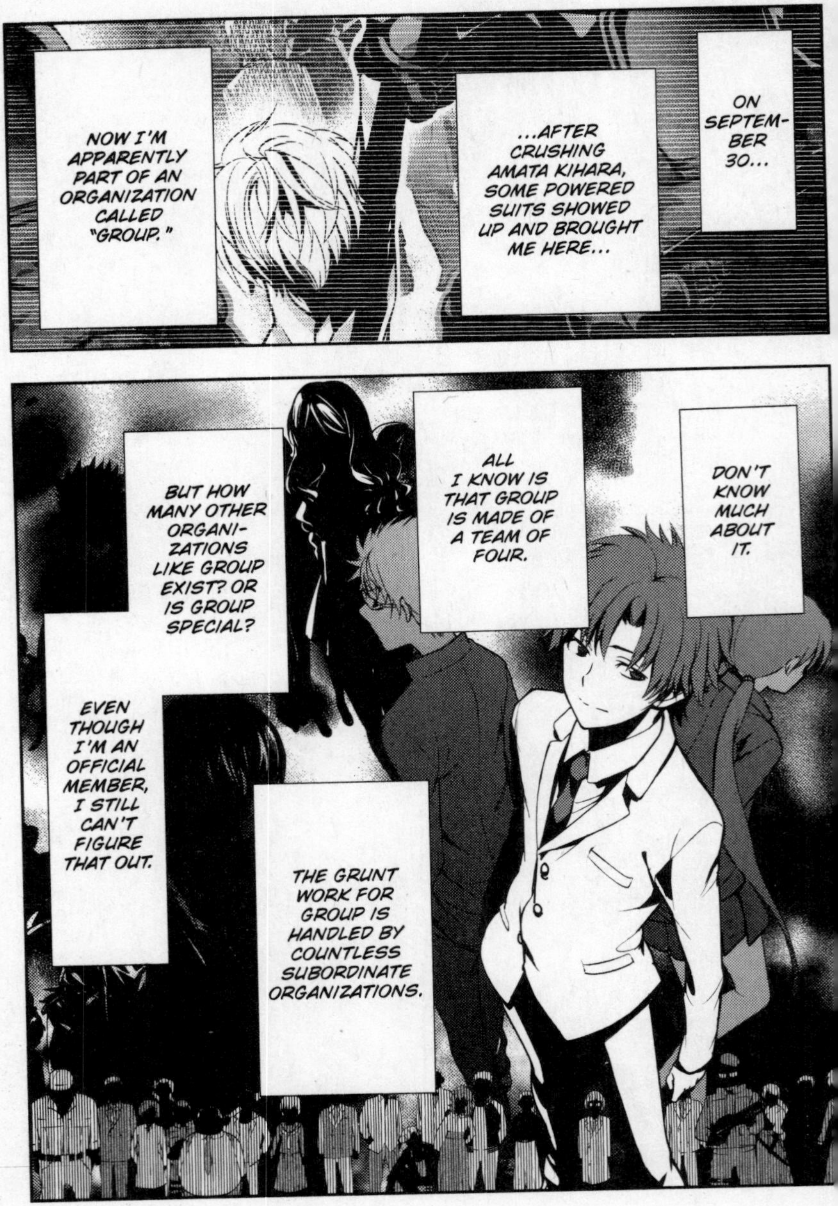
ON SEPTEMBER 30...
...AFTER CRUSHING AMATA KIHARA, SOME POWERED SUITS SHOWED UP AND BROUGHT ME HERE...
NOW I'M APPARENTLY PART OF AN ORGANIZATION CALLED "GROUP."
DON'T KNOW MUCH ABOUT IT.
ALL I KNOW IS THAT GROUP IS MADE OF A TEAM OF FOUR.
THE GRUNT WORK FOR GROUP IS HANDLED BY COUNTLESS SUBORDINATE ORGANIZATIONS.
BUT HOW MANY OTHER ORGANIZATIONS LIKE GROUP EXIST? OR IS GROUP SPECIAL?
EVEN THOUGH I'M AN OFFICIAL MEMBER, I STILL CAN'T FIGURE THAT OUT.

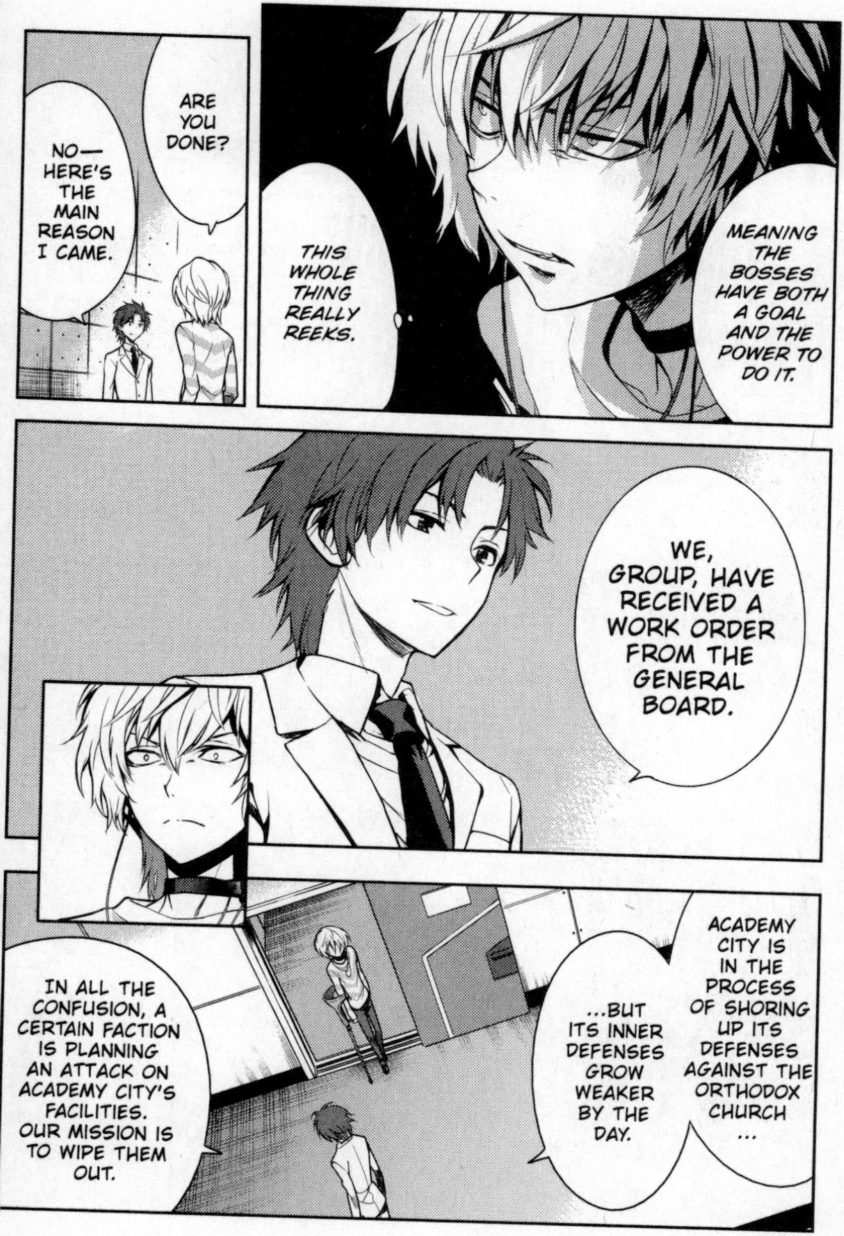
MEANING THE BOSSES HAVE BOTH A GOAL AND THE POWER TO DO IT.
THIS WHOLE THING REALLY REEKS.
ARE YOU DONE?
NO— HERE'S THE MAIN REASON I CAME.
WE, GROUP, HAVE RECEIVED A WORK ORDER FROM THE GENERAL BOARD.
ACADEMY CITY IS IN THE PROCESS OF SHORING UP ITS DEFENSES AGAINST THE ORTHODOX CHURCH ...
...BUT ITS INNER DEFENSES GROW WEAKER BY THE DAY.
IN ALL THE CONFUSION, A CERTAIN FACTION IS PLANNING AN ATTACK ON ACADEMY CITY'S FACILITIES. OUR MISSION IS TO WIPE THEM OUT.

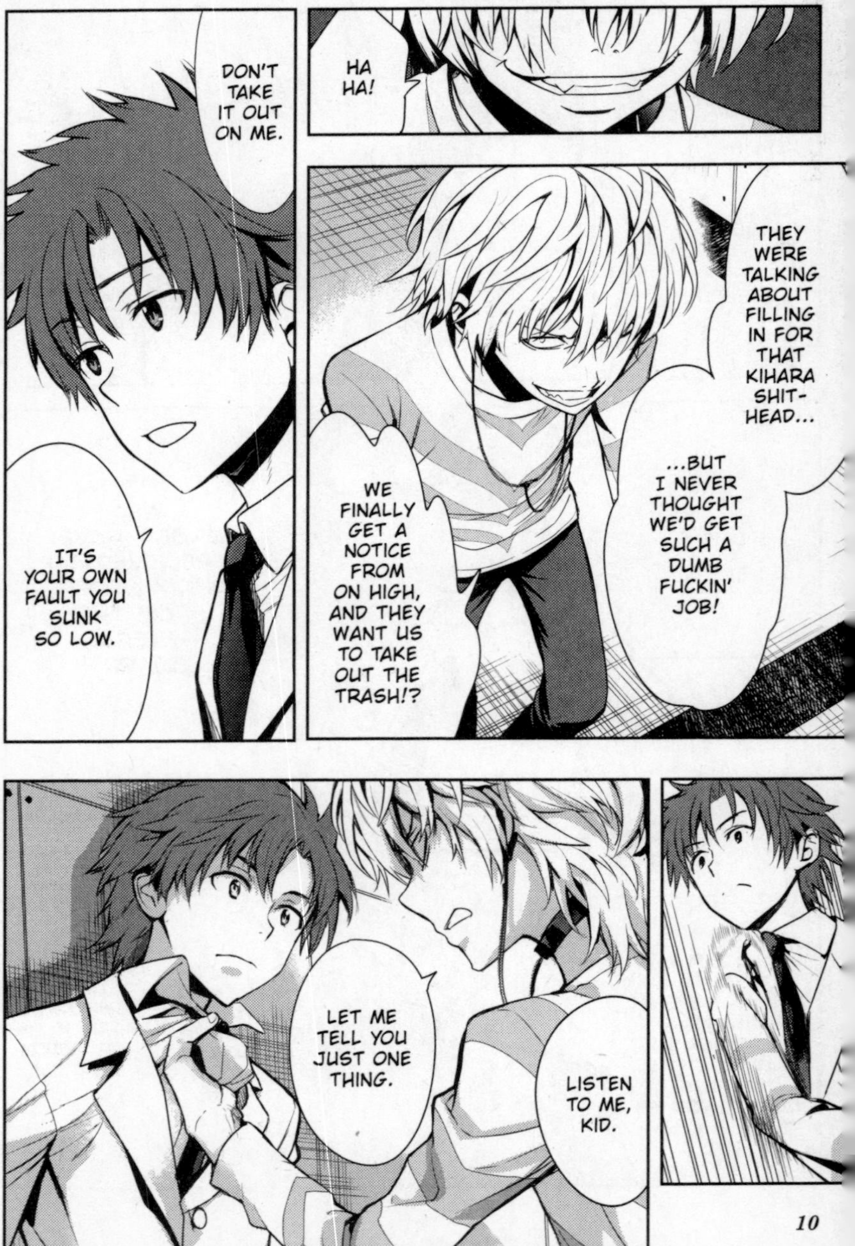
HA HA!
THEY WERE TALKING ABOUT FILLING IN FOR THAT KIHARA SHIT-HEAD...
...BUT I NEVER THOUGHT WE'D GET SUCH A DUMB FUCKIN' JOB!
WE FINALLY GET A NOTICE FROM ON HIGH, AND THEY WANT US TO TAKE OUT THE TRASH!?
DON'T TAKE IT OUT ON ME.
IT'S YOUR OWN FAULT YOU SUNK SO LOW.
LISTEN TO ME, KID.
LET ME TELL YOU JUST ONE THING.

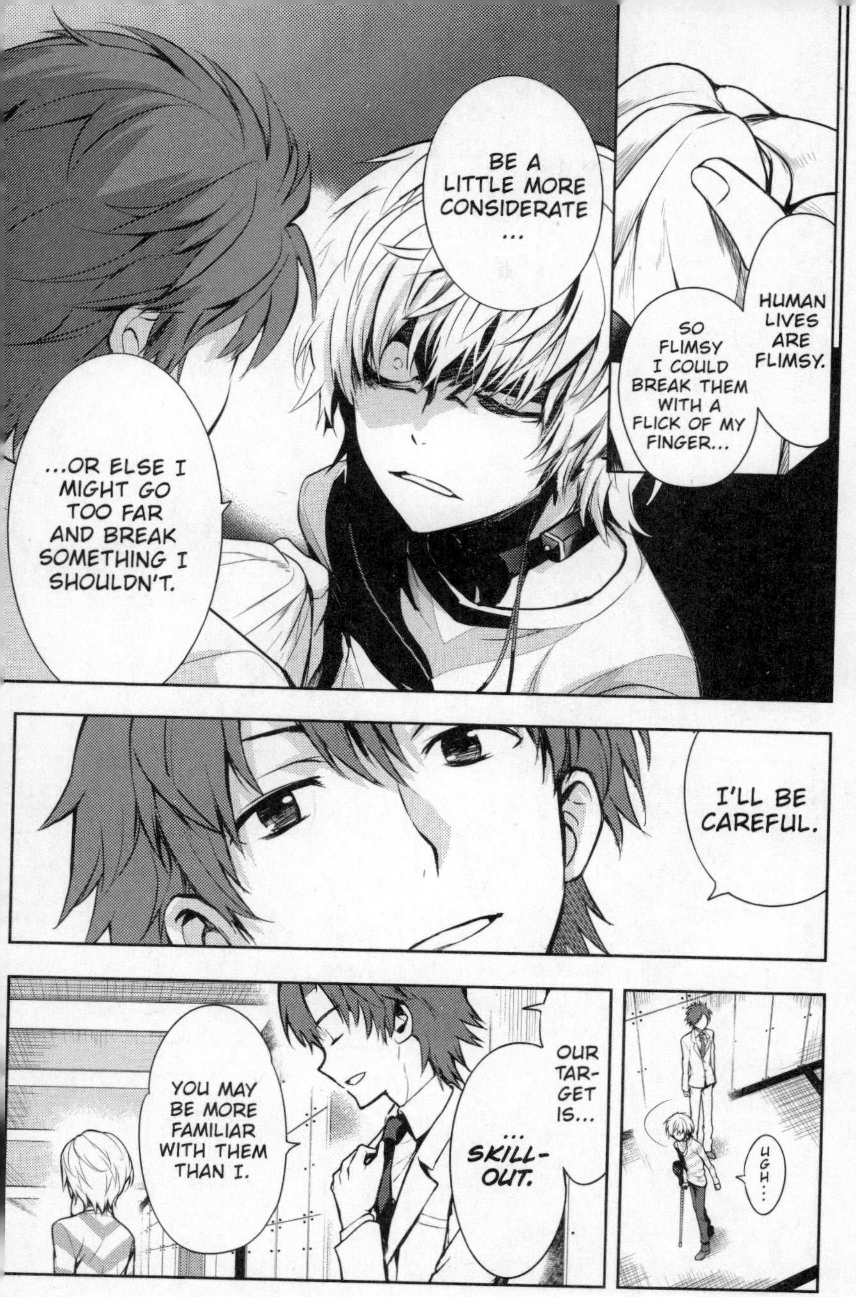
HUMAN LIVES ARE FLIMSY.
SO FLIMSY I COULD BREAK THEM WITH A FLICK OF MY FINGER...
BE A LITTLE MORE CONSIDERATE ...
...OR ELSE I MIGHT GO TOO FAR AND BREAK SOMETHING I SHOULDN'T.
I'LL BE CAREFUL.
UGH...
OUR TAR-GET IS...
... SKILL-OUT.
YOU MAY BE MORE FAMILIAR WITH THEM THAN I.

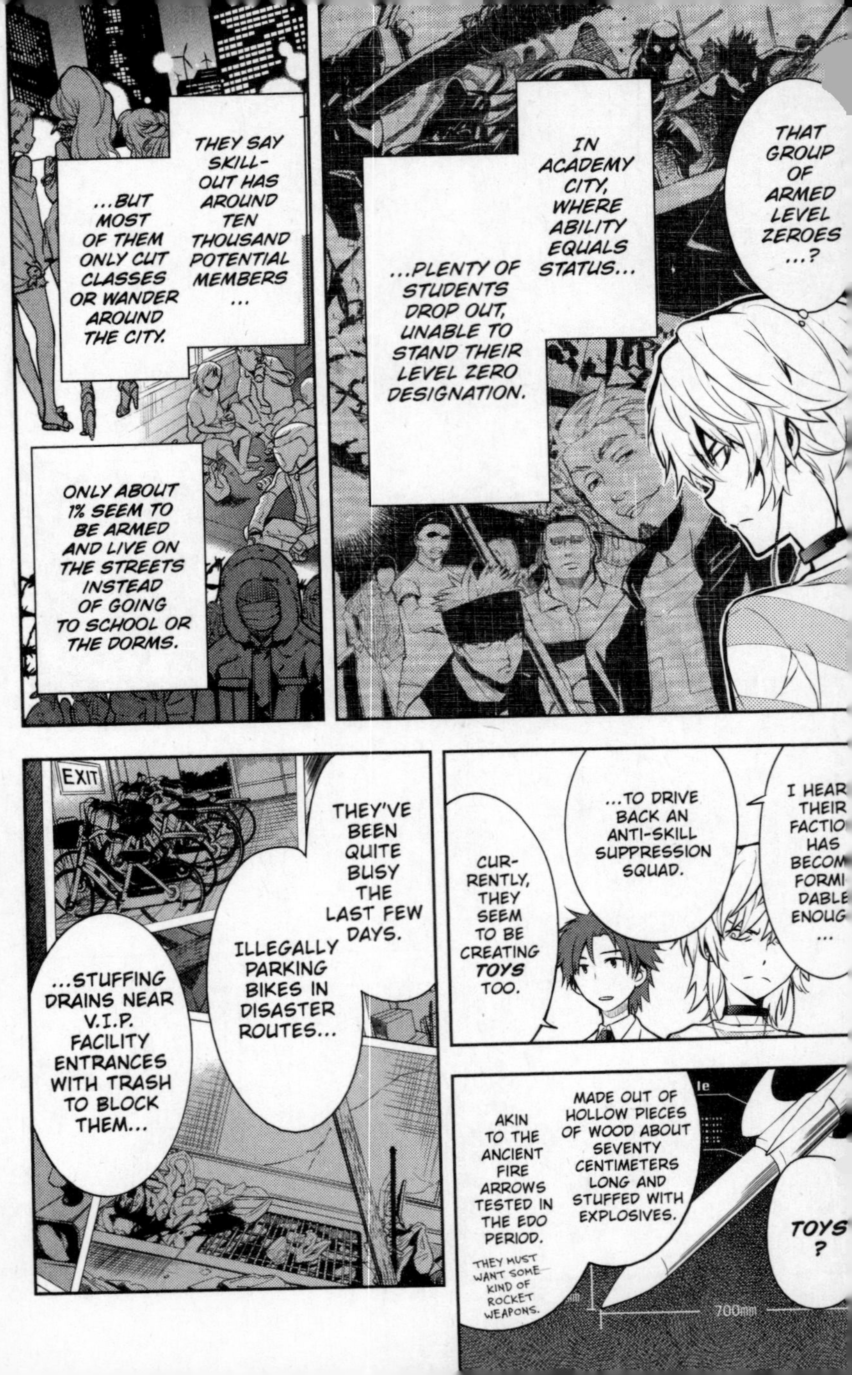
THAT GROUP OF ARMED LEVEL ZEROES ...?
IN ACADEMY CITY, WHERE ABILITY EQUALS STATUS...
...PLENTY OF STUDENTS DROP OUT, UNABLE TO STAND THEIR LEVEL ZERO DESIGNATION.
THEY SAY SKILL-OUT HAS AROUND TEN THOUSAND POTENTIAL MEMBERS ...
...BUT MOST OF THEM ONLY CUT CLASSES OR WANDER AROUND THE CITY.
ONLY ABOUT 1% SEEM TO BE ARMED AND LIVE ON THE STREETS INSTEAD OF GOING TO SCHOOL OR THE DORMS.
I HEAR THEIR FACTIO HAS BECOM FORMIDABLE ENOUG ...
...TO DRIVE BACK AN ANTI-SKILL SUPPRESSION SQUAD.
CURRENTLY, THEY SEEM TO BE CREATING TOYS TOO.
TOYS?
MADE OUT OF HOLLOW PIECES OF WOOD ABOUT SEVENTY CENTIMETERS LONG AND STUFFED WITH EXPLOSIVES.
AKIN TO THE ANCIENT FIRE ARROWS TESTED IN THE EDO PERIOD.
THEY MUST WANT SOME KIND OF ROCKET WEAPONS.
700mm
THEY'VE BEEN QUITE BUSY THE LAST FEW DAYS.
ILLEGALLY PARKING BIKES IN DISASTER ROUTES...
...STUFFING DRAINS NEAR V.I.P. FACILITY ENTRANCES WITH TRASH TO BLOCK THEM...
EXIT

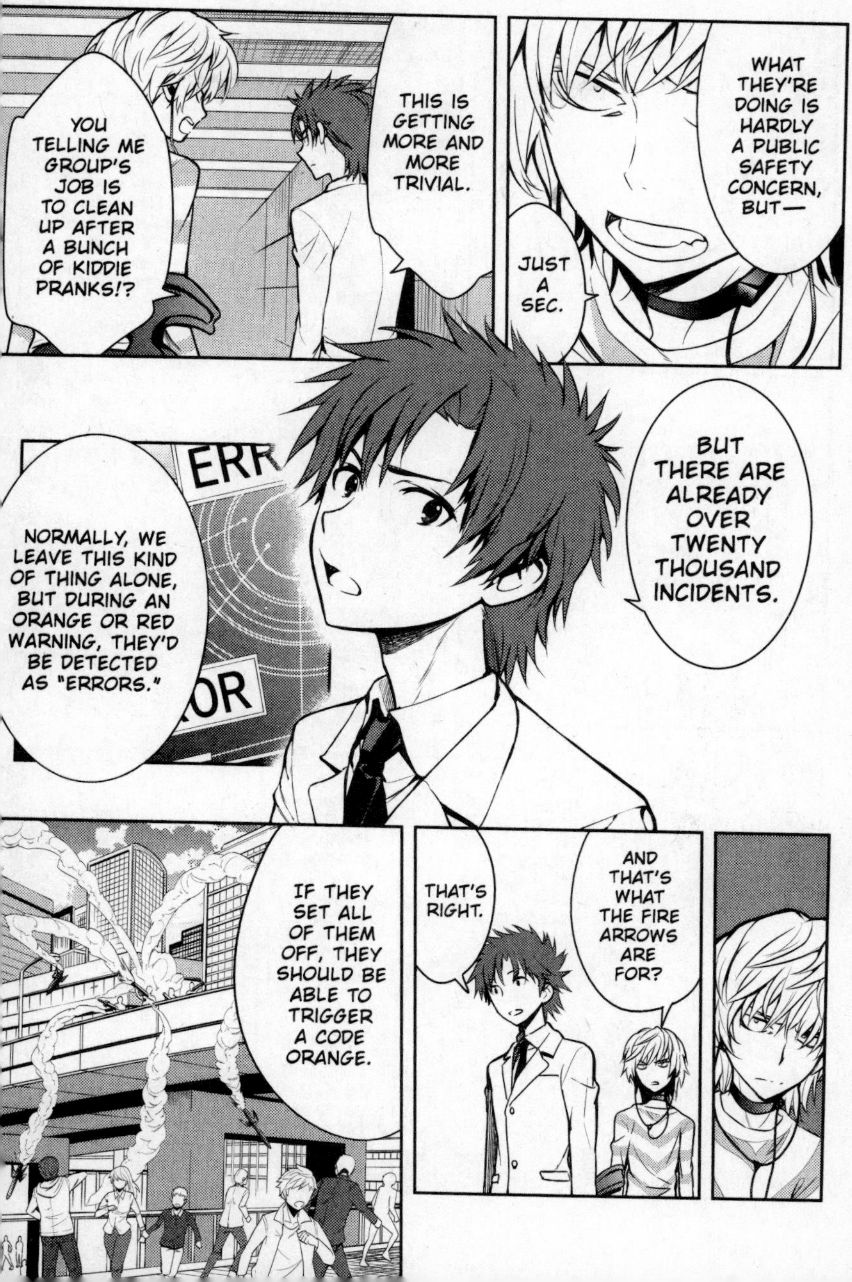
WHAT THEY'RE DOING IS HARDLY A PUBLIC SAFETY CONCERN, BUT—
JUST A SEC.
THIS IS GETTING MORE AND MORE TRIVIAL.
YOU TELLING ME GROUP'S JOB IS TO CLEAN UP AFTER A BUNCH OF KIDDIE PRANKS!?
BUT THERE ARE ALREADY OVER TWENTY THOUSAND INCIDENTS.
NORMALLY, WE LEAVE THIS KIND OF THING ALONE, BUT DURING AN ORANGE OR RED WARNING, THEY'D BE DETECTED AS "ERRORS."
AND THAT'S WHAT THE FIRE ARROWS ARE FOR?
THAT'S RIGHT.
IF THEY SET ALL OF THEM OFF, THEY SHOULD BE ABLE TO TRIGGER A CODE ORANGE.

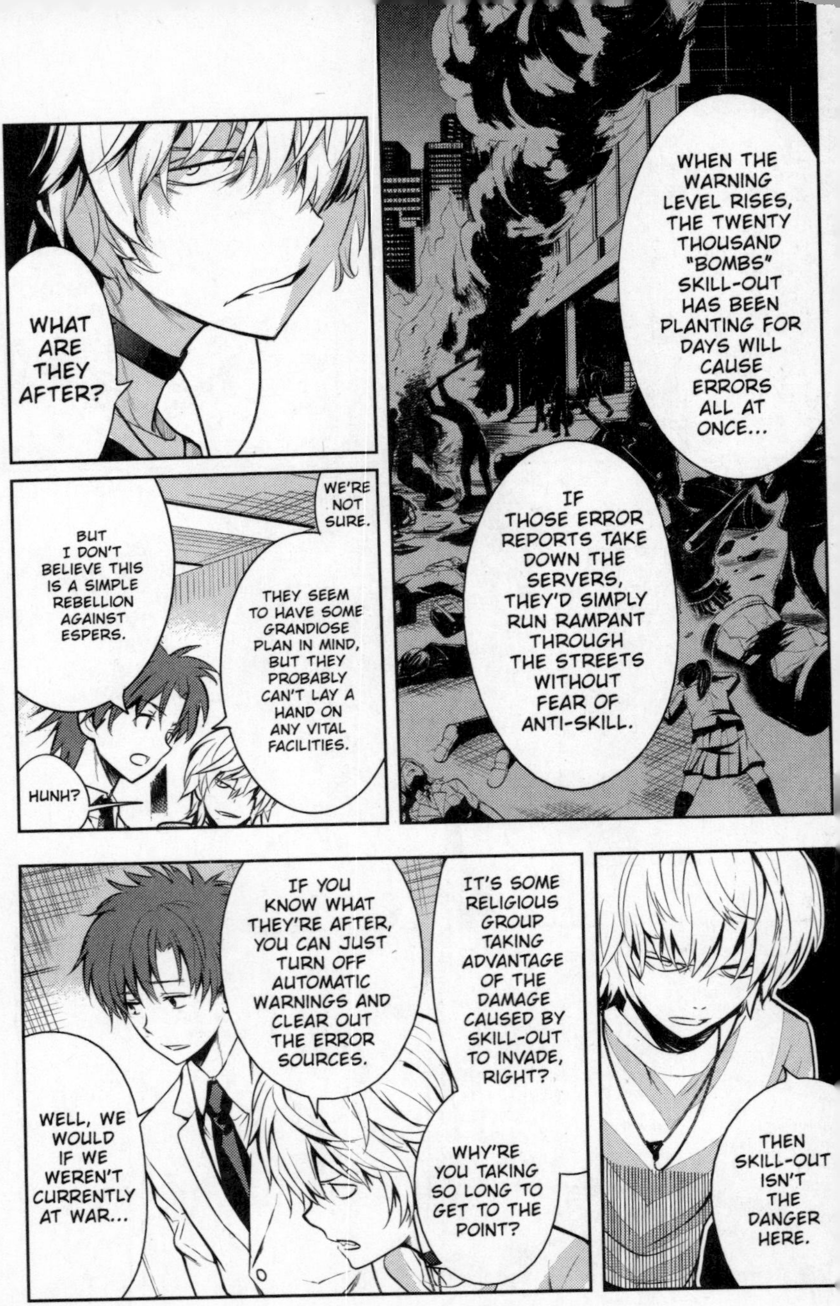

WHEN THE WARNING LEVEL RISES, THE TWENTY THOUSAND "BOMBS" SKILL-OUT HAS BEEN PLANTING FOR DAYS WILL CAUSE ERRORS ALL AT ONCE...
IF THOSE ERROR REPORTS TAKE DOWN THE SERVERS, THEY'D SIMPLY RUN RAMPANT THROUGH THE STREETS WITHOUT FEAR OF ANTI-SKILL.
WHAT ARE THEY AFTER?
WE'RE NOT SURE.
THEY SEEM TO HAVE SOME GRANDIOSE PLAN IN MIND, BUT THEY PROBABLY CAN'T LAY A HAND ON ANY VITAL FACILITIES.
BUT I DON'T BELIEVE THIS IS A SIMPLE REBELLION AGAINST ESPERS.
HUNH?
THEN SKILL-OUT ISN'T THE DANGER HERE.
IT'S SOME RELIGIOUS GROUP TAKING ADVANTAGE OF THE DAMAGE CAUSED BY SKILL-OUT TO INVADE, RIGHT?
IF YOU KNOW WHAT THEY'RE AFTER, YOU CAN JUST TURN OFF AUTOMATIC WARNINGS AND CLEAR OUT THE ERROR SOURCES.
WHY'RE YOU TAKING SO LONG TO GET TO THE POINT?
WELL, WE WOULD IF WE WEREN'T CURRENTLY AT WAR...

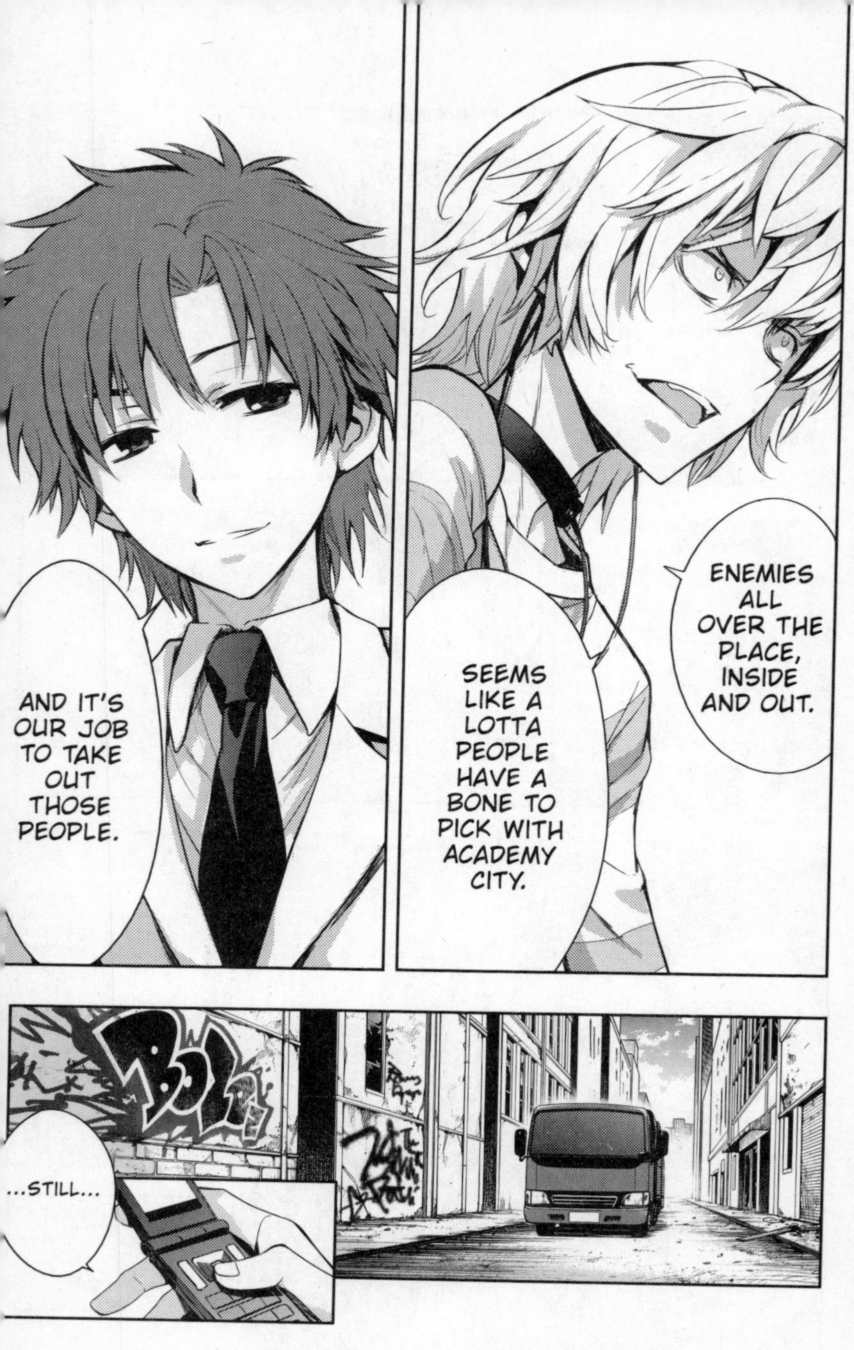
ENEMIES ALL OVER THE PLACE, INSIDE AND OUT.
SEEMS LIKE A LOTTA PEOPLE HAVE A BONE TO PICK WITH ACADEMY CITY.
AND IT'S OUR JOB TO TAKE OUT THOSE PEOPLE.
...STILL...

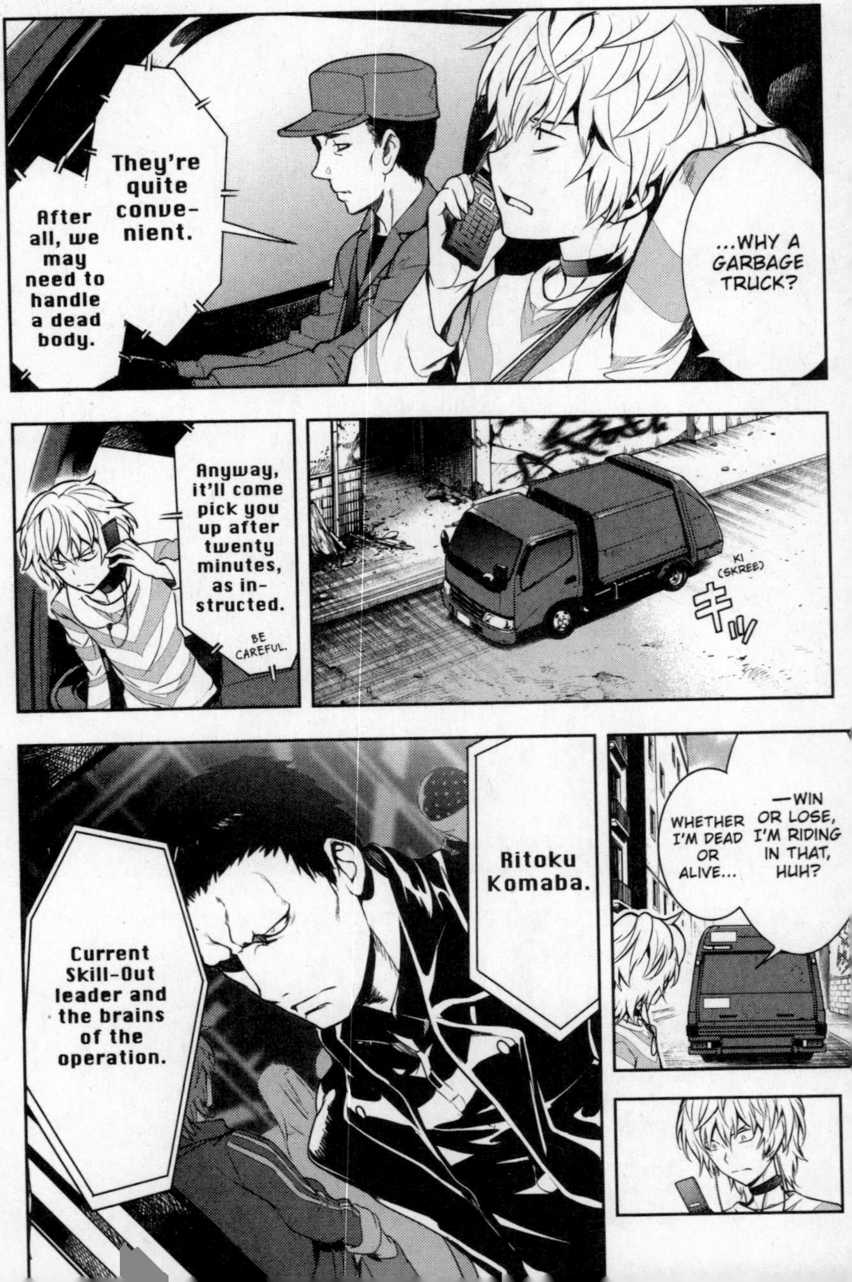
...WHY A GARBAGE TRUCK?
They're quite convenient.
After all, we may need to handle a dead body.
KI (SKREE)
キッ
Anyway, it'll come pick you up after twenty minutes, as instructed.
BE CAREFUL.
—WIN OR LOSE, I'M RIDING IN THAT, HUH?
WHETHER I'M DEAD OR ALIVE...
Ritoku Komaba.
Current Skill-Out leader and the brains of the operation.

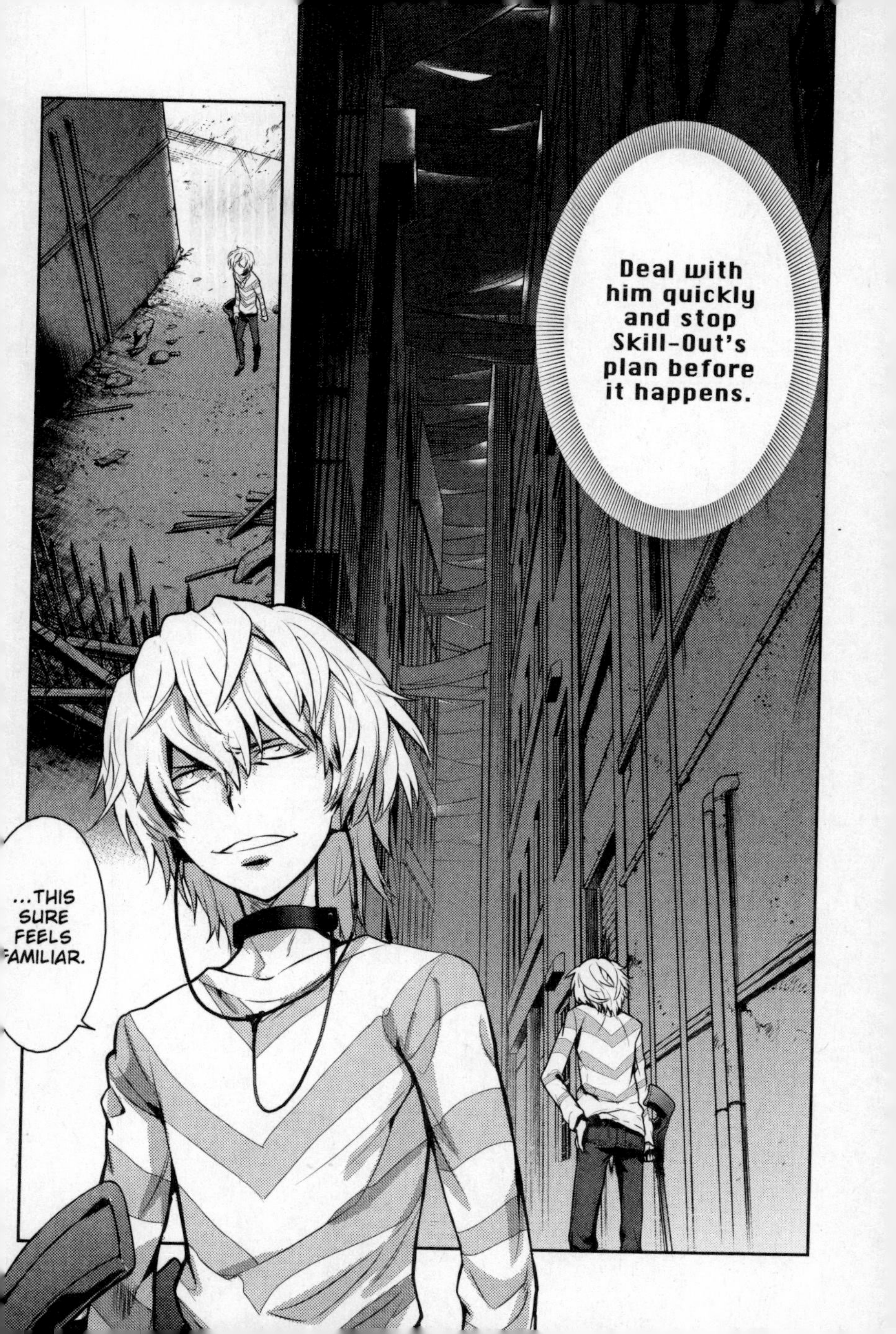
Deal with him quickly and stop Skill-Out's plan before it happens.
...THIS SURE FEELS FAMILIAR.

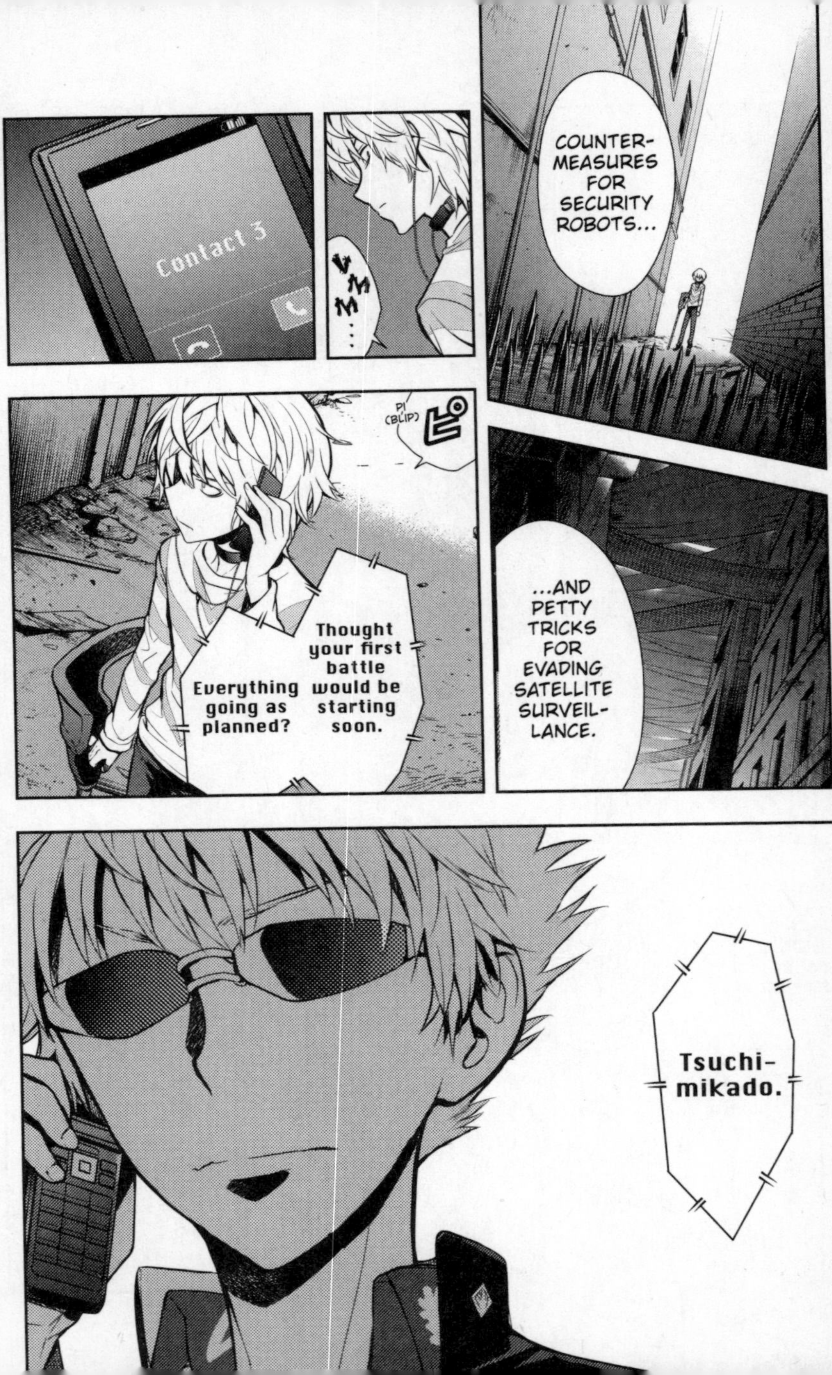
COUNTER-MEASURES FOR SECURITY ROBOTS...
VMM...
Contact 3
...AND PETTY TRICKS FOR EVADING SATELLITE SURVEIL-LANCE.
PI (BLIP)
Thought your first battle would be starting soon.
Everything going as planned?
Tsuchi-mikado.

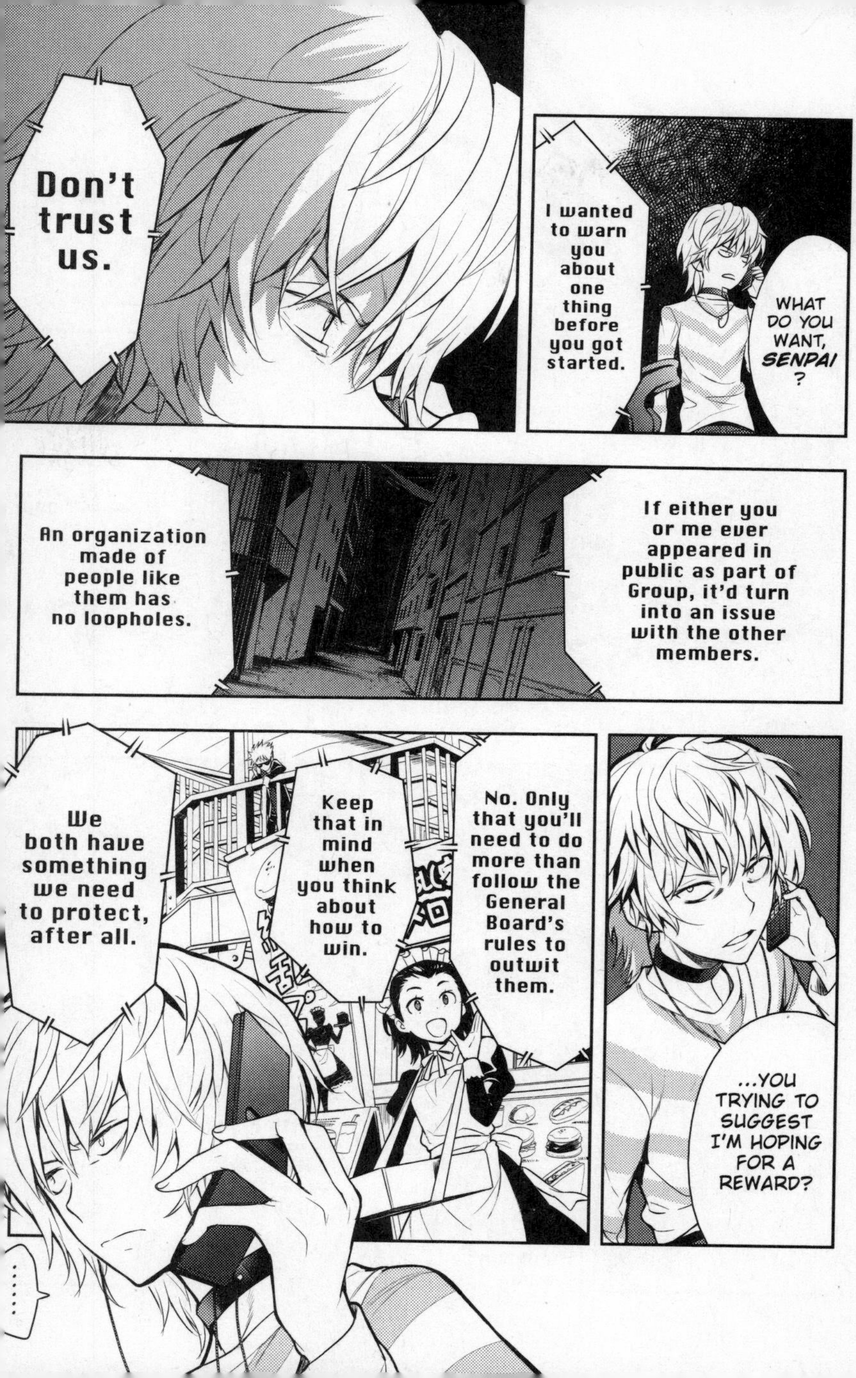
WHAT DO YOU WANT, *SENPAI*?
I wanted to warn you about one thing before you got started.
Don't trust us.
If either you or me ever appeared in public as part of Group, it'd turn into an issue with the other members.
An organization made of people like them has no loopholes.
...YOU TRYING TO SUGGEST I'M HOPING FOR A REWARD?
No. Only that you'll need to do more than follow the General Board's rules to outwit them.
Keep that in mind when you think about how to win.
We both have something we need to protect, after all.
......

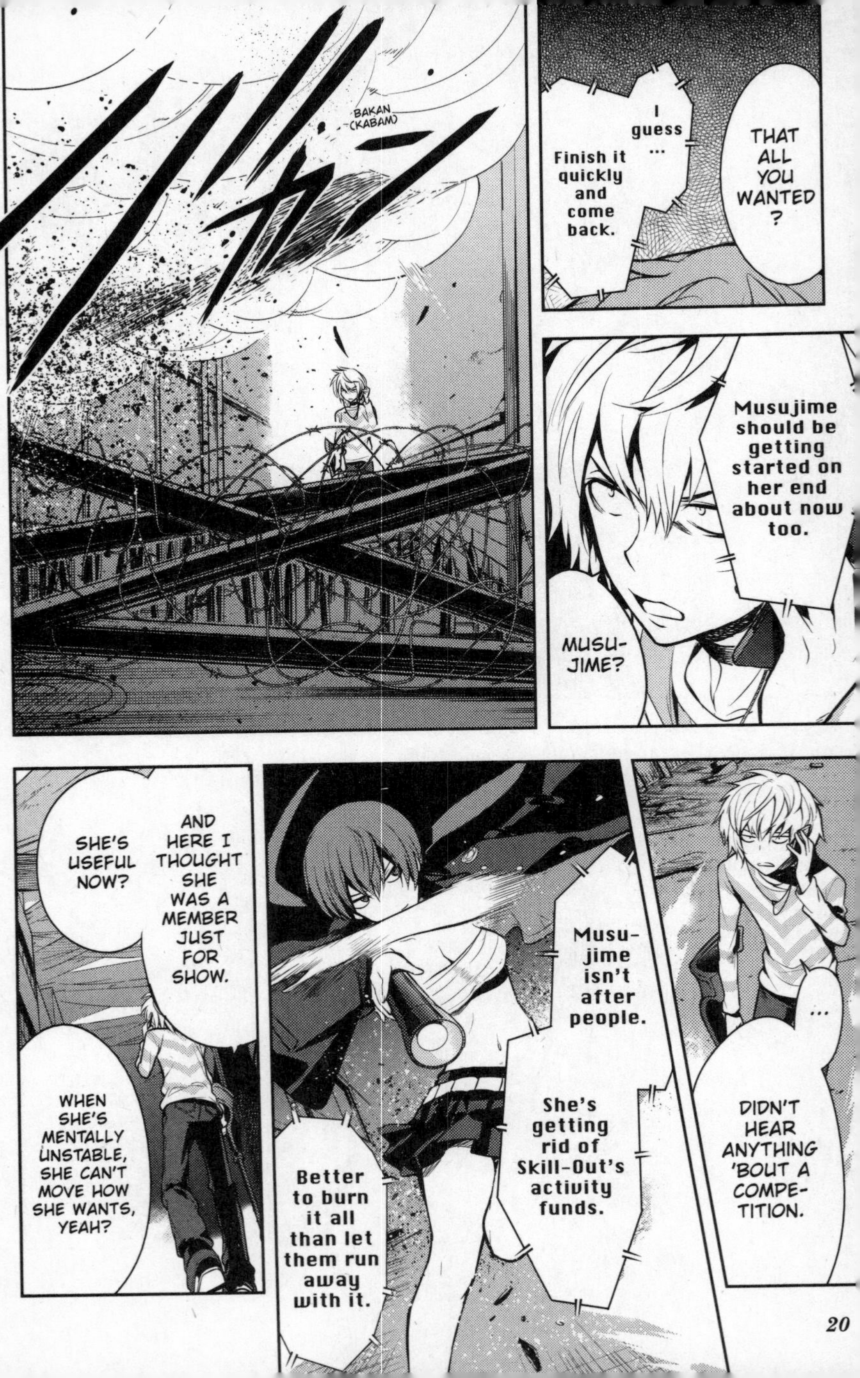
THAT ALL YOU WANTED?
I guess...
Finish it quickly and come back.
Musujime should be getting started on her end about now too.
MUSUJIME?
BAKAN (KABAM)
...
DIDN'T HEAR ANYTHING 'BOUT A COMPETITION.
Musujime isn't after people.
She's getting rid of Skill-Out's activity funds.
Better to burn it all than let them run away with it.
AND HERE I THOUGHT SHE WAS A MEMBER JUST FOR SHOW.
SHE'S USEFUL NOW?
WHEN SHE'S MENTALLY UNSTABLE, SHE CAN'T MOVE HOW SHE WANTS, YEAH?

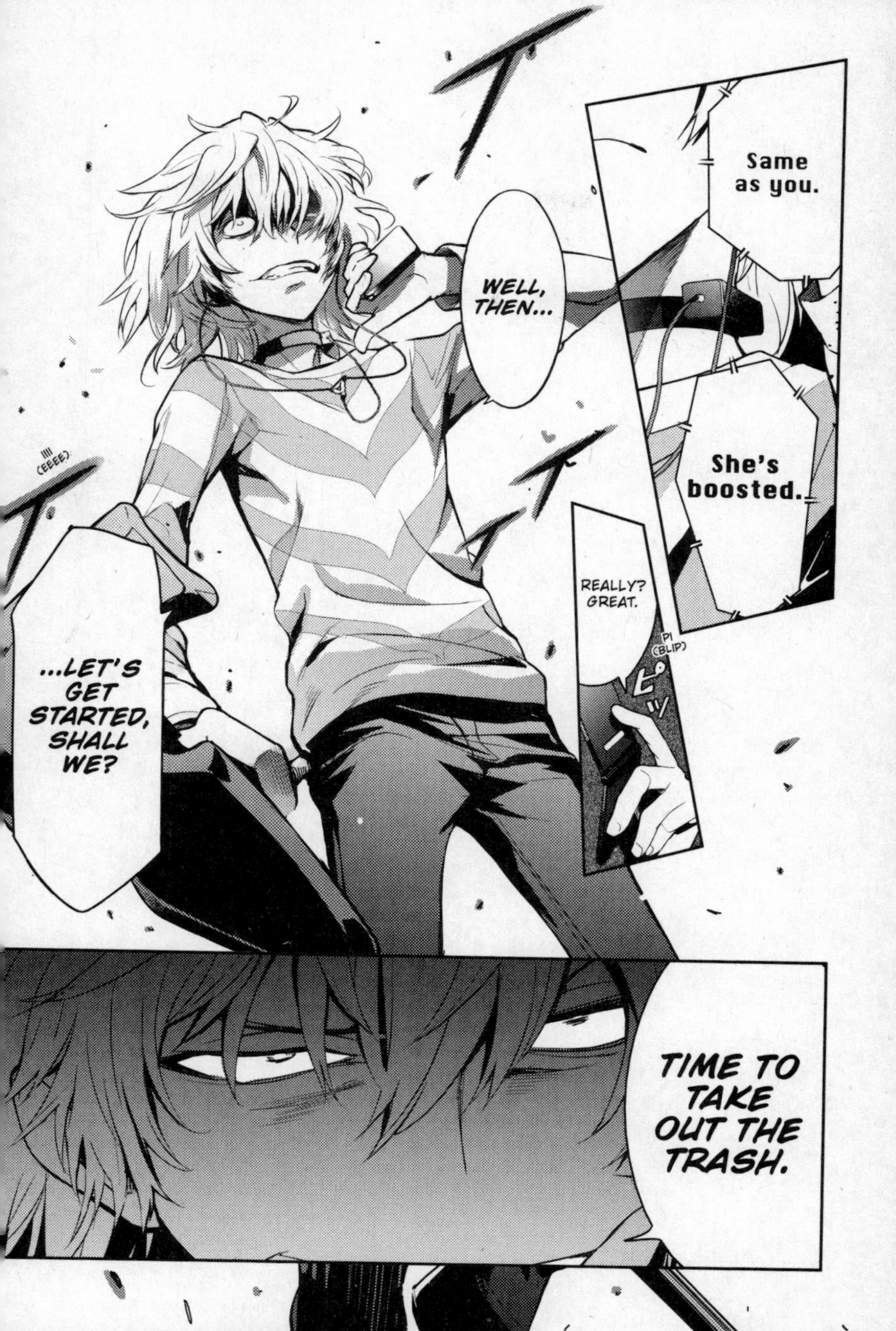
Same as you.
She's boosted.
REALLY? GREAT.
PI (BLIP)
WELL, THEN...
IIII (EEEE)
...LET'S GET STARTED, SHALL WE?
TIME TO TAKE OUT THE TRASH.

A Certain Magical

Index

#118 GROUP ②

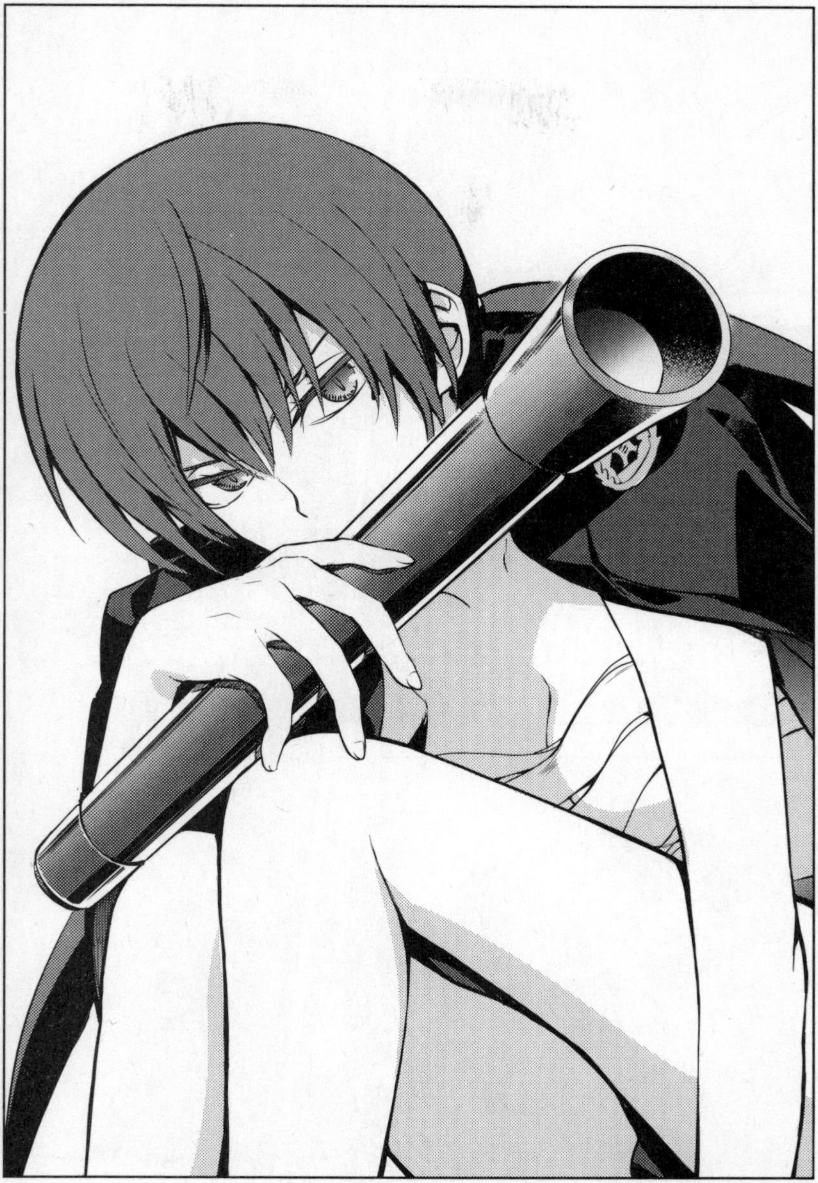

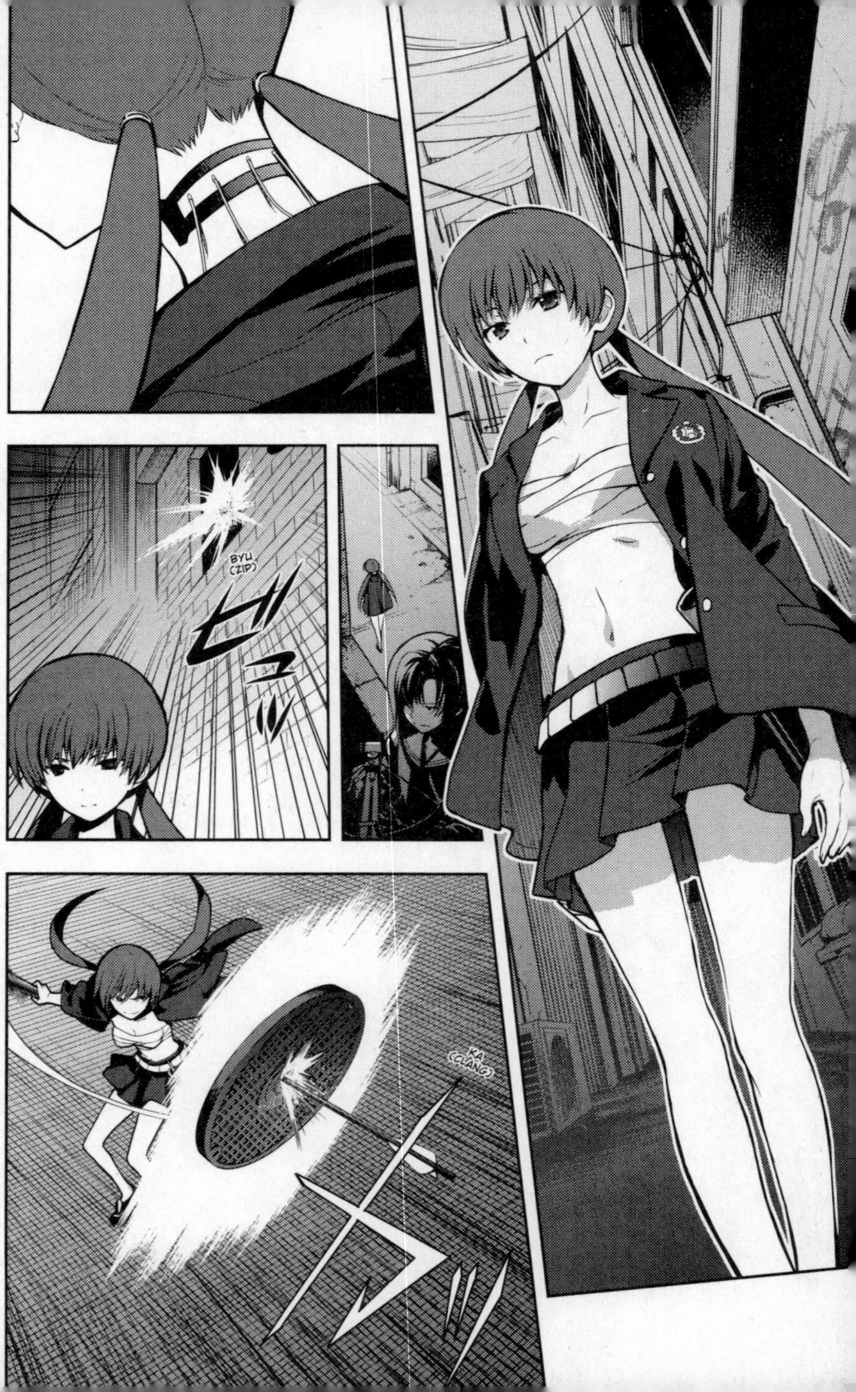
BYU (ZIP)
KA (CLANG)

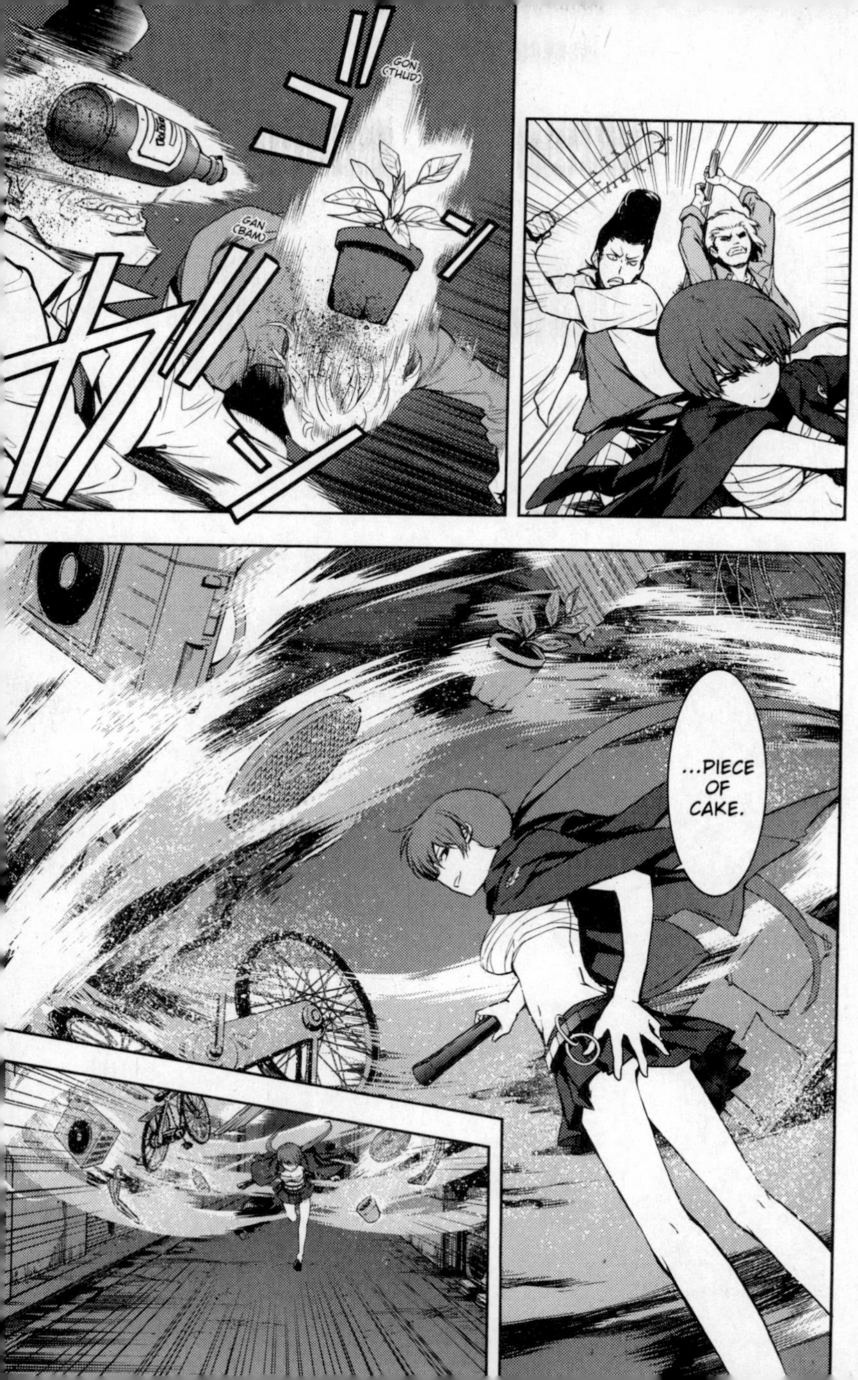
GON (THUD)
GAN (BAM)
...PIECE OF CAKE.

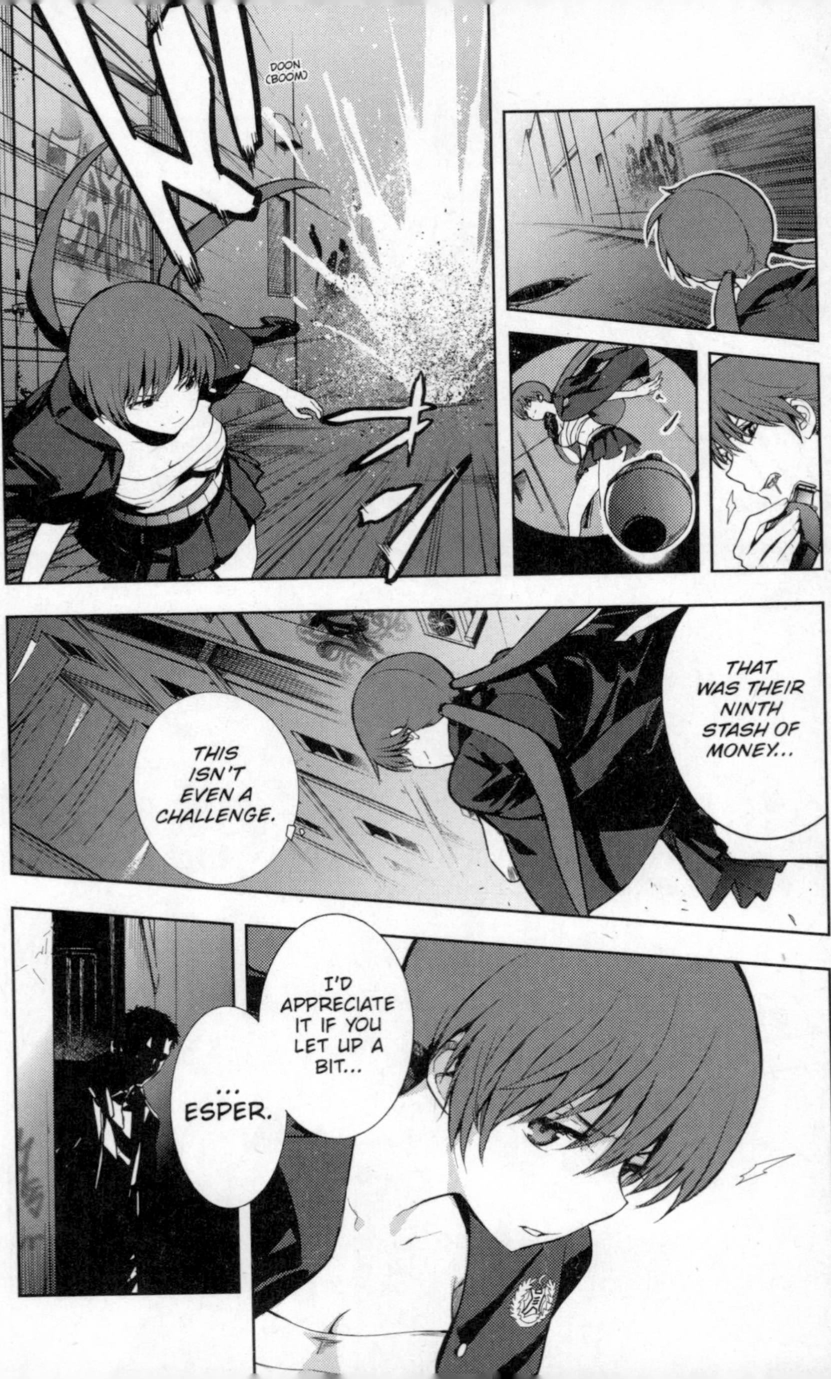
DOON (BOOM)
THAT WAS THEIR NINTH STASH OF MONEY...
THIS ISN'T EVEN A CHALLENGE.
I'D APPRECIATE IT IF YOU LET UP A BIT...
... ESPER.

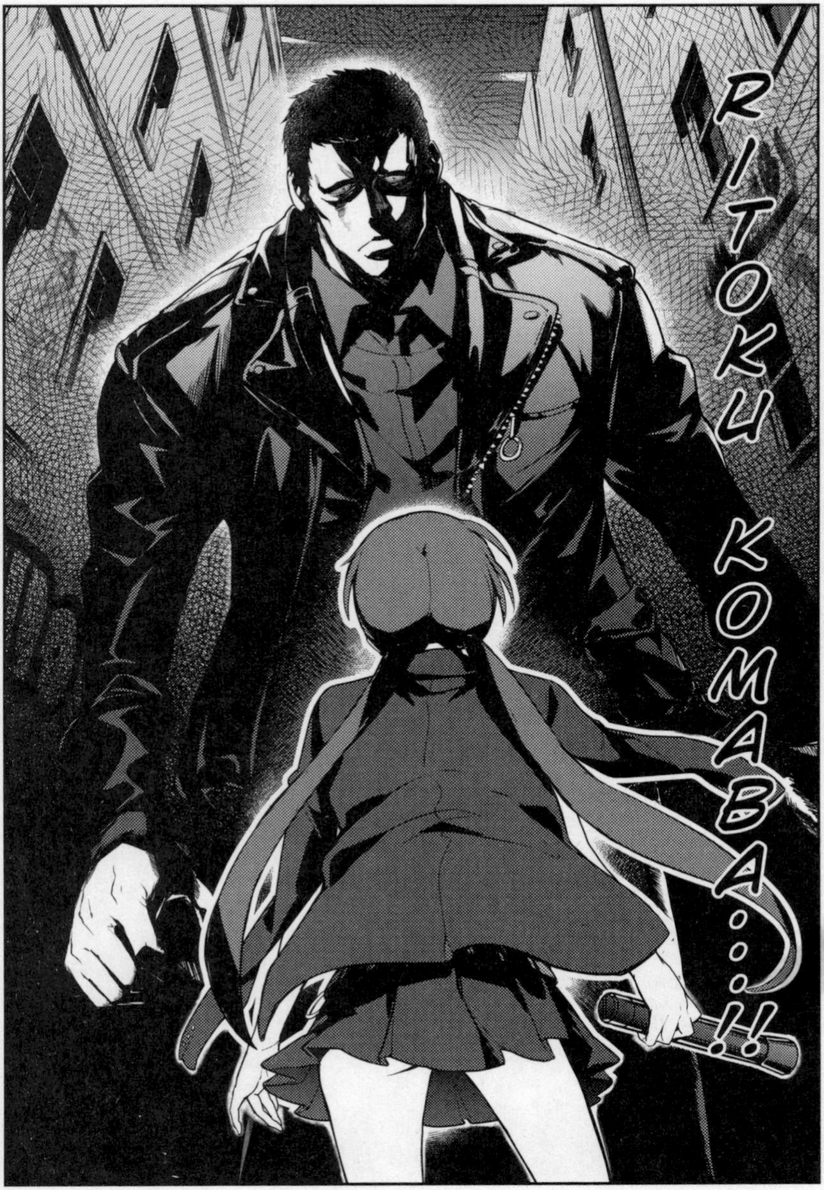
RITOKU KOMABA...!!

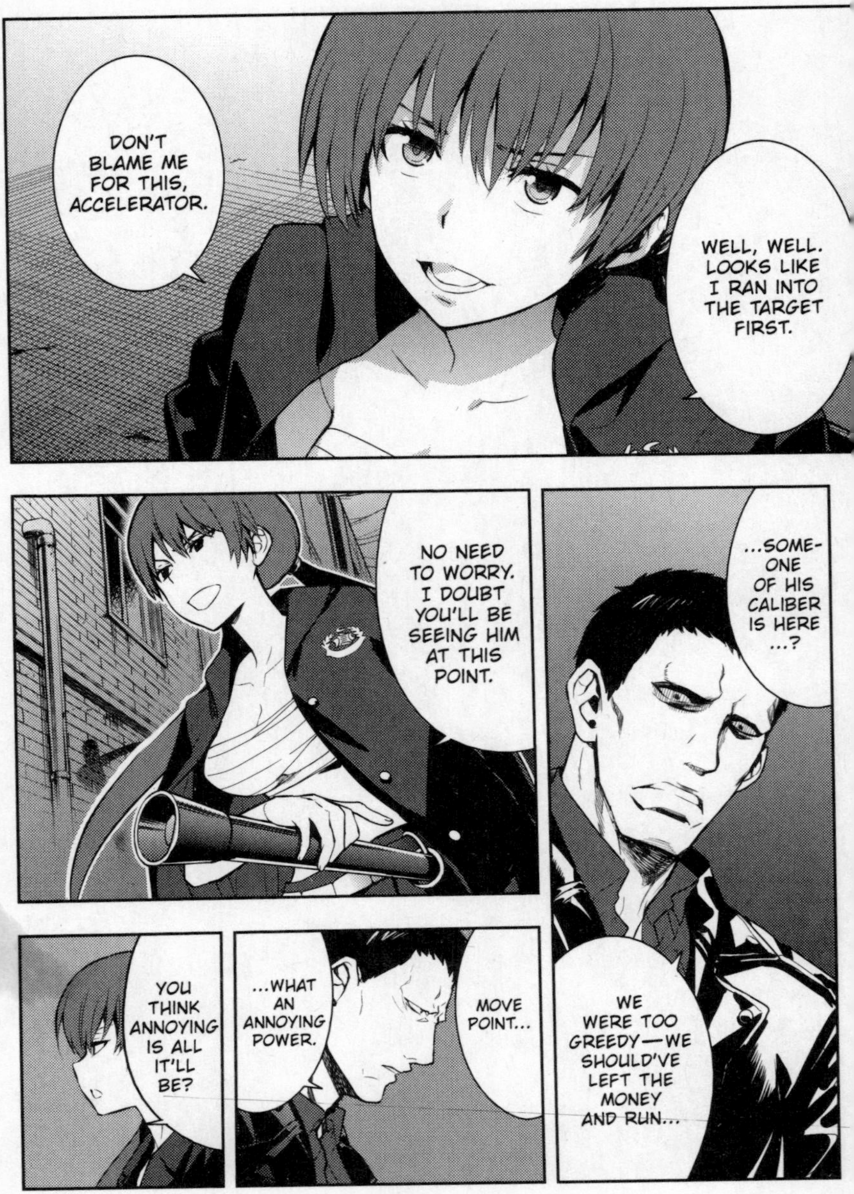
WELL, WELL. LOOKS LIKE I RAN INTO THE TARGET FIRST.
DON'T BLAME ME FOR THIS, ACCELERATOR.
...SOMEONE OF HIS CALIBER IS HERE ...?
WE WERE TOO GREEDY—WE SHOULD'VE LEFT THE MONEY AND RUN...
NO NEED TO WORRY. I DOUBT YOU'LL BE SEEING HIM AT THIS POINT.
MOVE POINT...
...WHAT AN ANNOYING POWER.
YOU THINK ANNOYING IS ALL IT'LL BE?

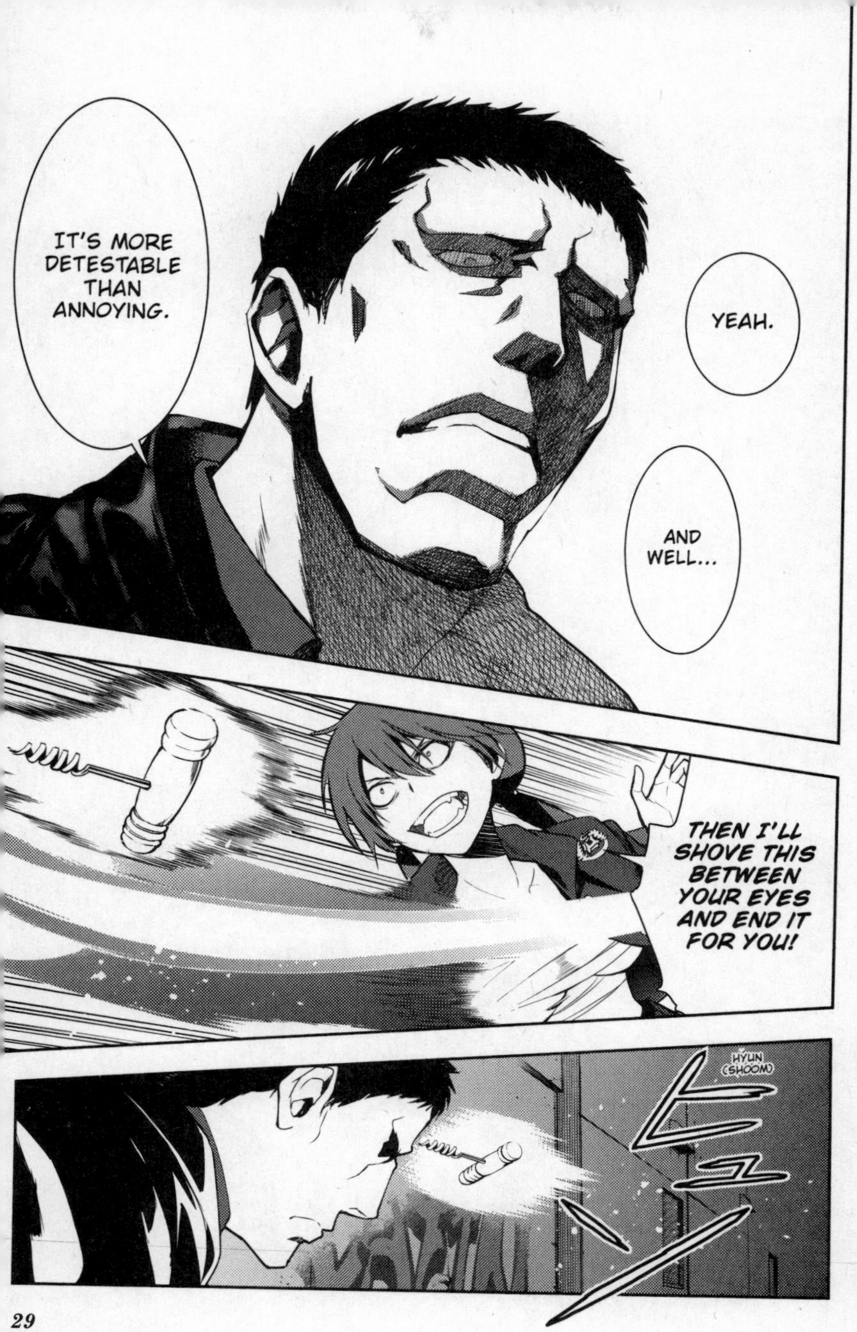
YEAH.
IT'S MORE DETESTABLE THAN ANNOYING.
AND WELL...
THEN I'LL SHOVE THIS BETWEEN YOUR EYES AND END IT FOR YOU!
HYUN (SHOOM)

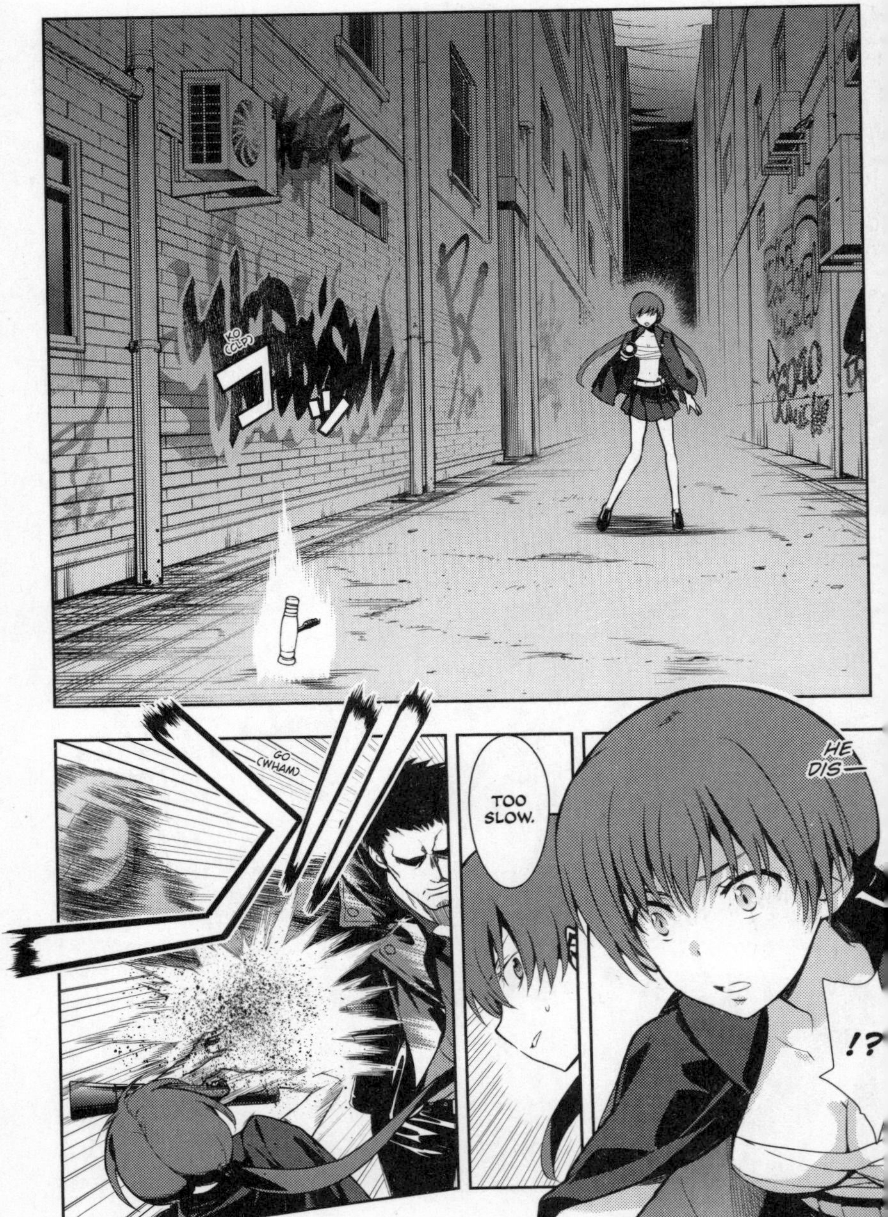
KO
(CLIP)
コッ
HE
DIS—
!?
TOO
SLOW.
GO
(WHAM)

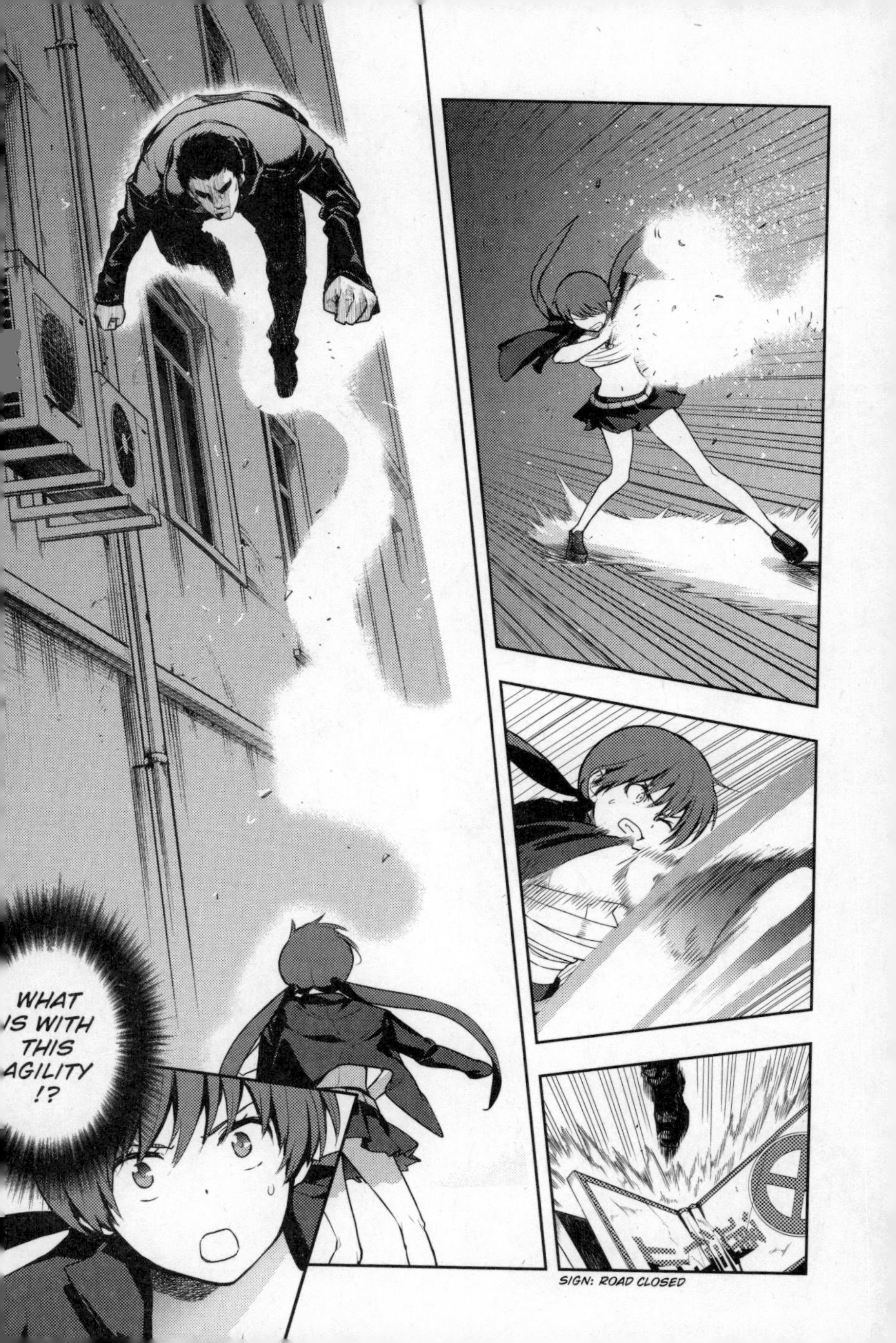
WHAT IS WITH THIS AGILITY !?
SIGN: ROAD CLOSED

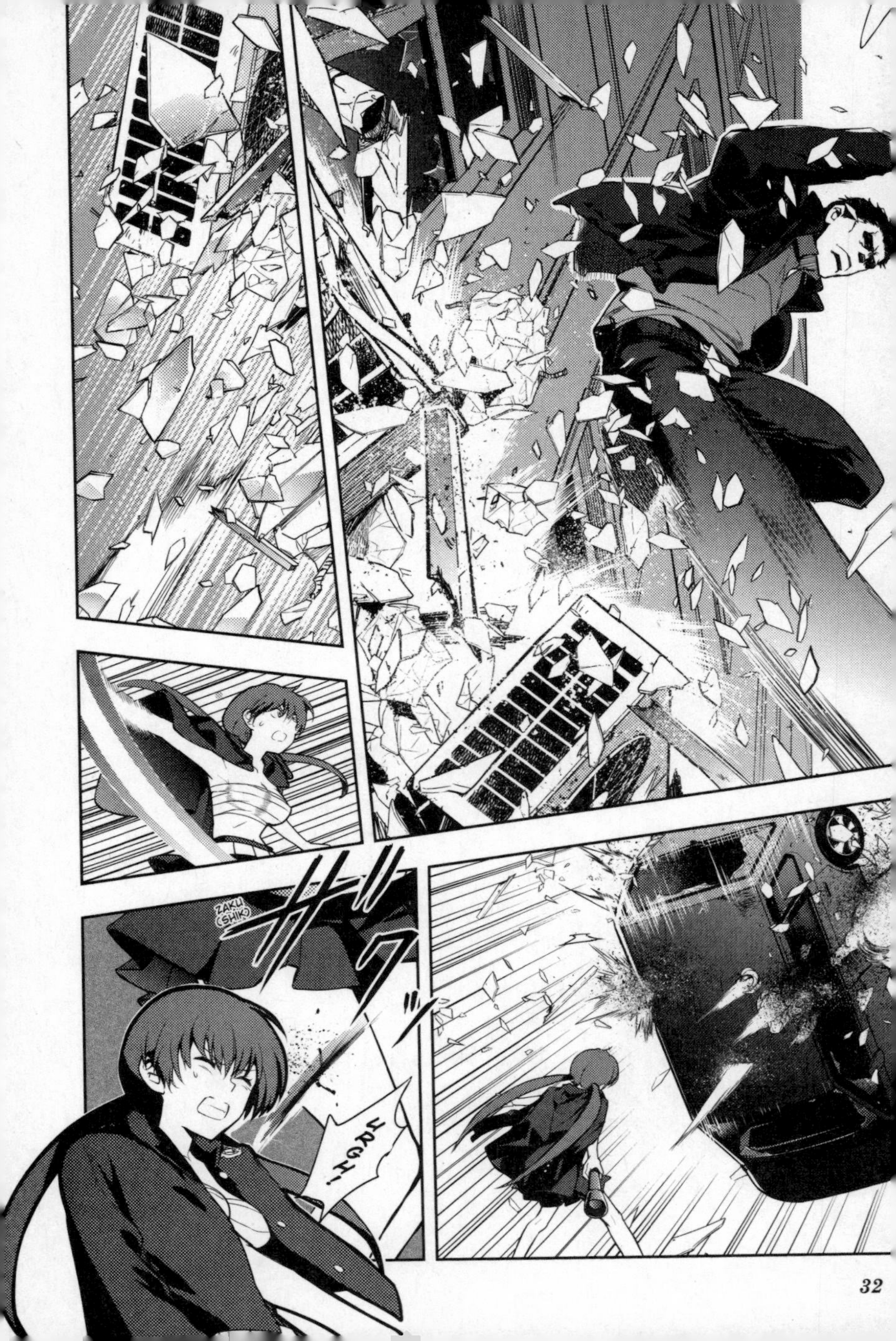
ZAKU (SHIK)
URGH!

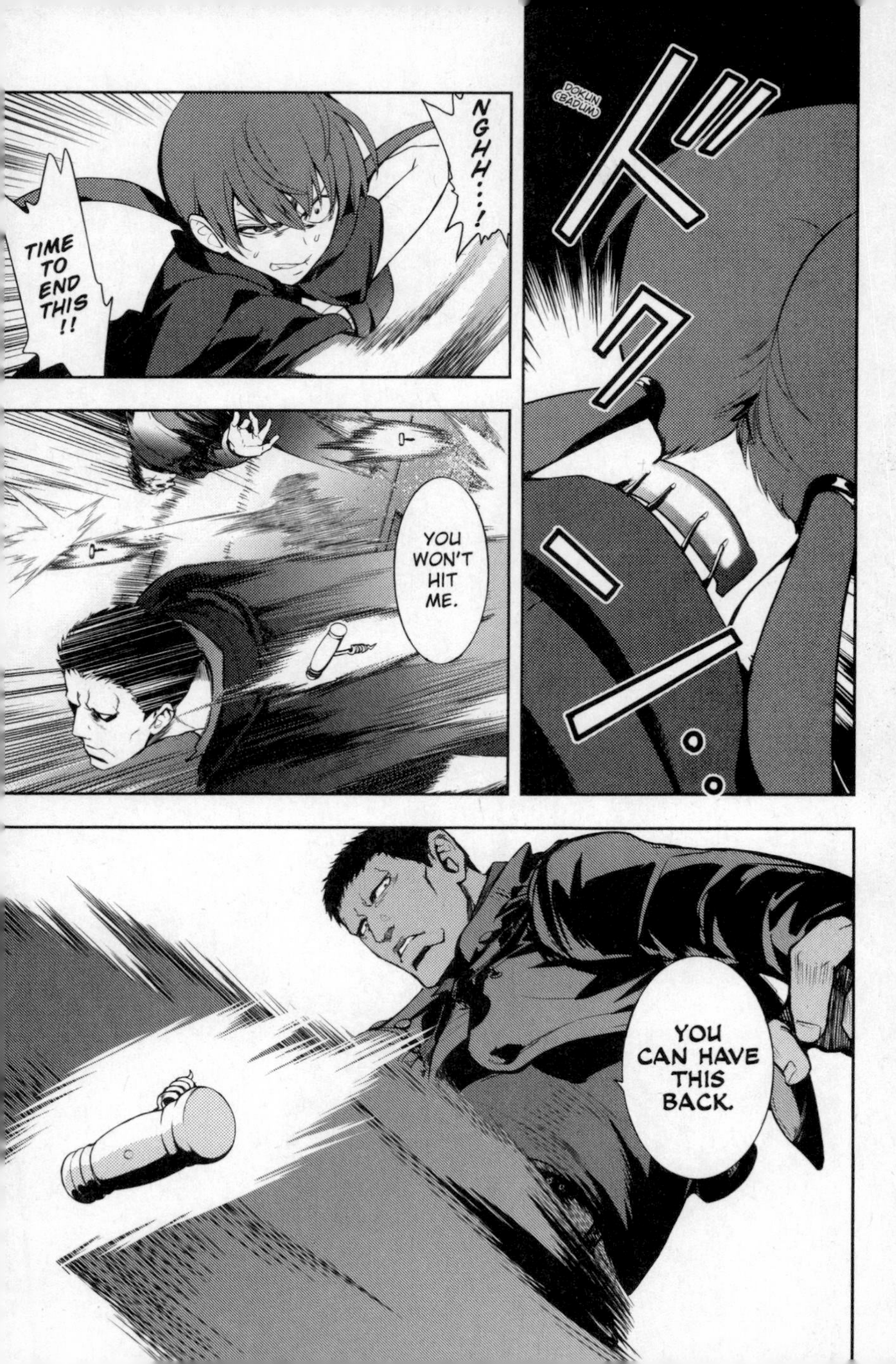
DOKUN (BADUM)
NGHH...!
TIME TO END THIS!!
YOU WON'T HIT ME.
YOU CAN HAVE THIS BACK.

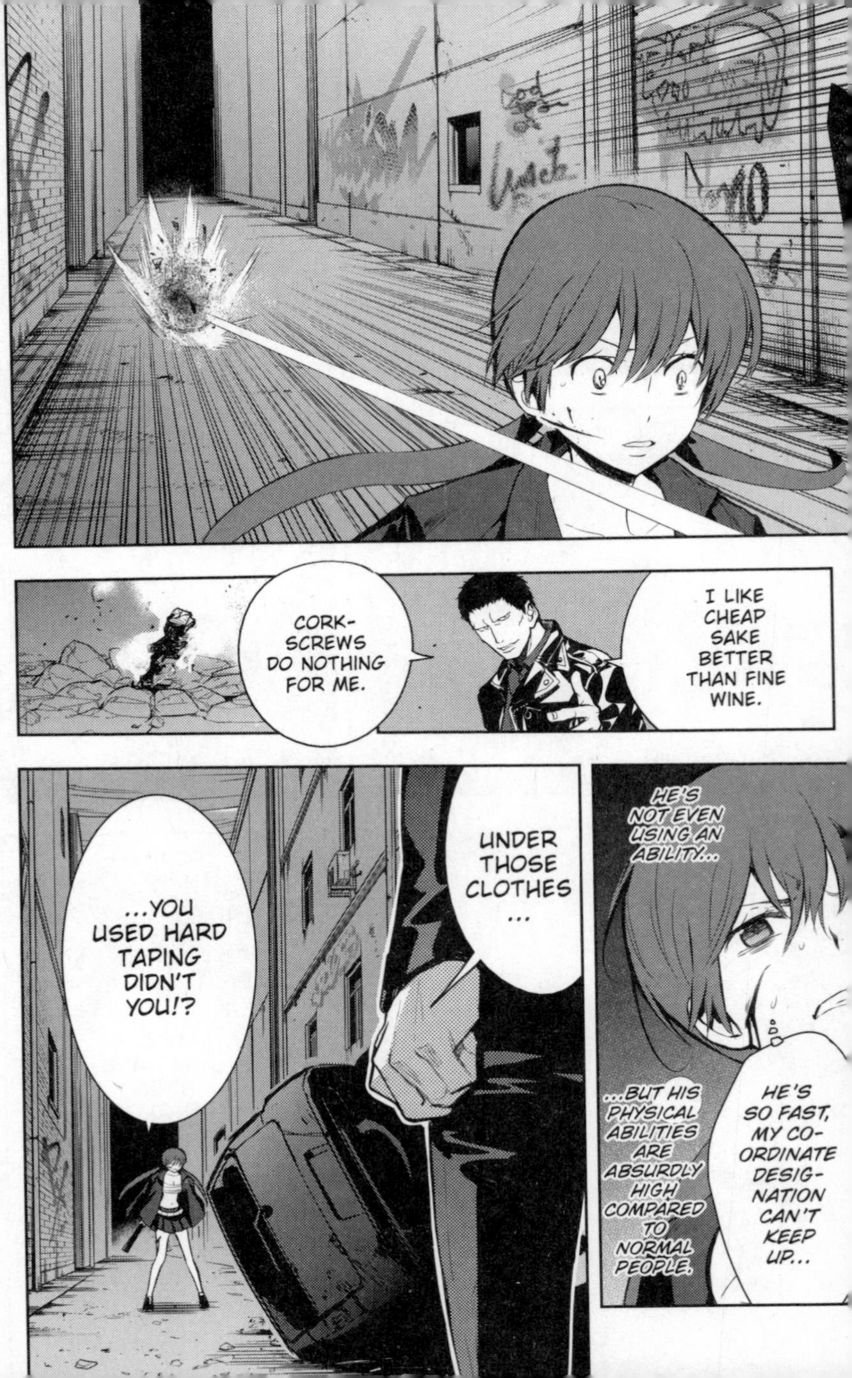
I LIKE CHEAP SAKE BETTER THAN FINE WINE.
CORK-SCREWS DO NOTHING FOR ME.
HE'S NOT EVEN USING AN ABILITY...
HE'S SO FAST, MY CO-ORDINATE DESIG-NATION CAN'T KEEP UP...
...BUT HIS PHYSICAL ABILITIES ARE ABSURDLY HIGH COMPARED TO NORMAL PEOPLE.
UNDER THOSE CLOTHES...
...YOU USED HARD TAPING DIDN'T YOU!?

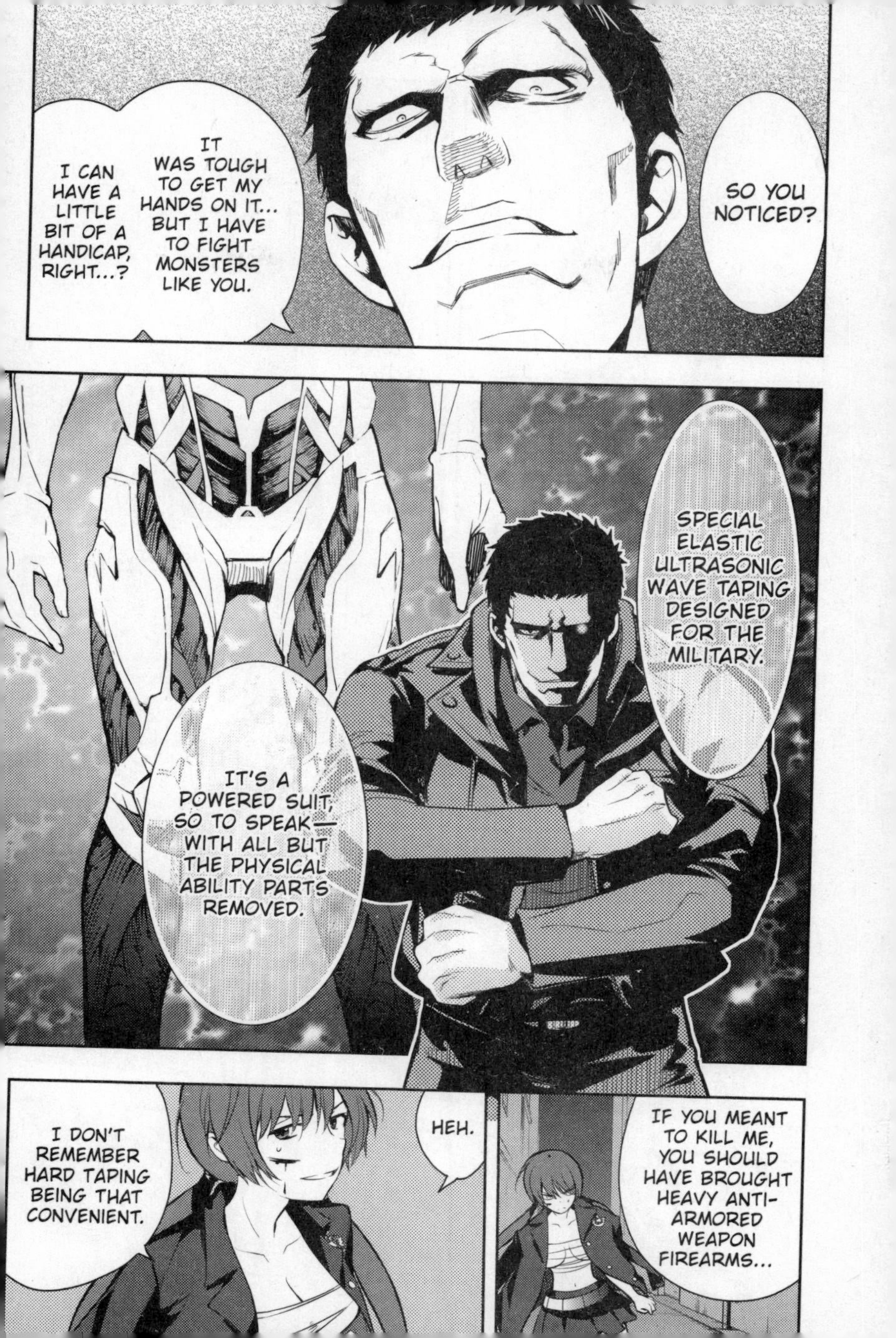
SO YOU NOTICED?
IT WAS TOUGH TO GET MY HANDS ON IT... BUT I HAVE TO FIGHT MONSTERS LIKE YOU.
I CAN HAVE A LITTLE BIT OF A HANDICAP, RIGHT...?
SPECIAL ELASTIC ULTRASONIC WAVE TAPING DESIGNED FOR THE MILITARY.
IT'S A POWERED SUIT, SO TO SPEAK—WITH ALL BUT THE PHYSICAL ABILITY PARTS REMOVED.
IF YOU MEANT TO KILL ME, YOU SHOULD HAVE BROUGHT HEAVY ANTI-ARMORED WEAPON FIREARMS...
HEH.
I DON'T REMEMBER HARD TAPING BEING THAT CONVENIENT.

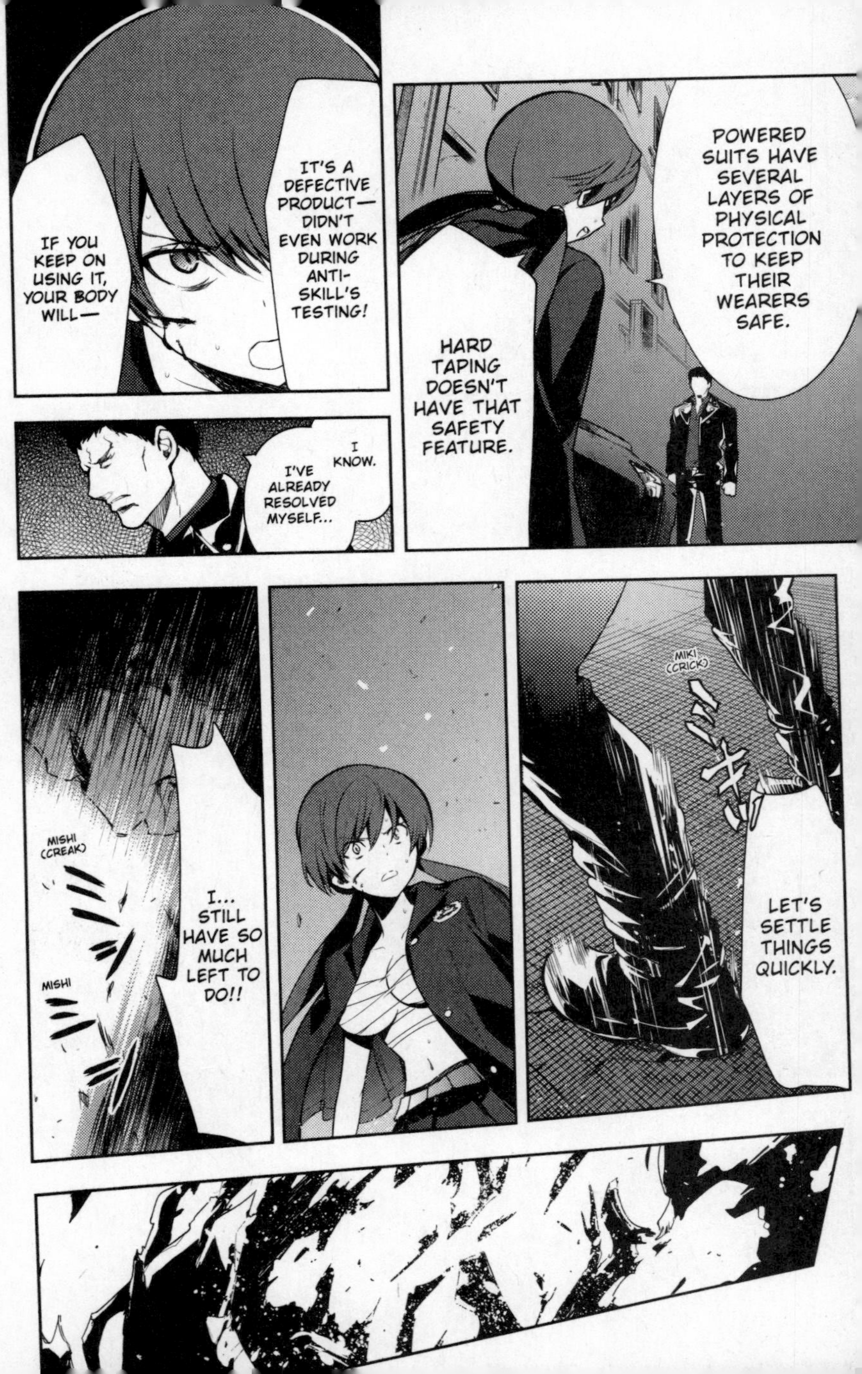
POWERED SUITS HAVE SEVERAL LAYERS OF PHYSICAL PROTECTION TO KEEP THEIR WEARERS SAFE.
HARD TAPING DOESN'T HAVE THAT SAFETY FEATURE.
IT'S A DEFECTIVE PRODUCT—DIDN'T EVEN WORK DURING ANTI-SKILL'S TESTING!
IF YOU KEEP ON USING IT, YOUR BODY WILL—
I KNOW.
I'VE ALREADY RESOLVED MYSELF...
MIKI (CRICK)
LET'S SETTLE THINGS QUICKLY.
I... STILL HAVE SO MUCH LEFT TO DO!!
MISHI (CREAK)
MISHI

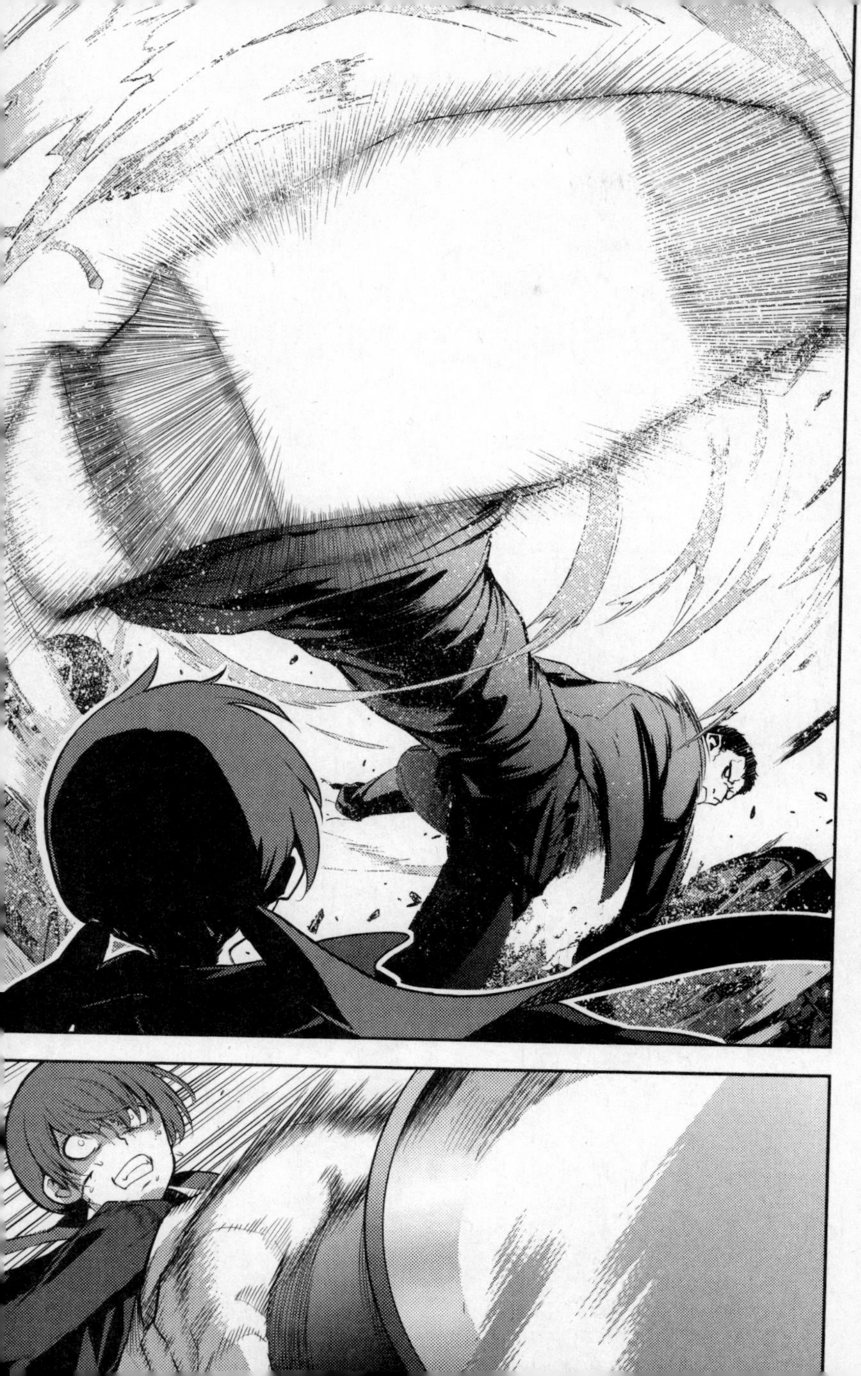

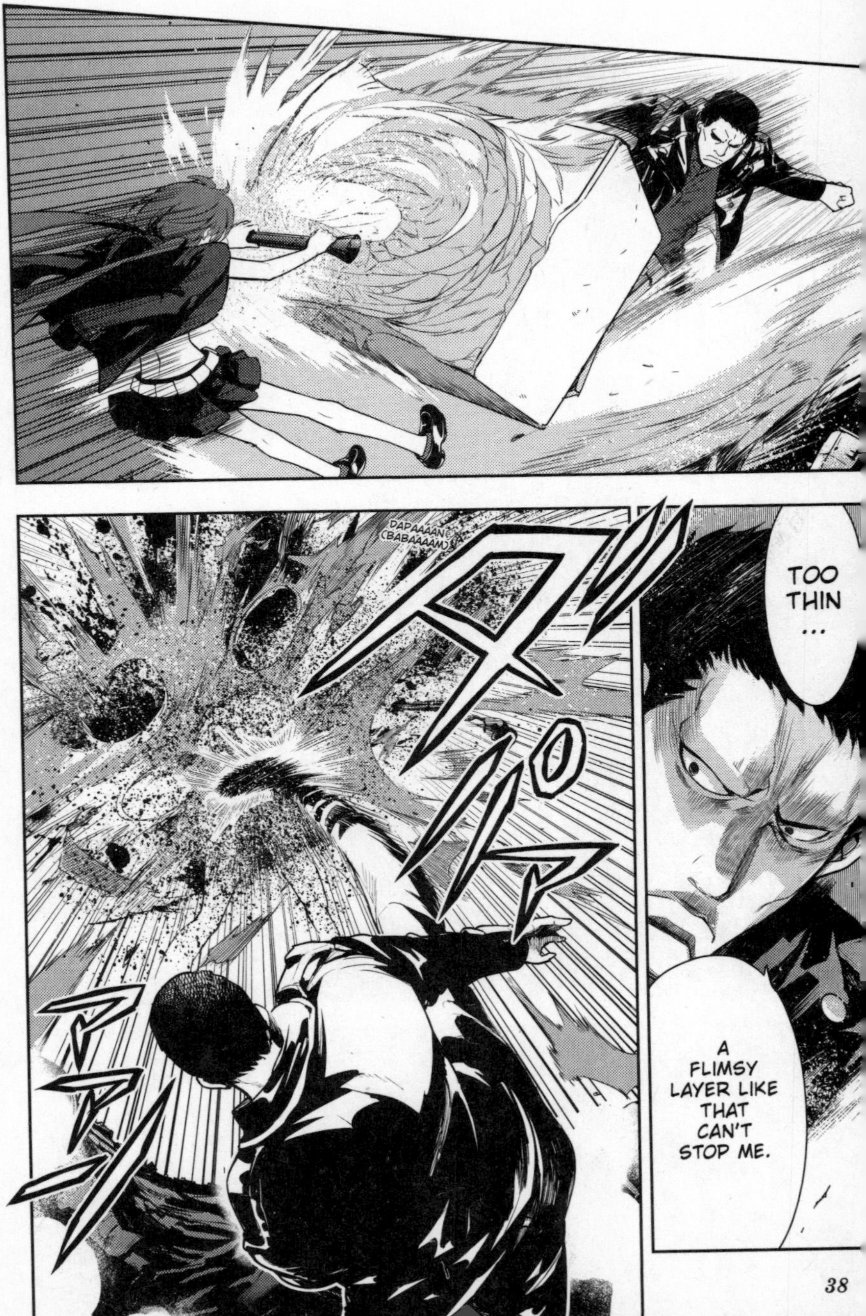
TOO THIN ...
A FLIMSY LAYER LIKE THAT CAN'T STOP ME.
DAPAAAAN
(BABAAAAM)

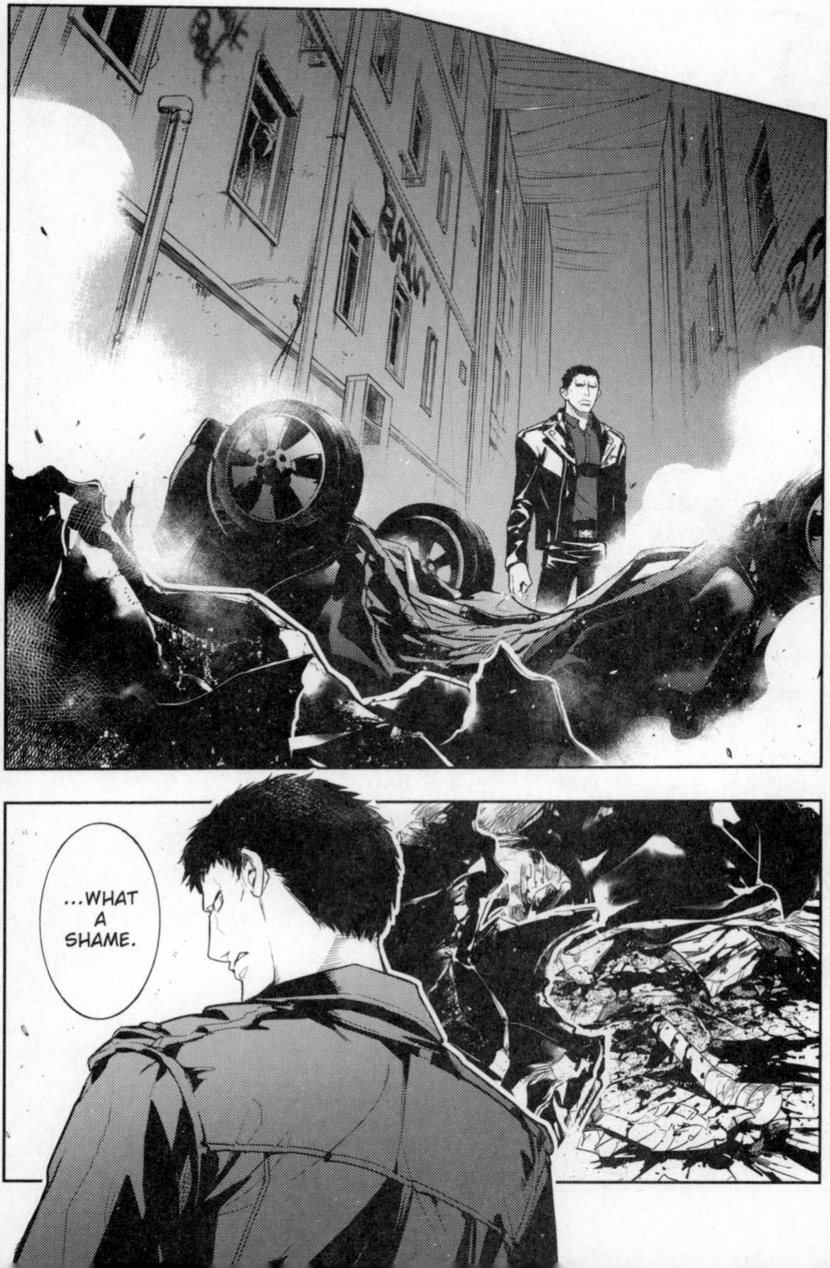
...WHAT A SHAME.

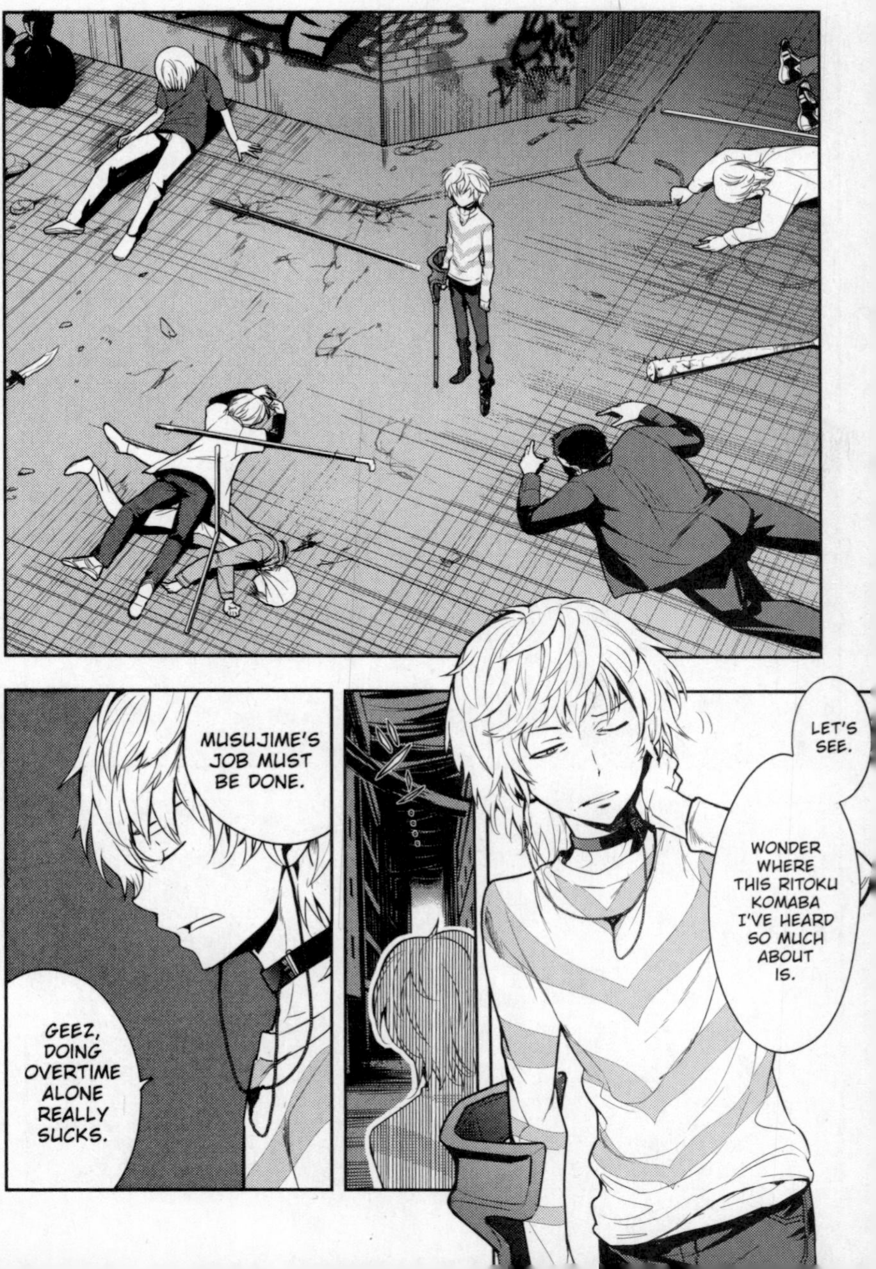
LET'S SEE.
WONDER WHERE THIS RITOKU KOMABA I'VE HEARD SO MUCH ABOUT IS.
MUSUJIME'S JOB MUST BE DONE.
GEEZ, DOING OVERTIME ALONE REALLY SUCKS.

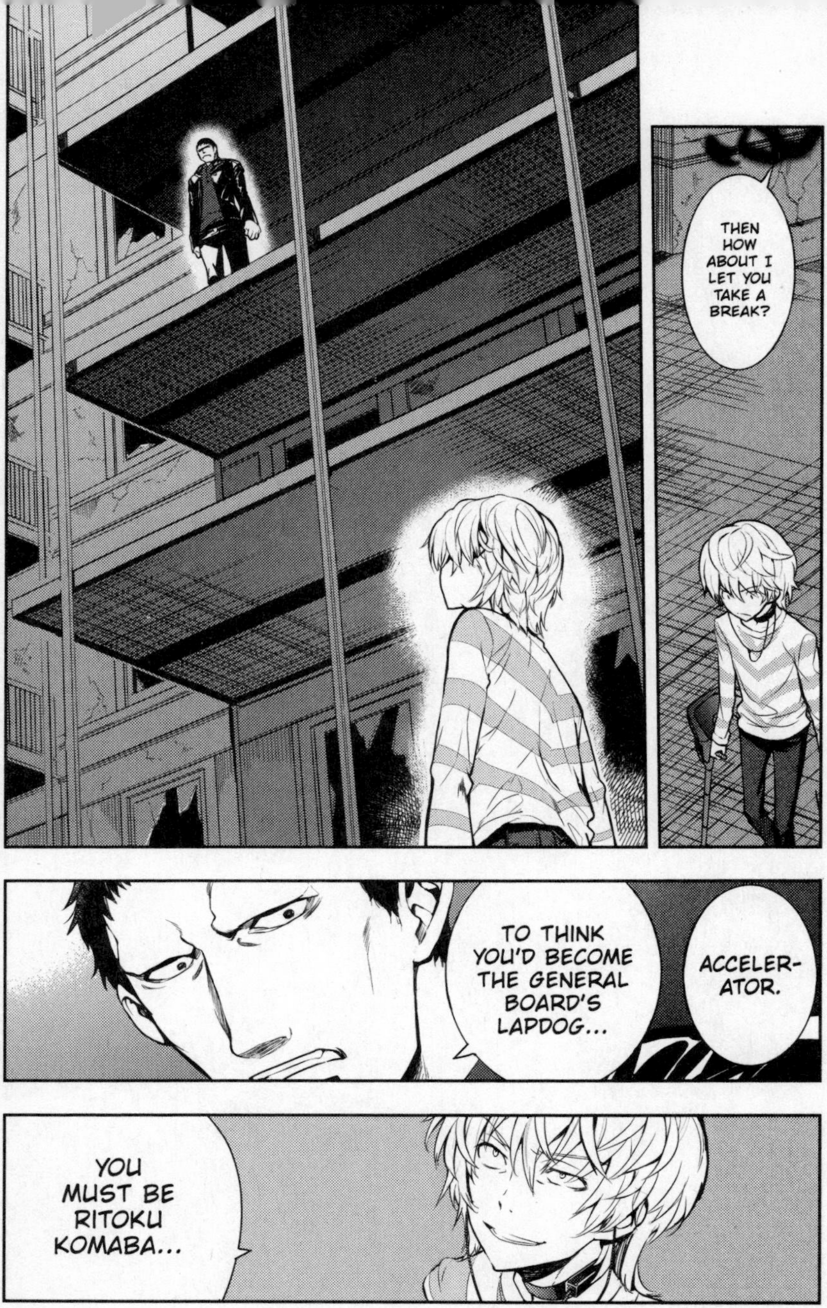
THEN HOW ABOUT I LET YOU TAKE A BREAK?
ACCELER-ATOR.
TO THINK YOU'D BECOME THE GENERAL BOARD'S LAPDOG...
YOU MUST BE RITOKU KOMABA...

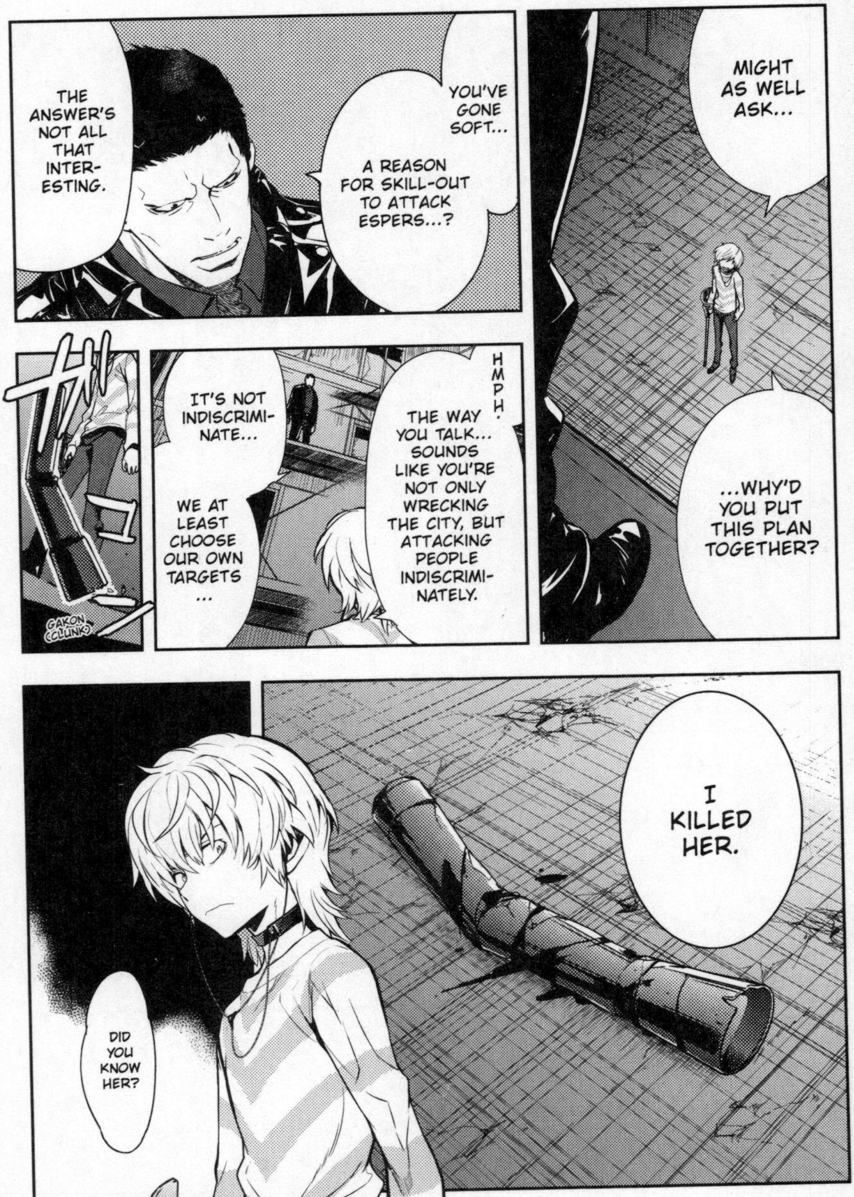
MIGHT AS WELL ASK...
...WHY'D YOU PUT THIS PLAN TOGETHER?
YOU'VE GONE SOFT...
A REASON FOR SKILL-OUT TO ATTACK ESPERS...?
THE ANSWER'S NOT ALL THAT INTERESTING.
HMPH.
THE WAY YOU TALK... SOUNDS LIKE YOU'RE NOT ONLY WRECKING THE CITY, BUT ATTACKING PEOPLE INDISCRIMINATELY.
IT'S NOT INDISCRIMINATE...
WE AT LEAST CHOOSE OUR OWN TARGETS...
GAKON (CLUNK)
I KILLED HER.
DID YOU KNOW HER?

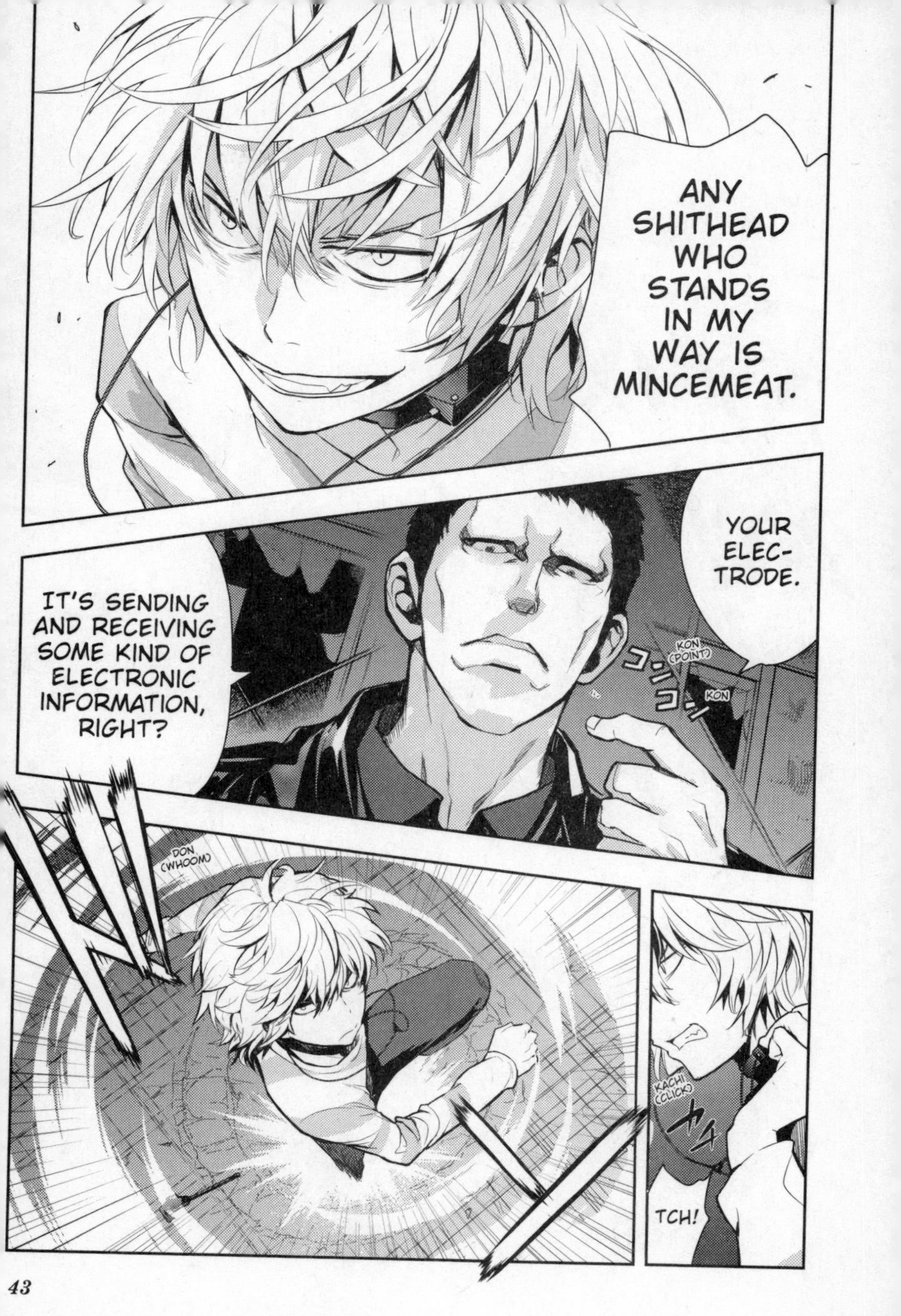
ANY SHITHEAD WHO STANDS IN MY WAY IS MINCEMEAT.
YOUR ELEC-TRODE.
KON (POINT)
KON
IT'S SENDING AND RECEIVING SOME KIND OF ELECTRONIC INFORMATION, RIGHT?
KACHI (CLICK)
TCH!
DON (WHOOM)

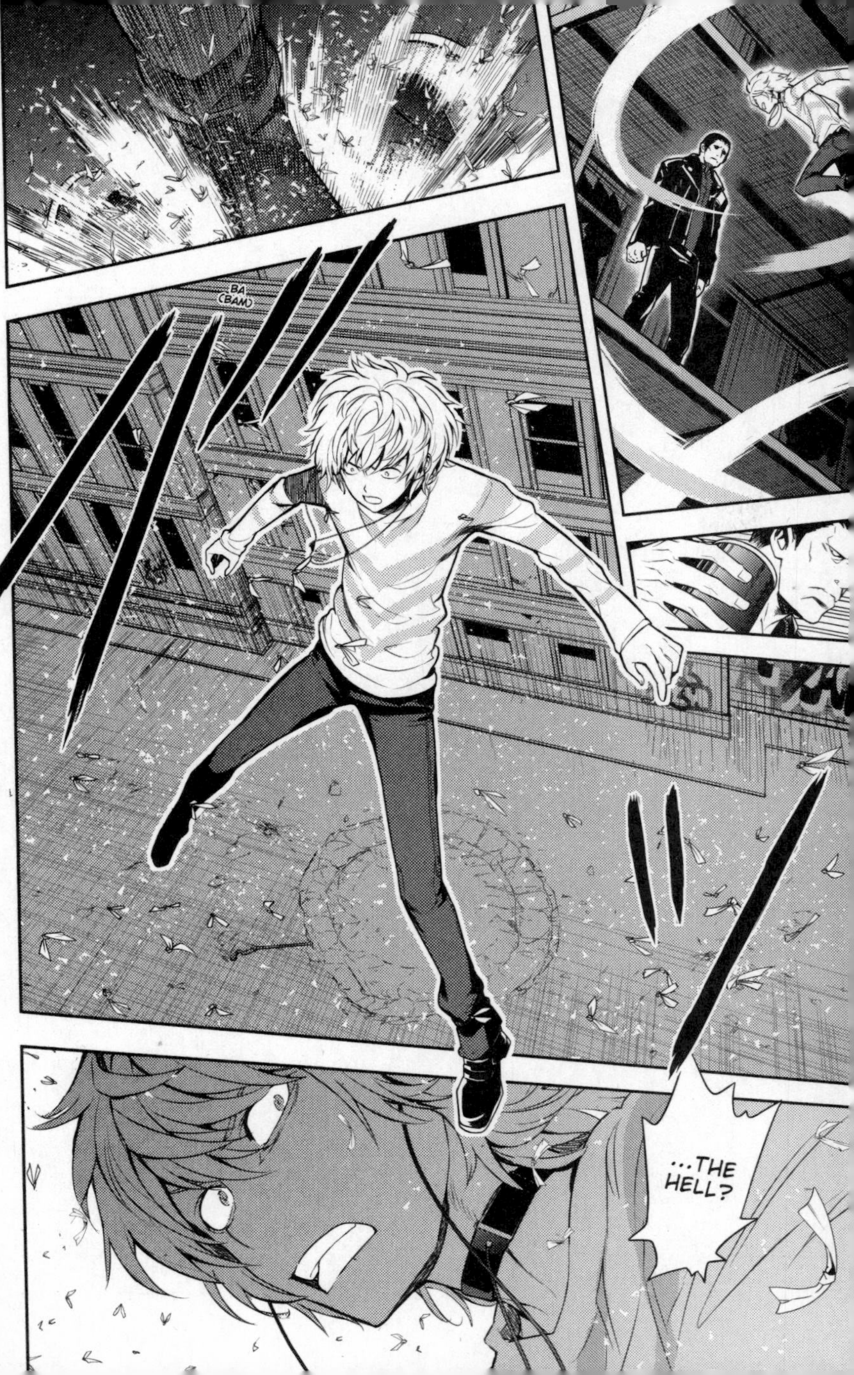
BA
(BAM)
...THE HELL?

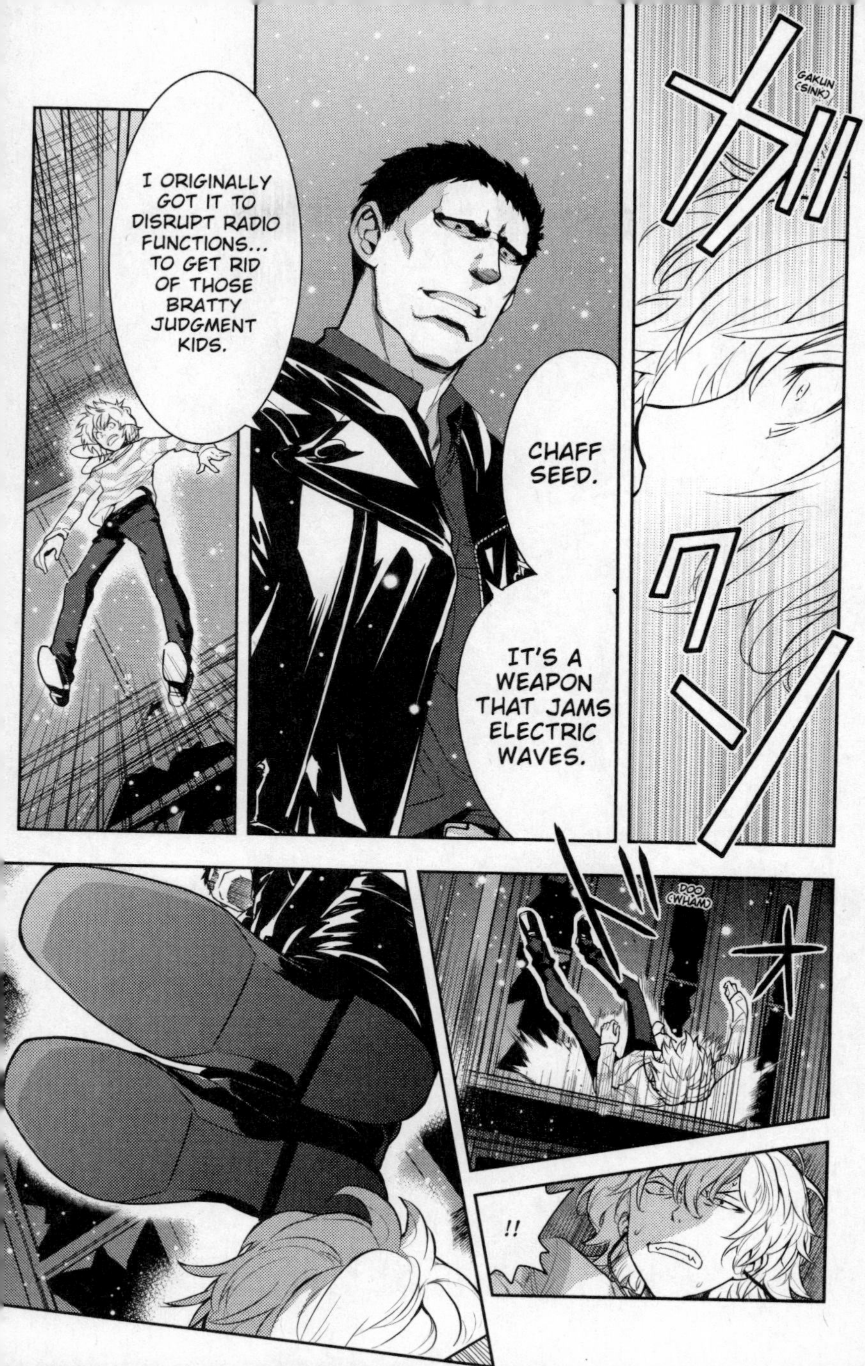
GAKUN (SINK)
CHAFF SEED.
IT'S A WEAPON THAT JAMS ELECTRIC WAVES.
I ORIGINALLY GOT IT TO DISRUPT RADIO FUNCTIONS... TO GET RID OF THOSE BRATTY JUDGMENT KIDS.
DOO (WHAM)
!!

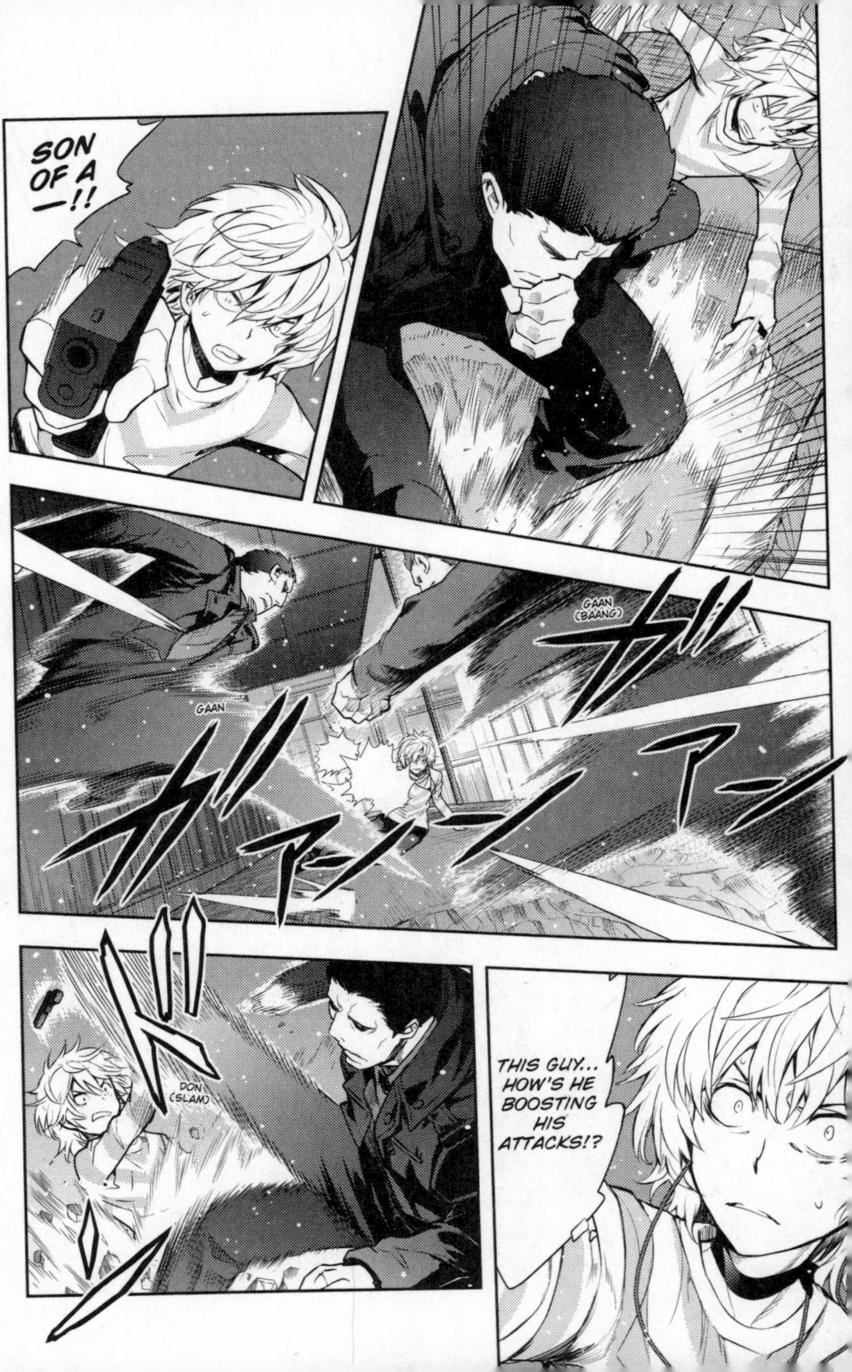
SON OF A —!!
GAAN (BAANG)
GAAN
THIS GUY... HOW'S HE BOOSTING HIS ATTACKS!?
DON (SLAM)

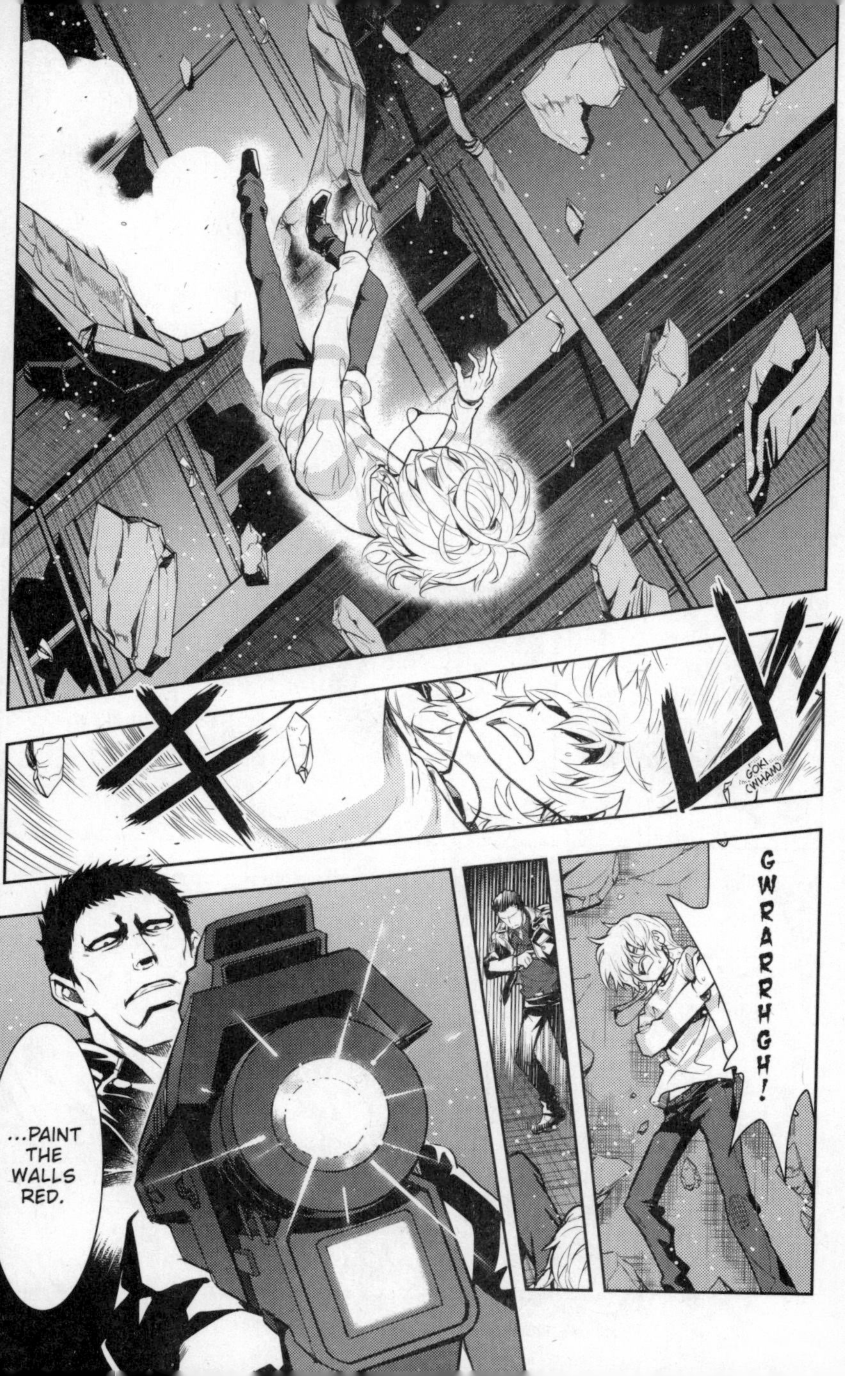
GOKI (WHAM)
GWRARRHGH!
...PAINT THE WALLS RED.

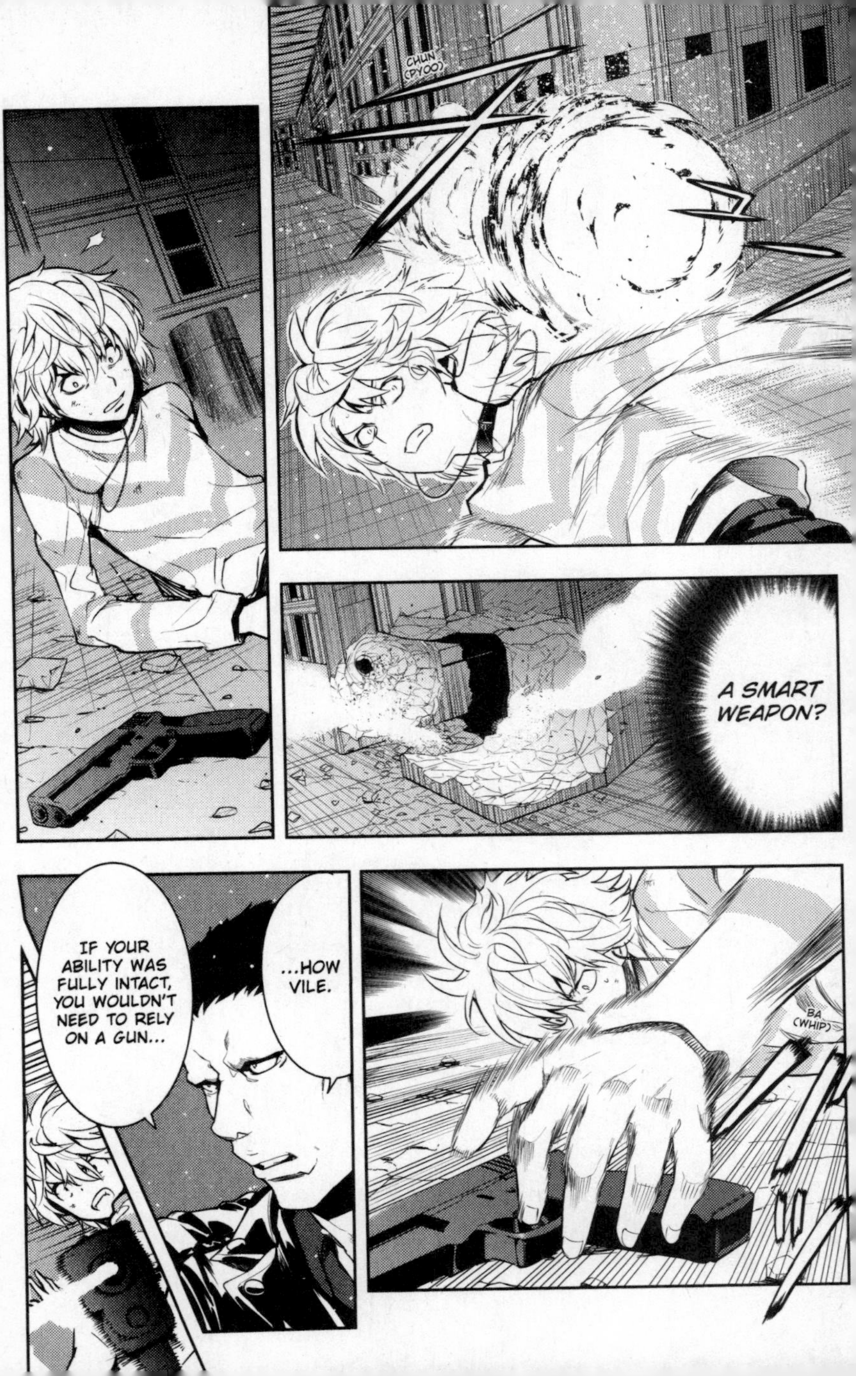
CHUN (PYOO)
A SMART WEAPON?
BA (WHIP)
...HOW VILE.
IF YOUR ABILITY WAS FULLY INTACT, YOU WOULDN'T NEED TO RELY ON A GUN...

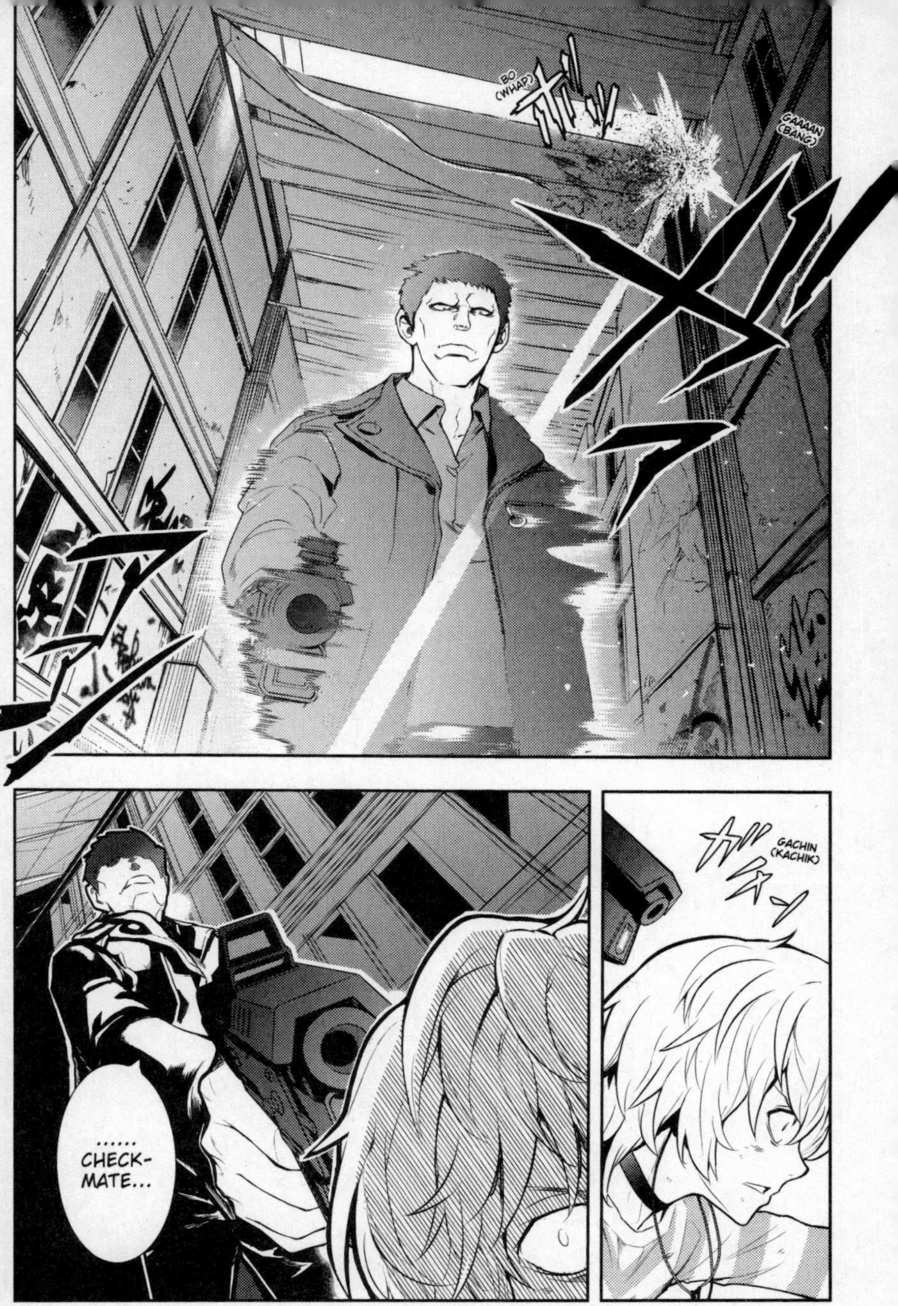
GAAAAN (BANG)
BO (WHAP)
GACHIN (KACHIK)
...... CHECK-MATE...

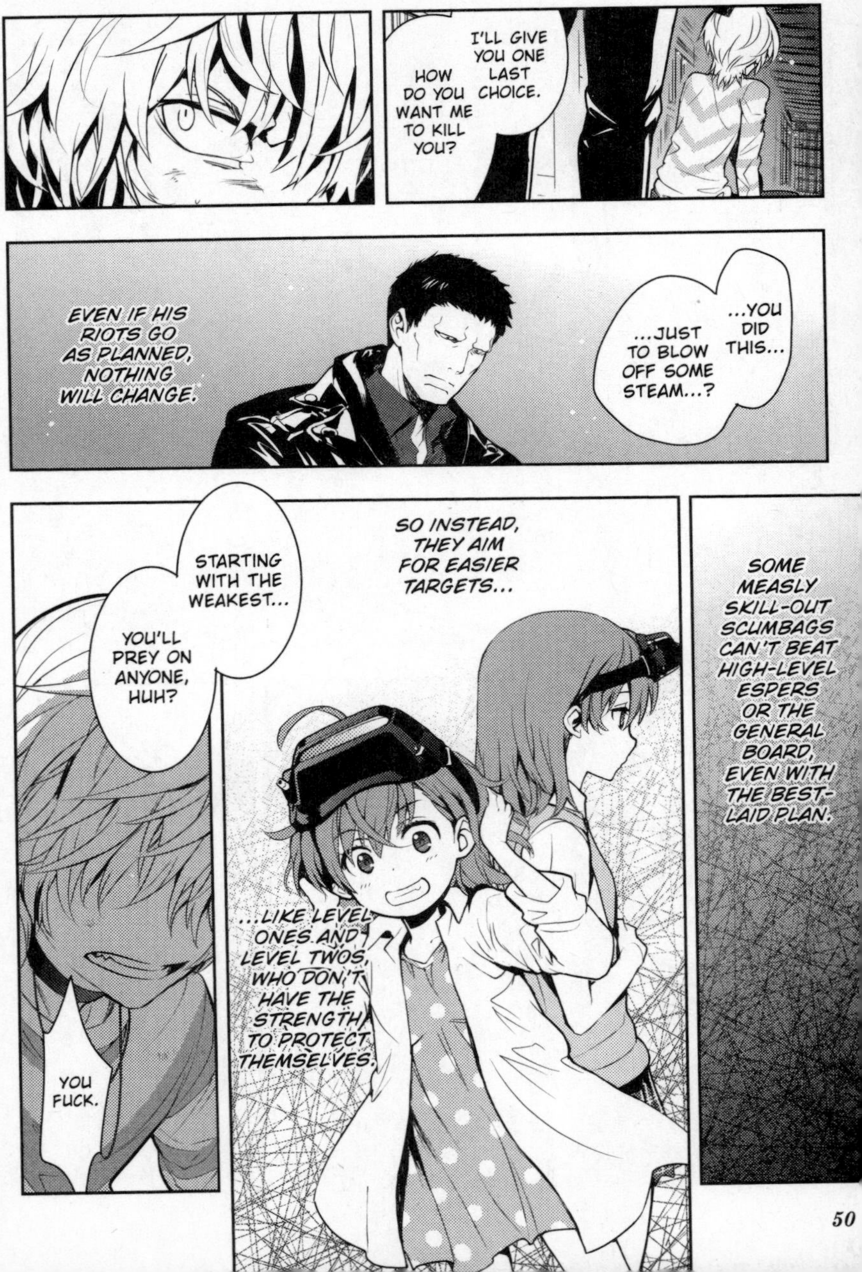
I'LL GIVE YOU ONE LAST CHOICE.
HOW DO YOU WANT ME TO KILL YOU?
...YOU DID THIS...
...JUST TO BLOW OFF SOME STEAM...?
EVEN IF HIS RIOTS GO AS PLANNED, NOTHING WILL CHANGE.
SOME MEASLY SKILL-OUT SCUMBAGS CAN'T BEAT HIGH-LEVEL ESPERS OR THE GENERAL BOARD, EVEN WITH THE BEST-LAID PLAN.
SO INSTEAD, THEY AIM FOR EASIER TARGETS...
...LIKE LEVEL ONES AND LEVEL TWOS, WHO DON'T HAVE THE STRENGTH TO PROTECT THEMSELVES.
STARTING WITH THE WEAKEST...
YOU'LL PREY ON ANYONE, HUH?
YOU FUCK.

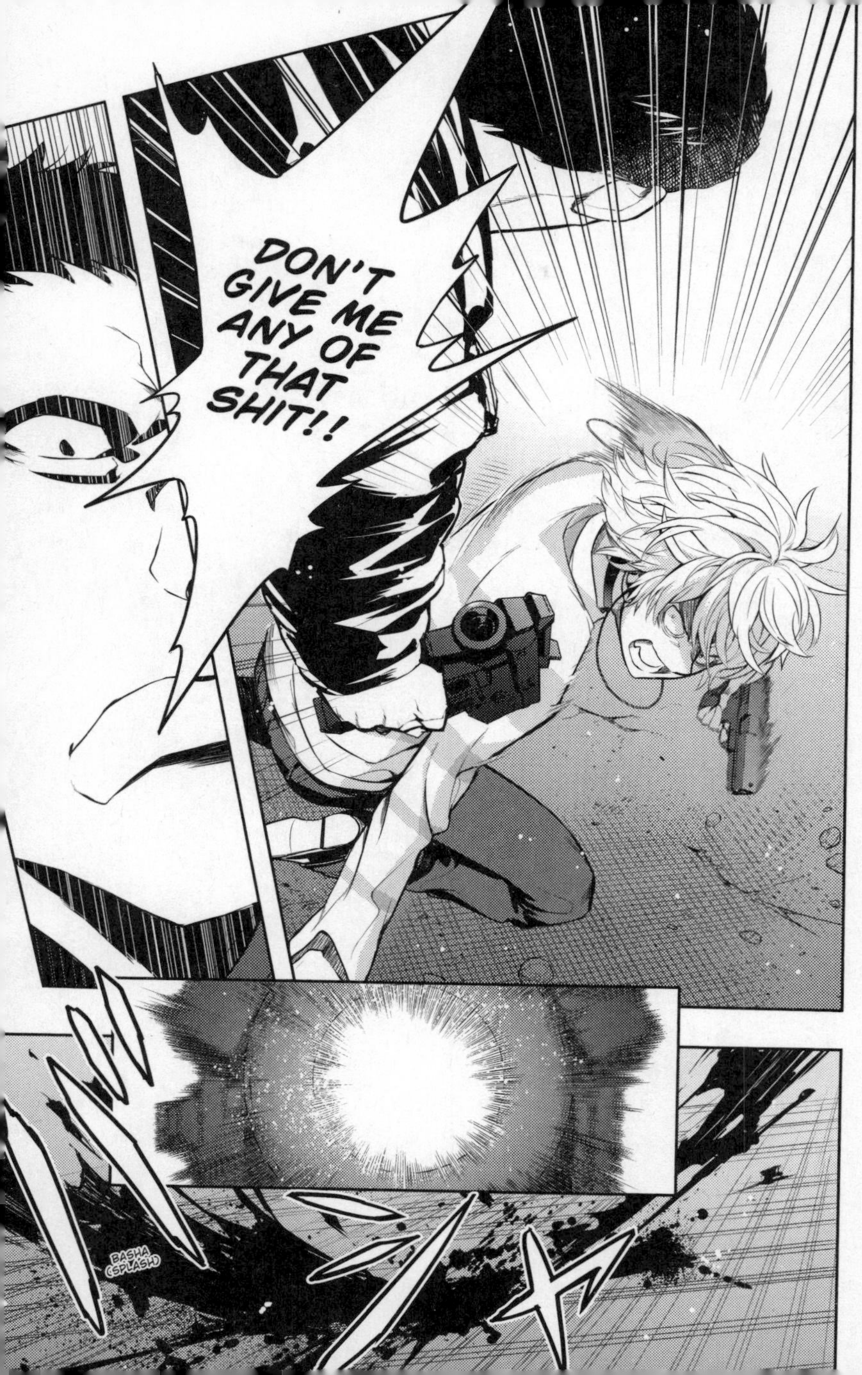
DON'T GIVE ME ANY OF THAT SHIT!!
BASHA (SPLASH)

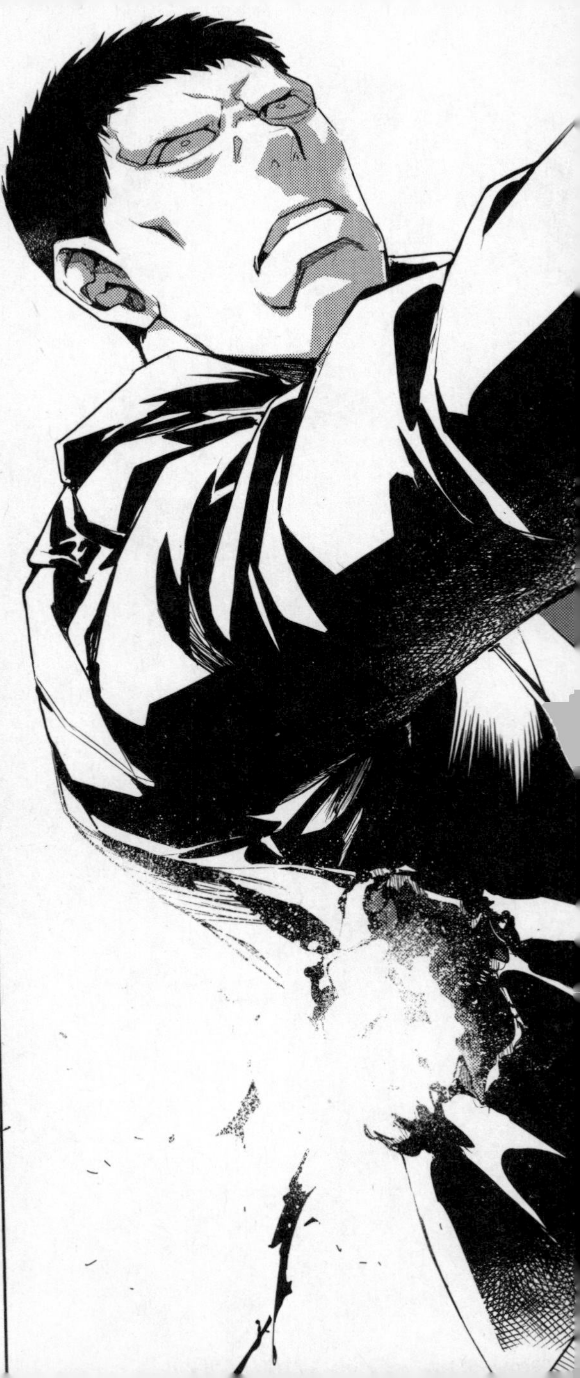

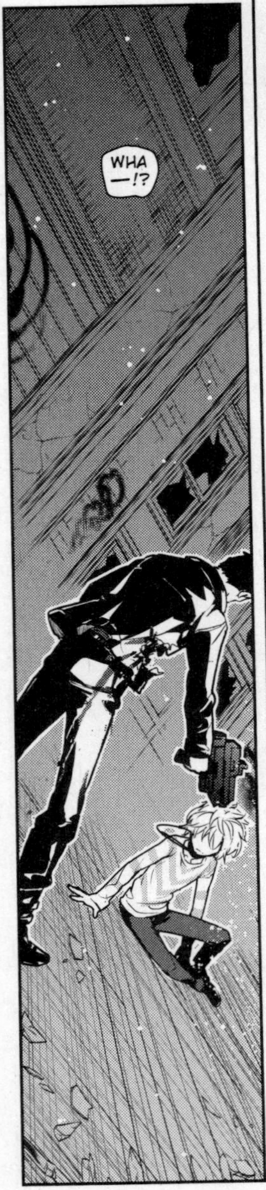
WHA —!?

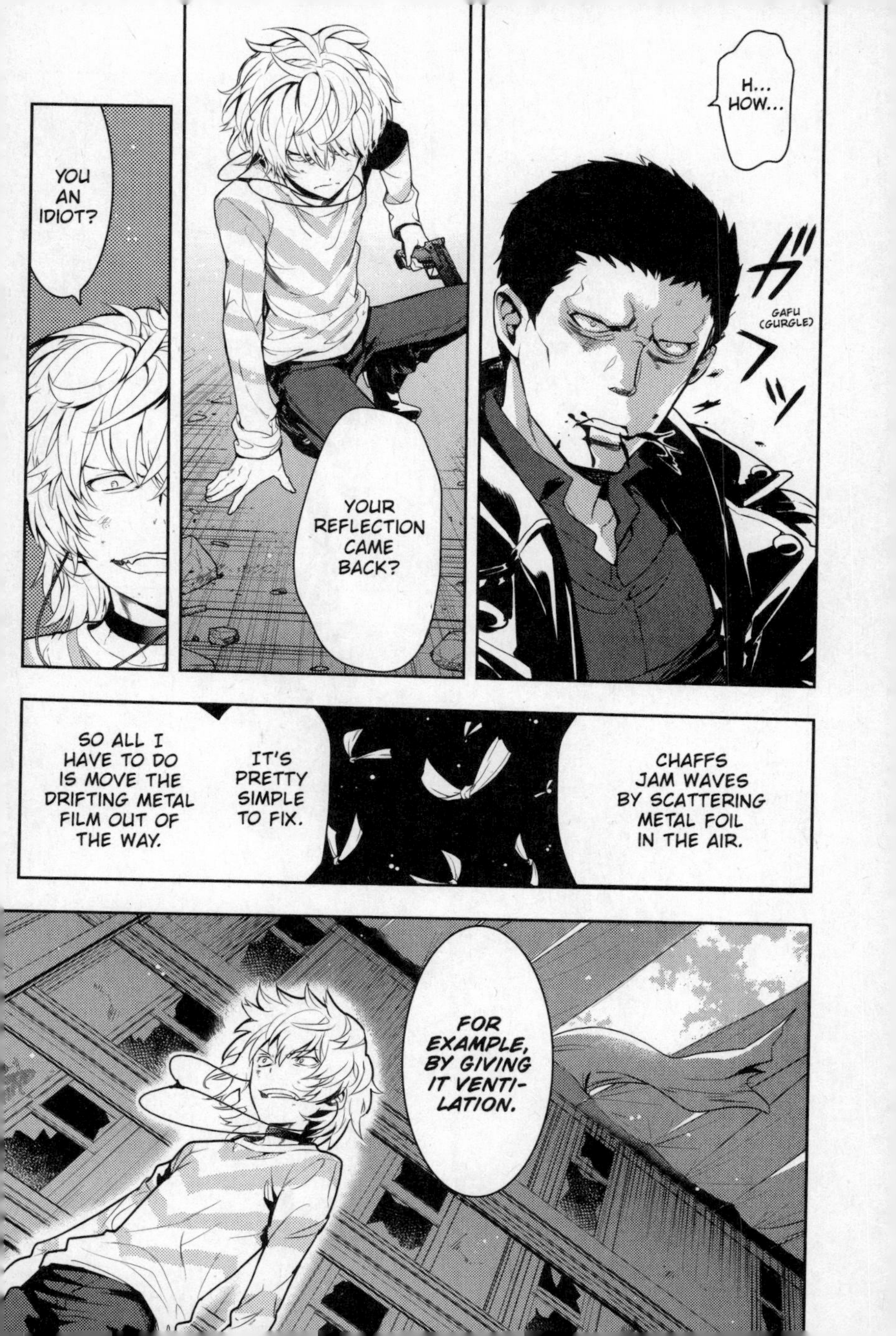
H...
HOW...
ガフッ
GAFU (GURGLE)
YOUR REFLECTION CAME BACK?
YOU AN IDIOT?
CHAFFS JAM WAVES BY SCATTERING METAL FOIL IN THE AIR.
IT'S PRETTY SIMPLE TO FIX.
SO ALL I HAVE TO DO IS MOVE THE DRIFTING METAL FILM OUT OF THE WAY.
FOR EXAMPLE, BY GIVING IT VENTI- LATION.

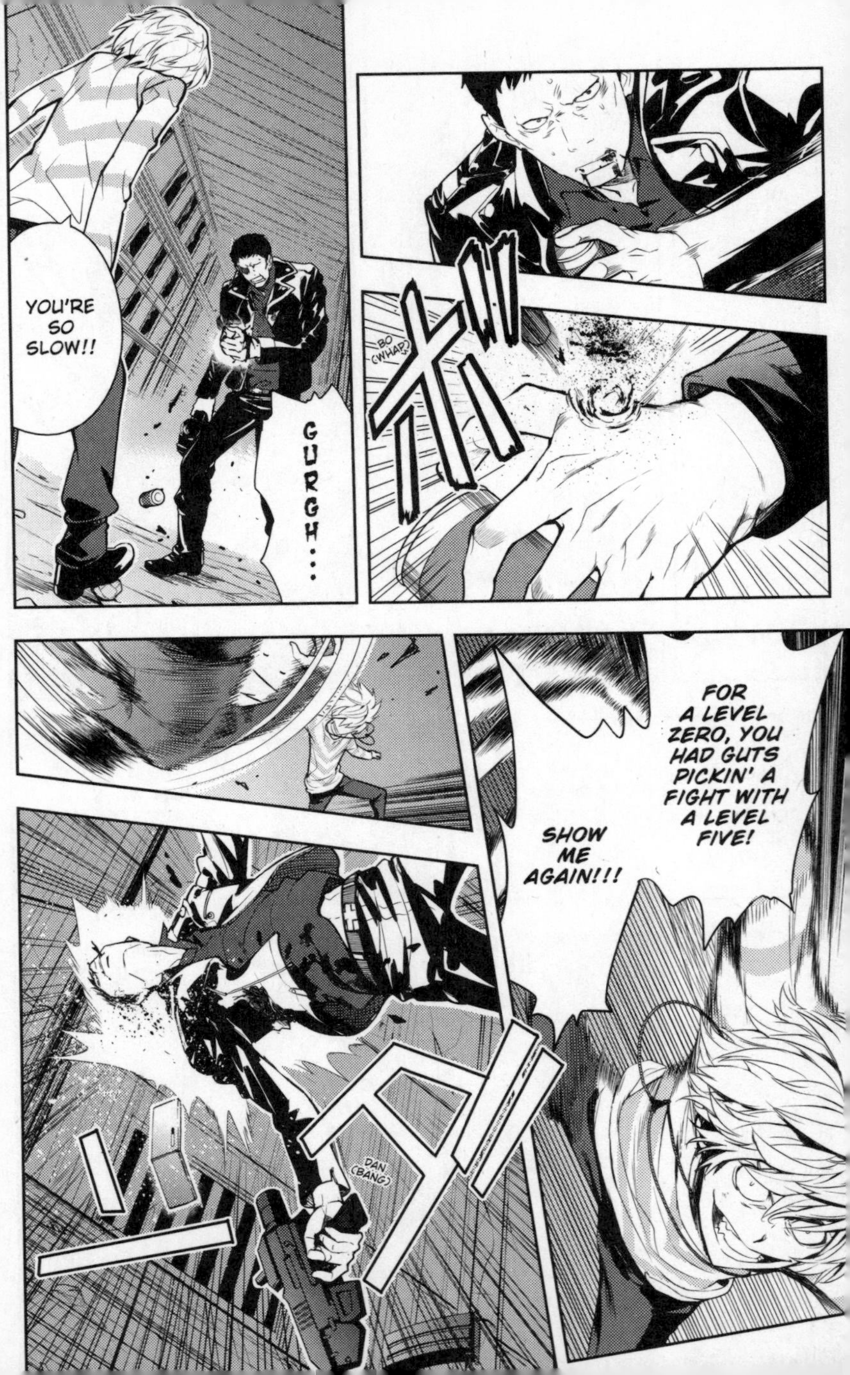
BO (WHAP)
YOU'RE SO SLOW!!
GURGH...
FOR A LEVEL ZERO, YOU HAD GUTS PICKIN' A FIGHT WITH A LEVEL FIVE!
SHOW ME AGAIN!!!
DAN (BANG)

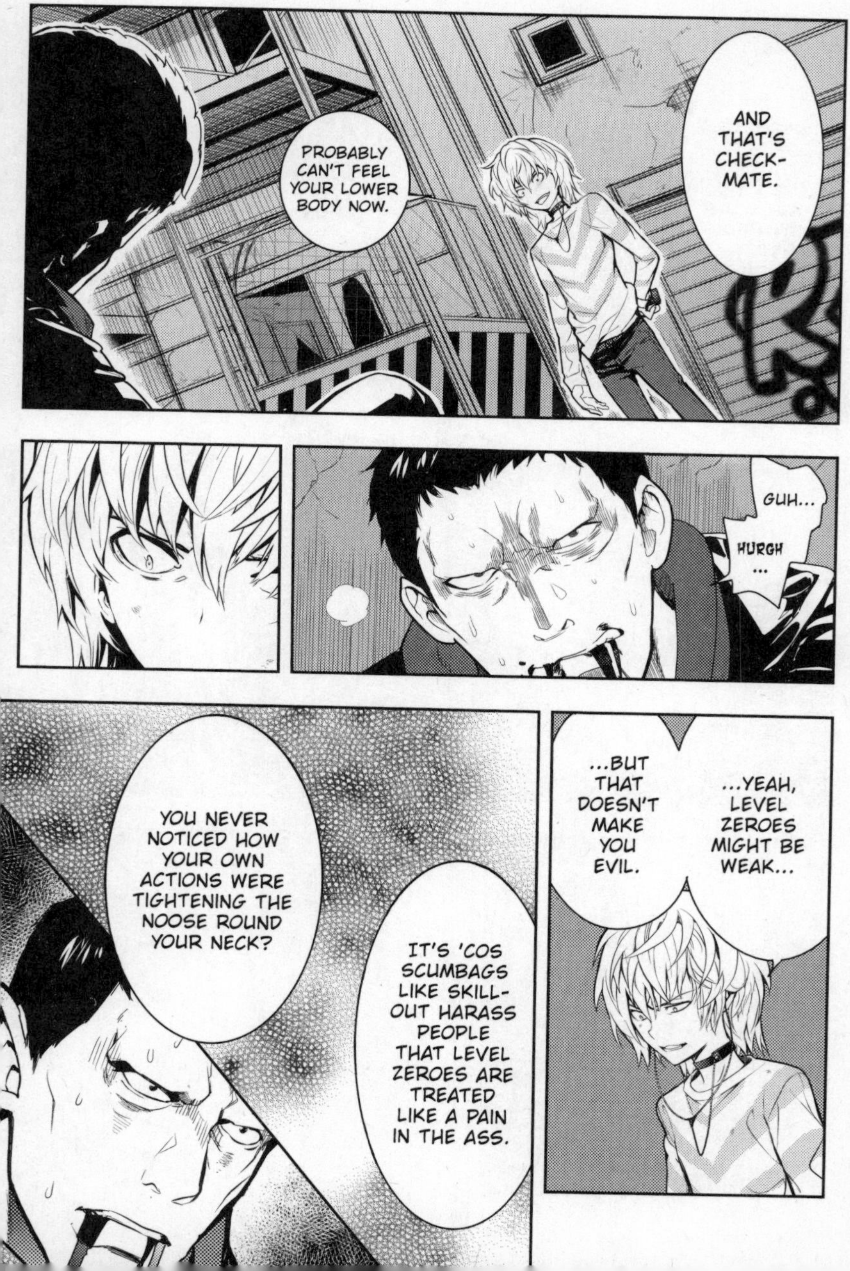
AND THAT'S CHECK-MATE.
PROBABLY CAN'T FEEL YOUR LOWER BODY NOW.
GUH...
HURGH ...
...YEAH, LEVEL ZEROES MIGHT BE WEAK...
...BUT THAT DOESN'T MAKE YOU EVIL.
IT'S 'COS SCUMBAGS LIKE SKILL-OUT HARASS PEOPLE THAT LEVEL ZEROES ARE TREATED LIKE A PAIN IN THE ASS.
YOU NEVER NOTICED HOW YOUR OWN ACTIONS WERE TIGHTENING THE NOOSE ROUND YOUR NECK?

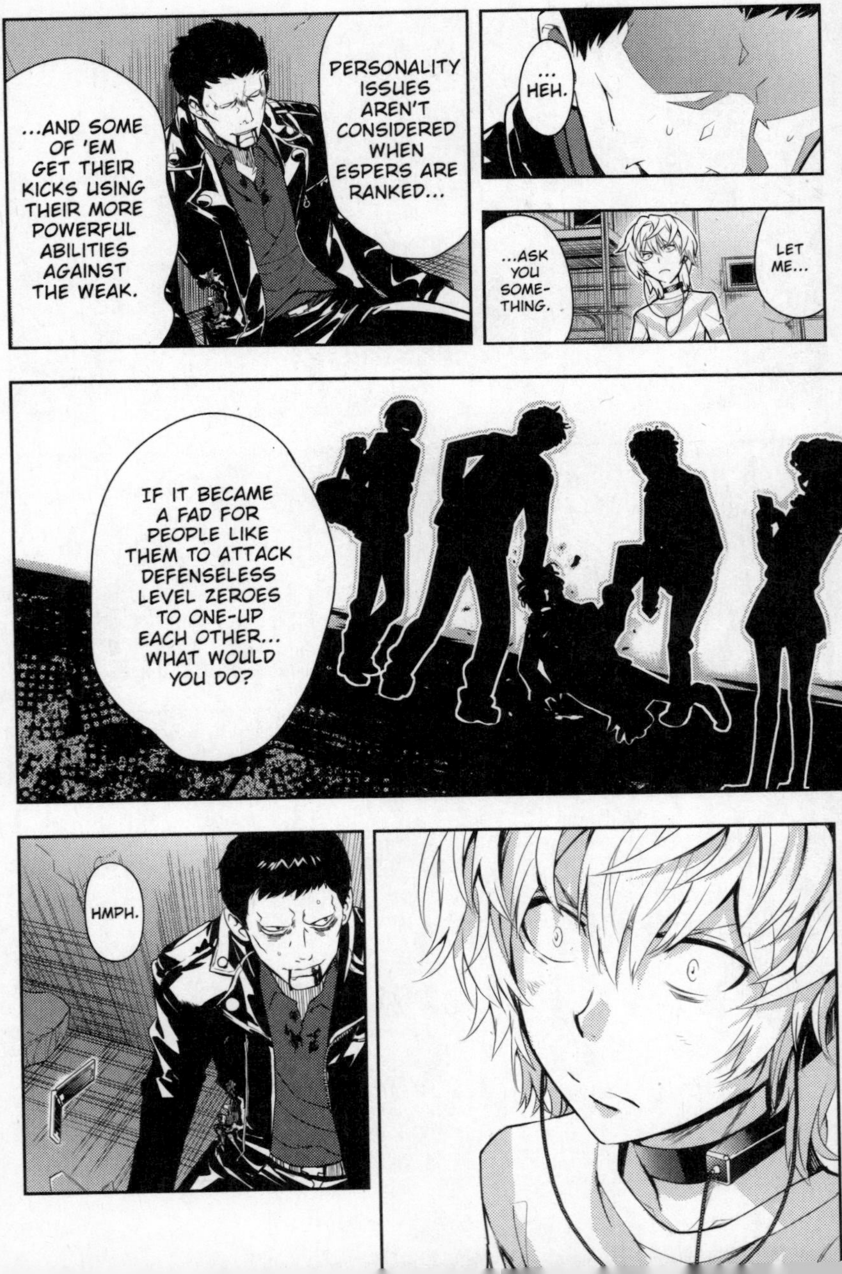
...HEH.
LET ME...
...ASK YOU SOMETHING.
PERSONALITY ISSUES AREN'T CONSIDERED WHEN ESPERS ARE RANKED...
...AND SOME OF 'EM GET THEIR KICKS USING THEIR MORE POWERFUL ABILITIES AGAINST THE WEAK.
IF IT BECAME A FAD FOR PEOPLE LIKE THEM TO ATTACK DEFENSELESS LEVEL ZEROES TO ONE-UP EACH OTHER... WHAT WOULD YOU DO?
HMPH.

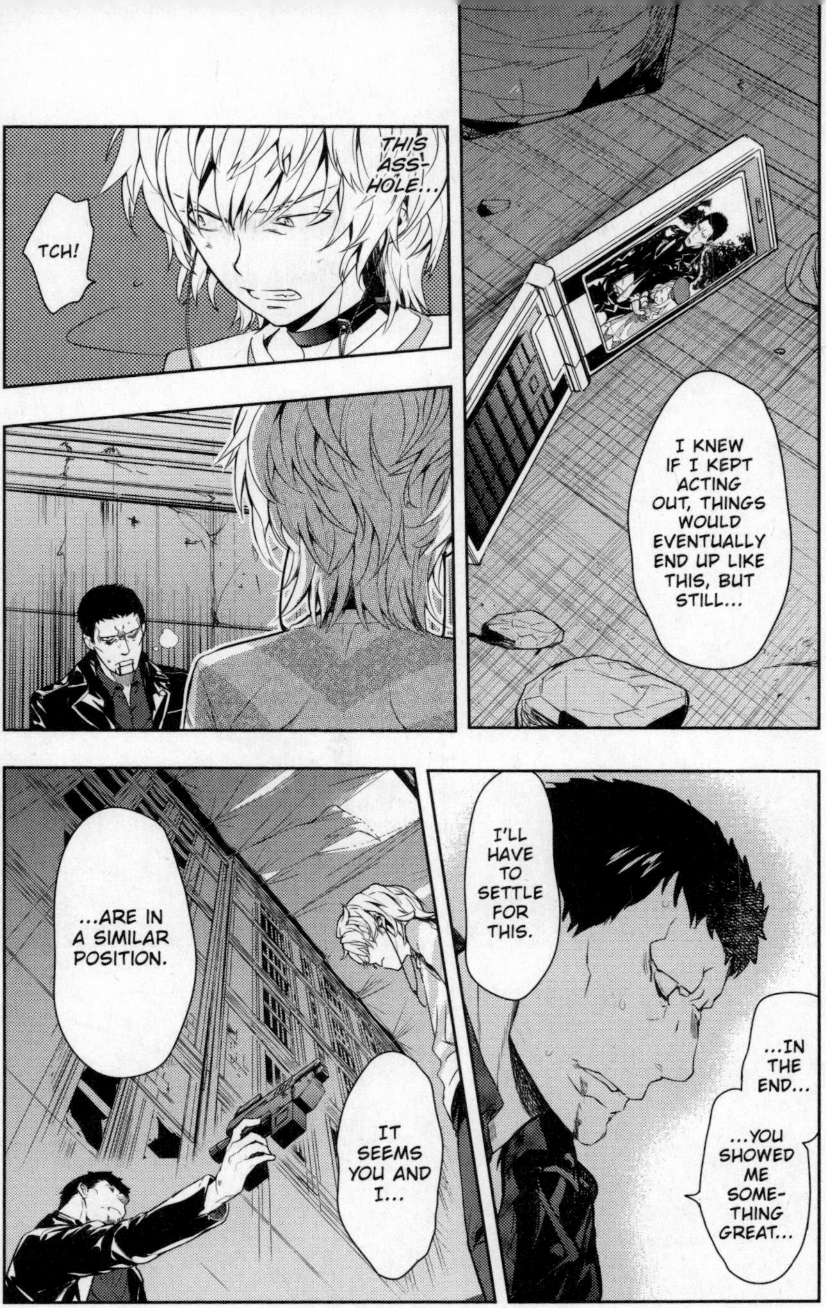
I KNEW IF I KEPT ACTING OUT, THINGS WOULD EVENTUALLY END UP LIKE THIS, BUT STILL...
THIS ASS-HOLE...
TCH!
...IN THE END...
...YOU SHOWED ME SOME-THING GREAT...
I'LL HAVE TO SETTLE FOR THIS.
IT SEEMS YOU AND I...
...ARE IN A SIMILAR POSITION.

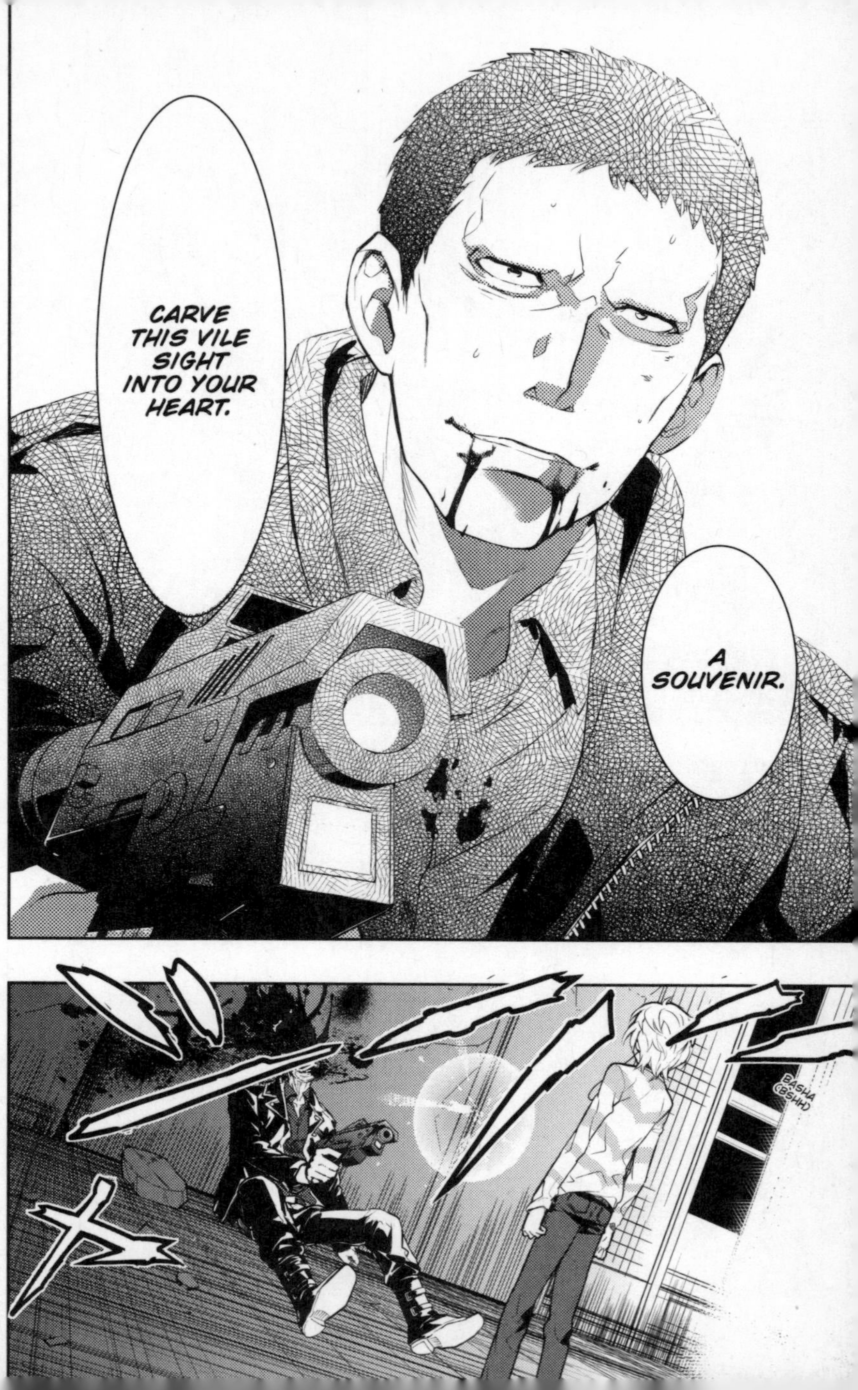
CARVE THIS VILE SIGHT INTO YOUR HEART.
A SOUVENIR.
BASHA (BSHH)

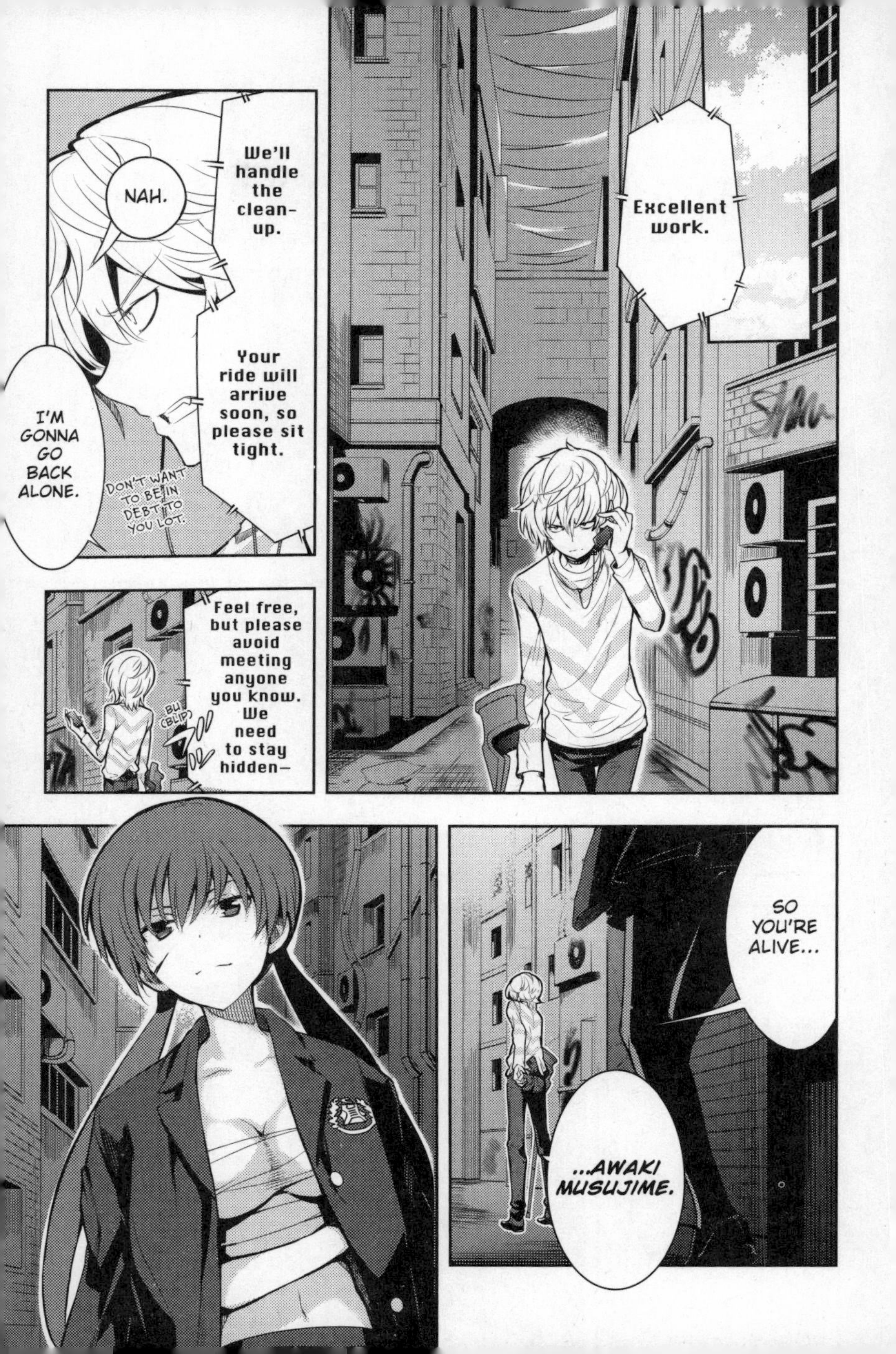
Excellent work.
We'll handle the clean-up.
NAH.
Your ride will arrive soon, so please sit tight.
I'M GONNA GO BACK ALONE.
DON'T WANT TO BE IN DEBT TO YOU LOT.
Feel free, but please avoid meeting anyone you know. We need to stay hidden–
BU (BLIP)
SO YOU'RE ALIVE...
...AWAKI MUSUJIME.

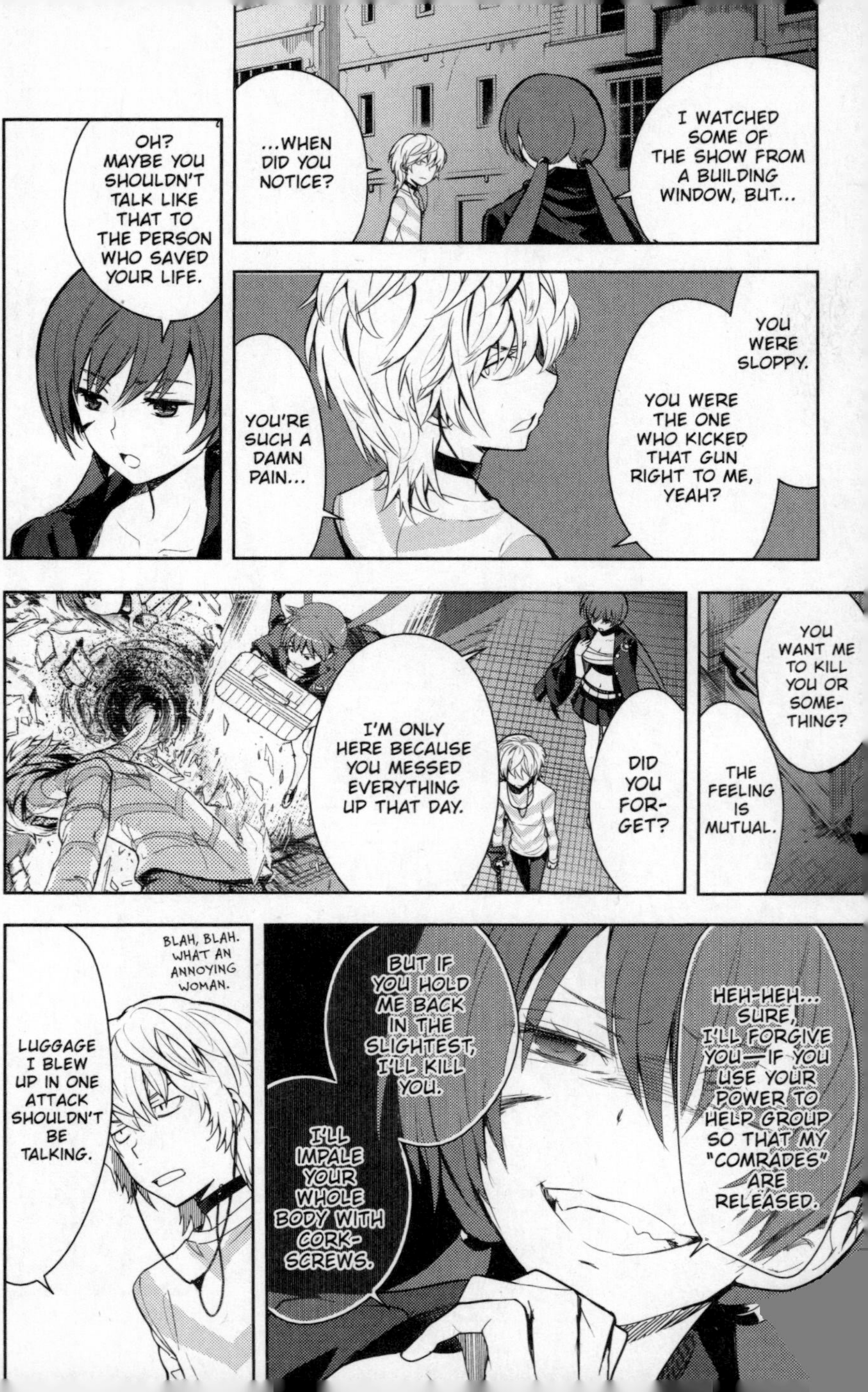
I WATCHED SOME OF THE SHOW FROM A BUILDING WINDOW, BUT...
...WHEN DID YOU NOTICE?
YOU WERE SLOPPY.
YOU WERE THE ONE WHO KICKED THAT GUN RIGHT TO ME, YEAH?
YOU'RE SUCH A DAMN PAIN...
OH? MAYBE YOU SHOULDN'T TALK LIKE THAT TO THE PERSON WHO SAVED YOUR LIFE.
YOU WANT ME TO KILL YOU OR SOME-THING?
THE FEELING IS MUTUAL.
DID YOU FOR-GET?
I'M ONLY HERE BECAUSE YOU MESSED EVERYTHING UP THAT DAY.
HEH-HEH... SURE, I'LL FORGIVE YOU—IF YOU USE YOUR POWER TO HELP GROUP SO THAT MY "COMRADES" ARE RELEASED.
BUT IF YOU HOLD ME BACK IN THE SLIGHTEST, I'LL KILL YOU.
I'LL IMPALE YOUR WHOLE BODY WITH CORK-SCREWS.
BLAH, BLAH. WHAT AN ANNOYING WOMAN.
LUGGAGE I BLEW UP IN ONE ATTACK SHOULDN'T BE TALKING.

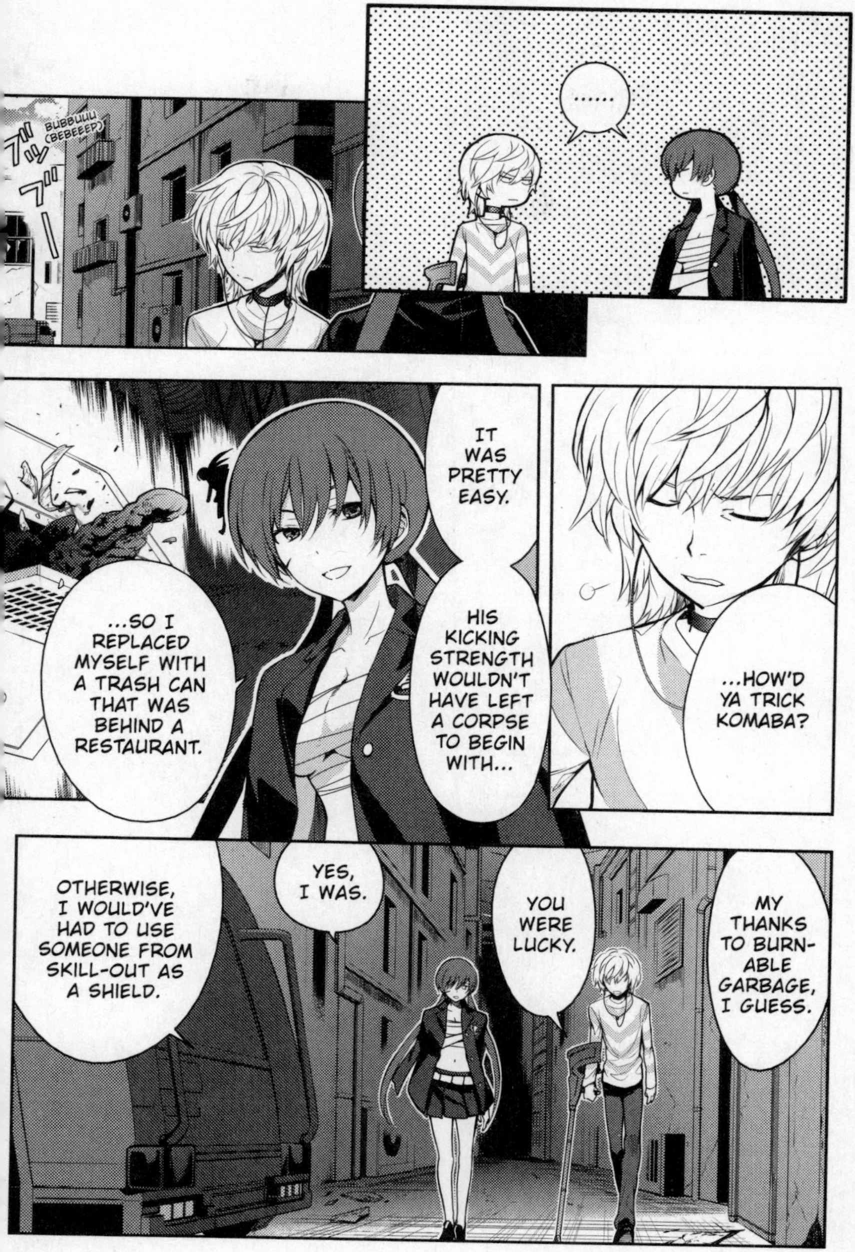
......
BUBBUUU (BEBEEEP)
...HOW'D YA TRICK KOMABA?
IT WAS PRETTY EASY.
HIS KICKING STRENGTH WOULDN'T HAVE LEFT A CORPSE TO BEGIN WITH...
...SO I REPLACED MYSELF WITH A TRASH CAN THAT WAS BEHIND A RESTAURANT.
MY THANKS TO BURN-ABLE GARBAGE, I GUESS.
YOU WERE LUCKY.
YES, I WAS.
OTHERWISE, I WOULD'VE HAD TO USE SOMEONE FROM SKILL-OUT AS A SHIELD.

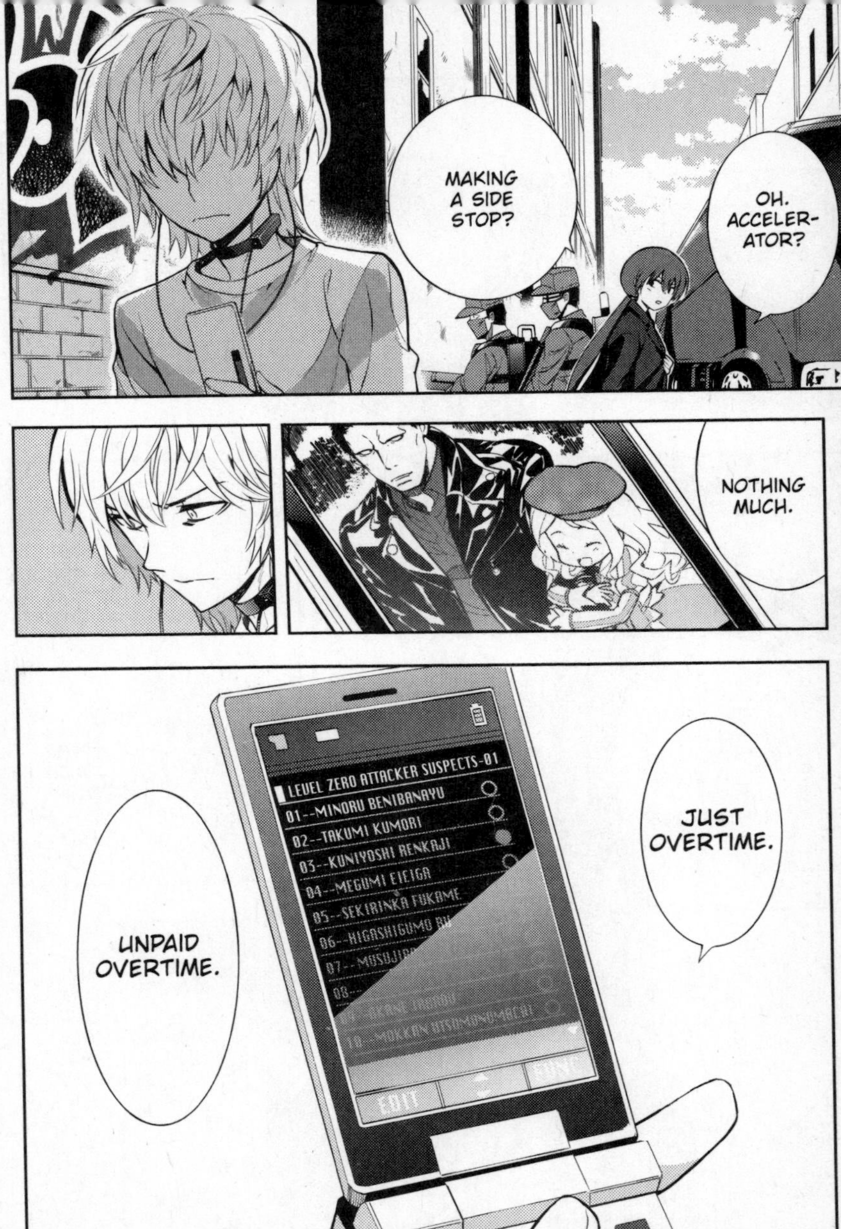
OH. ACCELER-ATOR?
MAKING A SIDE STOP?
NOTHING MUCH.
JUST OVERTIME.
LEVEL ZERO ATTACKER SUSPECTS-01
01--MINORU BENIBANAYU
02--TAKUMI KUMORI
03--KUNIYOSHI RENKAJI
04--MEGUMI EIEIGA
05--SEKIRINKA FUKAME
EDIT
UNPAID OVERTIME.

A Certain Magical Index

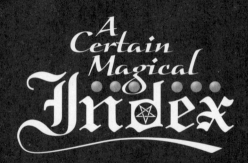

A Certain Magical Index

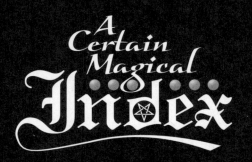

#119 THE ENGLISH PURITAN CHURCH WOMEN'S DORM

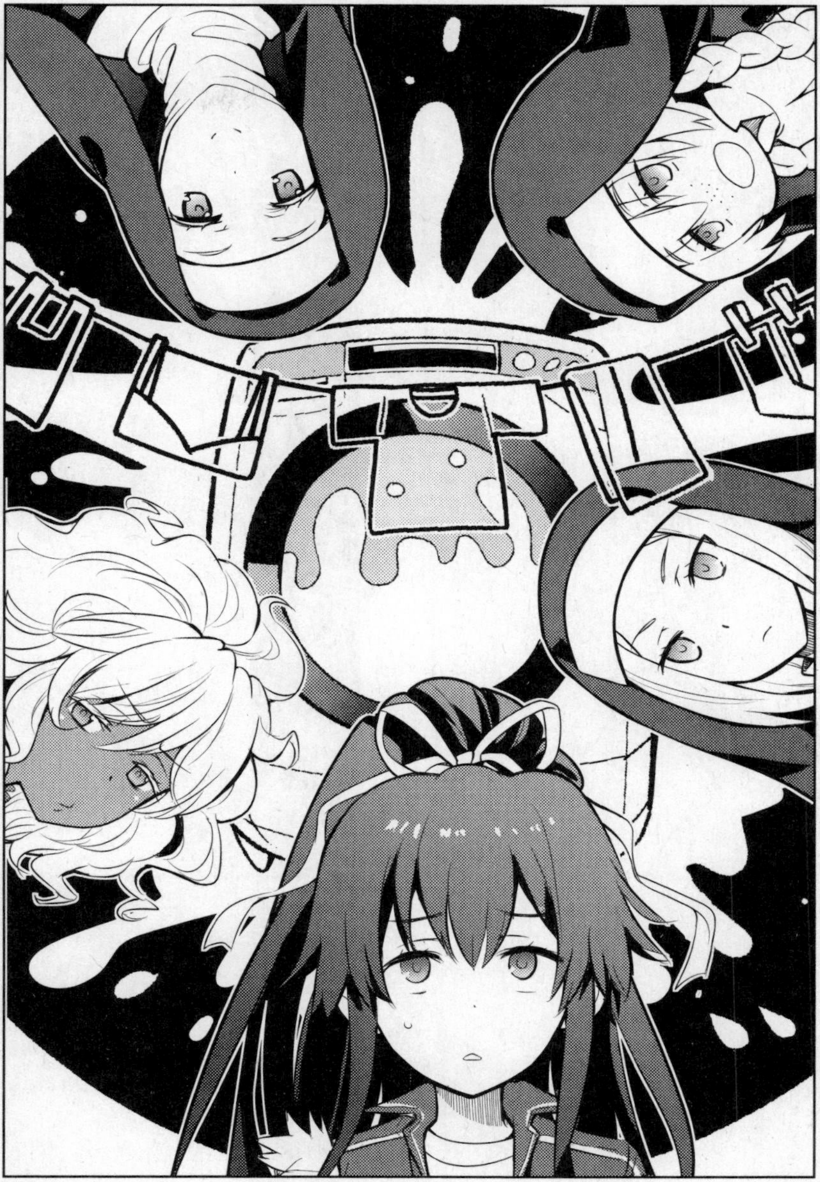

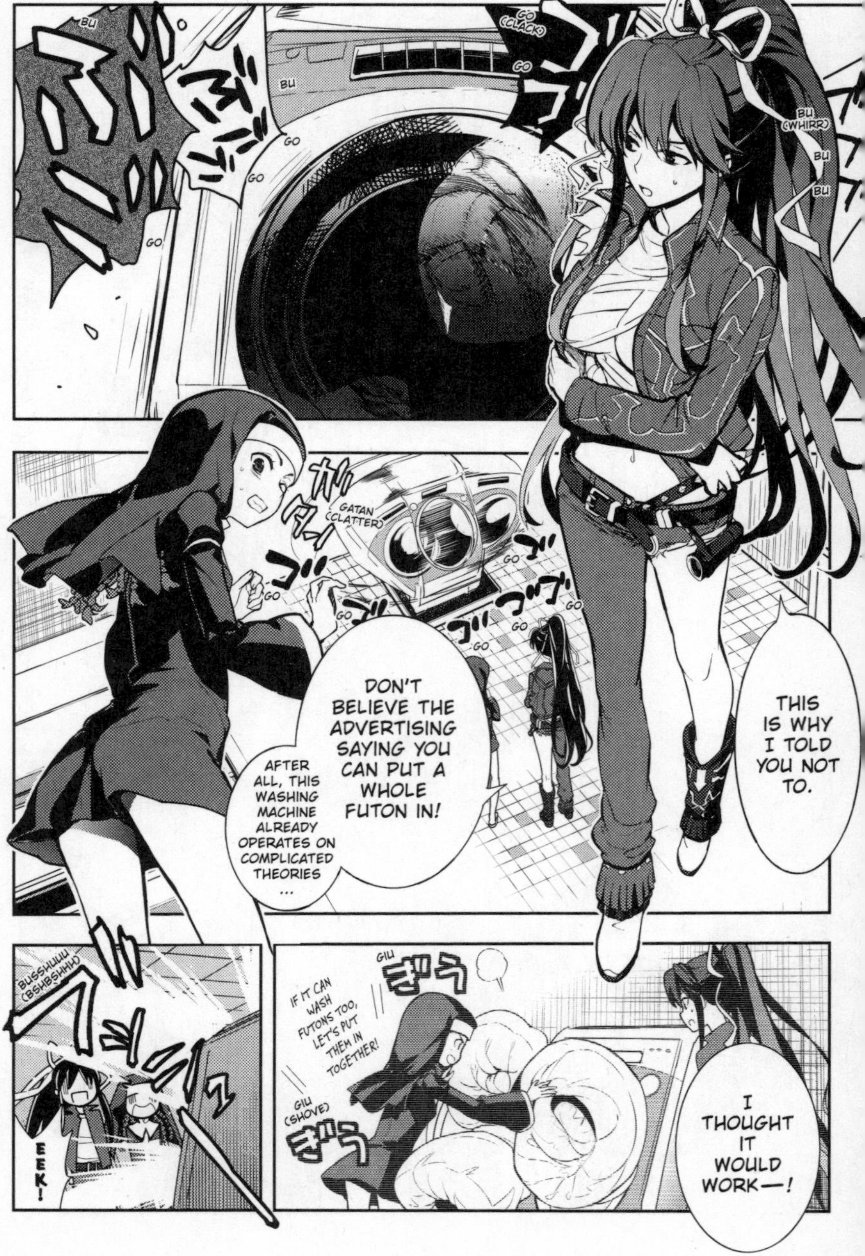
BU (WHIRR)
BU
BU
GO (CLACK)
GO
BU
BU
GO
GO
GO
THIS IS WHY I TOLD YOU NOT TO.
GATAN (CLATTER)
GO
GO
GO
GO
GO
GO
DON'T BELIEVE THE ADVERTISING SAYING YOU CAN PUT A WHOLE FUTON IN!
AFTER ALL, THIS WASHING MACHINE ALREADY OPERATES ON COMPLICATED THEORIES ...
I THOUGHT IT WOULD WORK—!
GIU
IF IT CAN WASH FUTONS TOO, LET'S PUT THEM IN TOGETHER!
GIU (SHOVE)
BUSSHUUU (BSHBSHHH)
EEK!

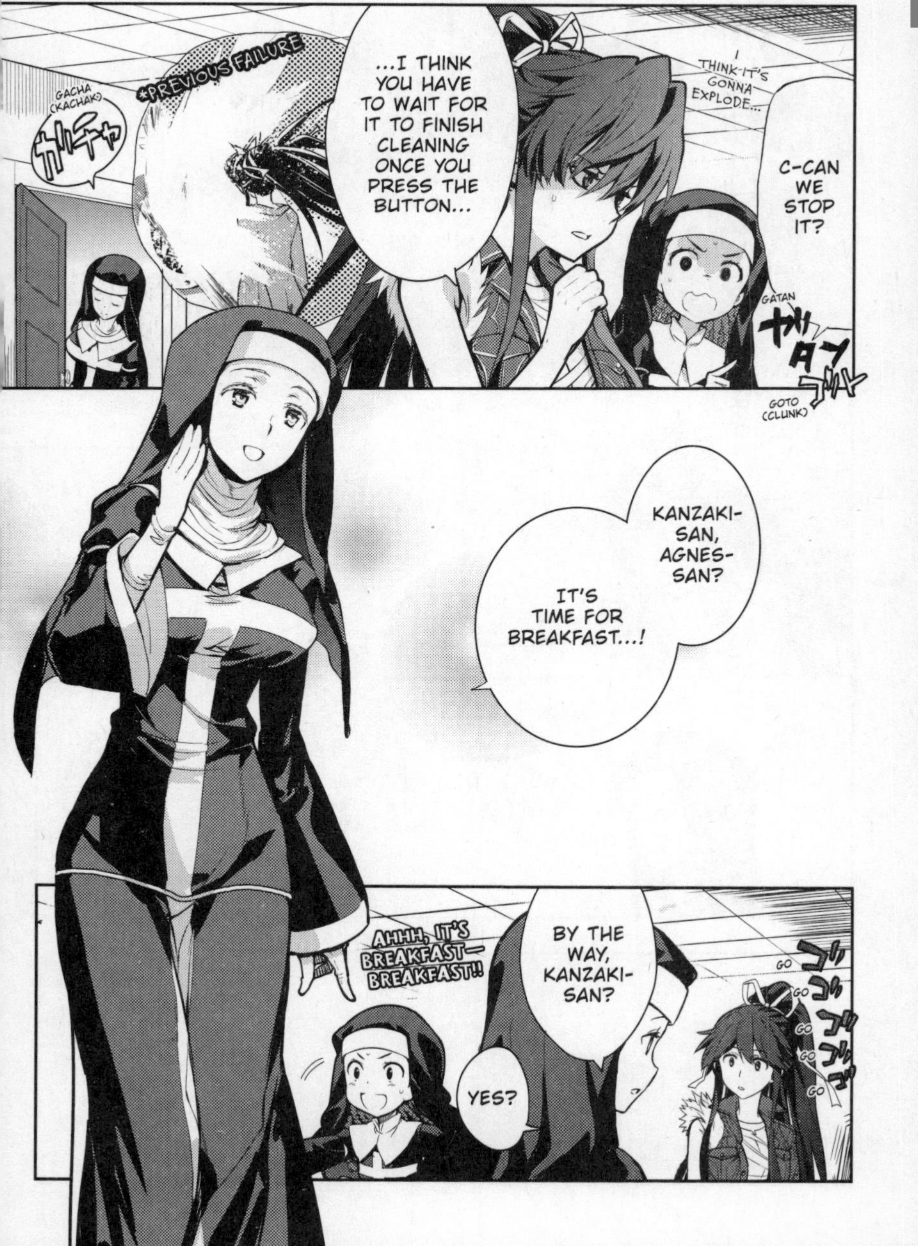
I THINK IT'S GONNA EXPLODE...
C-CAN WE STOP IT?
GATAN
GOTO (CLUNK)
...I THINK YOU HAVE TO WAIT FOR IT TO FINISH CLEANING ONCE YOU PRESS THE BUTTON...
*PREVIOUS FAILURE
GACHA (KACHAK)
KANZAKI-SAN, AGNES-SAN?
IT'S TIME FOR BREAKFAST...!
GO GO GO GO GO
BY THE WAY, KANZAKI-SAN?
YES?
AHHH, IT'S BREAKFAST— BREAKFAST!!

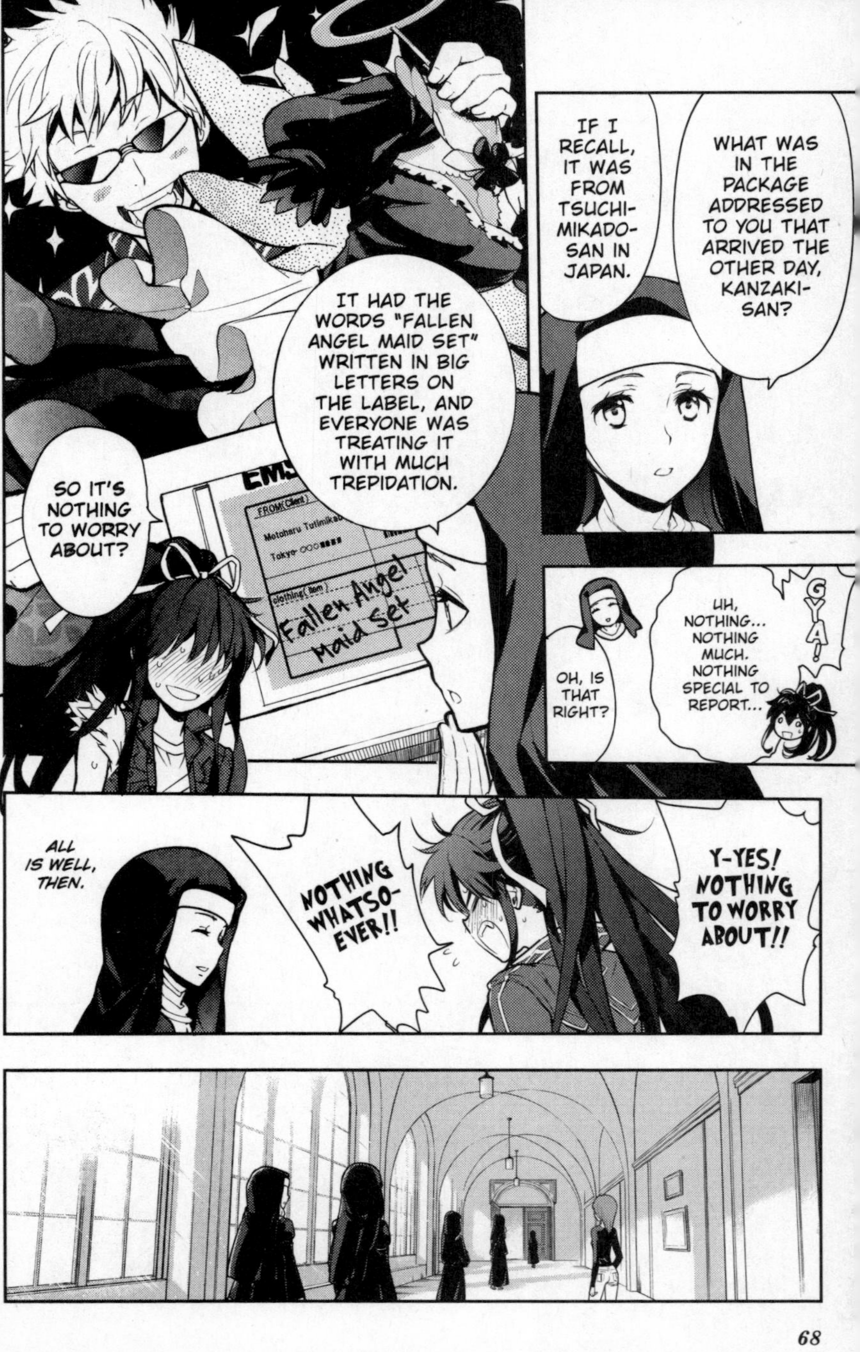
WHAT WAS IN THE PACKAGE ADDRESSED TO YOU THAT ARRIVED THE OTHER DAY, KANZAKI-SAN?
IF I RECALL, IT WAS FROM TSUCHI-MIKADO-SAN IN JAPAN.
GYA!
UH, NOTHING... NOTHING MUCH. NOTHING SPECIAL TO REPORT...
OH, IS THAT RIGHT?
IT HAD THE WORDS "FALLEN ANGEL MAID SET" WRITTEN IN BIG LETTERS ON THE LABEL, AND EVERYONE WAS TREATING IT WITH MUCH TREPIDATION.
SO IT'S NOTHING TO WORRY ABOUT?
EMS
FROM(Client)
Tokyo
clothing(Item)
Fallen Angel Maid Set
Y-YES! NOTHING TO WORRY ABOUT!!
NOTHING WHATSO-EVER!!
ALL IS WELL, THEN.

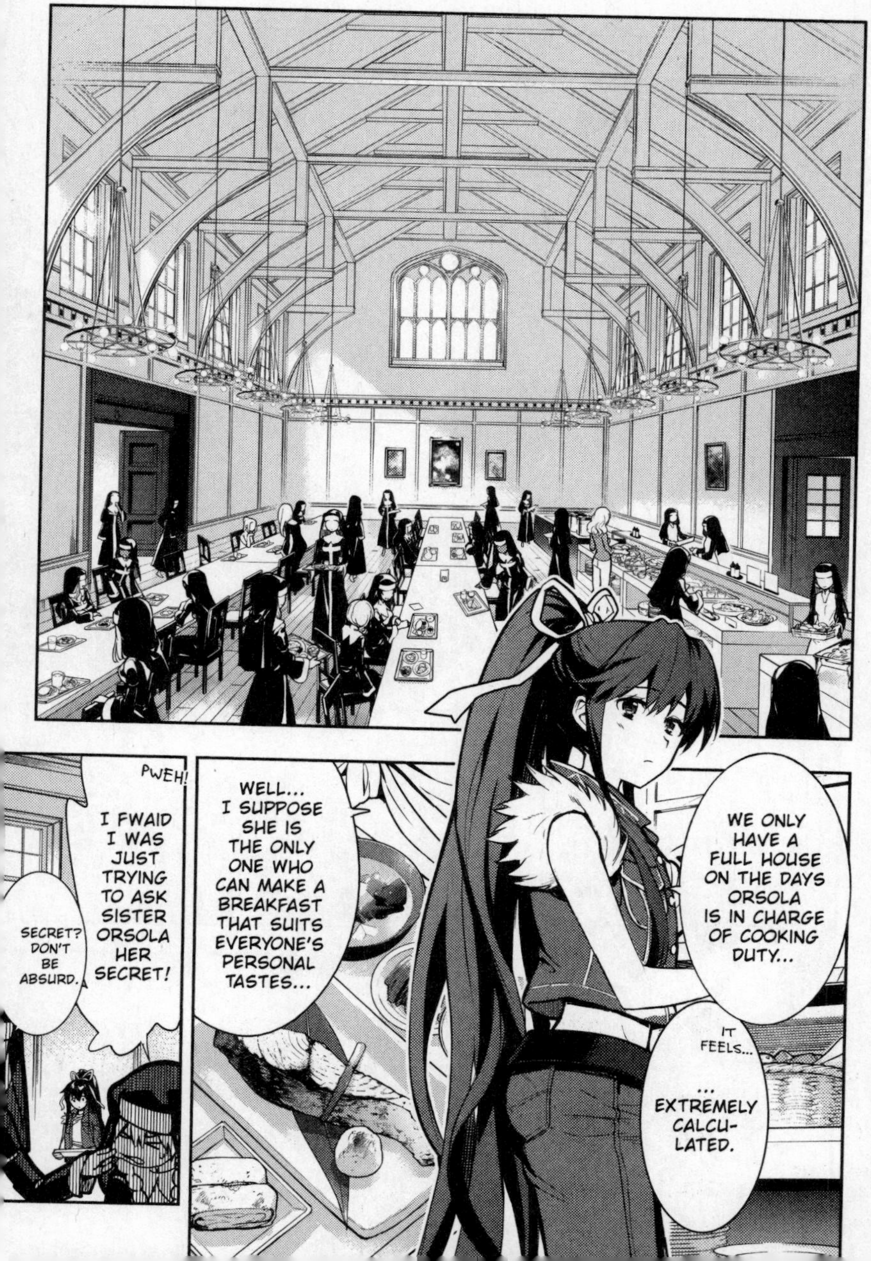
WE ONLY HAVE A FULL HOUSE ON THE DAYS ORSOLA IS IN CHARGE OF COOKING DUTY...
WELL... I SUPPOSE SHE IS THE ONLY ONE WHO CAN MAKE A BREAKFAST THAT SUITS EVERYONE'S PERSONAL TASTES...
IT FEELS...
... EXTREMELY CALCULATED.
PWEH!
I FWAID I WAS JUST TRYING TO ASK SISTER ORSOLA HER SECRET!
SECRET? DON'T BE ABSURD.

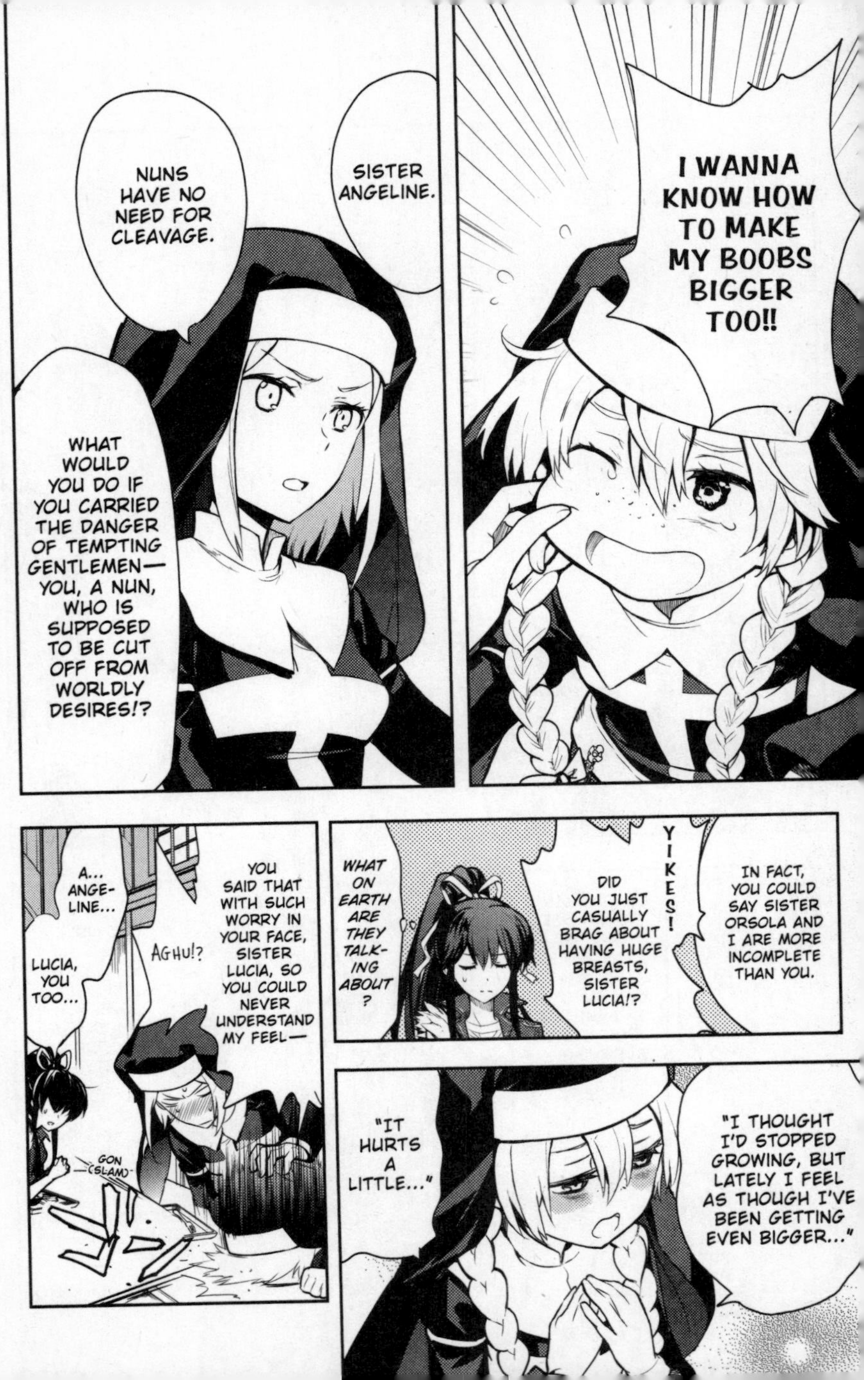
I WANNA KNOW HOW TO MAKE MY BOOBS BIGGER TOO!!
SISTER ANGELINE.
NUNS HAVE NO NEED FOR CLEAVAGE.
WHAT WOULD YOU DO IF YOU CARRIED THE DANGER OF TEMPTING GENTLEMEN— YOU, A NUN, WHO IS SUPPOSED TO BE CUT OFF FROM WORLDLY DESIRES!?
IN FACT, YOU COULD SAY SISTER ORSOLA AND I ARE MORE INCOMPLETE THAN YOU.
YIKES!
DID YOU JUST CASUALLY BRAG ABOUT HAVING HUGE BREASTS, SISTER LUCIA!?
WHAT ON EARTH ARE THEY TALKING ABOUT?
"I THOUGHT I'D STOPPED GROWING, BUT LATELY I FEEL AS THOUGH I'VE BEEN GETTING EVEN BIGGER..."
"IT HURTS A LITTLE..."
YOU SAID THAT WITH SUCH WORRY IN YOUR FACE, SISTER LUCIA, SO YOU COULD NEVER UNDERSTAND MY FEEL—
AGHU!?
A... ANGE-LINE...
LUCIA, YOU TOO...
GON (SLAM)

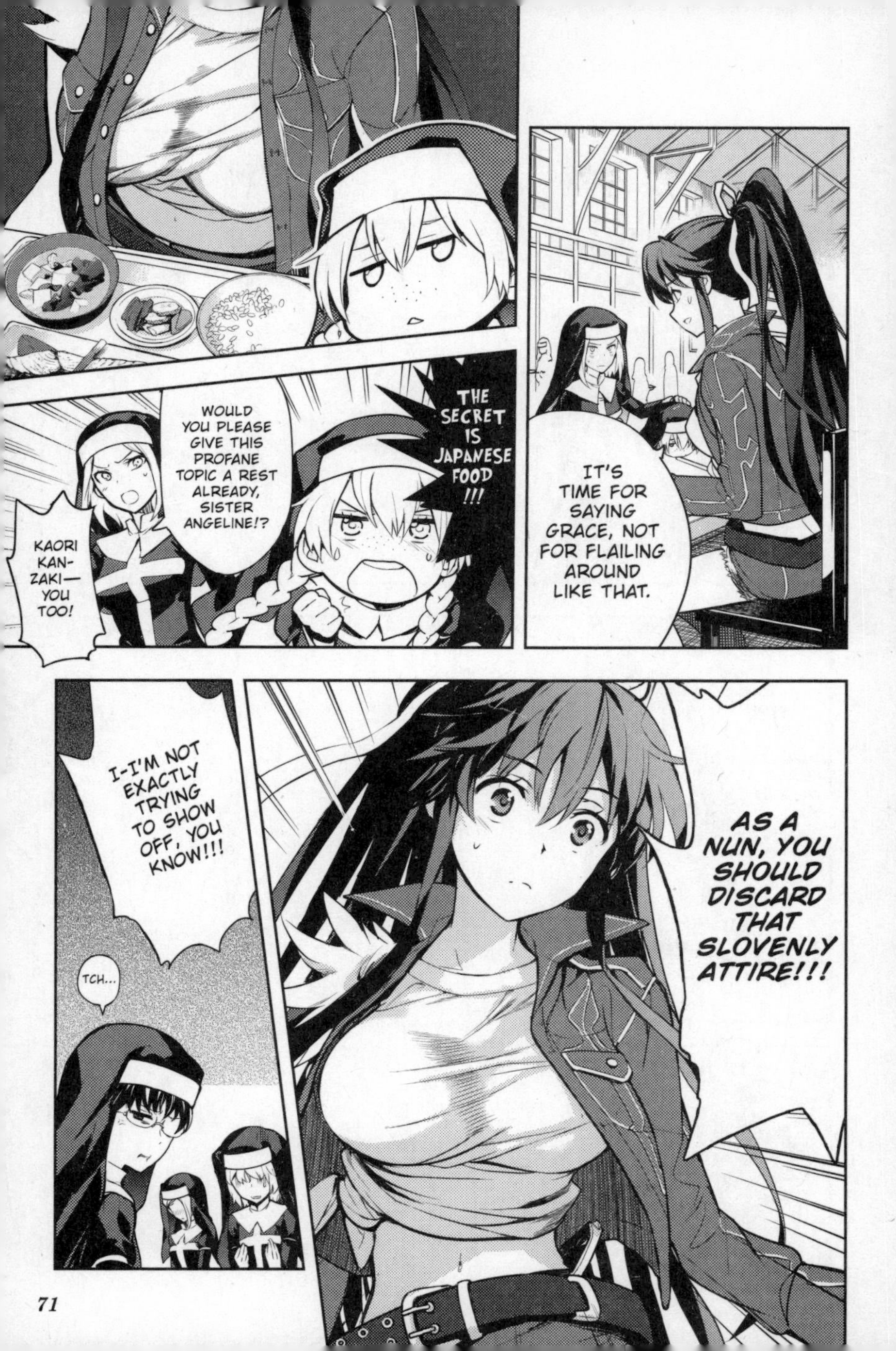
IT'S TIME FOR SAYING GRACE, NOT FOR FLAILING AROUND LIKE THAT.
THE SECRET IS JAPANESE FOOD!!!
WOULD YOU PLEASE GIVE THIS PROFANE TOPIC A REST ALREADY, SISTER ANGELINE!?
KAORI KANZAKI—YOU TOO!
AS A NUN, YOU SHOULD DISCARD THAT SLOVENLY ATTIRE!!!
I-I'M NOT EXACTLY TRYING TO SHOW OFF, YOU KNOW!!!
TCH...

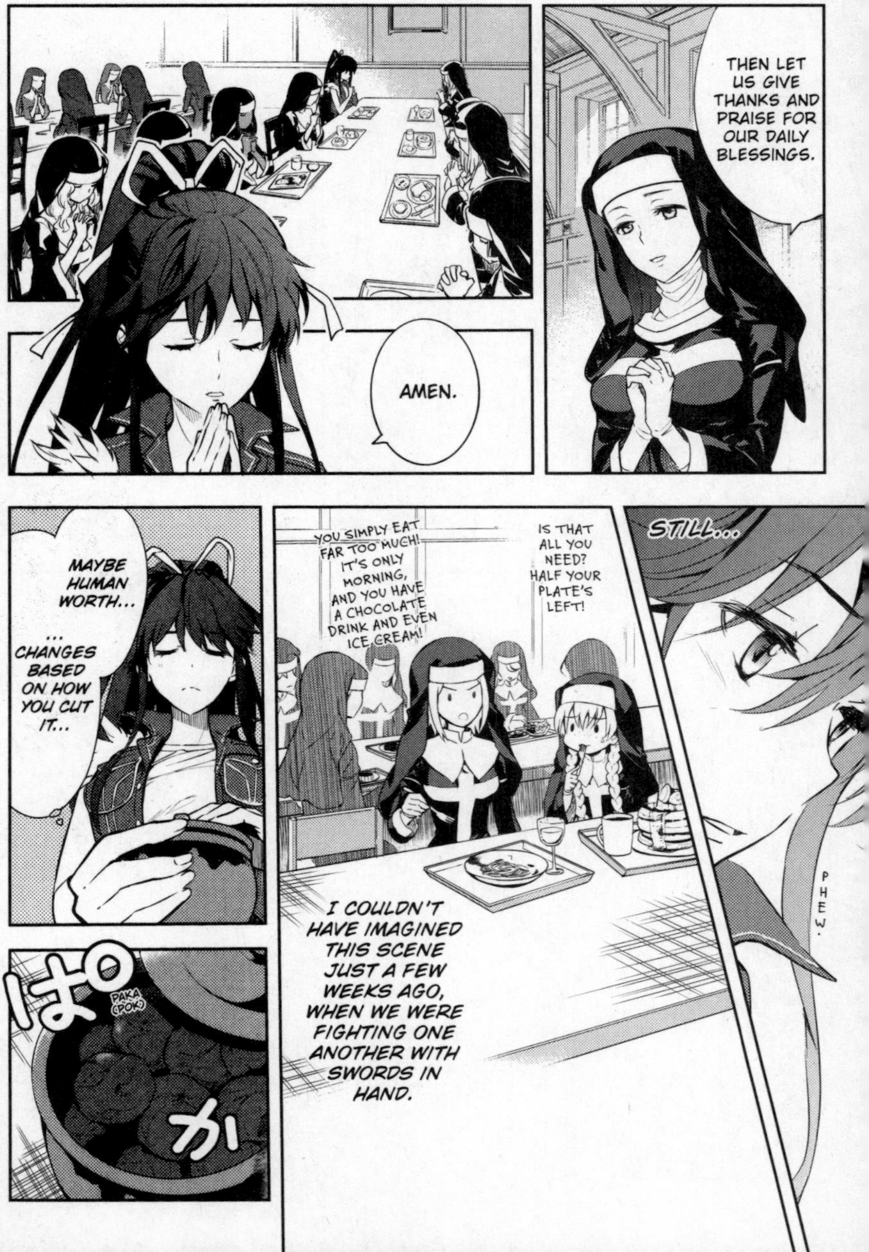

THEN LET US GIVE THANKS AND PRAISE FOR OUR DAILY BLESSINGS.
AMEN.
STILL...
PHEW.
IS THAT ALL YOU NEED? HALF YOUR PLATE'S LEFT!
YOU SIMPLY EAT FAR TOO MUCH! IT'S ONLY MORNING, AND YOU HAVE A CHOCOLATE DRINK AND EVEN ICE CREAM!
I COULDN'T HAVE IMAGINED THIS SCENE JUST A FEW WEEKS AGO, WHEN WE WERE FIGHTING ONE ANOTHER WITH SWORDS IN HAND.
MAYBE HUMAN WORTH...
...CHANGES BASED ON HOW YOU CUT IT...
ぱか
PAKA (POK)

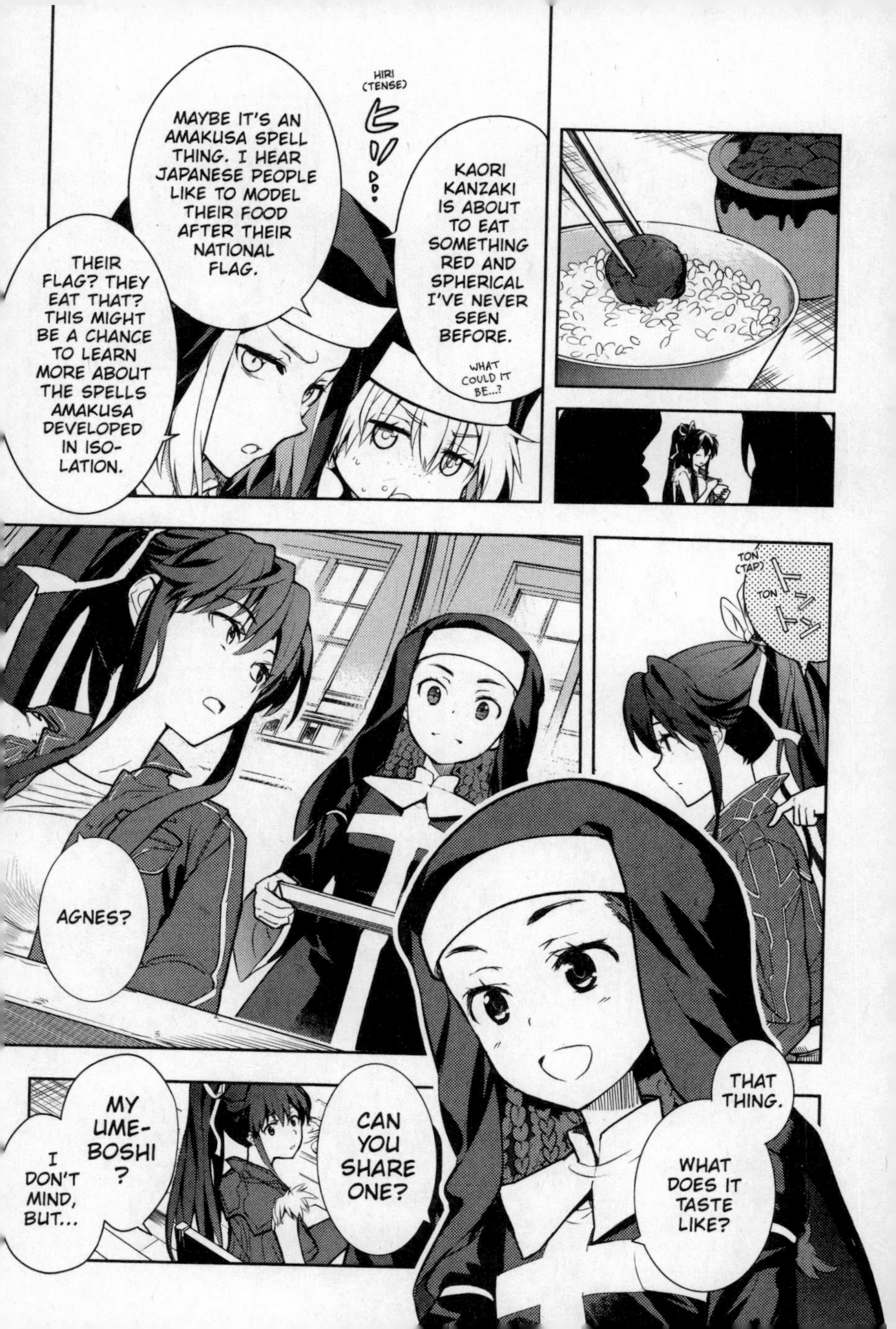
HIRI (TENSE)
KAORI KANZAKI IS ABOUT TO EAT SOMETHING RED AND SPHERICAL I'VE NEVER SEEN BEFORE.
WHAT COULD IT BE...?
MAYBE IT'S AN AMAKUSA SPELL THING. I HEAR JAPANESE PEOPLE LIKE TO MODEL THEIR FOOD AFTER THEIR NATIONAL FLAG.
THEIR FLAG? THEY EAT THAT? THIS MIGHT BE A CHANCE TO LEARN MORE ABOUT THE SPELLS AMAKUSA DEVELOPED IN ISO-LATION.
TON (TAP)
TON
AGNES?
THAT THING.
WHAT DOES IT TASTE LIKE?
CAN YOU SHARE ONE?
MY UME-BOSHI?
I DON'T MIND, BUT...

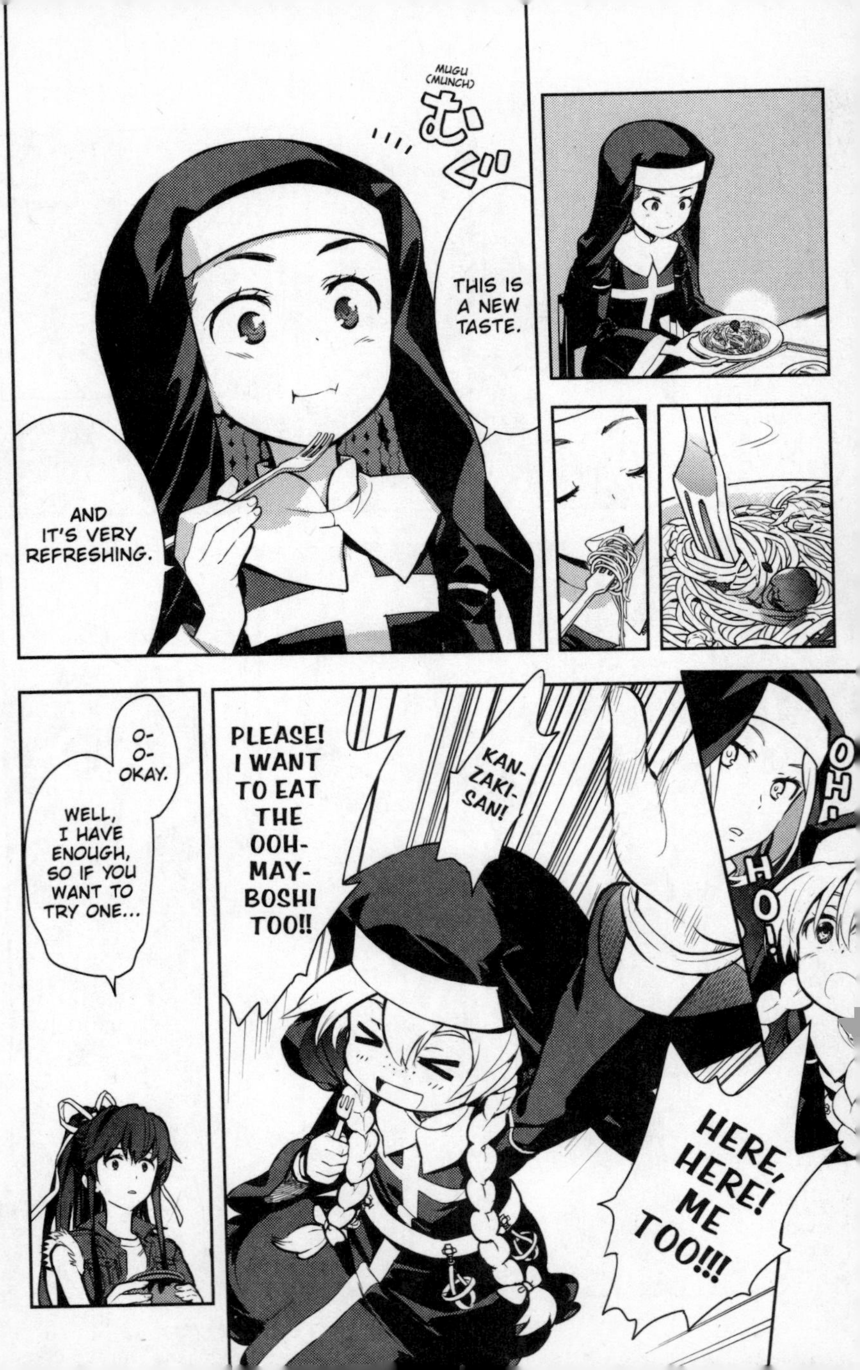

MUGU (MUNCH)
むぐ
THIS IS A NEW TASTE.
AND IT'S VERY REFRESHING.
KAN-ZAKI-SAN!
PLEASE! I WANT TO EAT THE OOH-MAY-BOSHI TOO!!
HERE, HERE! ME TOO!!!
O-O-OKAY.
WELL, I HAVE ENOUGH, SO IF YOU WANT TO TRY ONE...

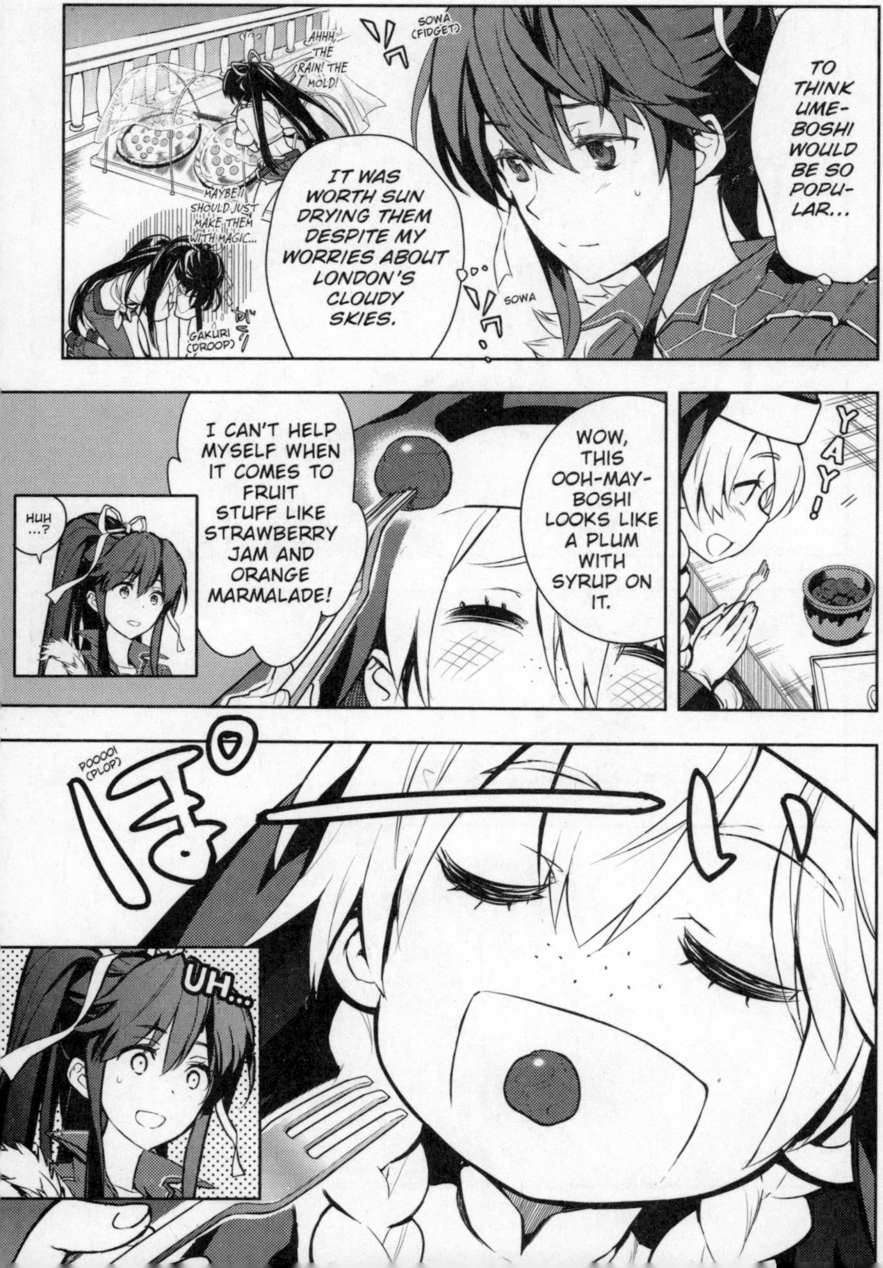
TO THINK UME-BOSHI WOULD BE SO POPU-LAR...
SOWA (FIDGET)
IT WAS WORTH SUN DRYING THEM DESPITE MY WORRIES ABOUT LONDON'S CLOUDY SKIES.
SOWA
AHHH, THE RAIN! THE MOLD!
MAYBE I SHOULD JUST MAKE THEM WITH MAGIC...
GAKURI (DROOP)
YAY!
WOW, THIS OOH-MAY-BOSHI LOOKS LIKE A PLUM WITH SYRUP ON IT.
I CAN'T HELP MYSELF WHEN IT COMES TO FRUIT STUFF LIKE STRAWBERRY JAM AND ORANGE MARMALADE!
HUH ...?
POOOOI (PLOP)
UH...

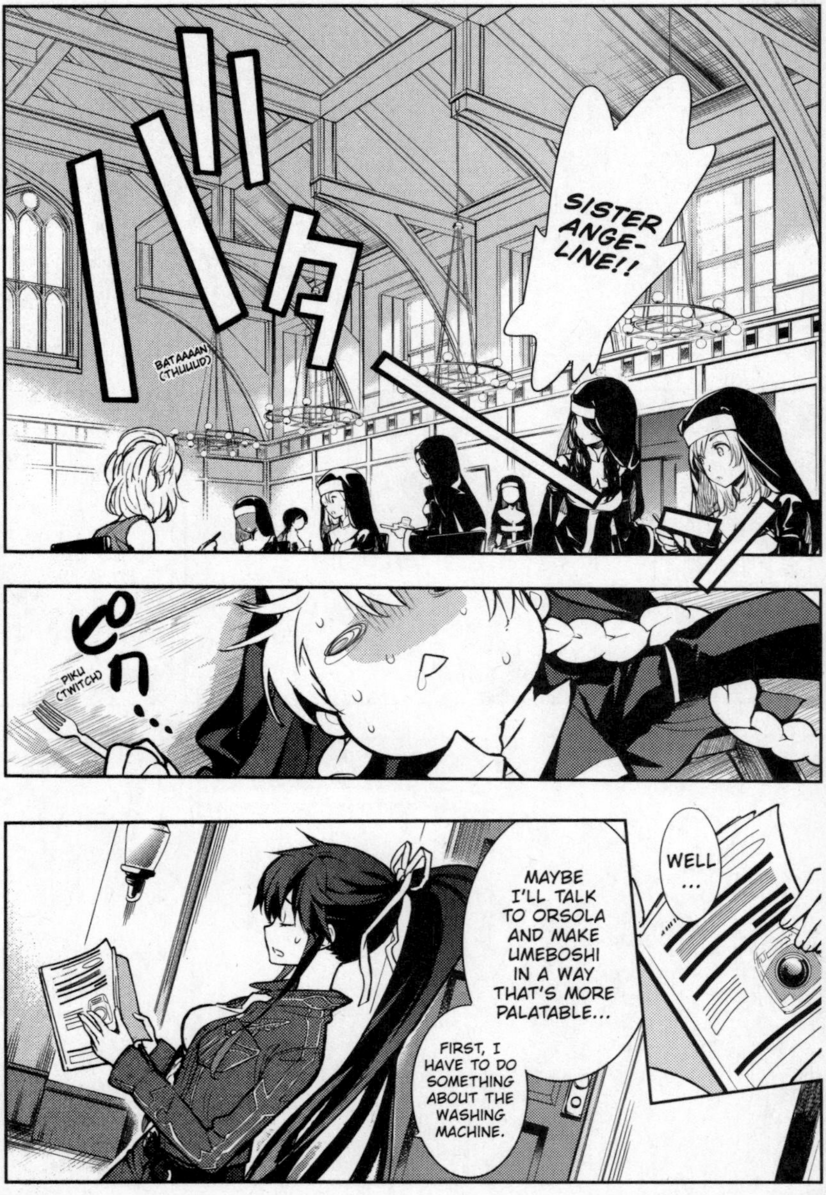
SISTER ANGELINE!!
BATAAAAN (THUUUD)
PIKU (TWITCH)
WELL...
MAYBE I'LL TALK TO ORSOLA AND MAKE UMEBOSHI IN A WAY THAT'S MORE PALATABLE...
FIRST, I HAVE TO DO SOMETHING ABOUT THE WASHING MACHINE.

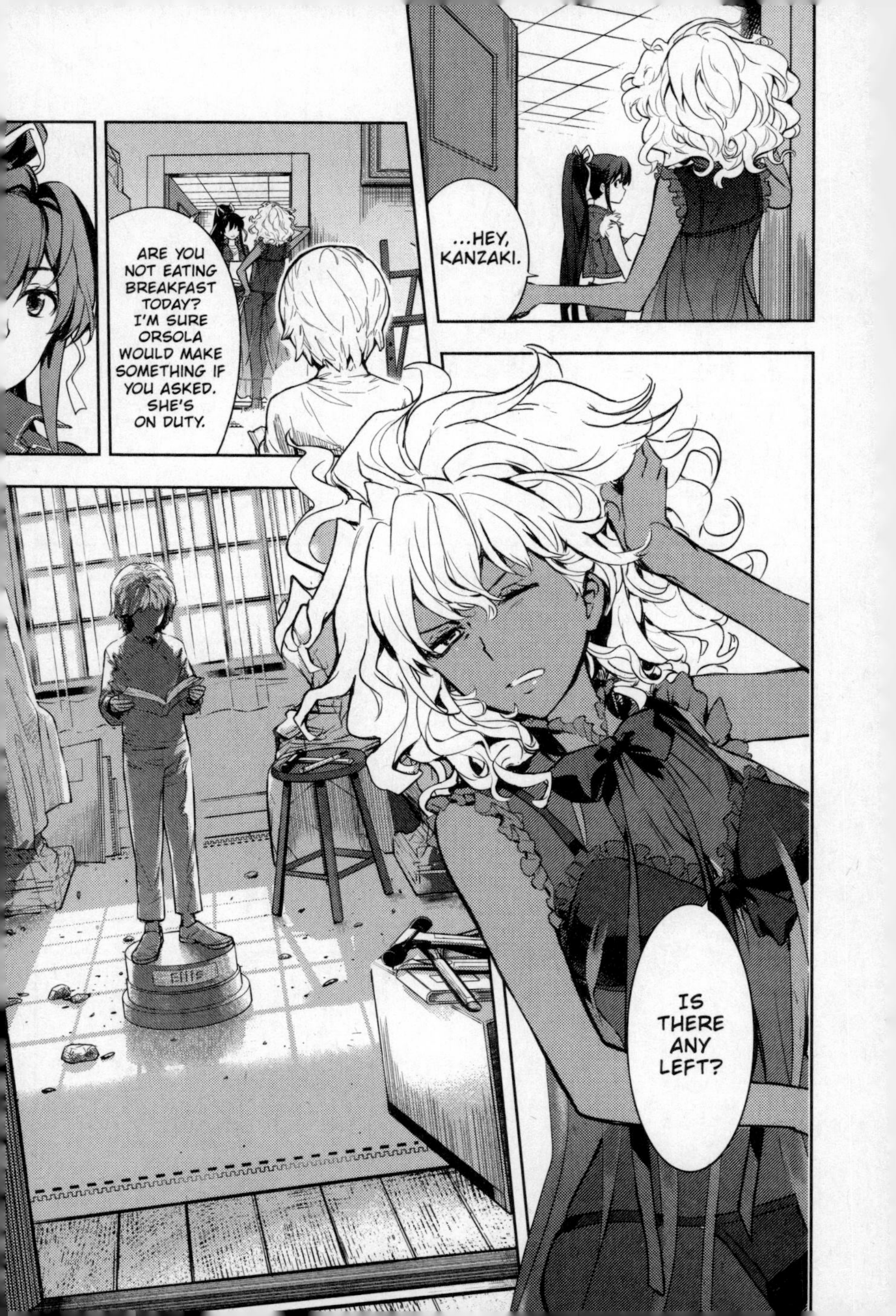
...HEY, KANZAKI.
ARE YOU NOT EATING BREAKFAST TODAY? I'M SURE ORSOLA WOULD MAKE SOMETHING IF YOU ASKED. SHE'S ON DUTY.
IS THERE ANY LEFT?

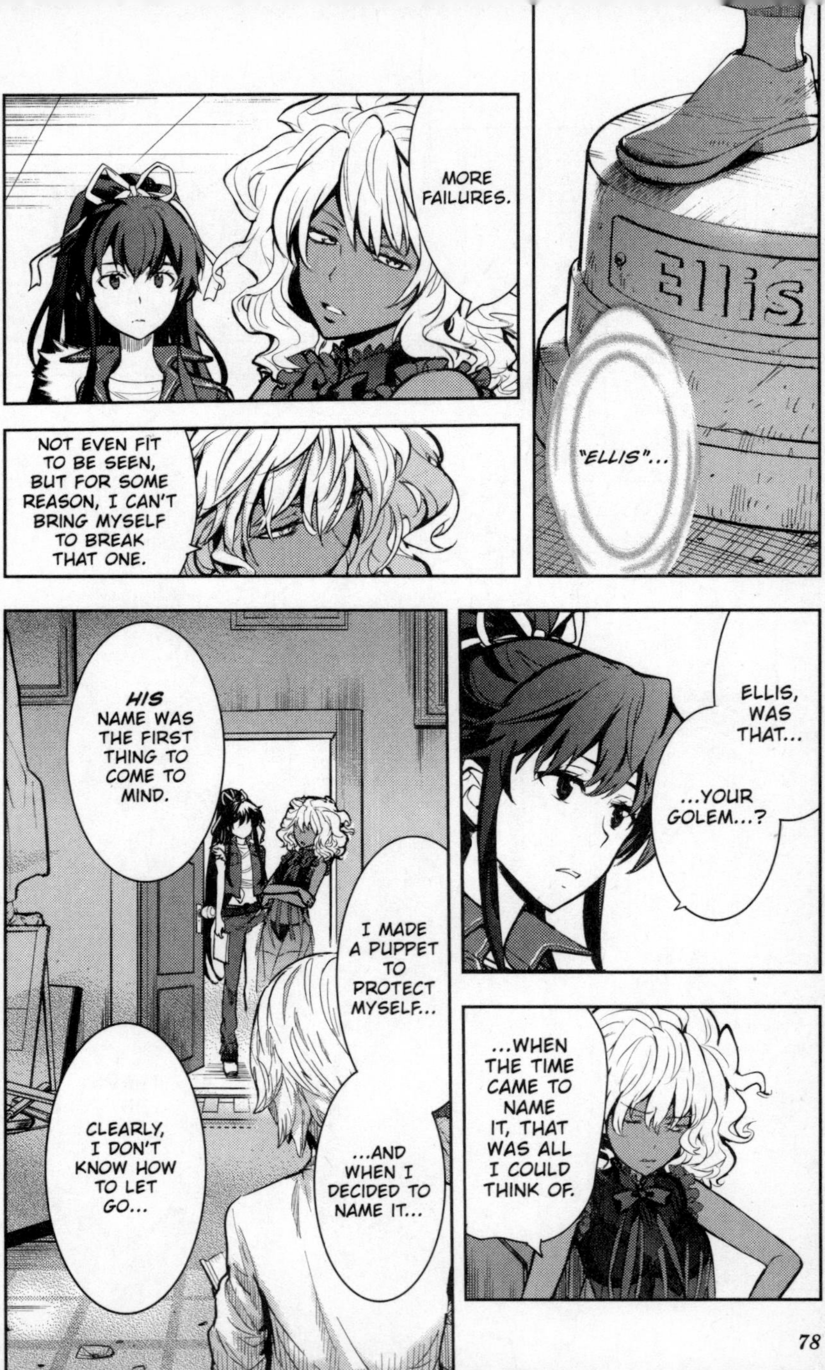
"ELLIS"...
MORE FAILURES.
NOT EVEN FIT TO BE SEEN, BUT FOR SOME REASON, I CAN'T BRING MYSELF TO BREAK THAT ONE.
ELLIS, WAS THAT...
...YOUR GOLEM...?
...WHEN THE TIME CAME TO NAME IT, THAT WAS ALL I COULD THINK OF.
I MADE A PUPPET TO PROTECT MYSELF...
...AND WHEN I DECIDED TO NAME IT...
HIS NAME WAS THE FIRST THING TO COME TO MIND.
CLEARLY, I DON'T KNOW HOW TO LET GO...

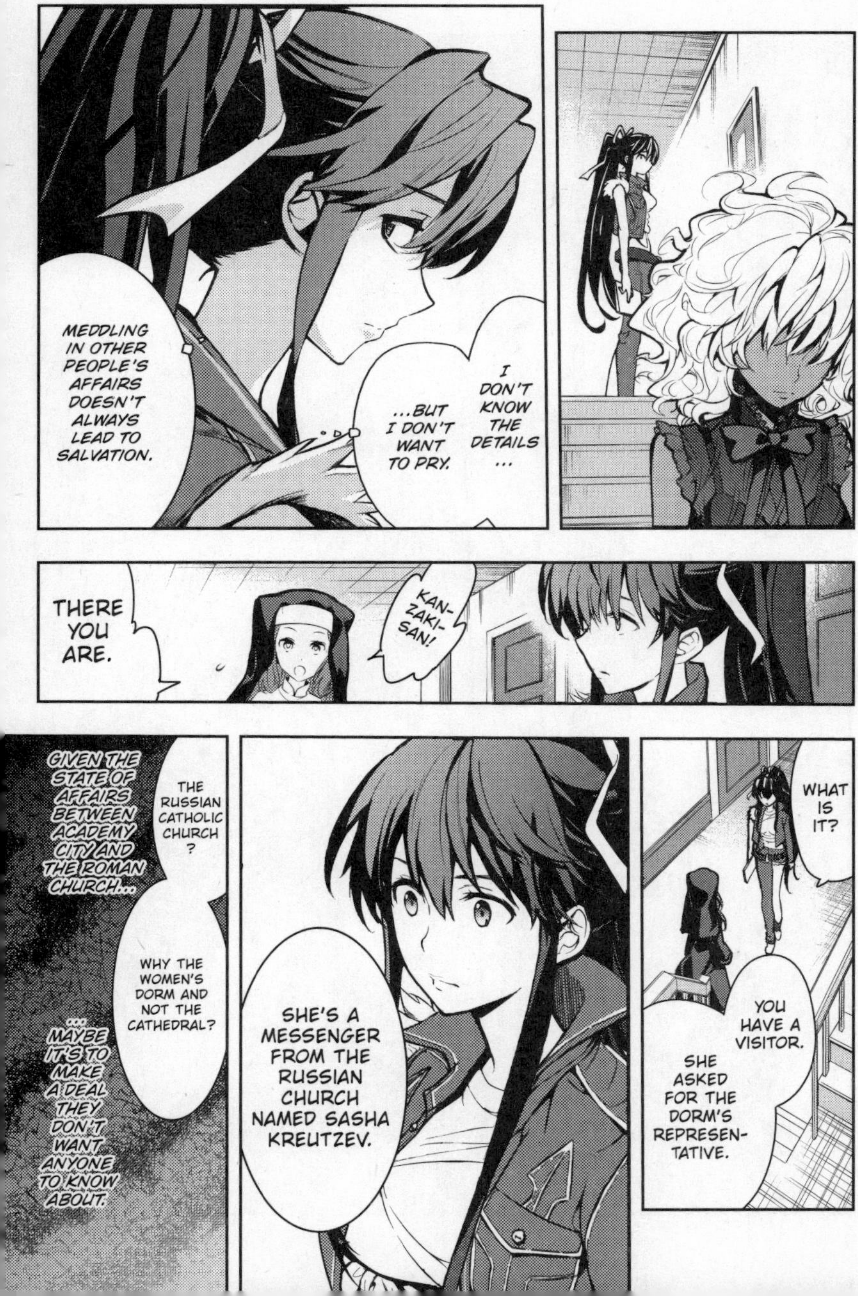
I DON'T KNOW THE DETAILS...
...BUT I DON'T WANT TO PRY.
MEDDLING IN OTHER PEOPLE'S AFFAIRS DOESN'T ALWAYS LEAD TO SALVATION.
KAN-ZAKI-SAN!
THERE YOU ARE.
WHAT IS IT?
YOU HAVE A VISITOR.
SHE ASKED FOR THE DORM'S REPRESEN-TATIVE.
SHE'S A MESSENGER FROM THE RUSSIAN CHURCH NAMED SASHA KREUTZEV.
THE RUSSIAN CATHOLIC CHURCH?
WHY THE WOMEN'S DORM AND NOT THE CATHEDRAL?
GIVEN THE STATE OF AFFAIRS BETWEEN ACADEMY CITY AND THE ROMAN CHURCH...
...MAYBE IT'S TO MAKE A DEAL THEY DON'T WANT ANYONE TO KNOW ABOUT.

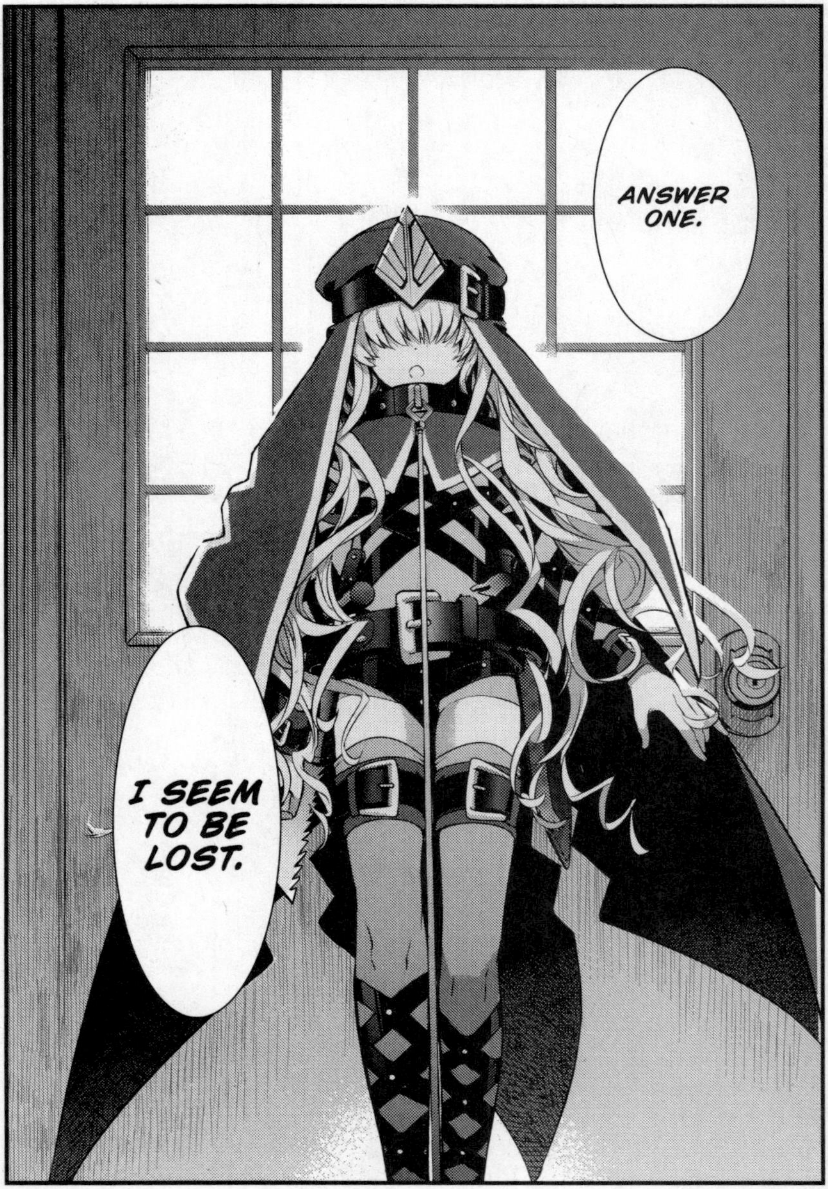
ANSWER ONE.
I SEEM TO BE LOST.

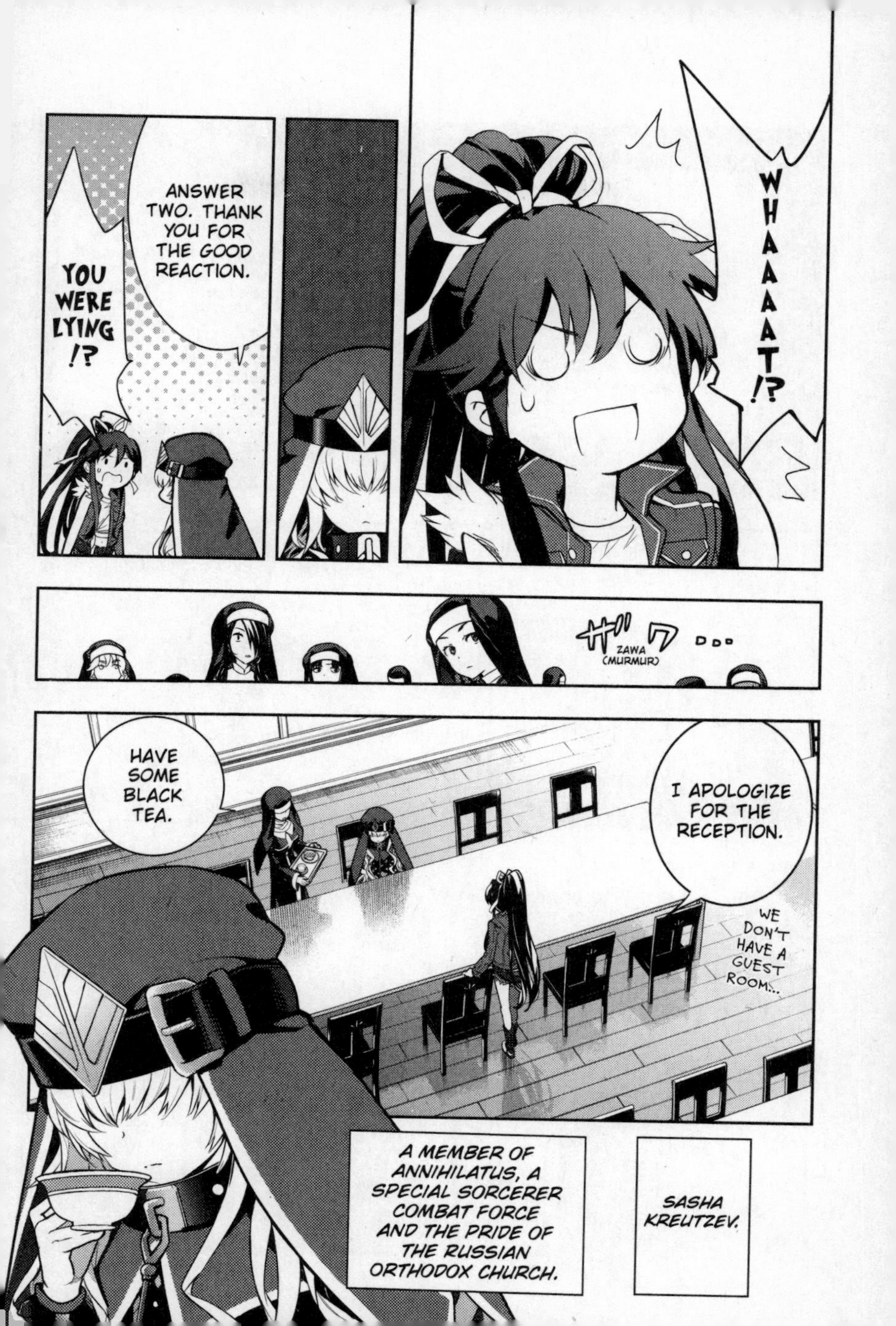
WHAAAAT!?
ANSWER TWO. THANK YOU FOR THE GOOD REACTION.
YOU WERE LYING!?
ザワ…
ZAWA (MURMUR)
I APOLOGIZE FOR THE RECEPTION.
WE DON'T HAVE A GUEST ROOM...
HAVE SOME BLACK TEA.
SASHA KREUTZEV.
A MEMBER OF ANNIHILATUS, A SPECIAL SORCERER COMBAT FORCE AND THE PRIDE OF THE RUSSIAN ORTHODOX CHURCH.

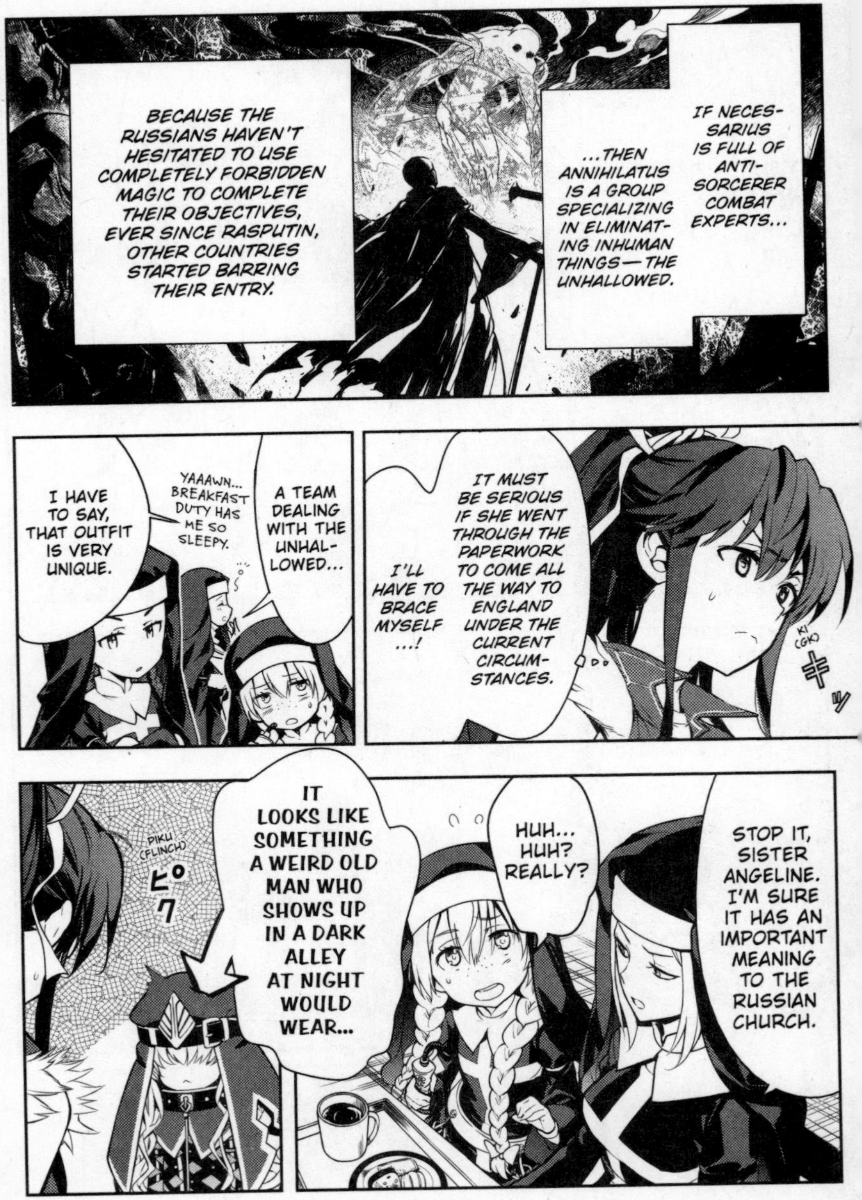
IF NECESSARIUS IS FULL OF ANTI-SORCERER COMBAT EXPERTS...
...THEN ANNIHILATUS IS A GROUP SPECIALIZING IN ELIMINATING INHUMAN THINGS—THE UNHALLOWED.
BECAUSE THE RUSSIANS HAVEN'T HESITATED TO USE COMPLETELY FORBIDDEN MAGIC TO COMPLETE THEIR OBJECTIVES, EVER SINCE RASPUTIN, OTHER COUNTRIES STARTED BARRING THEIR ENTRY.
IT MUST BE SERIOUS IF SHE WENT THROUGH THE PAPERWORK TO COME ALL THE WAY TO ENGLAND UNDER THE CURRENT CIRCUMSTANCES.
I'LL HAVE TO BRACE MYSELF ...!
KI (GK)
A TEAM DEALING WITH THE UNHALLOWED...
YAAAWN... BREAKFAST DUTY HAS ME SO SLEEPY.
I HAVE TO SAY, THAT OUTFIT IS VERY UNIQUE.
STOP IT, SISTER ANGELINE. I'M SURE IT HAS AN IMPORTANT MEANING TO THE RUSSIAN CHURCH.
HUH... HUH? REALLY?
IT LOOKS LIKE SOMETHING A WEIRD OLD MAN WHO SHOWS UP IN A DARK ALLEY AT NIGHT WOULD WEAR...
PIKU (FLINCH)

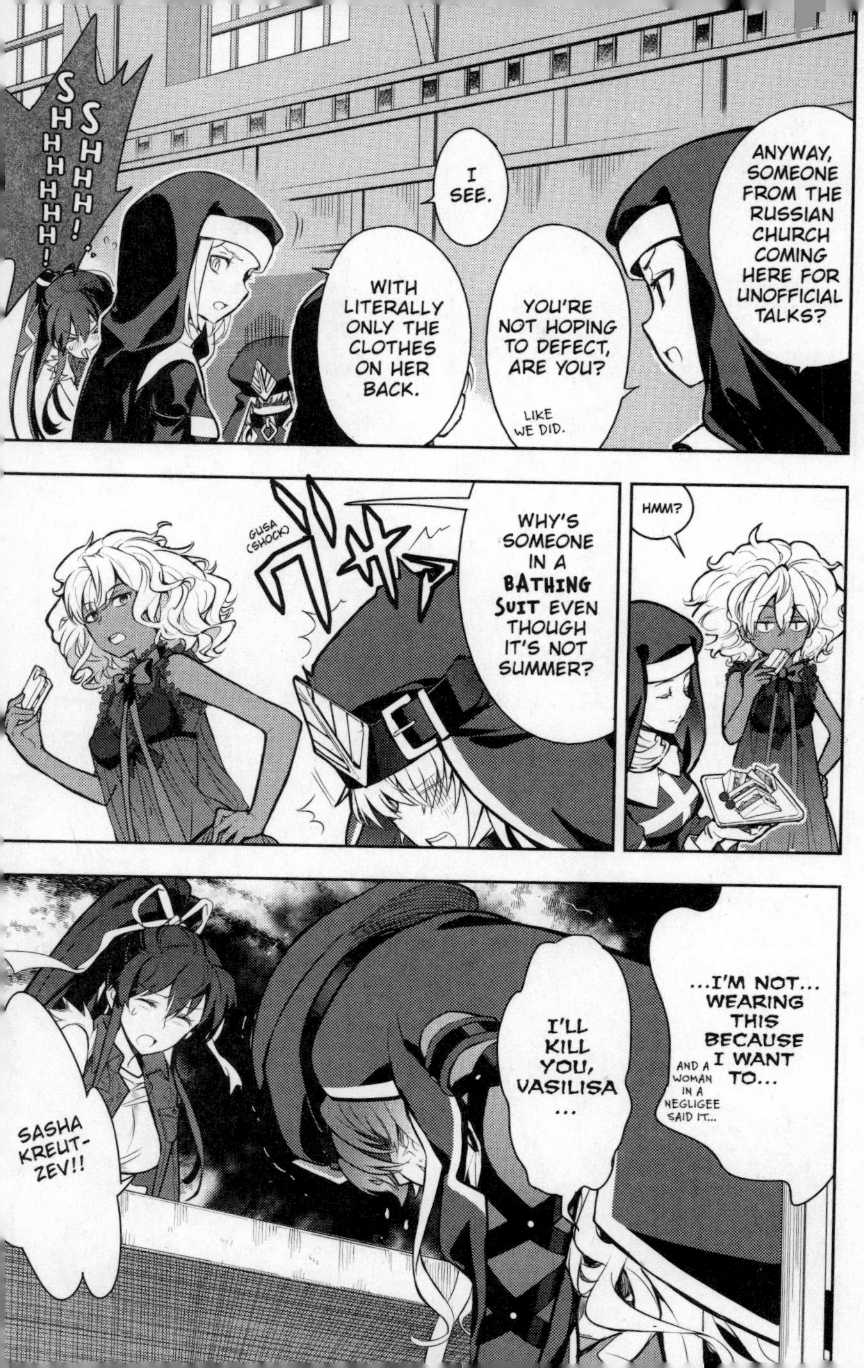
ANYWAY, SOMEONE FROM THE RUSSIAN CHURCH COMING HERE FOR UNOFFICIAL TALKS?
YOU'RE NOT HOPING TO DEFECT, ARE YOU?
LIKE WE DID.
I SEE.
WITH LITERALLY ONLY THE CLOTHES ON HER BACK.
SHHHH!
SHHHHHHH!
HMM?
WHY'S SOMEONE IN A BATHING SUIT EVEN THOUGH IT'S NOT SUMMER?
グサァ
GUSA (SHOCK)
...I'M NOT... WEARING THIS BECAUSE I WANT TO...
AND A WOMAN IN A NEGLIGEE SAID IT...
I'LL KILL YOU, VASILISA...
SASHA KREUTZEV!!

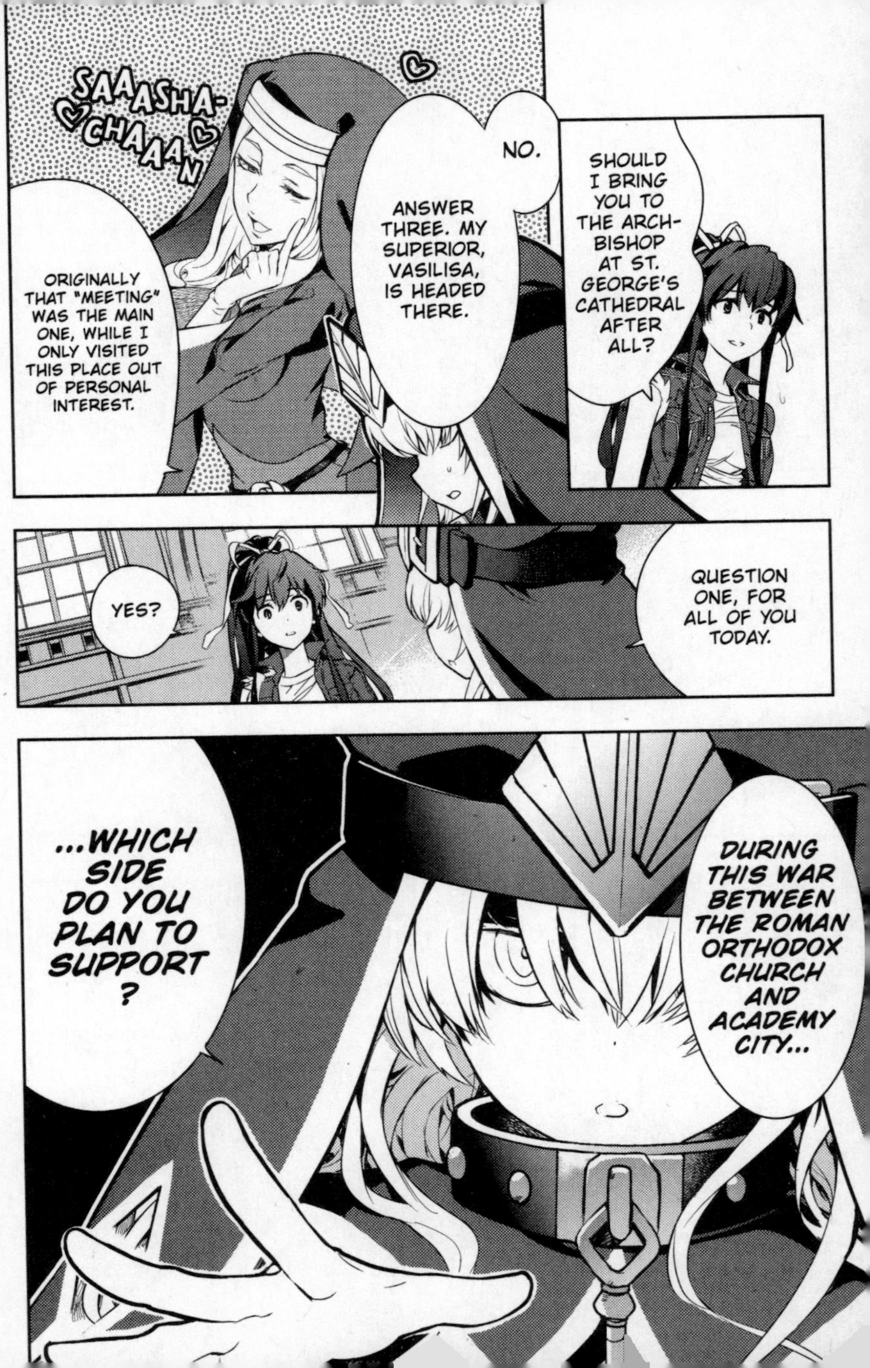
SHOULD I BRING YOU TO THE ARCH-BISHOP AT ST. GEORGE'S CATHEDRAL AFTER ALL?
NO.
ANSWER THREE. MY SUPERIOR, VASILISA, IS HEADED THERE.
SAAASHA-CHAAAN
ORIGINALLY THAT "MEETING" WAS THE MAIN ONE, WHILE I ONLY VISITED THIS PLACE OUT OF PERSONAL INTEREST.
QUESTION ONE, FOR ALL OF YOU TODAY.
YES?
DURING THIS WAR BETWEEN THE ROMAN ORTHODOX CHURCH AND ACADEMY CITY...
...WHICH SIDE DO YOU PLAN TO SUPPORT?

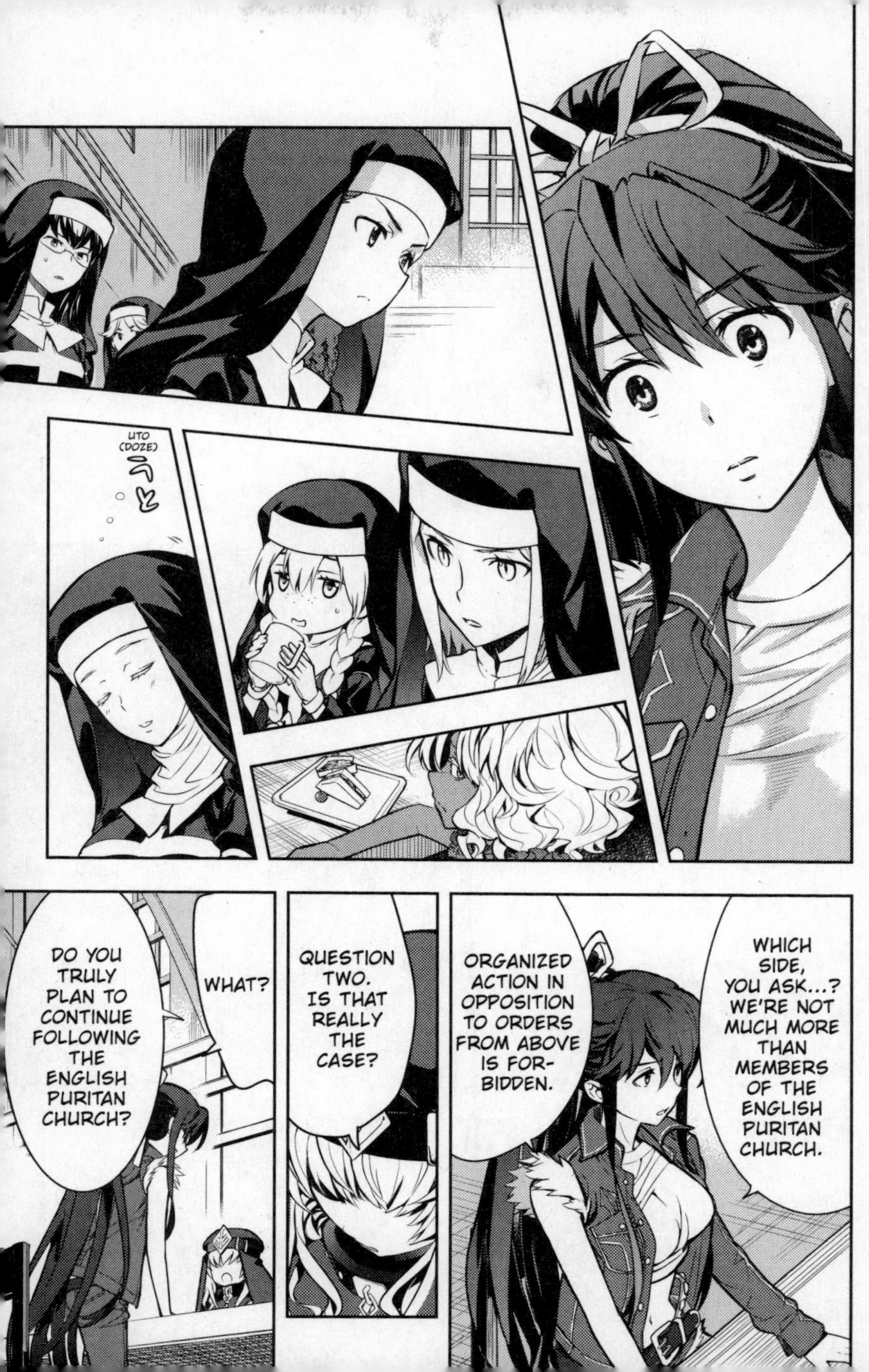
UTO (DOZE)
WHICH SIDE, YOU ASK...? WE'RE NOT MUCH MORE THAN MEMBERS OF THE ENGLISH PURITAN CHURCH.
ORGANIZED ACTION IN OPPOSITION TO ORDERS FROM ABOVE IS FOR-BIDDEN.
QUESTION TWO. IS THAT REALLY THE CASE?
WHAT?
DO YOU TRULY PLAN TO CONTINUE FOLLOWING THE ENGLISH PURITAN CHURCH?

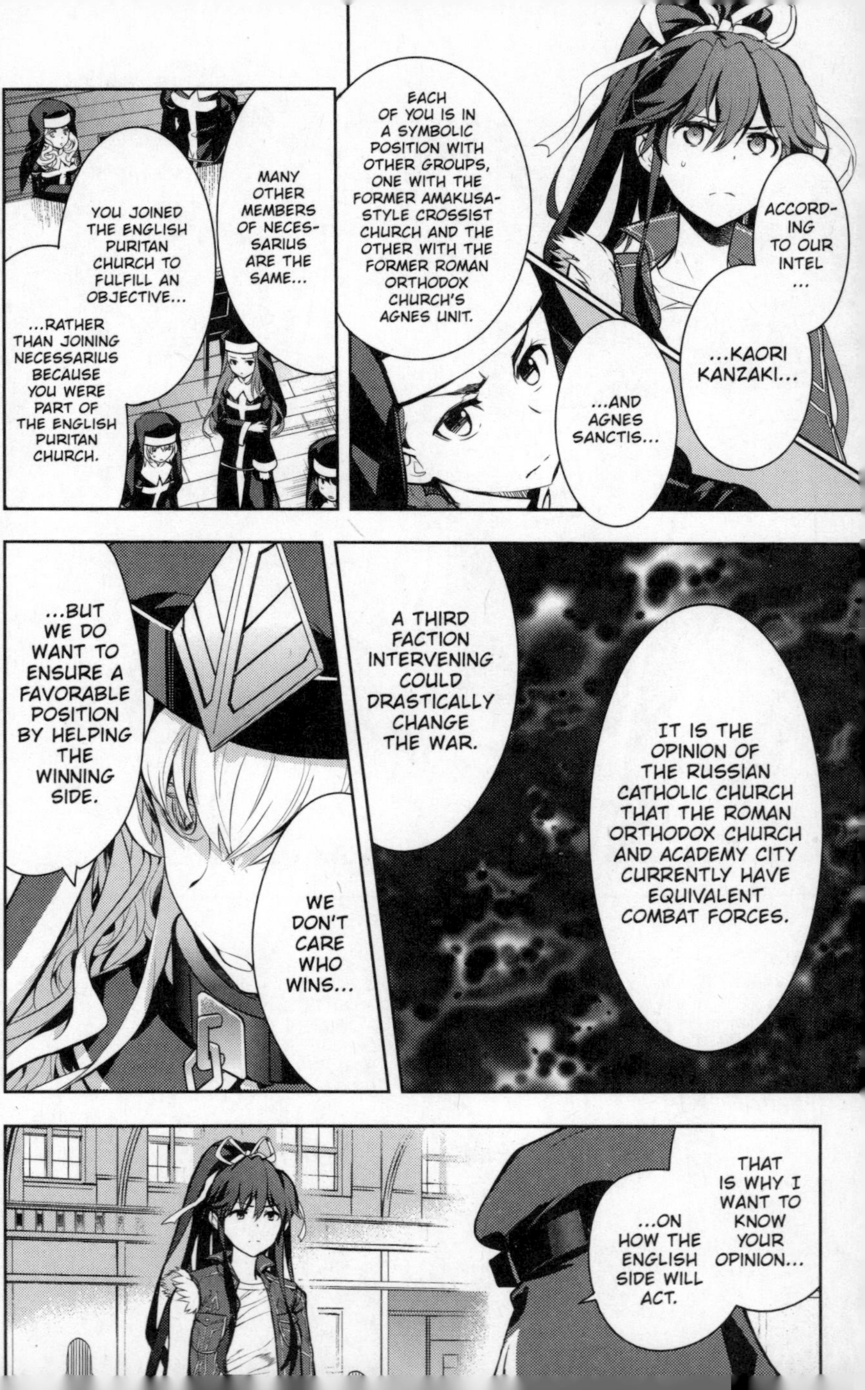
ACCORDING TO OUR INTEL...
...KAORI KANZAKI...
...AND AGNES SANCTIS...
EACH OF YOU IS IN A SYMBOLIC POSITION WITH OTHER GROUPS, ONE WITH THE FORMER AMAKUSA-STYLE CROSSIST CHURCH AND THE OTHER WITH THE FORMER ROMAN ORTHODOX CHURCH'S AGNES UNIT.
MANY OTHER MEMBERS OF NECESSARIUS ARE THE SAME...
YOU JOINED THE ENGLISH PURITAN CHURCH TO FULFILL AN OBJECTIVE...
...RATHER THAN JOINING NECESSARIUS BECAUSE YOU WERE PART OF THE ENGLISH PURITAN CHURCH.
IT IS THE OPINION OF THE RUSSIAN CATHOLIC CHURCH THAT THE ROMAN ORTHODOX CHURCH AND ACADEMY CITY CURRENTLY HAVE EQUIVALENT COMBAT FORCES.
A THIRD FACTION INTERVENING COULD DRASTICALLY CHANGE THE WAR.
WE DON'T CARE WHO WINS...
...BUT WE DO WANT TO ENSURE A FAVORABLE POSITION BY HELPING THE WINNING SIDE.
THAT IS WHY I WANT TO KNOW YOUR OPINION...
...ON HOW THE ENGLISH SIDE WILL ACT.

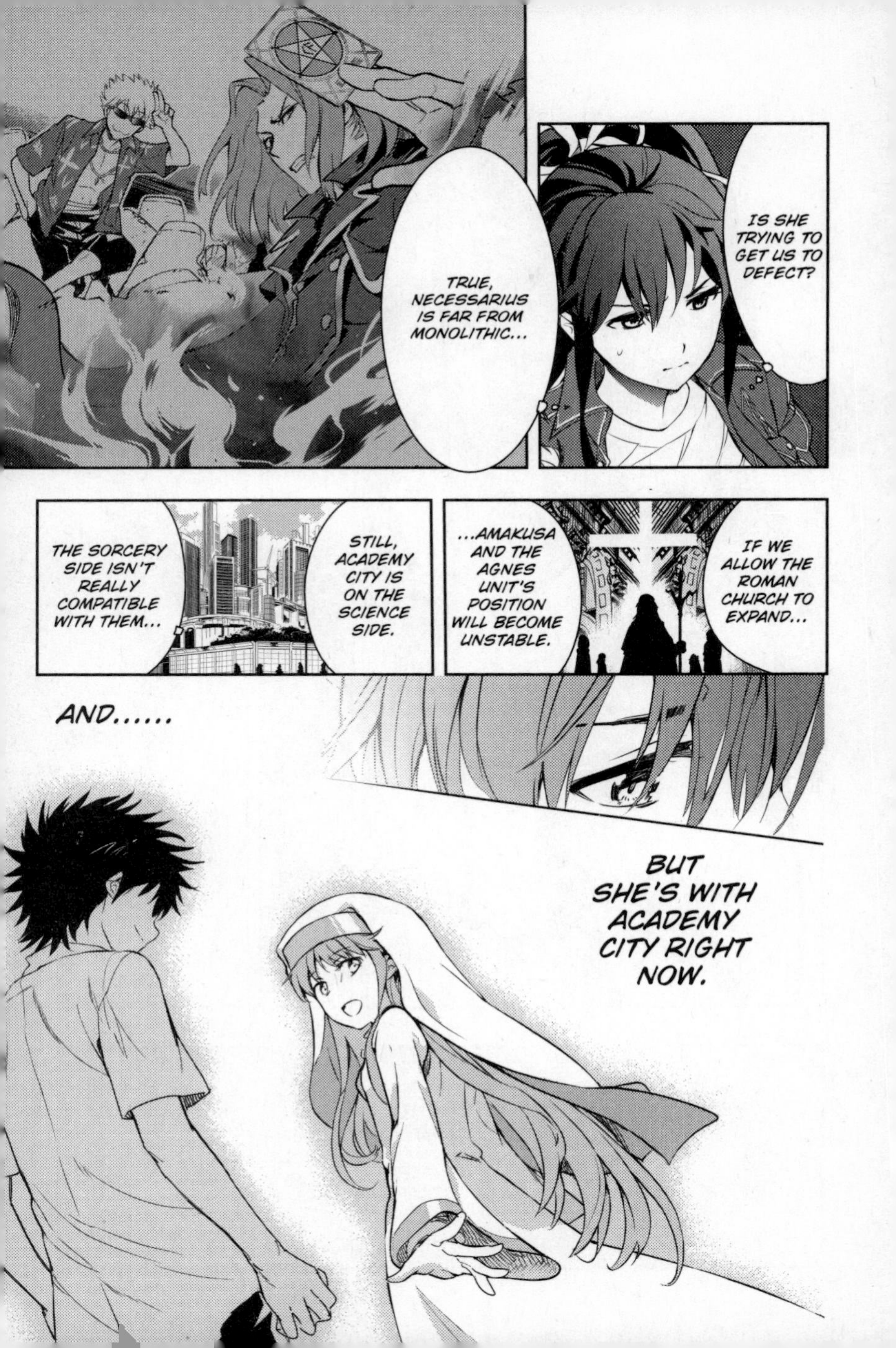
IS SHE TRYING TO GET US TO DEFECT?
TRUE, NECESSARIUS IS FAR FROM MONOLITHIC...
IF WE ALLOW THE ROMAN CHURCH TO EXPAND...
...AMAKUSA AND THE AGNES UNIT'S POSITION WILL BECOME UNSTABLE.
STILL, ACADEMY CITY IS ON THE SCIENCE SIDE.
THE SORCERY SIDE ISN'T REALLY COMPATIBLE WITH THEM...
AND......
BUT SHE'S WITH ACADEMY CITY RIGHT NOW.

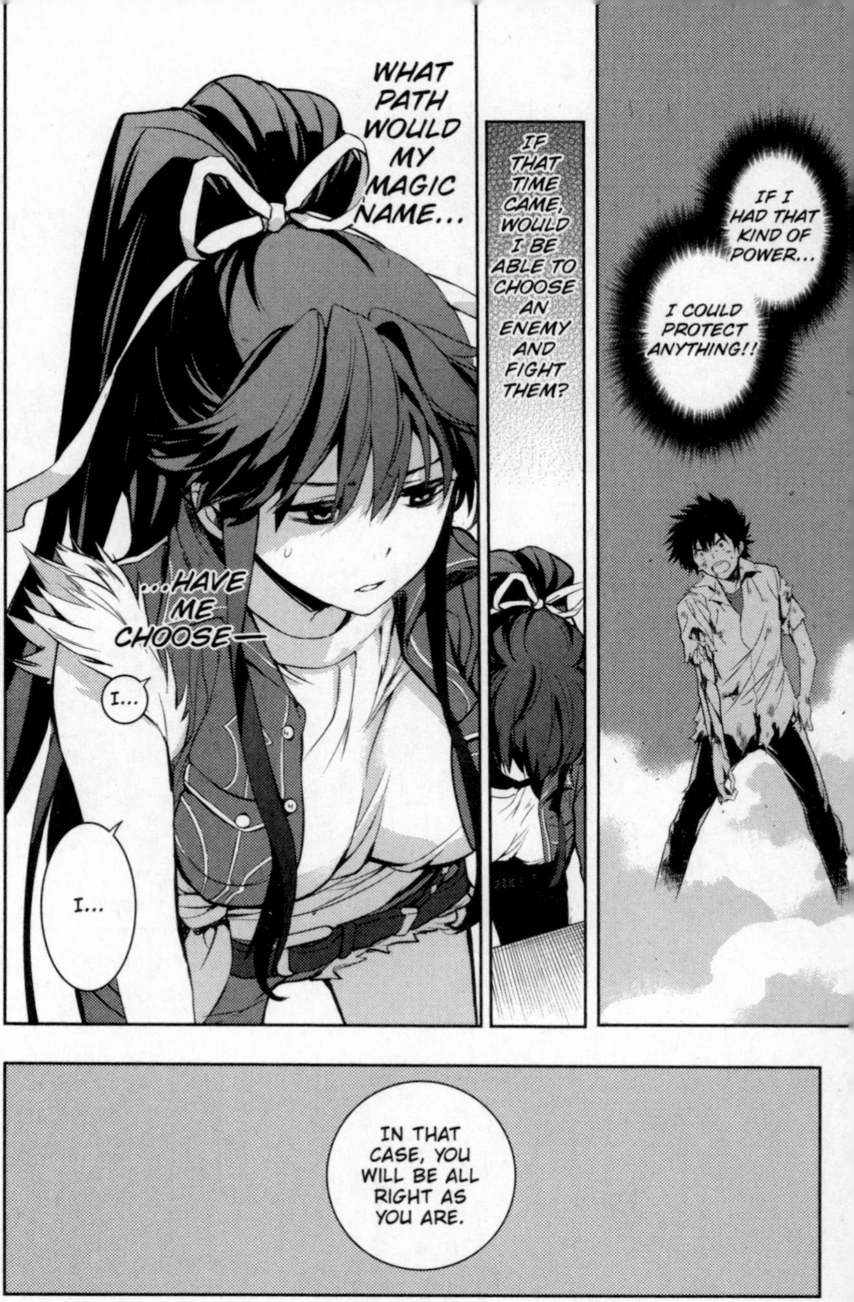
IF I HAD THAT KIND OF POWER...
I COULD PROTECT ANYTHING!!
IF THAT TIME CAME, WOULD I BE ABLE TO CHOOSE AN ENEMY AND FIGHT THEM?
WHAT PATH WOULD MY MAGIC NAME...
...HAVE ME CHOOSE—
I...
I...
IN THAT CASE, YOU WILL BE ALL RIGHT AS YOU ARE.

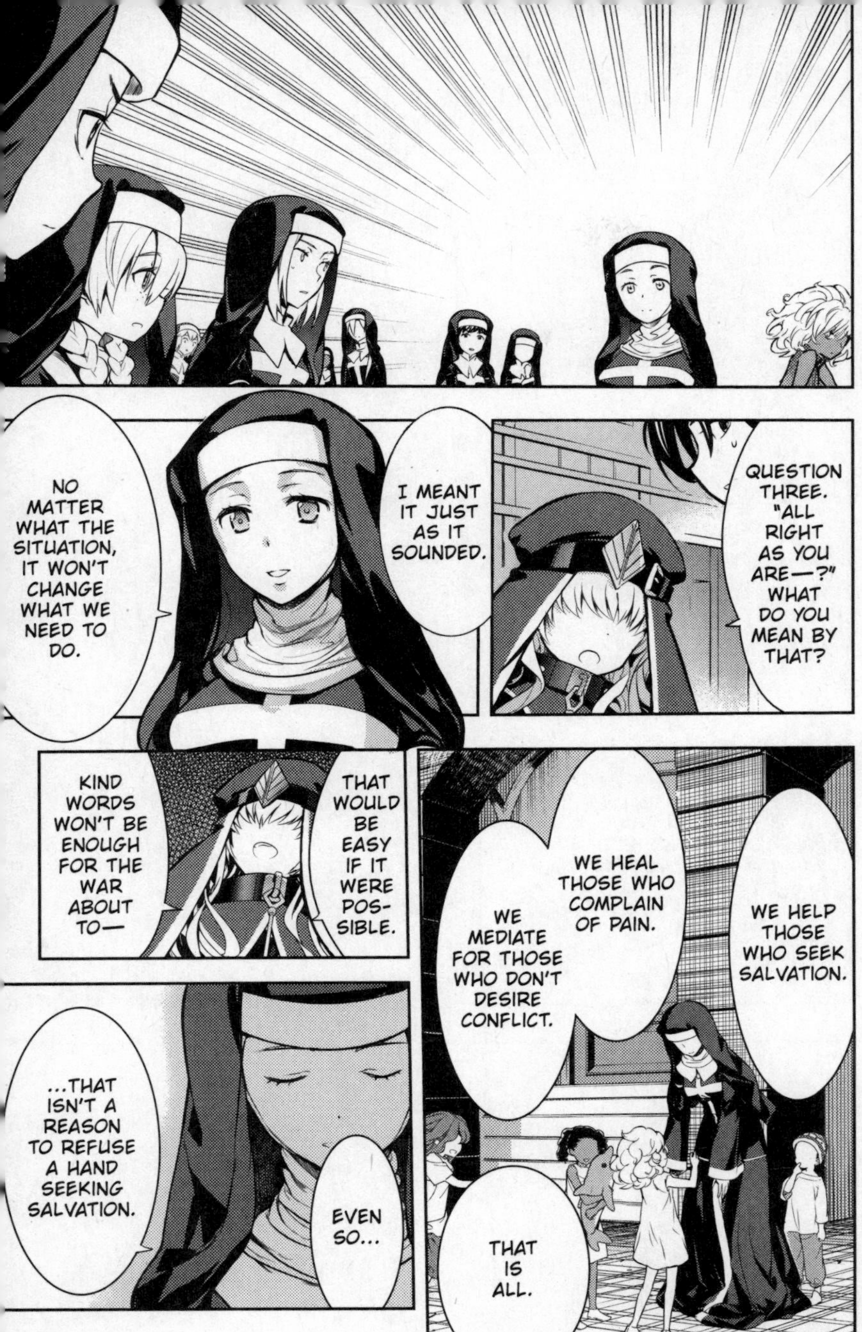
QUESTION THREE. "ALL RIGHT AS YOU ARE—?" WHAT DO YOU MEAN BY THAT?
I MEANT IT JUST AS IT SOUNDED.
NO MATTER WHAT THE SITUATION, IT WON'T CHANGE WHAT WE NEED TO DO.
WE HELP THOSE WHO SEEK SALVATION.
WE HEAL THOSE WHO COMPLAIN OF PAIN.
WE MEDIATE FOR THOSE WHO DON'T DESIRE CONFLICT.
THAT IS ALL.
THAT WOULD BE EASY IF IT WERE POS-SIBLE.
KIND WORDS WON'T BE ENOUGH FOR THE WAR ABOUT TO—
EVEN SO...
...THAT ISN'T A REASON TO REFUSE A HAND SEEKING SALVATION.

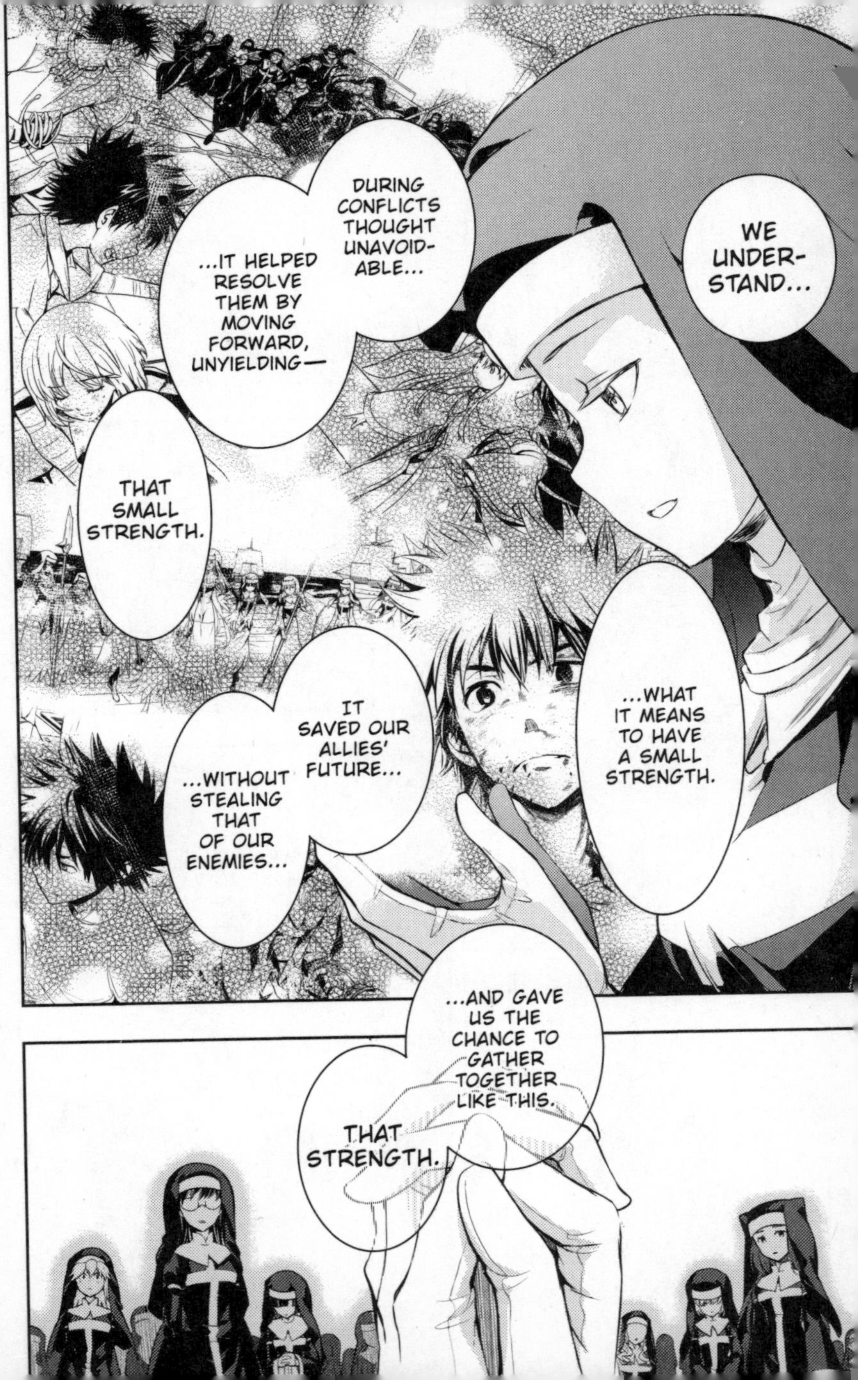
WE UNDER-STAND...
...WHAT IT MEANS TO HAVE A SMALL STRENGTH.
DURING CONFLICTS THOUGHT UNAVOID-ABLE...
...IT HELPED RESOLVE THEM BY MOVING FORWARD, UNYIELDING—
THAT SMALL STRENGTH.
IT SAVED OUR ALLIES' FUTURE...
...WITHOUT STEALING THAT OF OUR ENEMIES...
...AND GAVE US THE CHANCE TO GATHER TOGETHER LIKE THIS.
THAT STRENGTH.

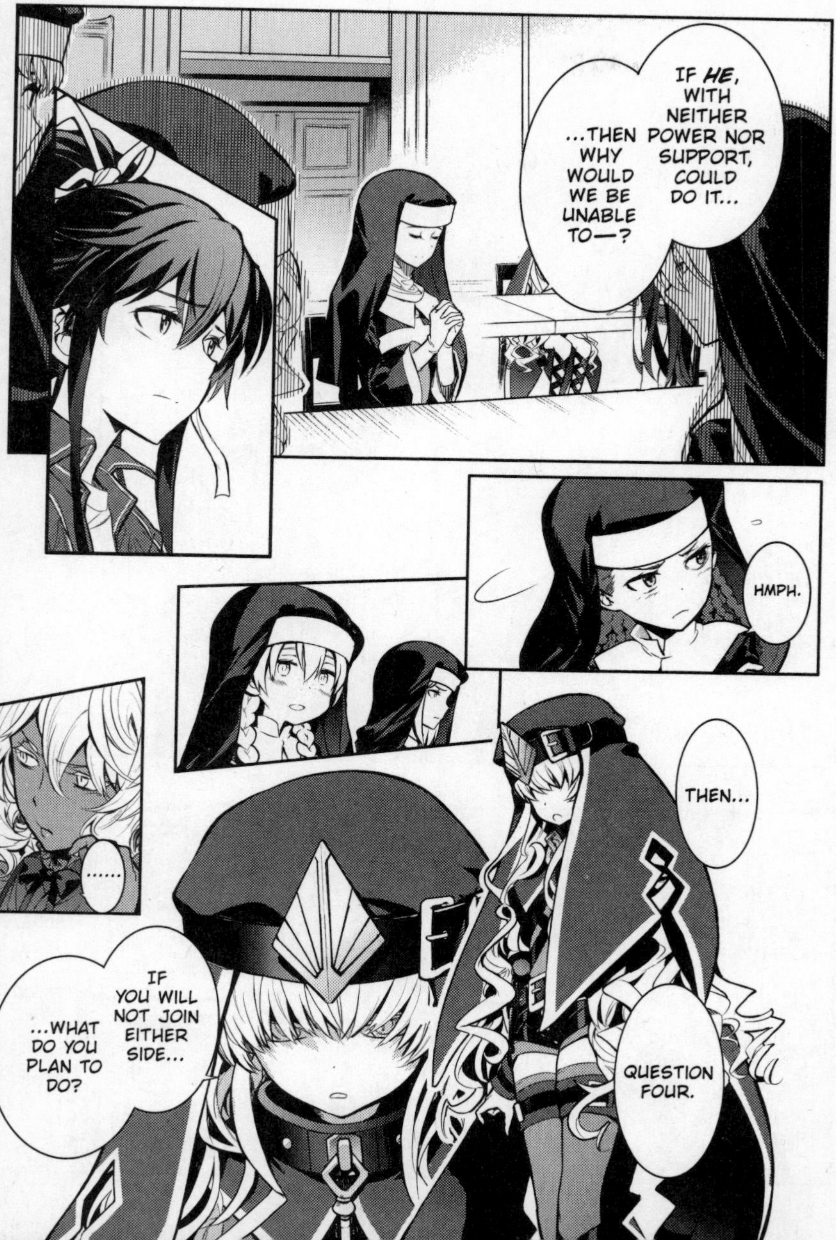
IF *HE*, WITH NEITHER POWER NOR SUPPORT, COULD DO IT...
...THEN WHY WOULD WE BE UNABLE TO—?
HMPH.
THEN...
......
QUESTION FOUR.
IF YOU WILL NOT JOIN EITHER SIDE...
...WHAT DO YOU PLAN TO DO?

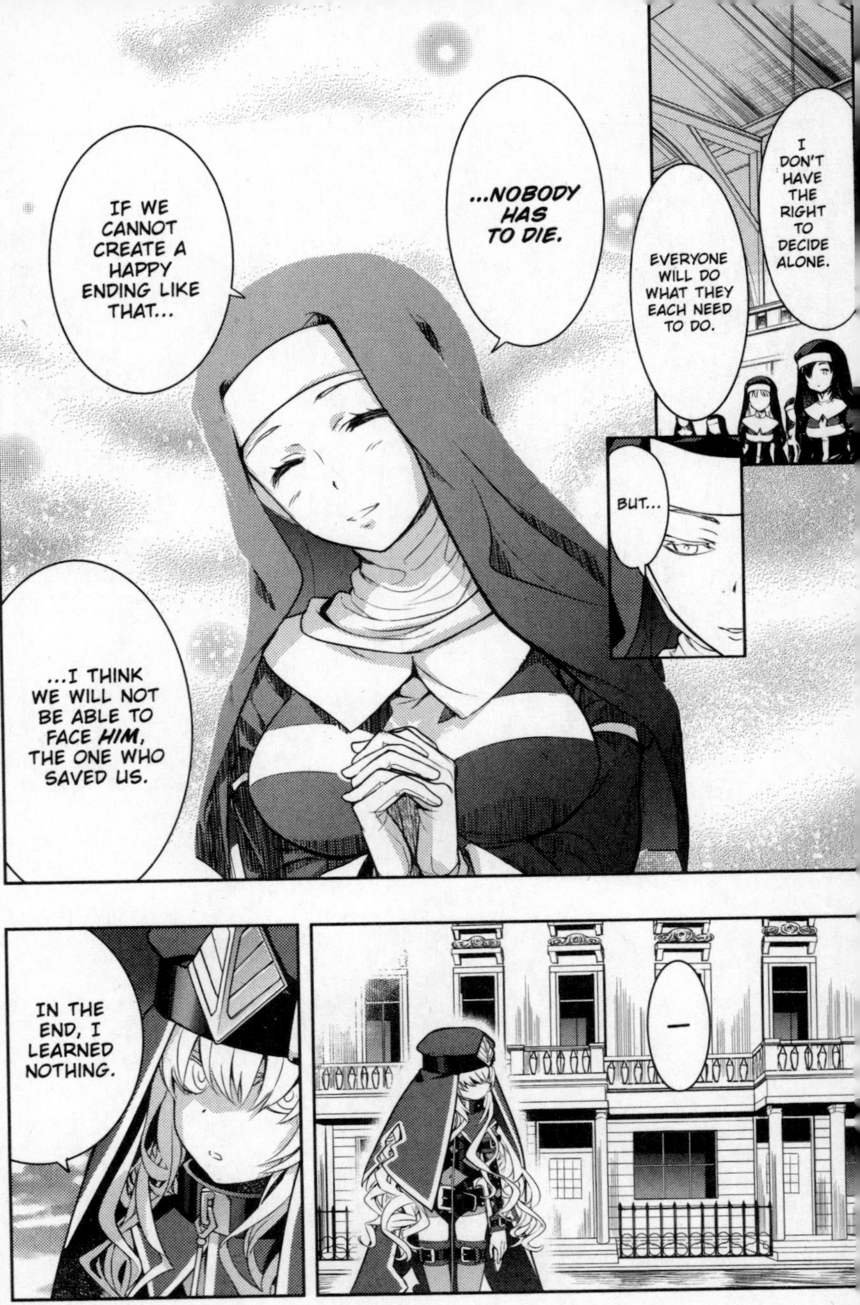
I DON'T HAVE THE RIGHT TO DECIDE ALONE.
EVERYONE WILL DO WHAT THEY EACH NEED TO DO.
BUT...
...NOBODY HAS TO DIE.
IF WE CANNOT CREATE A HAPPY ENDING LIKE THAT...
...I THINK WE WILL NOT BE ABLE TO FACE *HIM*, THE ONE WHO SAVED US.
—
IN THE END, I LEARNED NOTHING.

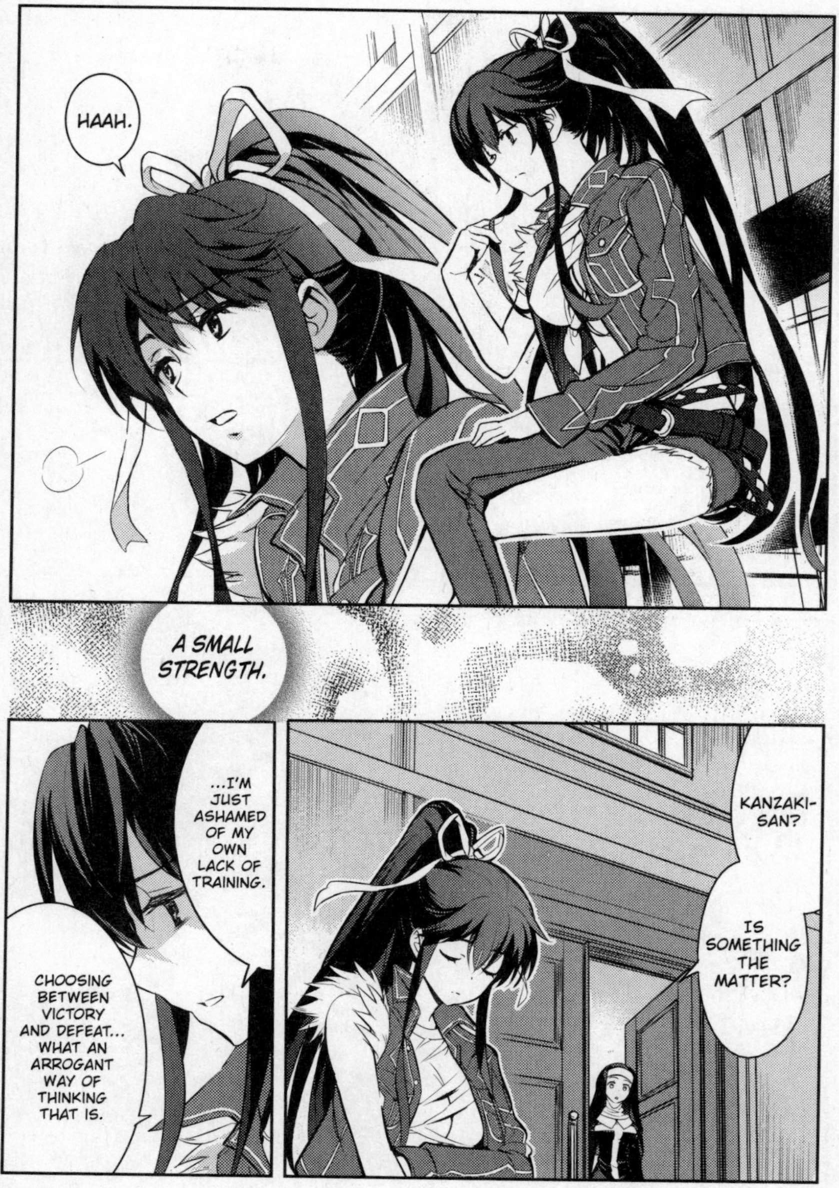
HAAH.
A SMALL STRENGTH.
KANZAKI-SAN?
IS SOMETHING THE MATTER?
...I'M JUST ASHAMED OF MY OWN LACK OF TRAINING.
CHOOSING BETWEEN VICTORY AND DEFEAT... WHAT AN ARROGANT WAY OF THINKING THAT IS.

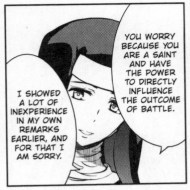

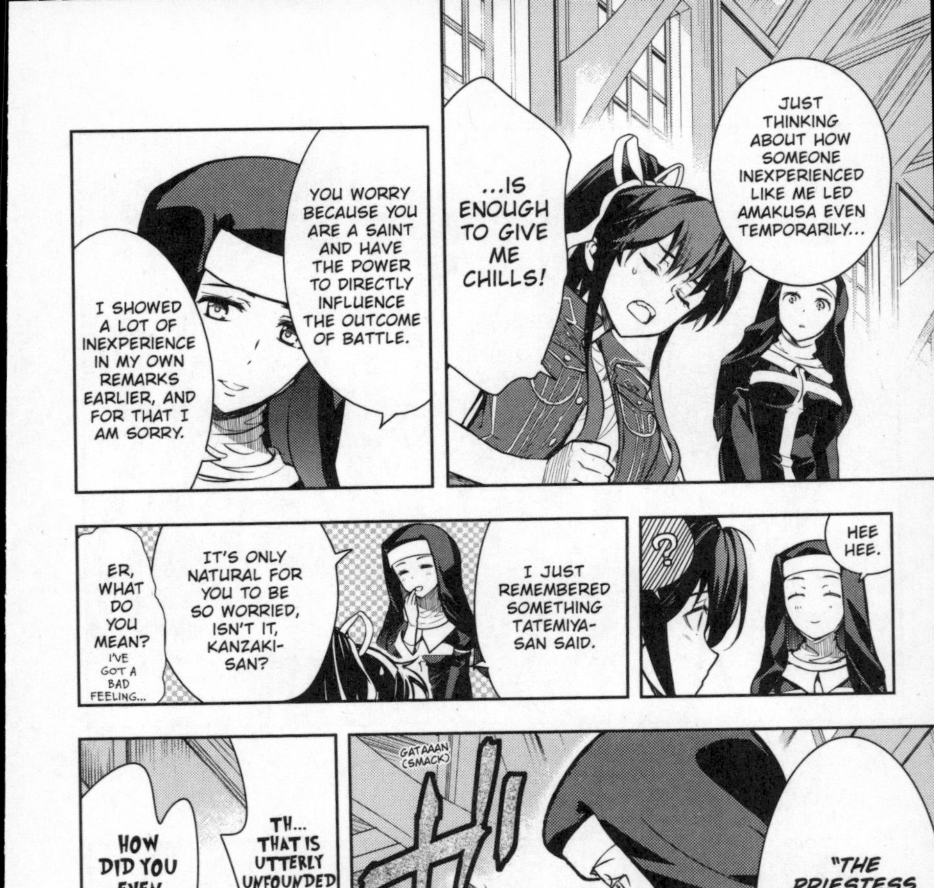

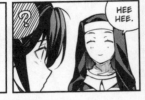

JUST THINKING ABOUT HOW SOMEONE INEXPERIENCED LIKE ME LED AMAKUSA EVEN TEMPORARILY...
...IS ENOUGH TO GIVE ME CHILLS!
YOU WORRY BECAUSE YOU ARE A SAINT AND HAVE THE POWER TO DIRECTLY INFLUENCE THE OUTCOME OF BATTLE.
I SHOWED A LOT OF INEXPERIENCE IN MY OWN REMARKS EARLIER, AND FOR THAT I AM SORRY.
?
HEE HEE.
I JUST REMEMBERED SOMETHING TATEMIYA-SAN SAID.
IT'S ONLY NATURAL FOR YOU TO BE SO WORRIED, ISN'T IT, KANZAKI-SAN?
ER, WHAT DO YOU MEAN?
I'VE GOT A BAD FEELING...
"THE PRIESTESS LOVES SOMEONE FROM ACADEMY CITY..."
GATAAAN (SMACK)
...HE SAID.
TH... THAT IS UTTERLY UNFOUNDED—!!
HOW DID YOU EVEN END UP TALKING ABOUT THAT ANYWAY—!??
OH MY.

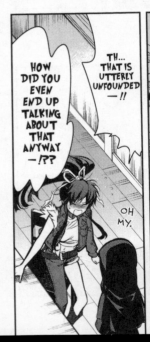

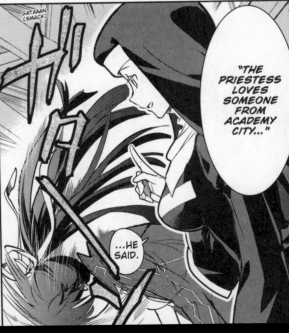

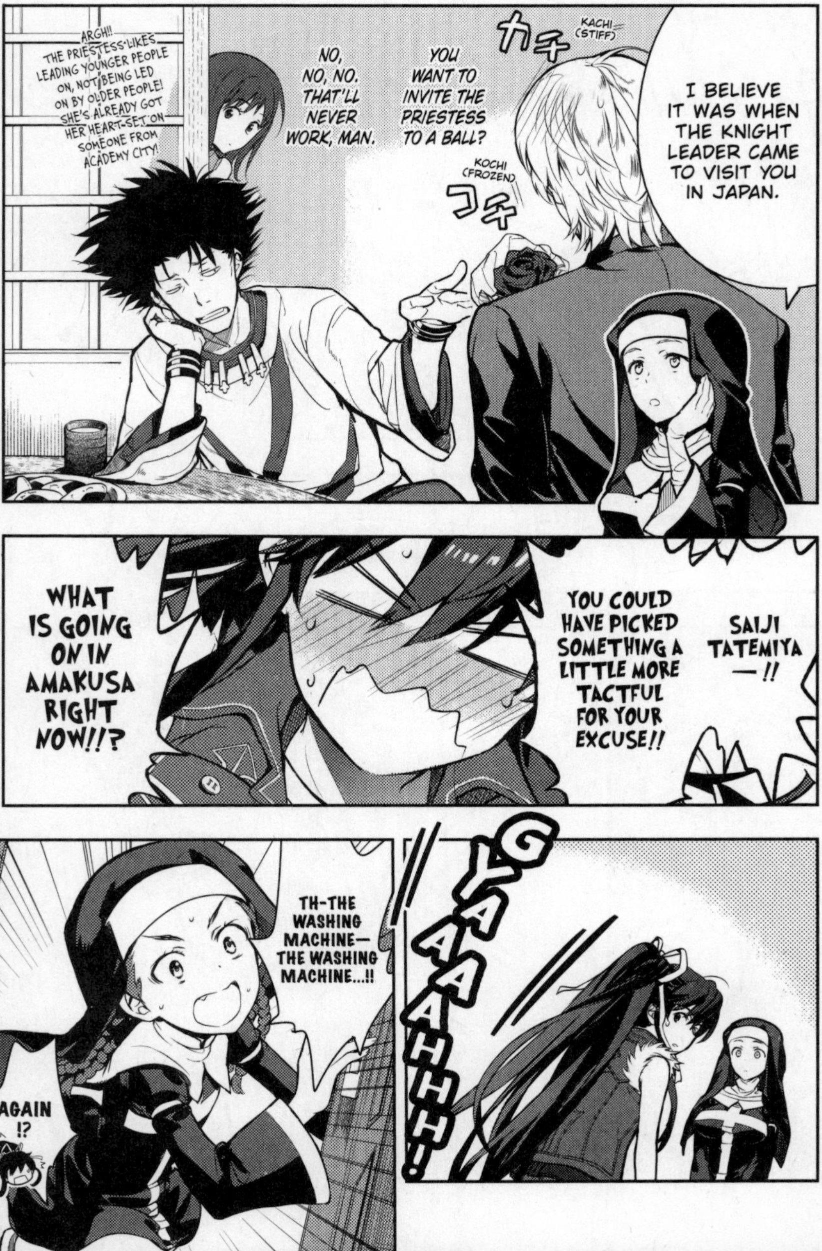
I BELIEVE IT WAS WHEN THE KNIGHT LEADER CAME TO VISIT YOU IN JAPAN.
カチ KACHI (STIFF)
コチ KOCHI (FROZEN)
YOU WANT TO INVITE THE PRIESTESS TO A BALL?
NO, NO, NO. THAT'LL NEVER WORK, MAN.
ARGH!! THE PRIESTESS LIKES LEADING YOUNGER PEOPLE ON, NOT BEING LED ON BY OLDER PEOPLE! SHE'S ALREADY GOT HER HEART SET ON SOMEONE FROM ACADEMY CITY!
SAIJI TATEMIYA —!!
YOU COULD HAVE PICKED SOMETHING A LITTLE MORE TACTFUL FOR YOUR EXCUSE!!
WHAT IS GOING ON IN AMAKUSA RIGHT NOW!!?
GYAAAAAHHH!
TH-THE WASHING MACHINE—THE WASHING MACHINE...!!
AGAIN !?

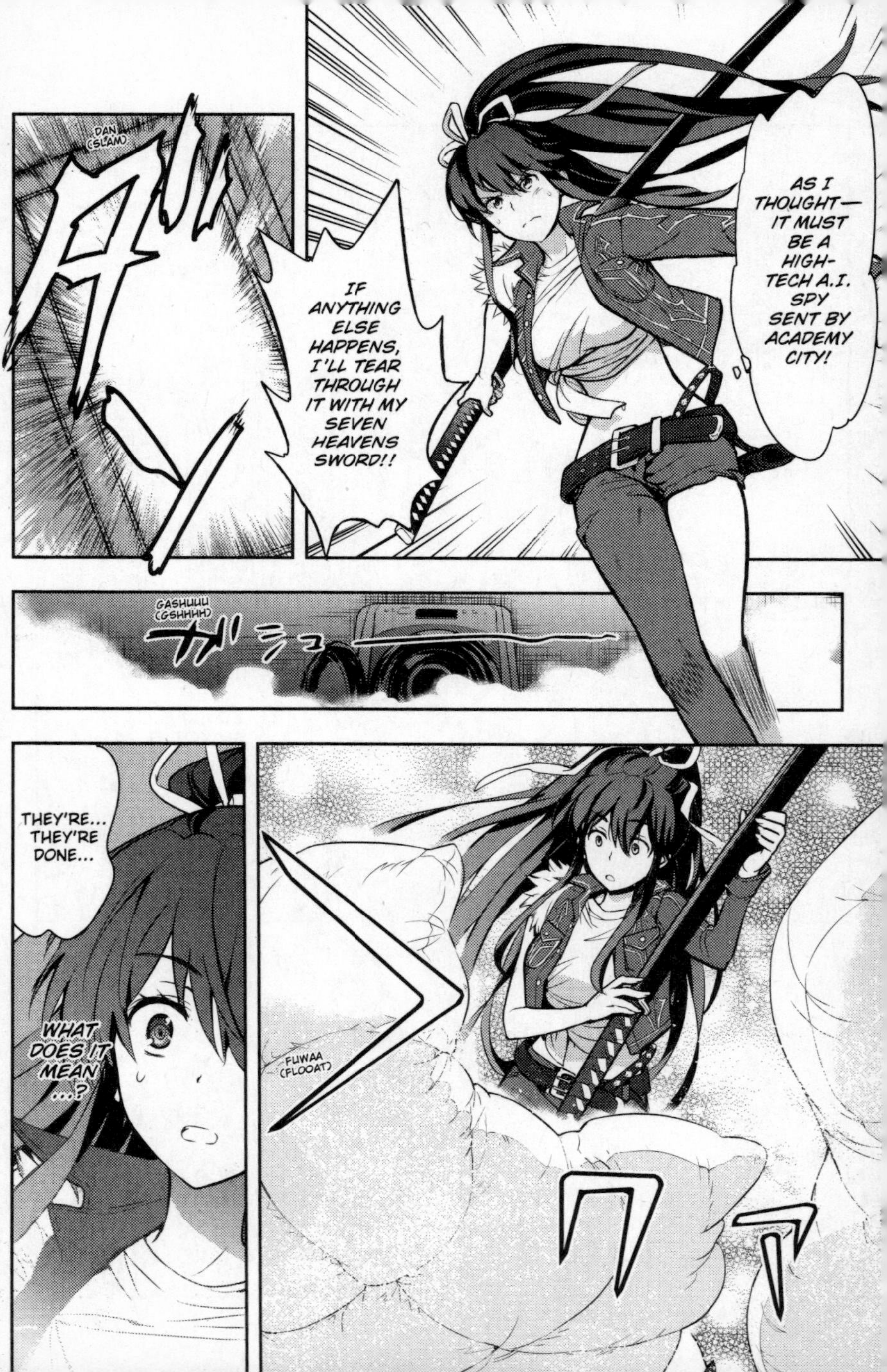
AS I THOUGHT—IT MUST BE A HIGH-TECH A.I. SPY SENT BY ACADEMY CITY!
IF ANYTHING ELSE HAPPENS, I'LL TEAR THROUGH IT WITH MY SEVEN HEAVENS SWORD!!
DAN (SLAM)
GASHUUU (GSHHHH)
FUWAA (FLOOAT)
THEY'RE... THEY'RE DONE...
WHAT DOES IT MEAN...?

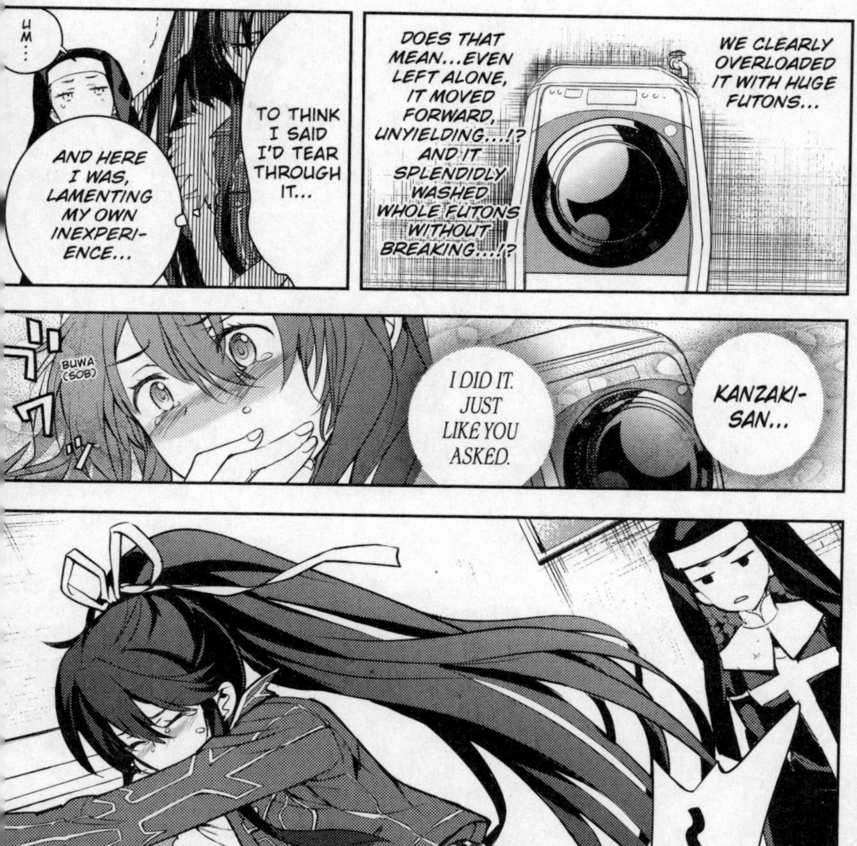
WE CLEARLY OVERLOADED IT WITH HUGE FUTONS...
DOES THAT MEAN...EVEN LEFT ALONE, IT MOVED FORWARD, UNYIELDING...!? AND IT SPLENDIDLY WASHED WHOLE FUTONS WITHOUT BREAKING...!?
TO THINK I SAID I'D TEAR THROUGH IT...
UM...
AND HERE I WAS, LAMENTING MY OWN INEXPERI-ENCE...
KANZAKI-SAN...
I DID IT. JUST LIKE YOU ASKED.
BUWA (SOB)
——!!

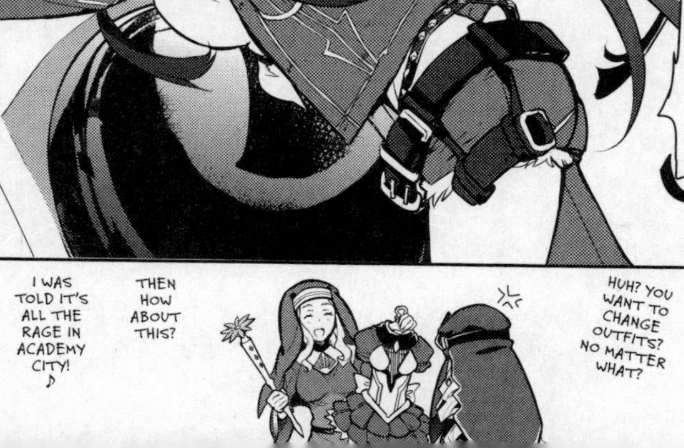
HUH? YOU WANT TO CHANGE OUTFITS? NO MATTER WHAT?
THEN HOW ABOUT THIS?
I WAS TOLD IT'S ALL THE RAGE IN ACADEMY CITY! ♪

A Certain Magical Index

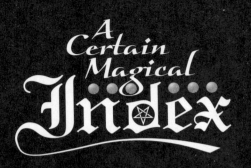

#120 MISUZU MISAKA ①

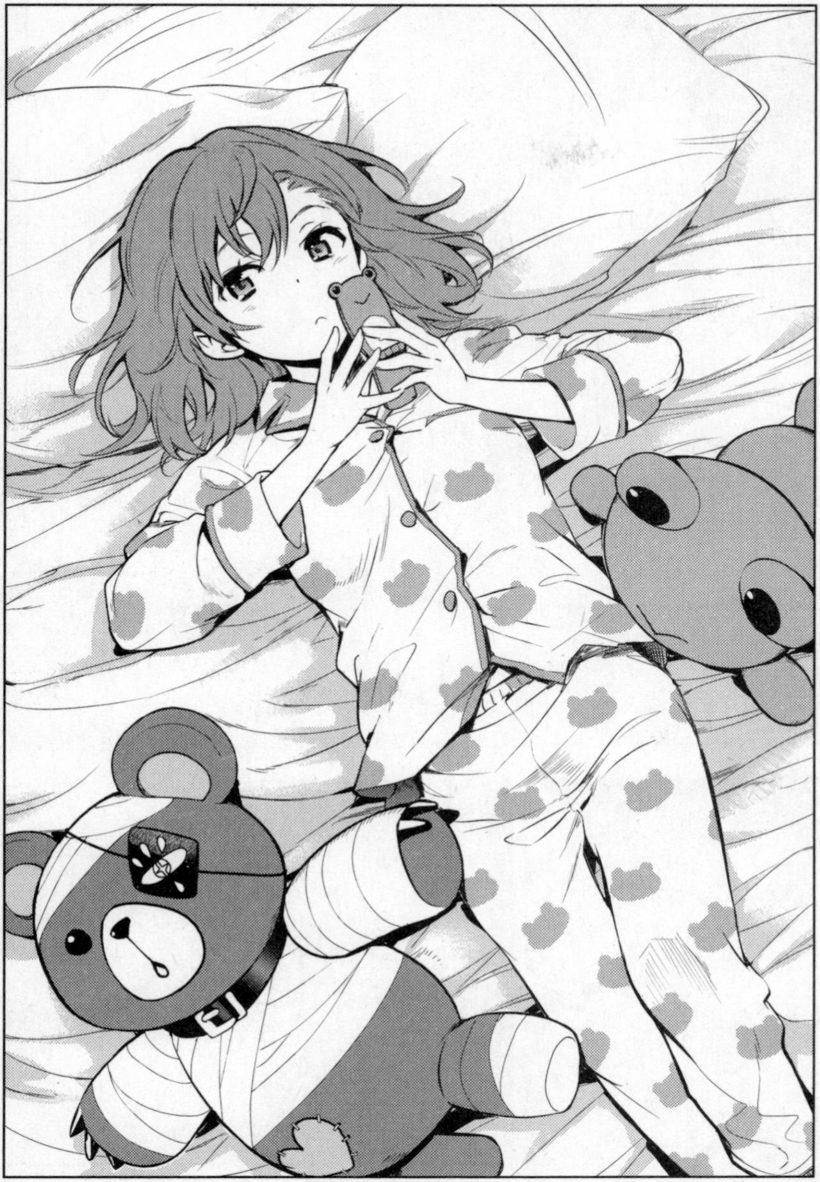

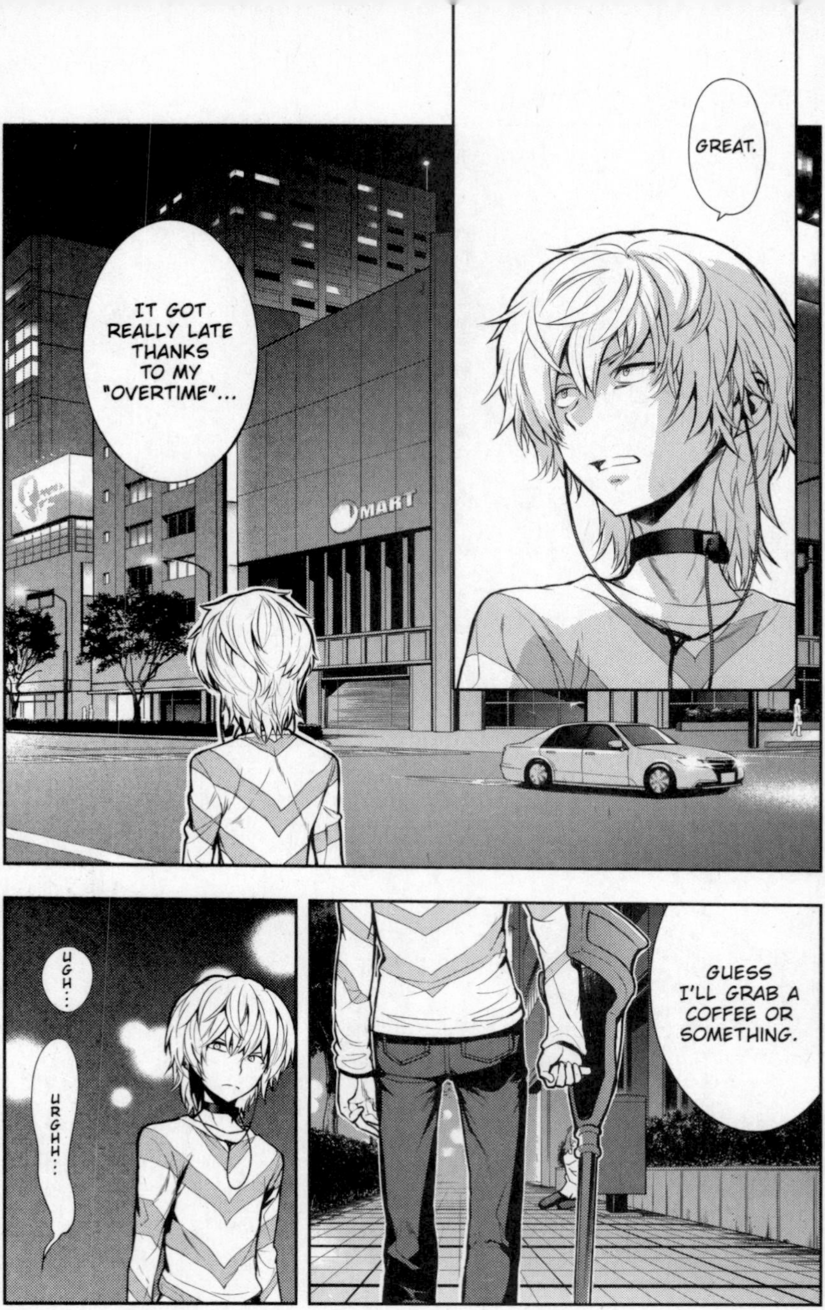
GREAT.
IT GOT REALLY LATE THANKS TO MY "OVERTIME"...
MART
GUESS I'LL GRAB A COFFEE OR SOMETHING.
UGH...
URGHH...

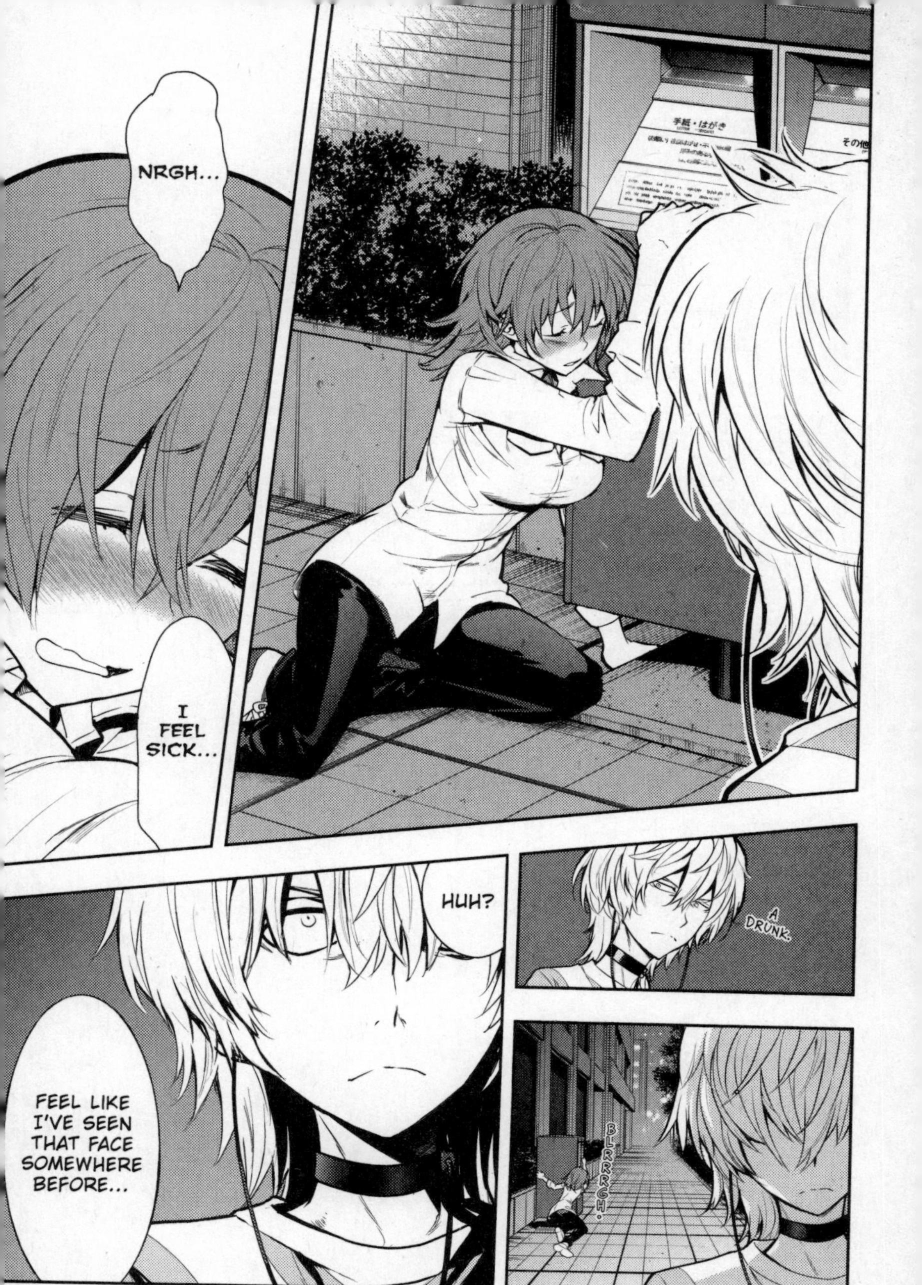
手紙・はがき
その他
NRGH...
I FEEL SICK...
A DRUNK.
BLRRRGH.
HUH?
FEEL LIKE I'VE SEEN THAT FACE SOMEWHERE BEFORE...

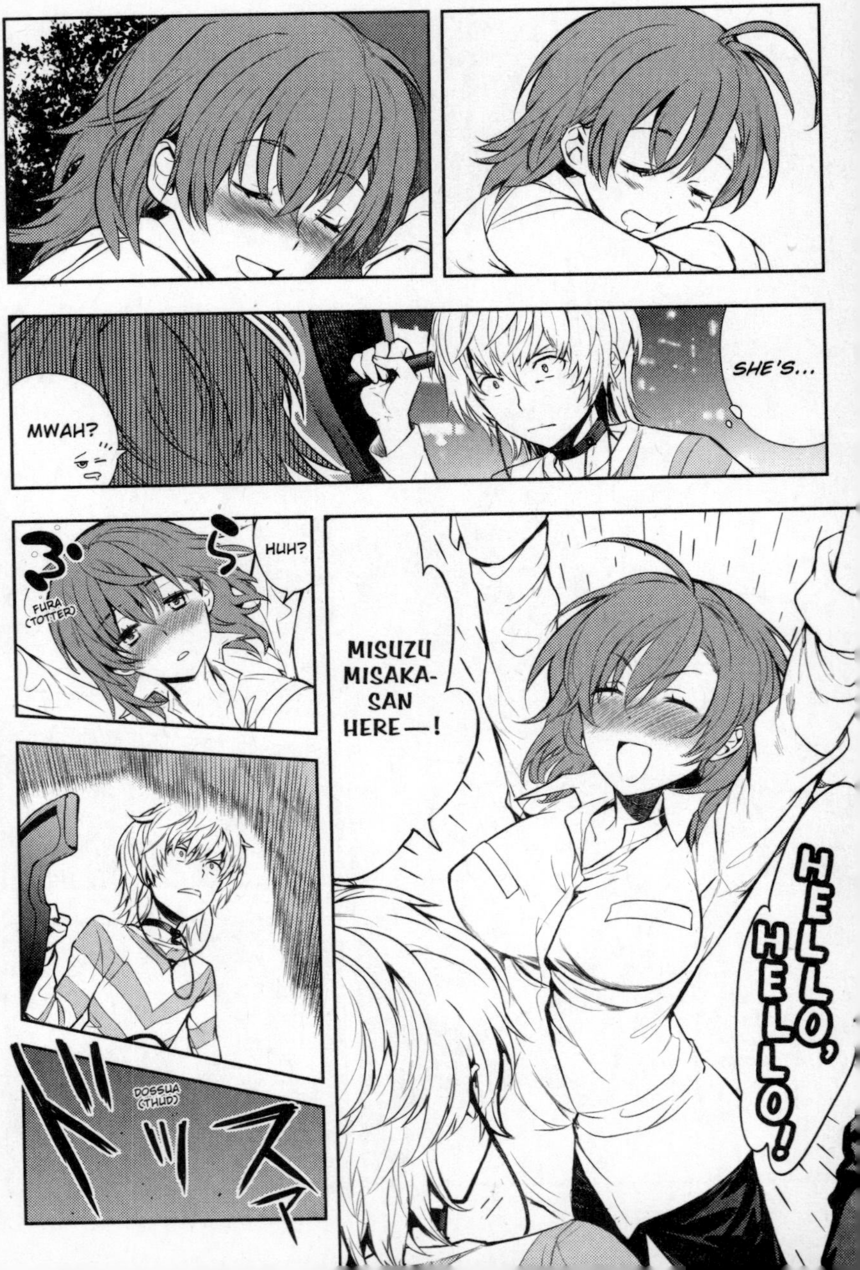
SHE'S...
MWAH?
HELLO, HELLO!
MISUZU MISAKA-SAN HERE—!
HUH?
FURA (TOTTER)
DOSSUA (THUD)

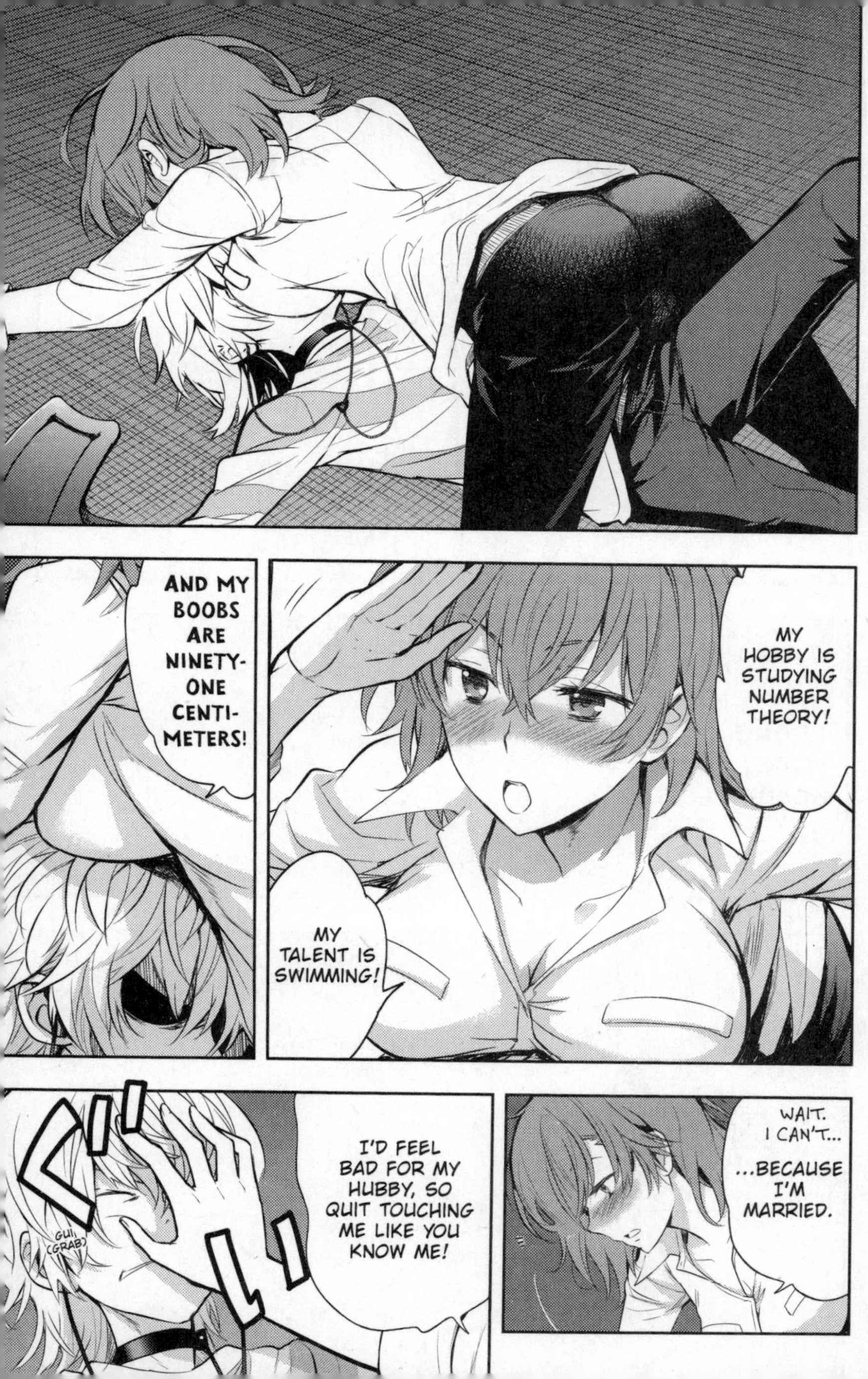
MY HOBBY IS STUDYING NUMBER THEORY!
MY TALENT IS SWIMMING!
AND MY BOOBS ARE NINETY-ONE CENTIMETERS!
WAIT. I CAN'T...
...BECAUSE I'M MARRIED.
I'D FEEL BAD FOR MY HUBBY, SO QUIT TOUCHING ME LIKE YOU KNOW ME!
GUI (GRAB)

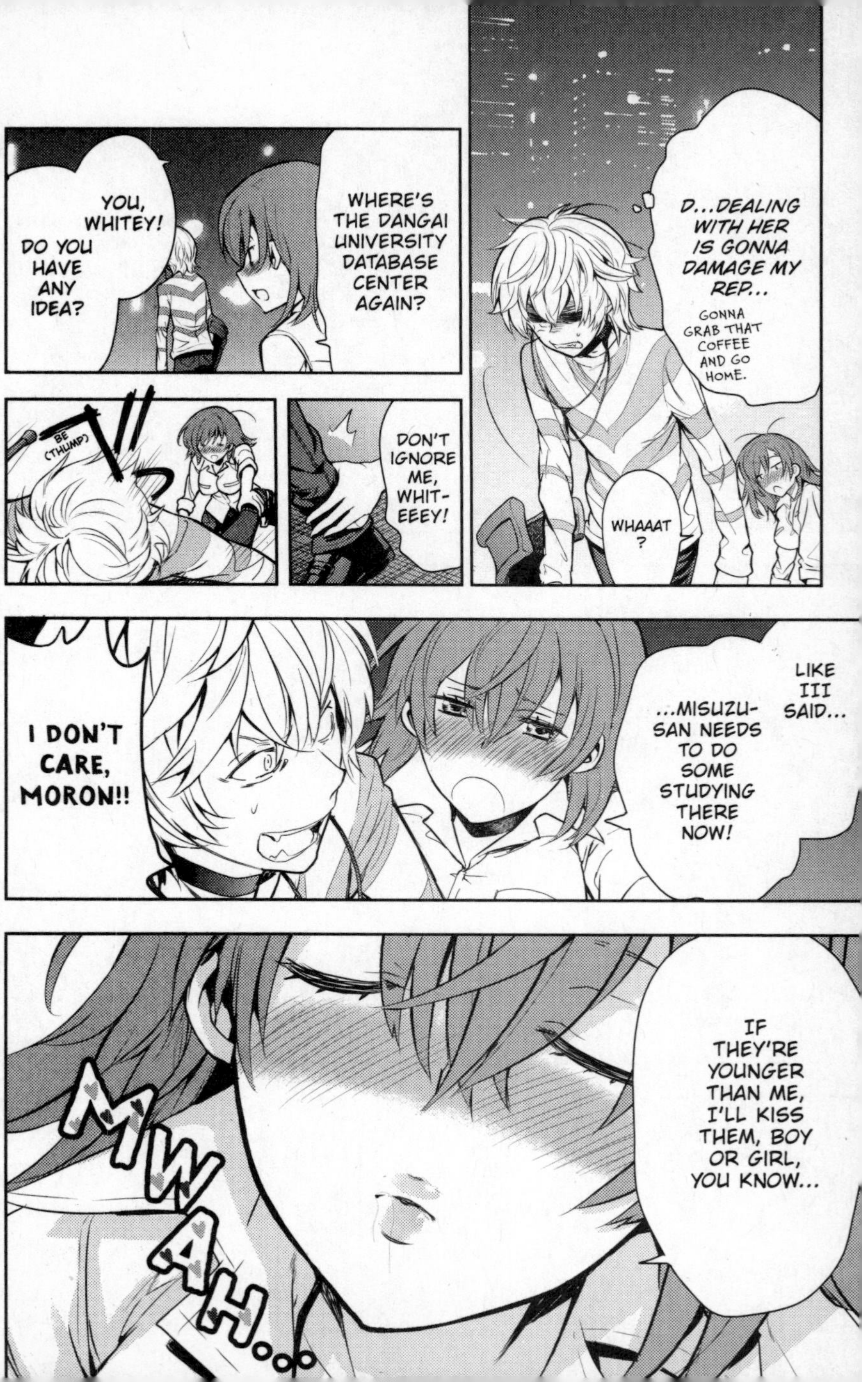
D...DEALING WITH HER IS GONNA DAMAGE MY REP...
GONNA GRAB THAT COFFEE AND GO HOME.
WHAAAT?
WHERE'S THE DANGAI UNIVERSITY DATABASE CENTER AGAIN?
YOU, WHITEY! DO YOU HAVE ANY IDEA?
DON'T IGNORE ME, WHIT-EEEY!
BE (THUMP)
LIKE III SAID...
...MISUZU-SAN NEEDS TO DO SOME STUDYING THERE NOW!
I DON'T CARE, MORON!!
IF THEY'RE YOUNGER THAN ME, I'LL KISS THEM, BOY OR GIRL, YOU KNOW...
MWAH...

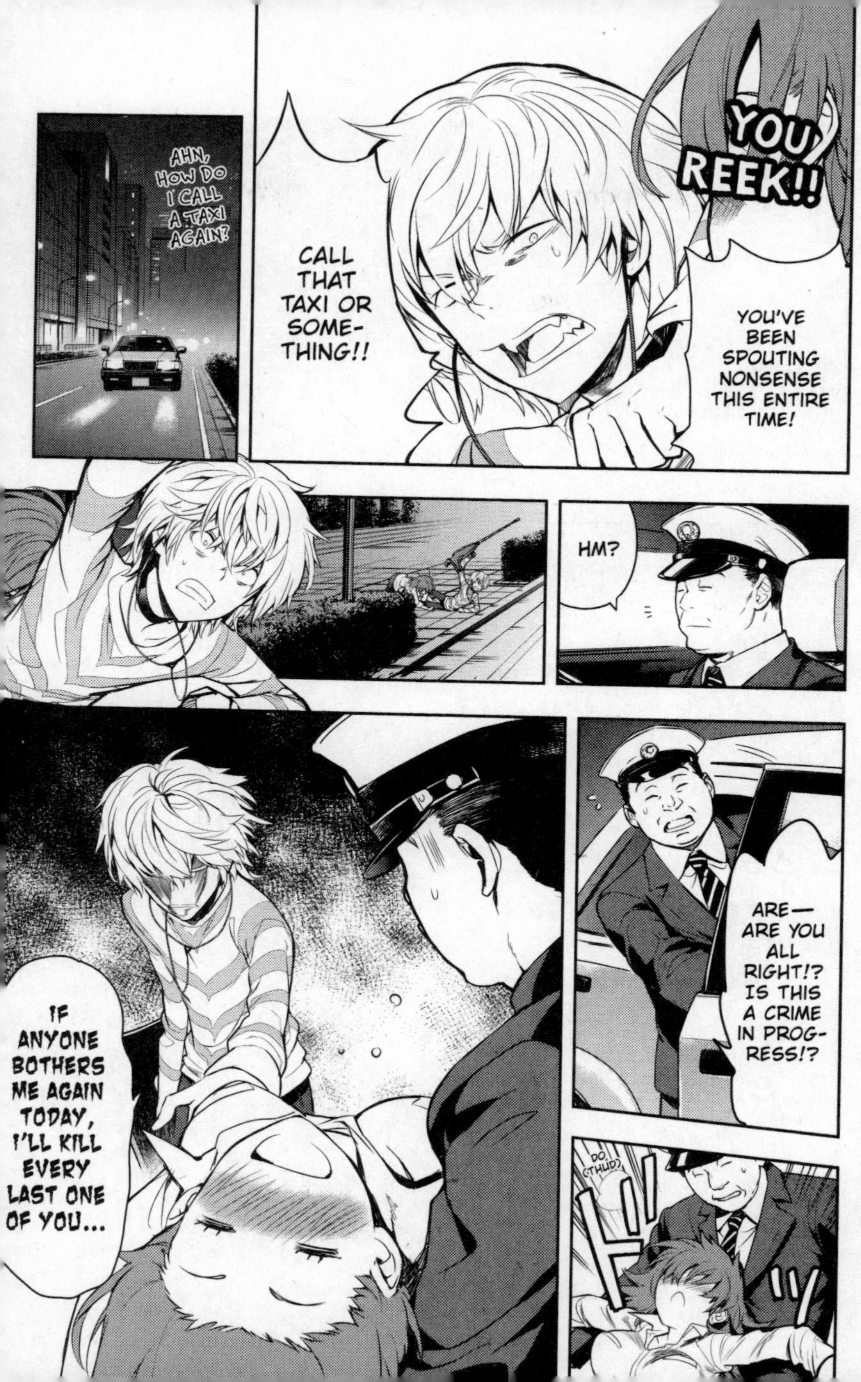
YOU REEK!!
YOU'VE BEEN SPOUTING NONSENSE THIS ENTIRE TIME!
CALL THAT TAXI OR SOME-THING!!
AHN, HOW DO I CALL A TAXI AGAIN?
HM?
ARE— ARE YOU ALL RIGHT!? IS THIS A CRIME IN PROG-RESS!?
DO (THUD)
IF ANYONE BOTHERS ME AGAIN TODAY, I'LL KILL EVERY LAST ONE OF YOU...

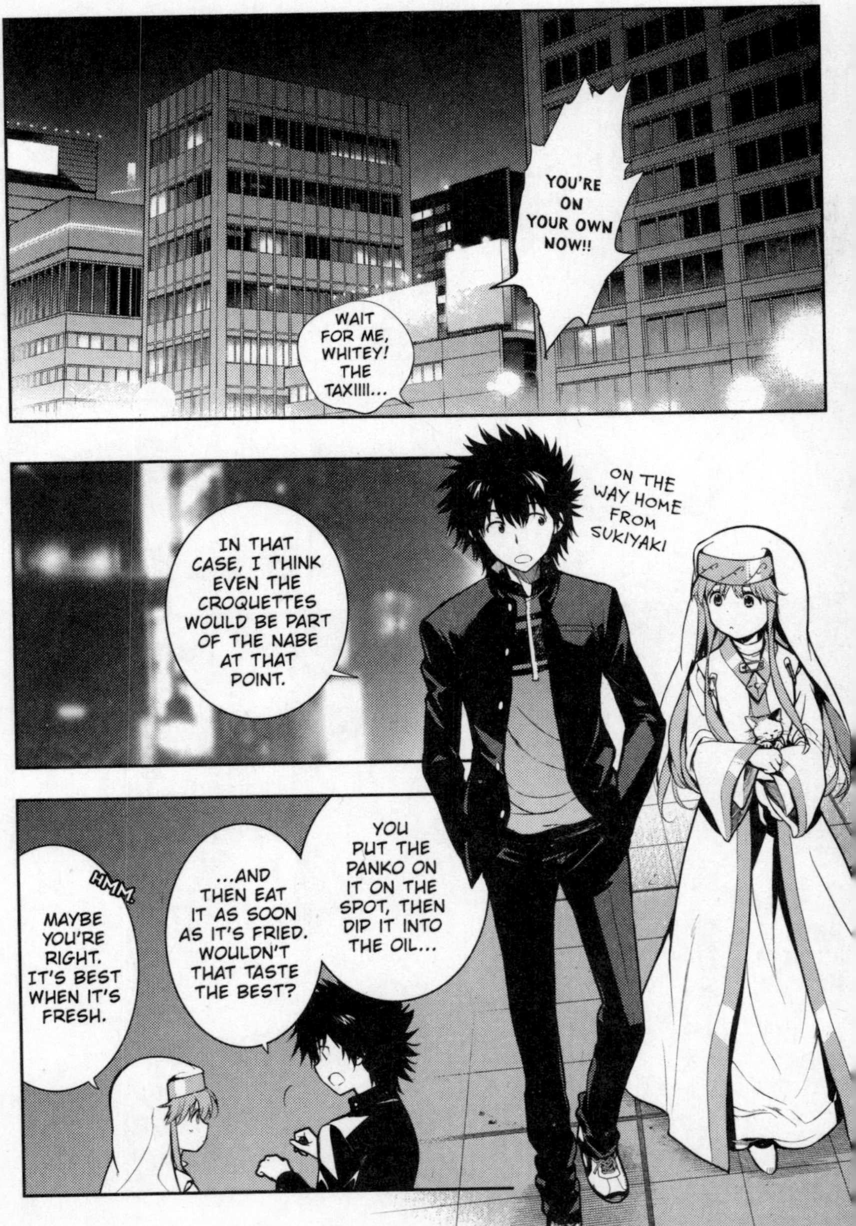
YOU'RE ON YOUR OWN NOW!!
WAIT FOR ME, WHITEY! THE TAXIIII...
ON THE WAY HOME FROM SUKIYAKI
IN THAT CASE, I THINK EVEN THE CROQUETTES WOULD BE PART OF THE NABE AT THAT POINT.
YOU PUT THE PANKO ON IT ON THE SPOT, THEN DIP IT INTO THE OIL...
...AND THEN EAT IT AS SOON AS IT'S FRIED. WOULDN'T THAT TASTE THE BEST?
HMM.
MAYBE YOU'RE RIGHT. IT'S BEST WHEN IT'S FRESH.

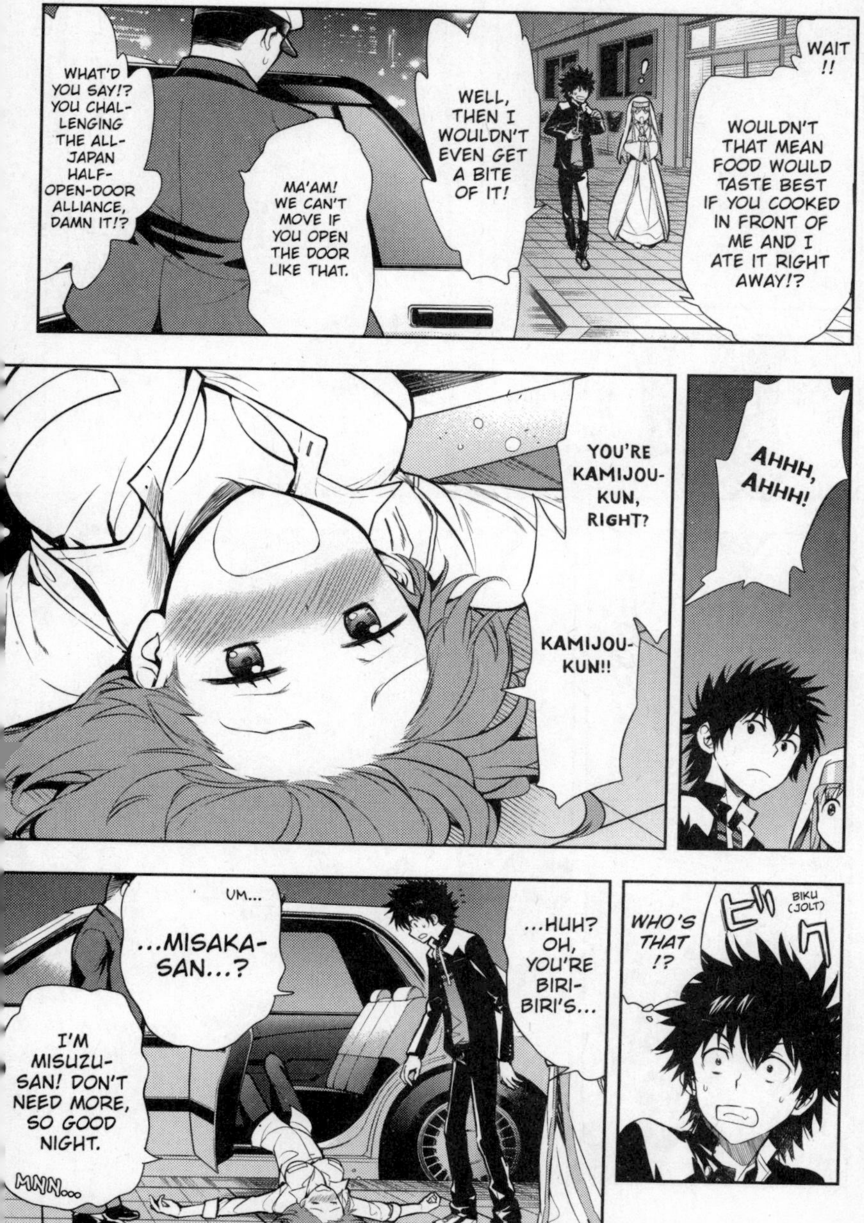
WAIT!!
WOULDN'T THAT MEAN FOOD WOULD TASTE BEST IF YOU COOKED IN FRONT OF ME AND I ATE IT RIGHT AWAY!?
WELL, THEN I WOULDN'T EVEN GET A BITE OF IT!
MA'AM! WE CAN'T MOVE IF YOU OPEN THE DOOR LIKE THAT.
WHAT'D YOU SAY!? YOU CHAL-LENGING THE ALL-JAPAN HALF-OPEN-DOOR ALLIANCE, DAMN IT!?
AHHH, AHHH!
YOU'RE KAMIJOU-KUN, RIGHT?
KAMIJOU-KUN!!
BIKU (JOLT)
WHO'S THAT!?
...HUH? OH, YOU'RE BIRI-BIRI'S...
UM...
...MISAKA-SAN...?
I'M MISUZU-SAN! DON'T NEED MORE, SO GOOD NIGHT.
MNN...

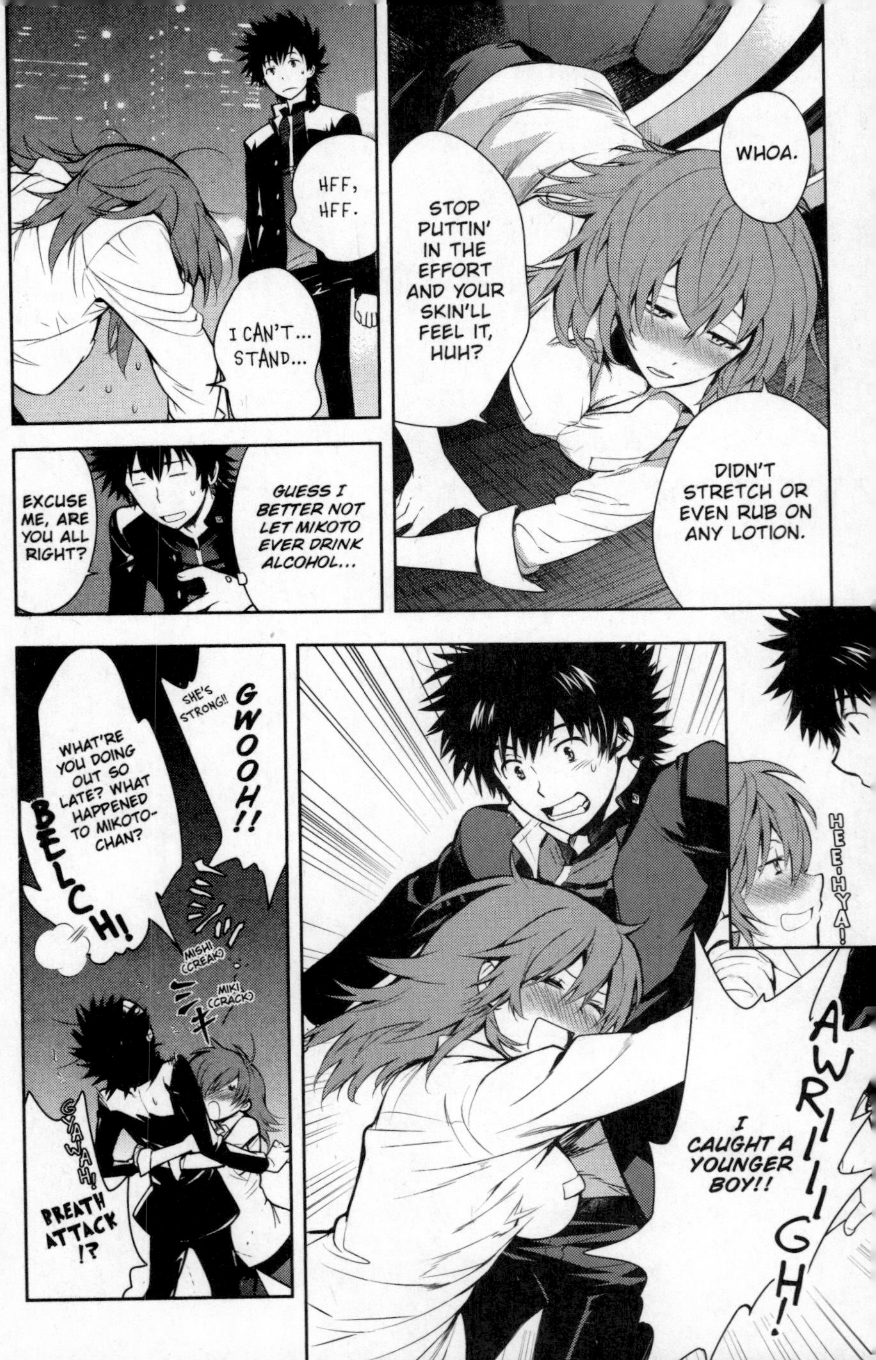
WHOA.
STOP PUTTIN' IN THE EFFORT AND YOUR SKIN'LL FEEL IT, HUH?
DIDN'T STRETCH OR EVEN RUB ON ANY LOTION.
HFF, HFF.
I CAN'T... STAND...
GUESS I BETTER NOT LET MIKOTO EVER DRINK ALCOHOL...
EXCUSE ME, ARE YOU ALL RIGHT?
HEE-HYA!
AWRIIIIGH!
I CAUGHT A YOUNGER BOY!!
GWOOOH!!
SHE'S STRONG!!
WHAT'RE YOU DOING OUT SO LATE? WHAT HAPPENED TO MIKOTO-CHAN?
BELCH!
MISHI (CREAK)
MIKI (CRACK)
GYAAAH!
BREATH ATTACK!?

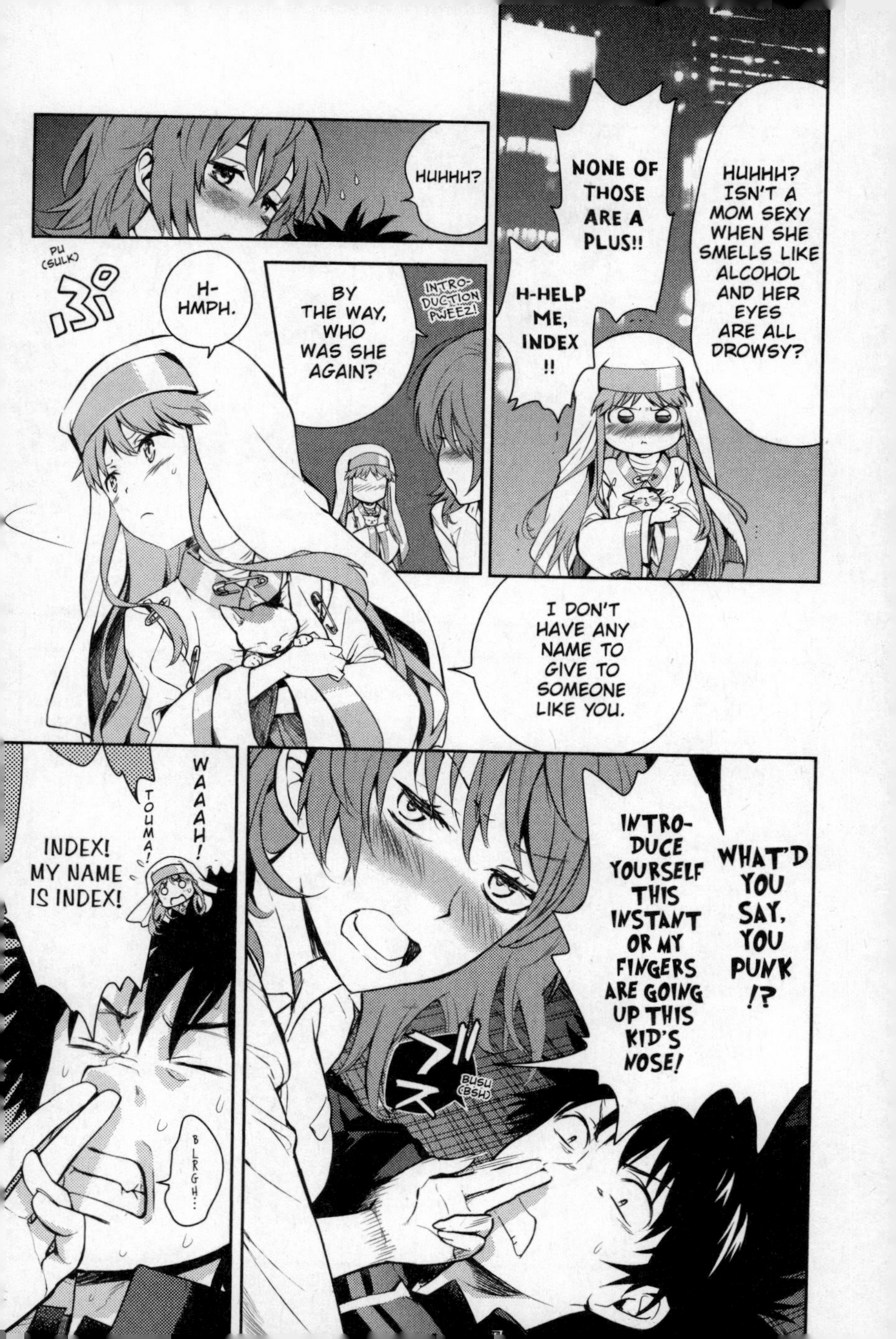
HUHHH? ISN'T A MOM SEXY WHEN SHE SMELLS LIKE ALCOHOL AND HER EYES ARE ALL DROWSY?
NONE OF THOSE ARE A PLUS!!
H-HELP ME, INDEX!!
HUHHH?
INTRO-DUCTION PWEEZ!
BY THE WAY, WHO WAS SHE AGAIN?
H-HMPH.
PU (SULK)
I DON'T HAVE ANY NAME TO GIVE TO SOMEONE LIKE YOU.
WHAT'D YOU SAY, YOU PUNK!?
INTRO-DUCE YOURSELF THIS INSTANT OR MY FINGERS ARE GOING UP THIS KID'S NOSE!
BUSU (BSH)
WAAAAH!
TOUMA!
INDEX! MY NAME IS INDEX!
BLRGH...

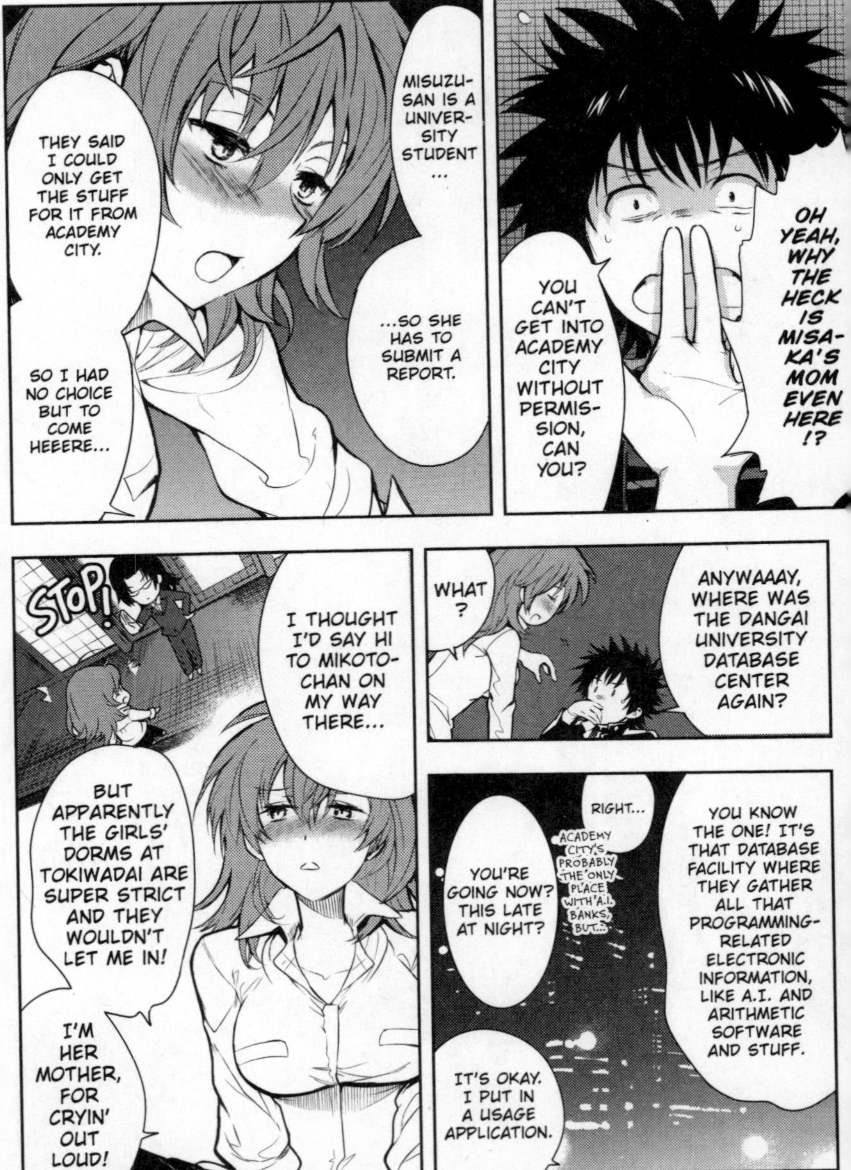
OH YEAH, WHY THE HECK IS MISAKA'S MOM EVEN HERE!?
YOU CAN'T GET INTO ACADEMY CITY WITHOUT PERMISSION, CAN YOU?
MISUZU-SAN IS A UNIVERSITY STUDENT ...
...SO SHE HAS TO SUBMIT A REPORT.
THEY SAID I COULD ONLY GET THE STUFF FOR IT FROM ACADEMY CITY.
SO I HAD NO CHOICE BUT TO COME HEEERE...
ANYWAAAY, WHERE WAS THE DANGAI UNIVERSITY DATABASE CENTER AGAIN?
WHAT?
YOU KNOW THE ONE! IT'S THAT DATABASE FACILITY WHERE THEY GATHER ALL THAT PROGRAMMING-RELATED ELECTRONIC INFORMATION, LIKE A.I. AND ARITHMETIC SOFTWARE AND STUFF.
RIGHT...
ACADEMY CITY'S PROBABLY THE ONLY PLACE WITH A.I. BANKS, BUT...
YOU'RE GOING NOW? THIS LATE AT NIGHT?
IT'S OKAY. I PUT IN A USAGE APPLICATION.
I THOUGHT I'D SAY HI TO MIKOTO-CHAN ON MY WAY THERE...
STOP!
BUT APPARENTLY THE GIRLS' DORMS AT TOKIWADAI ARE SUPER STRICT AND THEY WOULDN'T LET ME IN!
I'M HER MOTHER, FOR CRYIN' OUT LOUD!

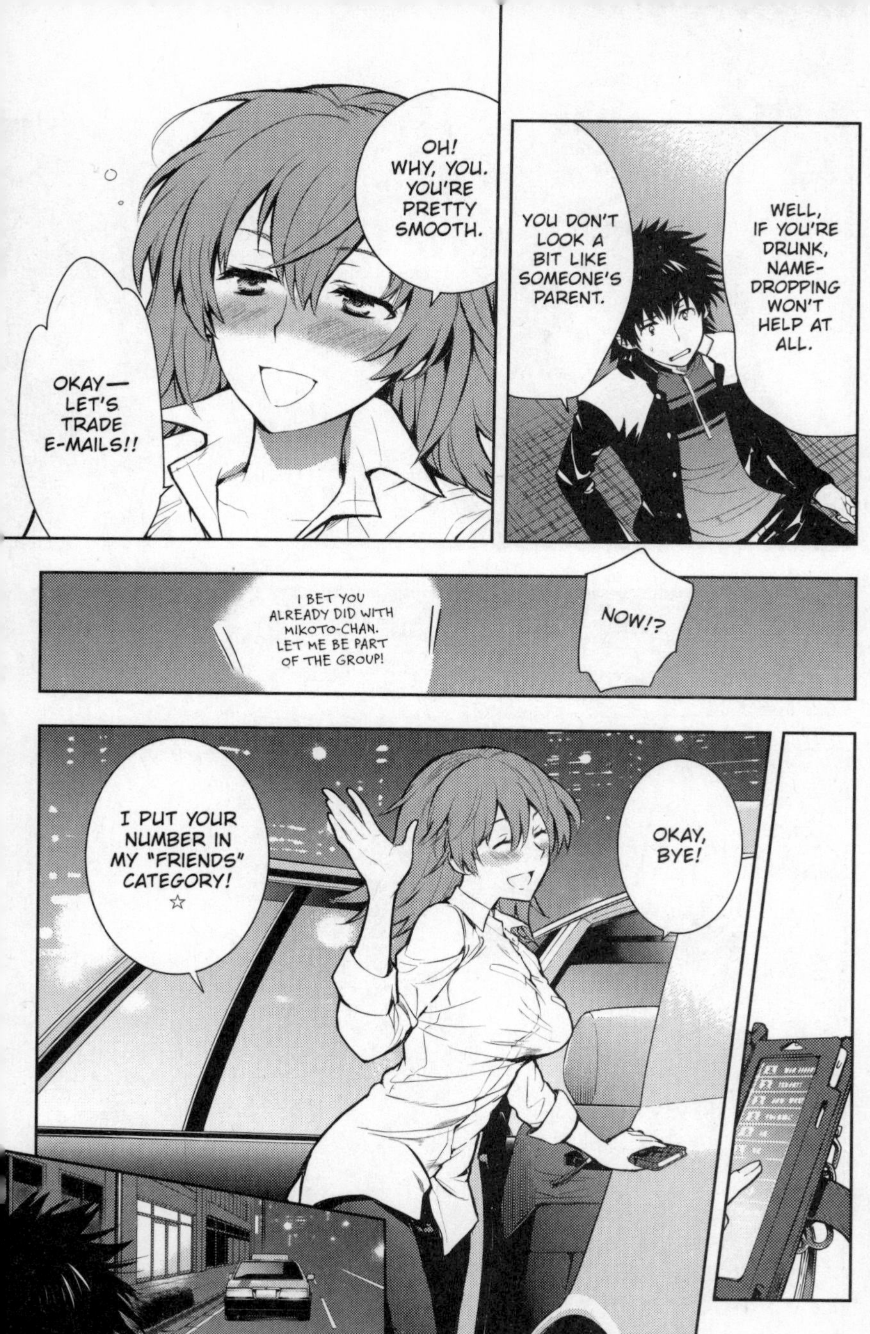
WELL, IF YOU'RE DRUNK, NAME-DROPPING WON'T HELP AT ALL.
YOU DON'T LOOK A BIT LIKE SOMEONE'S PARENT.
OH! WHY, YOU. YOU'RE PRETTY SMOOTH.
OKAY— LET'S TRADE E-MAILS!!
NOW!?
I BET YOU ALREADY DID WITH MIKOTO-CHAN. LET ME BE PART OF THE GROUP!
OKAY, BYE!
I PUT YOUR NUMBER IN MY "FRIENDS" CATEGORY! ☆

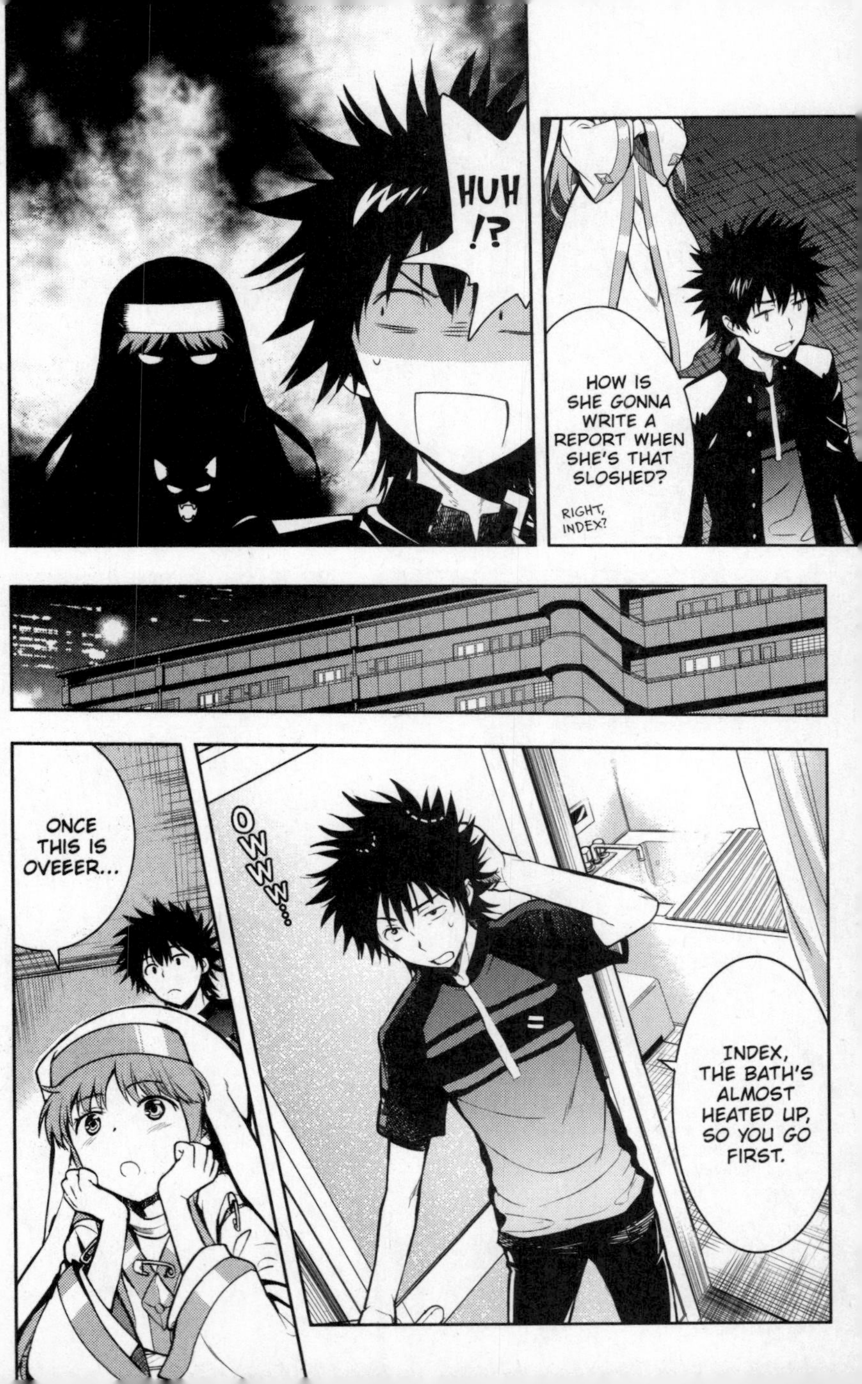
HOW IS SHE GONNA WRITE A REPORT WHEN SHE'S THAT SLOSHED?
RIGHT, INDEX?
HUH !?
OWWW...
INDEX, THE BATH'S ALMOST HEATED UP, SO YOU GO FIRST.
ONCE THIS IS OVEEER...

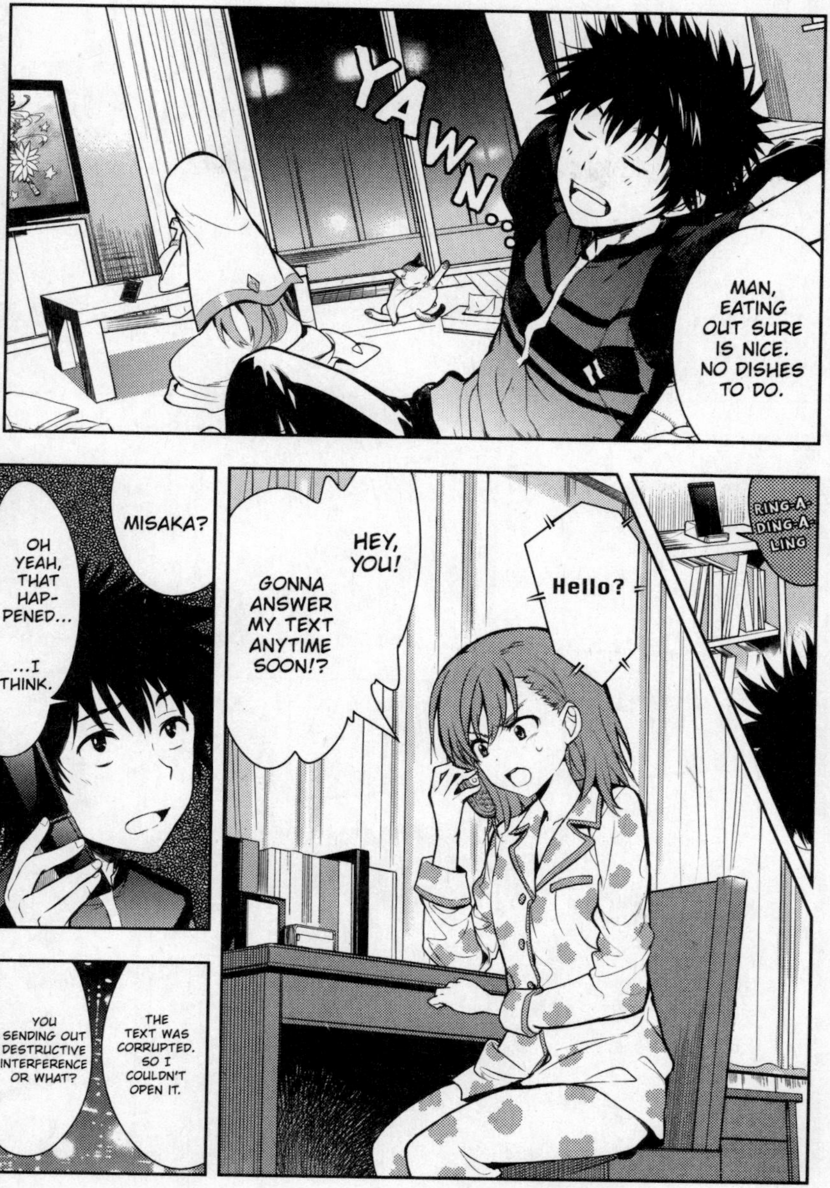
YAWN...
MAN, EATING OUT SURE IS NICE. NO DISHES TO DO.
RING-A-DING-A-LING
Hello?
HEY, YOU!
GONNA ANSWER MY TEXT ANYTIME SOON!?
MISAKA?
OH YEAH, THAT HAP-PENED...
...I THINK.
THE TEXT WAS CORRUPTED. SO I COULDN'T OPEN IT.
YOU SENDING OUT DESTRUCTIVE INTERFERENCE OR WHAT?

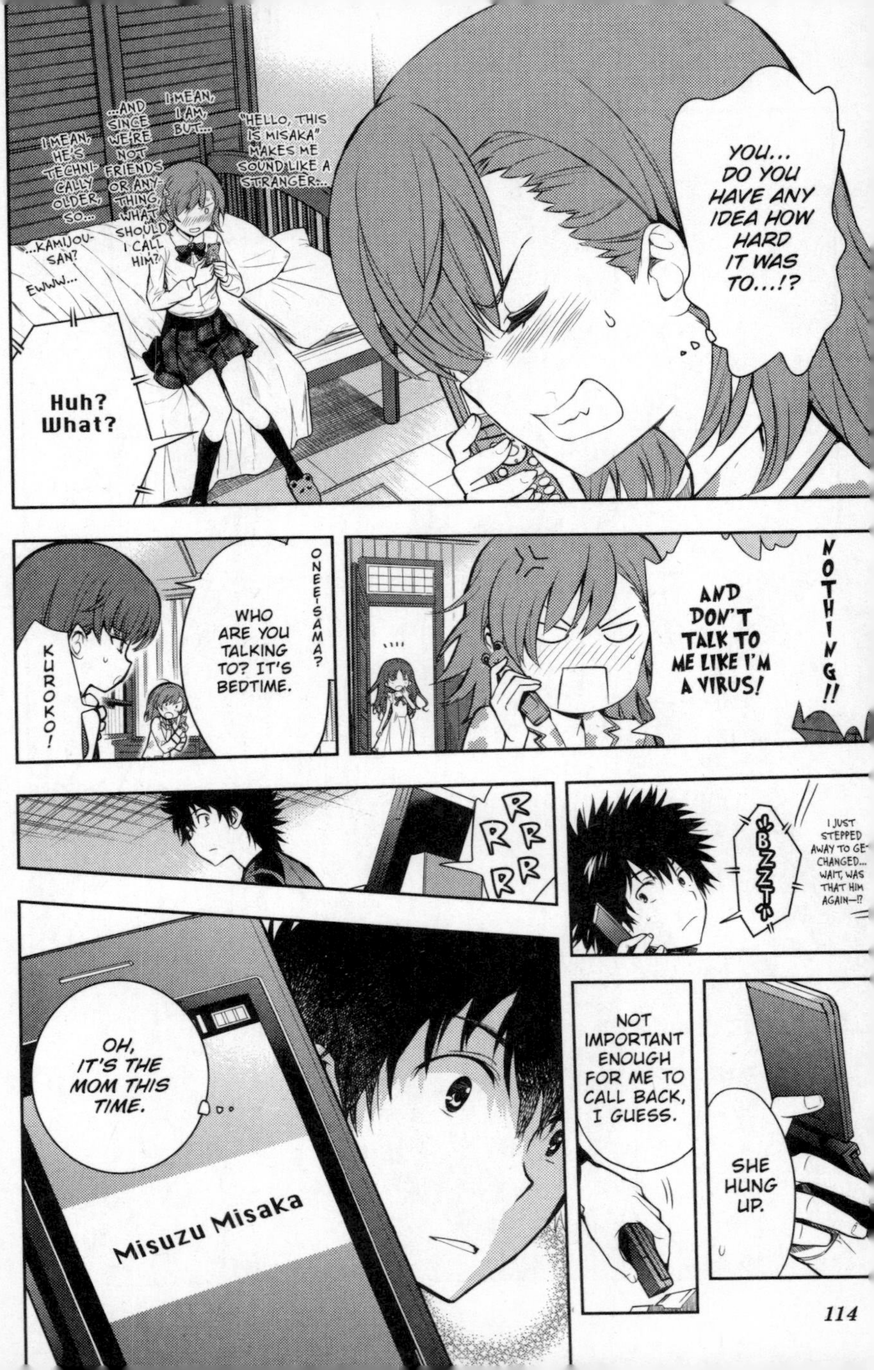
YOU... DO YOU HAVE ANY IDEA HOW HARD IT WAS TO...!?
"HELLO, THIS IS MISAKA" MAKES ME SOUND LIKE A STRANGER...
I MEAN, I AM, BUT...
...AND SINCE WE'RE NOT FRIENDS OR ANYTHING, WHAT SHOULD I CALL HIM?
I MEAN, HE'S TECHNICALLY OLDER, SO...
...KAMIJOU-SAN?
EWWW...
Huh? What?
NOTHING!!
AND DON'T TALK TO ME LIKE I'M A VIRUS!
ONEE-SAMA?
WHO ARE YOU TALKING TO? IT'S BEDTIME.
KUROKO!
I JUST STEPPED AWAY TO GET CHANGED... WAIT, WAS THAT HIM AGAIN—!?
BZZT
RRRRRRR
SHE HUNG UP.
NOT IMPORTANT ENOUGH FOR ME TO CALL BACK, I GUESS.
OH, IT'S THE MOM THIS TIME.
Misuzu Misaka

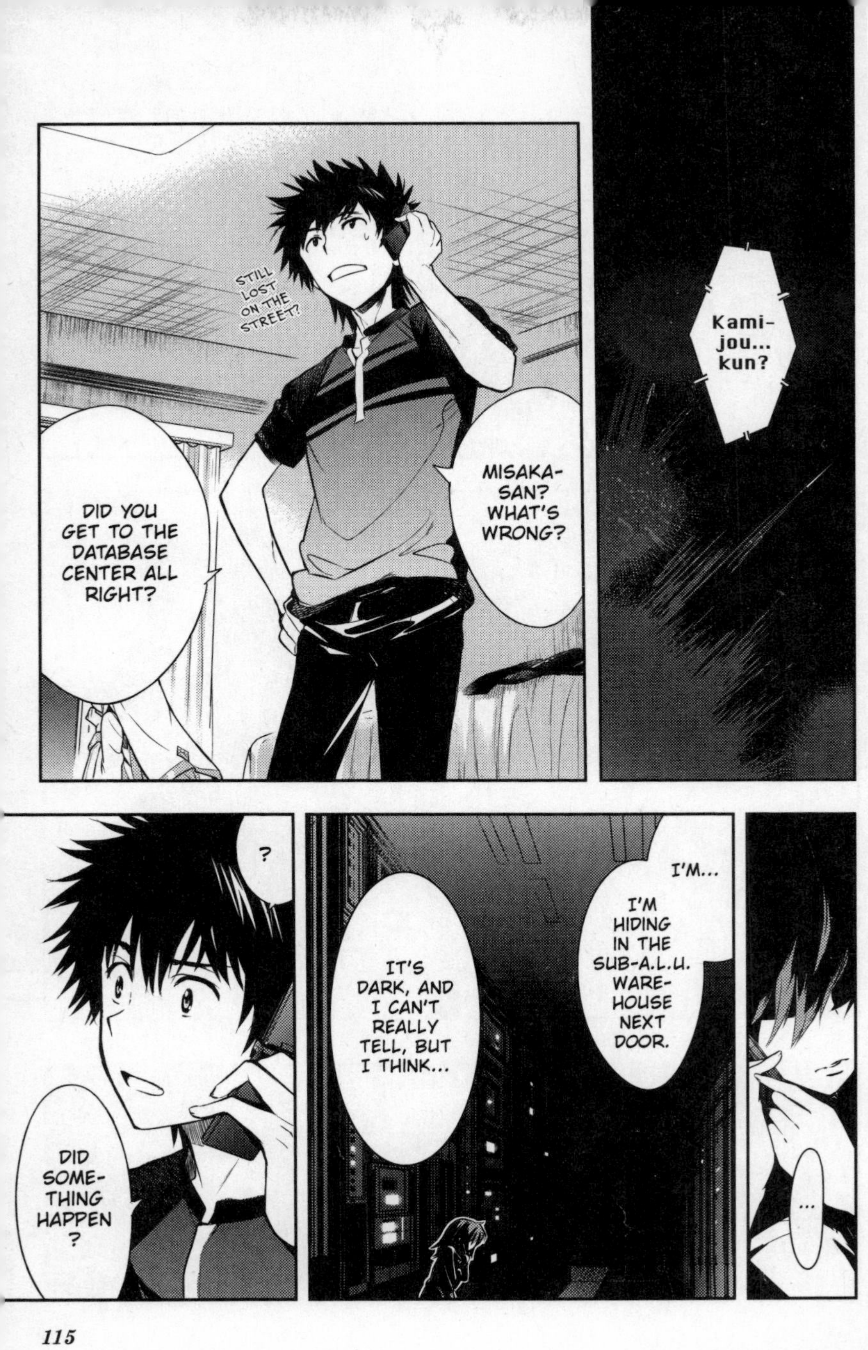
Kami-jou... kun?
MISAKA-SAN? WHAT'S WRONG?
STILL LOST ON THE STREET?
DID YOU GET TO THE DATABASE CENTER ALL RIGHT?
...
I'M...
I'M HIDING IN THE SUB-A.L.U. WARE-HOUSE NEXT DOOR.
IT'S DARK, AND I CAN'T REALLY TELL, BUT I THINK...
?
DID SOME-THING HAPPEN?

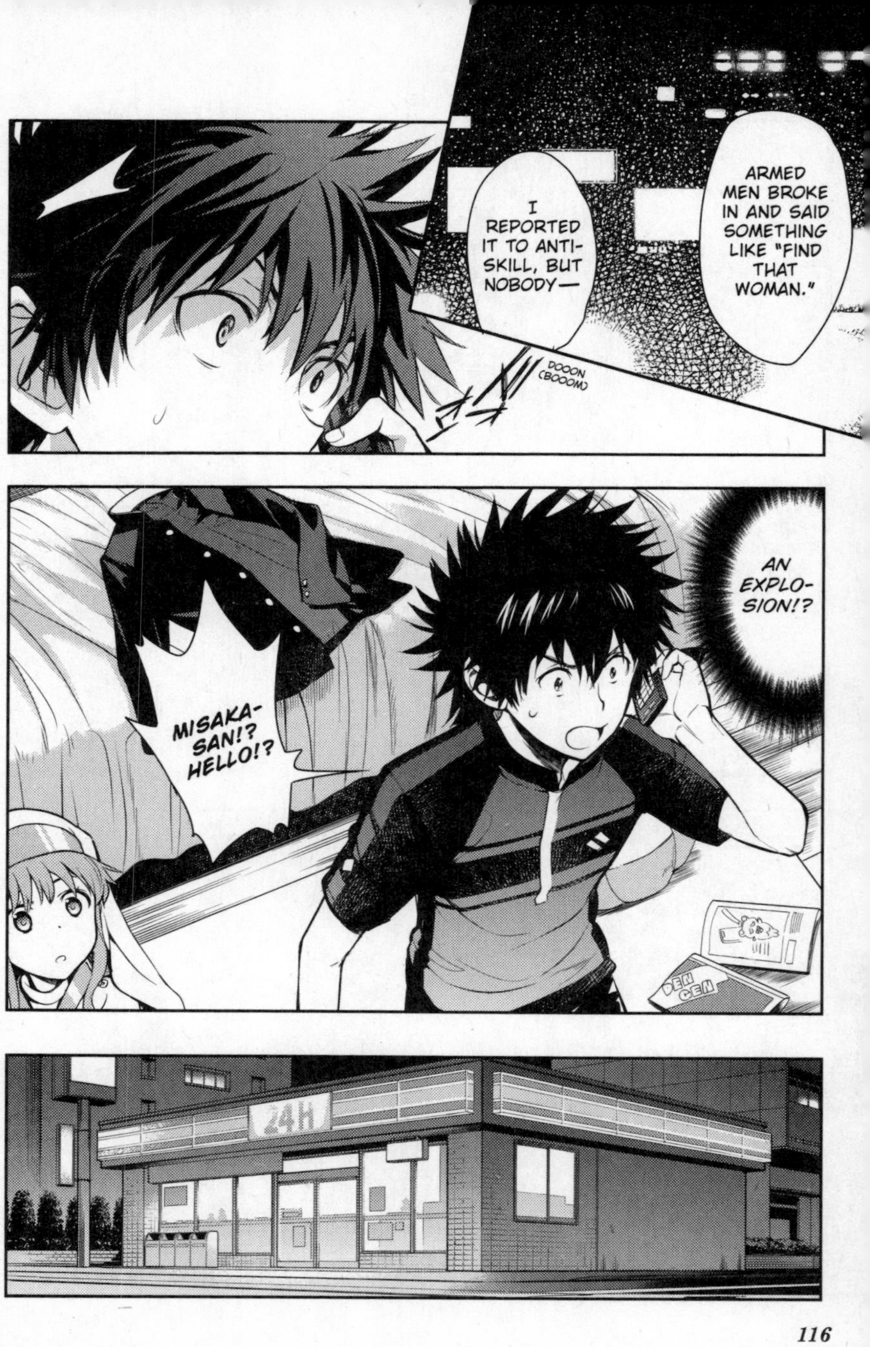
ARMED MEN BROKE IN AND SAID SOMETHING LIKE "FIND THAT WOMAN."
I REPORTED IT TO ANTI-SKILL, BUT NOBODY—
DOOON (BOOOM)
AN EXPLOSION!?
MISAKA-SAN!? HELLO!?
DEN GEN
24H

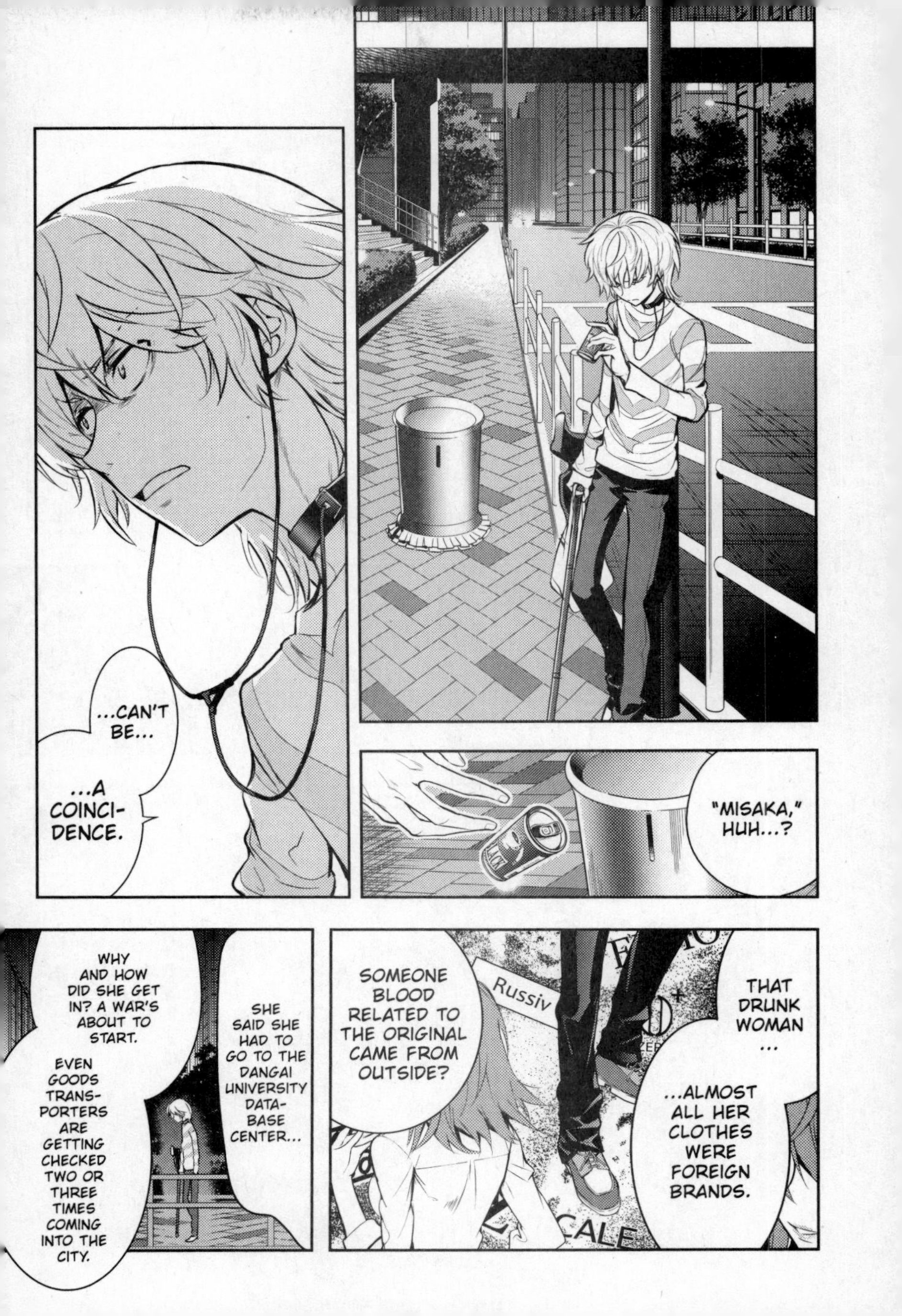
"MISAKA," HUH...?
...CAN'T BE...
...A COINCIDENCE.
THAT DRUNK WOMAN ...
...ALMOST ALL HER CLOTHES WERE FOREIGN BRANDS.
SOMEONE BLOOD RELATED TO THE ORIGINAL CAME FROM OUTSIDE?
SHE SAID SHE HAD TO GO TO THE DANGAI UNIVERSITY DATABASE CENTER...
WHY AND HOW DID SHE GET IN? A WAR'S ABOUT TO START.
EVEN GOODS TRANSPORTERS ARE GETTING CHECKED TWO OR THREE TIMES COMING INTO THE CITY.

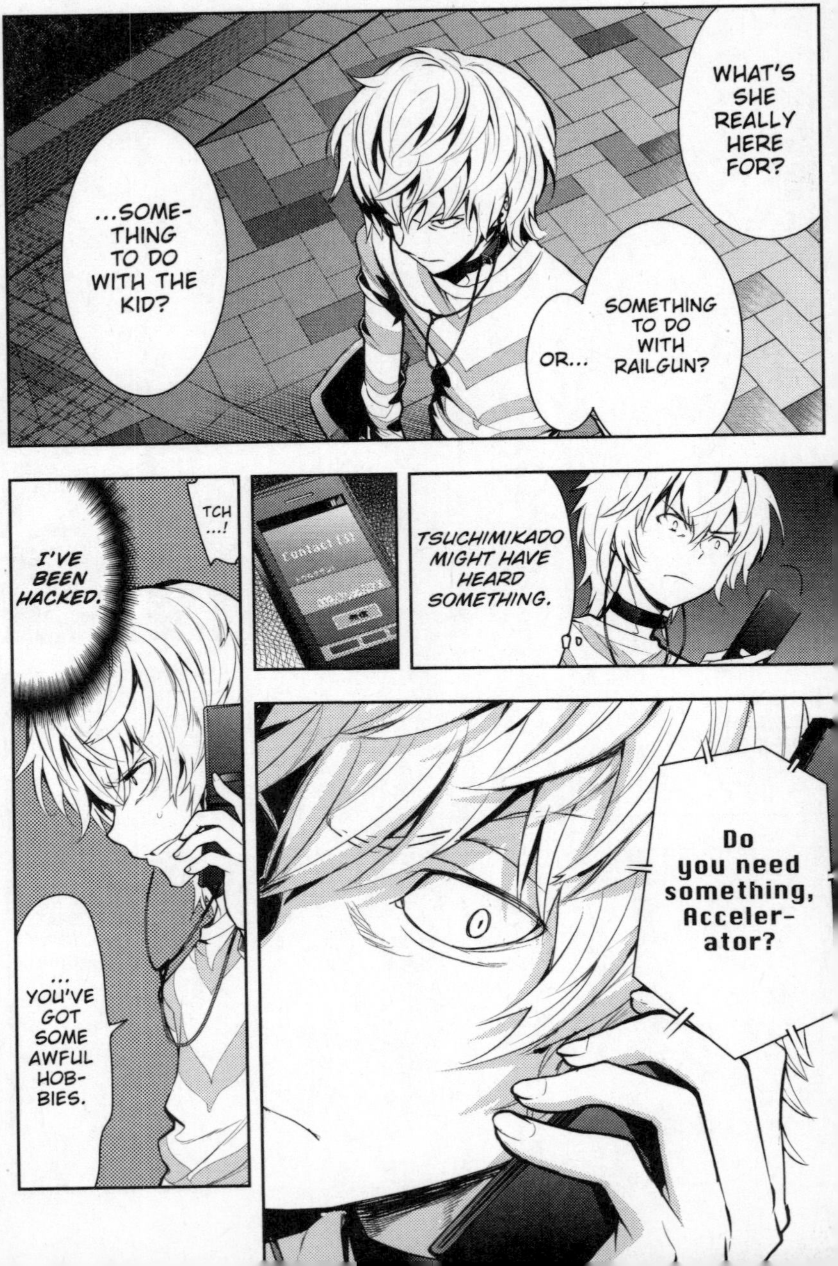
WHAT'S SHE REALLY HERE FOR?
...SOME-THING TO DO WITH THE KID?
OR...
SOMETHING TO DO WITH RAILGUN?
TSUCHIMIKADO MIGHT HAVE HEARD SOMETHING.
Do you need something, Acceler-ator?
TCH ...!
I'VE BEEN HACKED.
... YOU'VE GOT SOME AWFUL HOB-BIES.

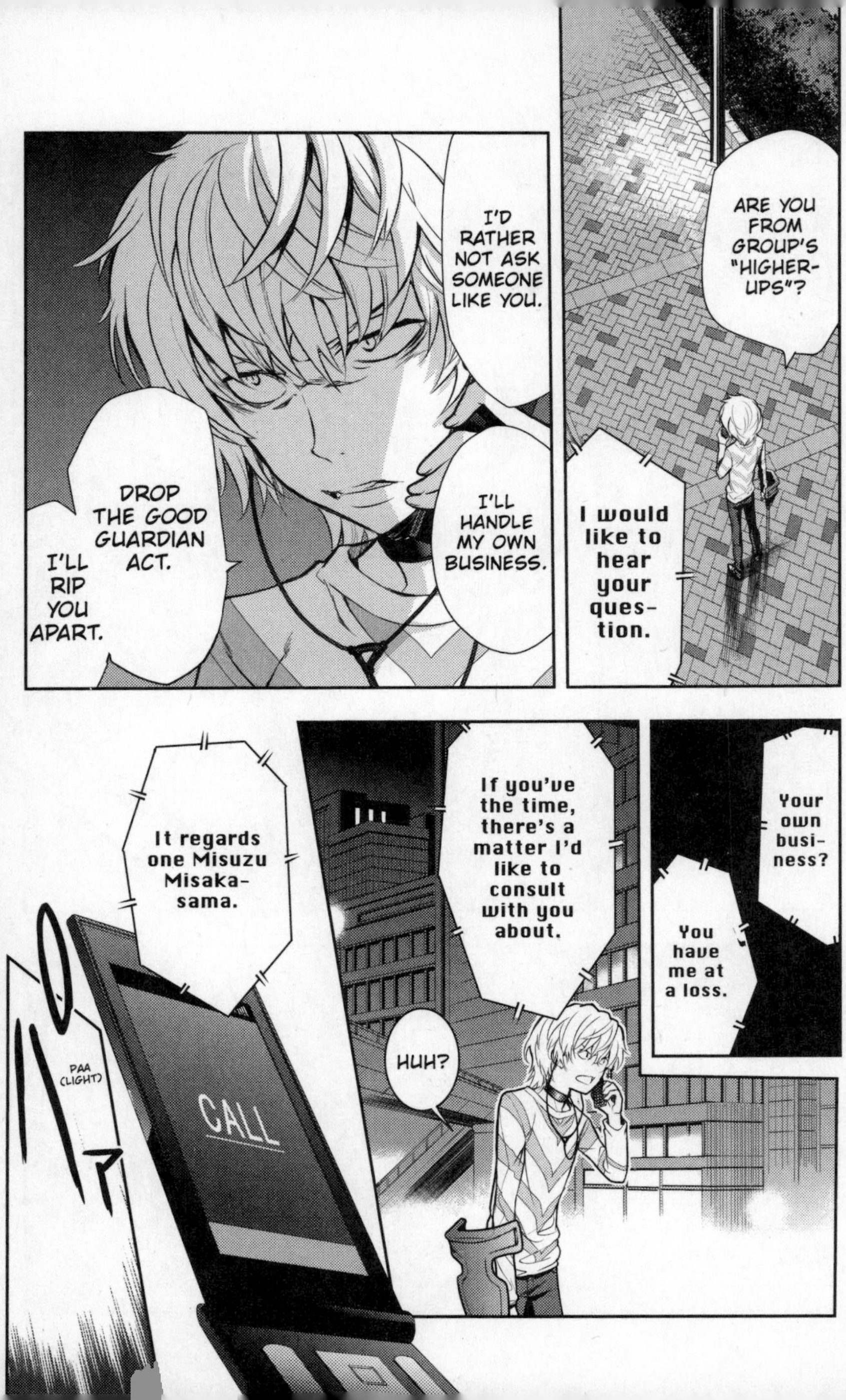
ARE YOU FROM GROUP'S "HIGHER-UPS"?
I would like to hear your question.
I'D RATHER NOT ASK SOMEONE LIKE YOU.
I'LL HANDLE MY OWN BUSINESS.
DROP THE GOOD GUARDIAN ACT.
I'LL RIP YOU APART.
Your own business?
You have me at a loss.
If you've the time, there's a matter I'd like to consult with you about.
HUH?
It regards one Misuzu Misaka-sama.
PAA (LIGHT)
CALL

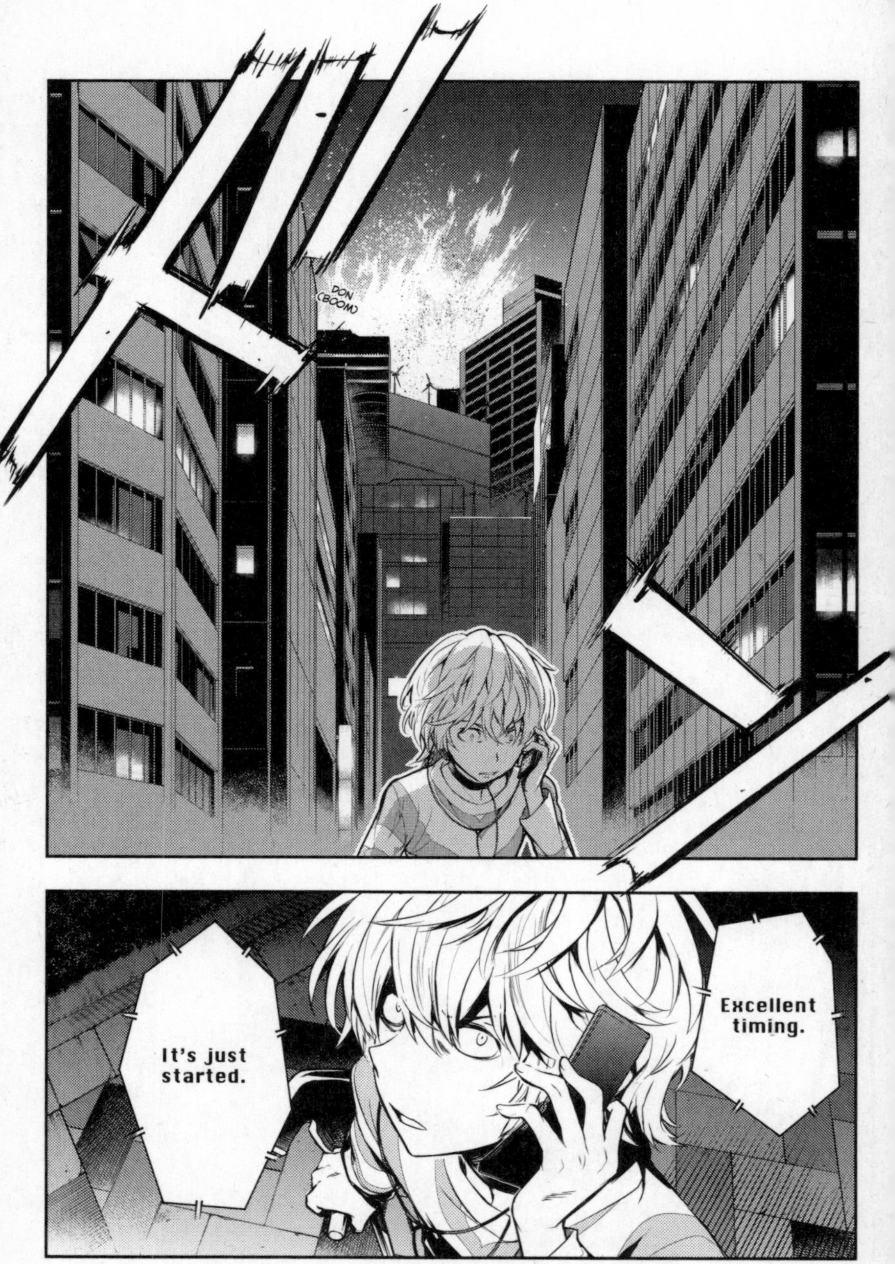
DON (BOOM)
Excellent timing.
It's just started.

A Certain Magical Index

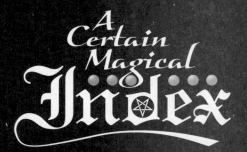

A Certain Magical Index

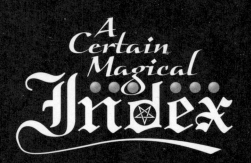

#121 MISUZU MISAKA ②

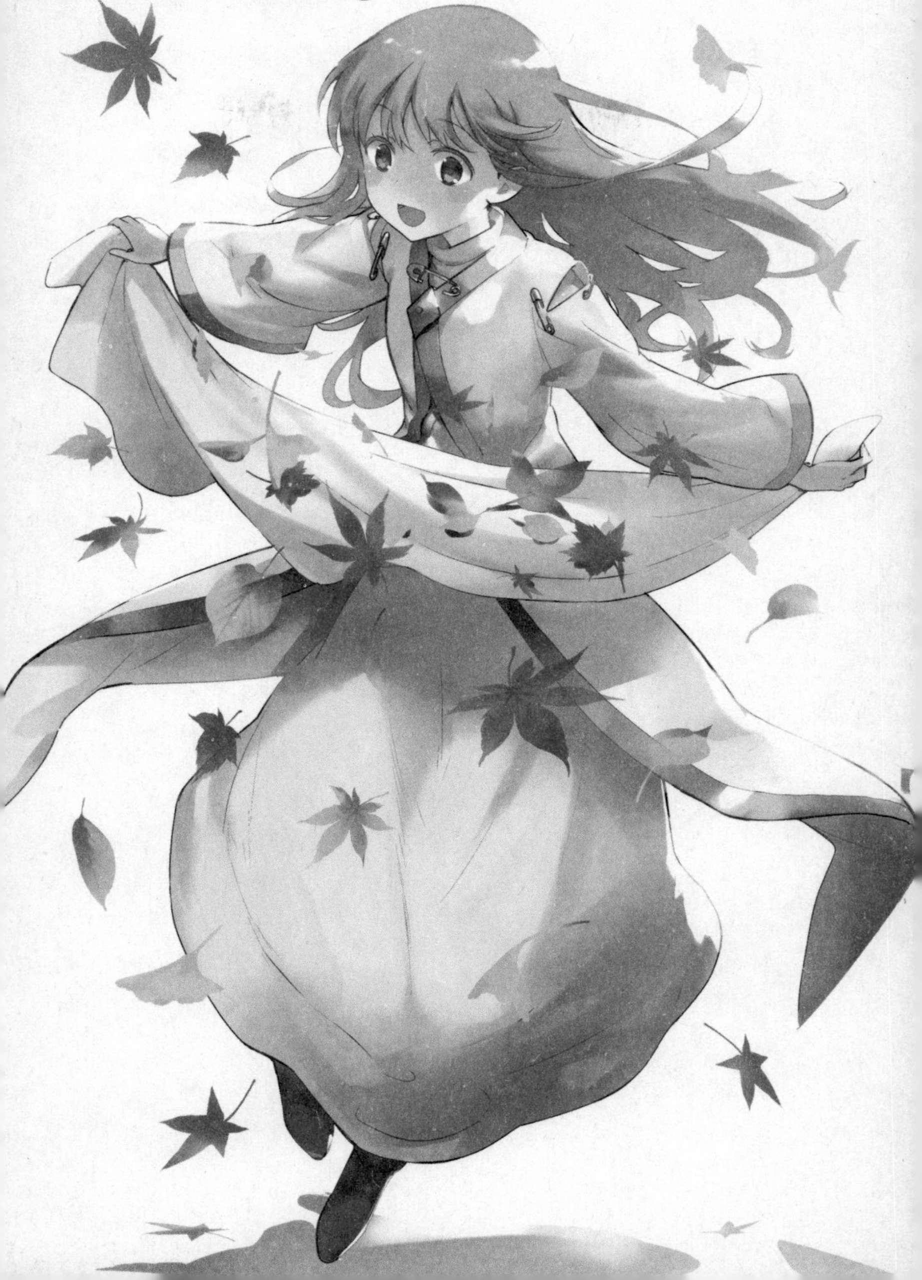

A Certain Magical Index

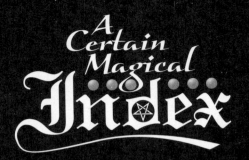

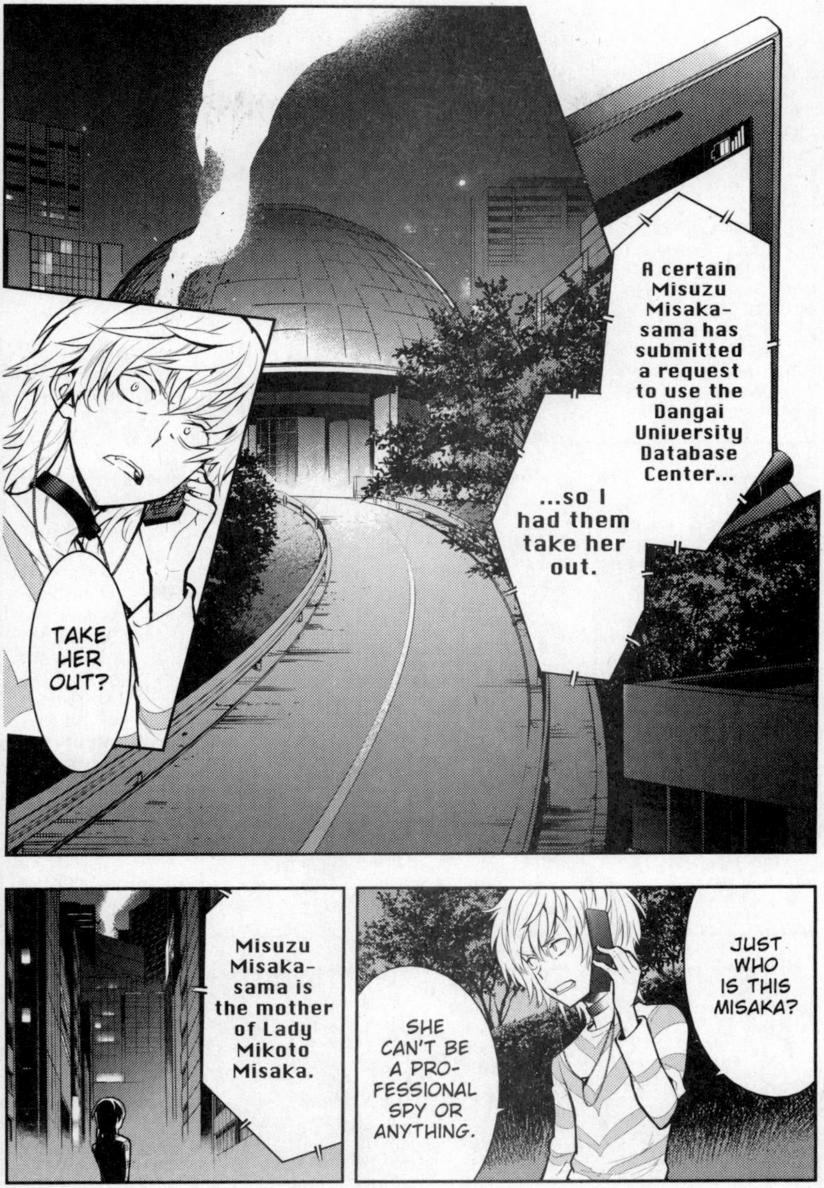
A certain Misuzu Misaka-sama has submitted a request to use the Dangai University Database Center...
...so I had them take her out.
TAKE HER OUT?
JUST WHO IS THIS MISAKA?
SHE CAN'T BE A PROFESSIONAL SPY OR ANYTHING.
Misuzu Misaka-sama is the mother of Lady Mikoto Misaka.

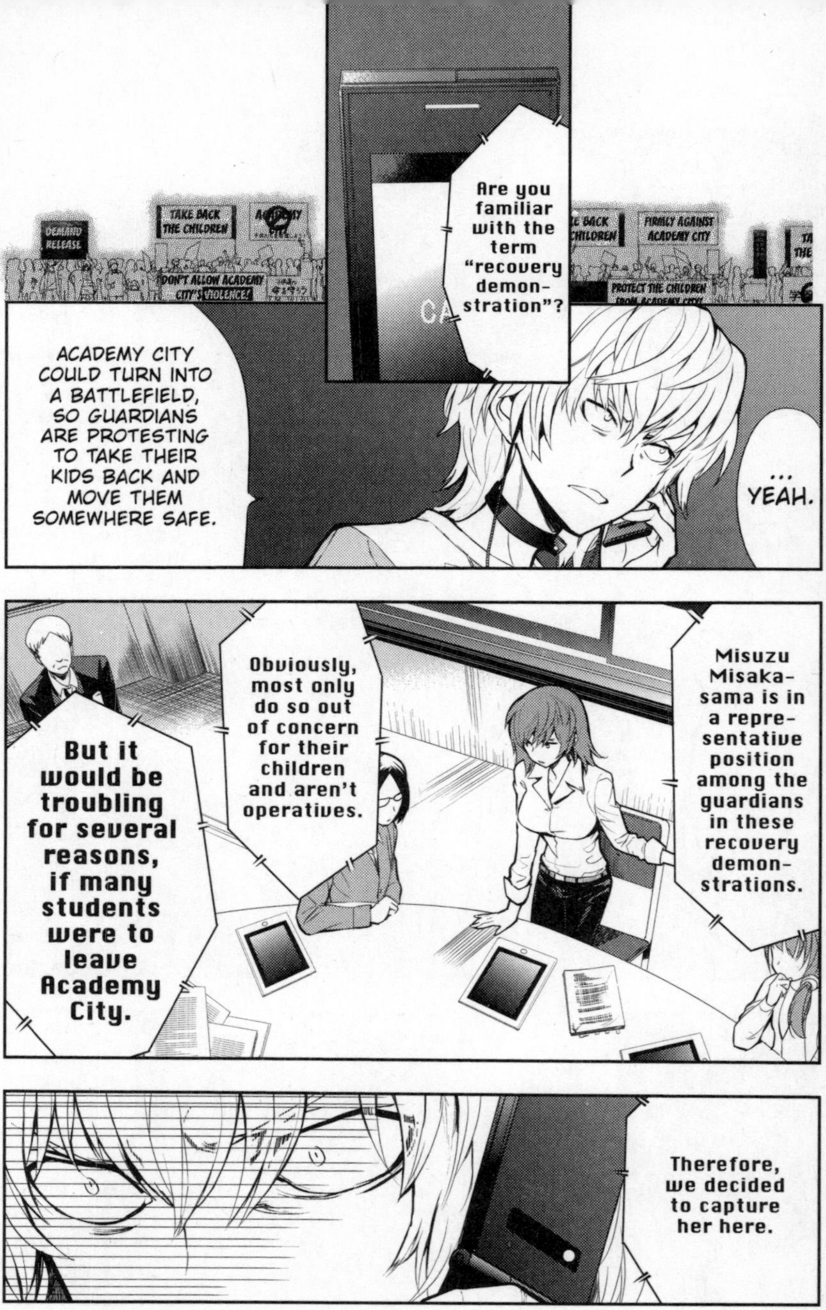
FIRMLY AGAINST ACADEMY CITY
PROTECT THE CHILDREN FROM ACADEMY CITY!
TAKE BACK THE CHILDREN
DON'T ALLOW ACADEMY CITY'S VIOLENCE!
DEMAND RELEASE
Are you familiar with the term "recovery demonstration"?
... YEAH.
ACADEMY CITY COULD TURN INTO A BATTLEFIELD, SO GUARDIANS ARE PROTESTING TO TAKE THEIR KIDS BACK AND MOVE THEM SOMEWHERE SAFE.
Misuzu Misaka-sama is in a representative position among the guardians in these recovery demonstrations.
Obviously, most only do so out of concern for their children and aren't operatives.
But it would be troubling for several reasons, if many students were to leave Academy City.
Therefore, we decided to capture her here.

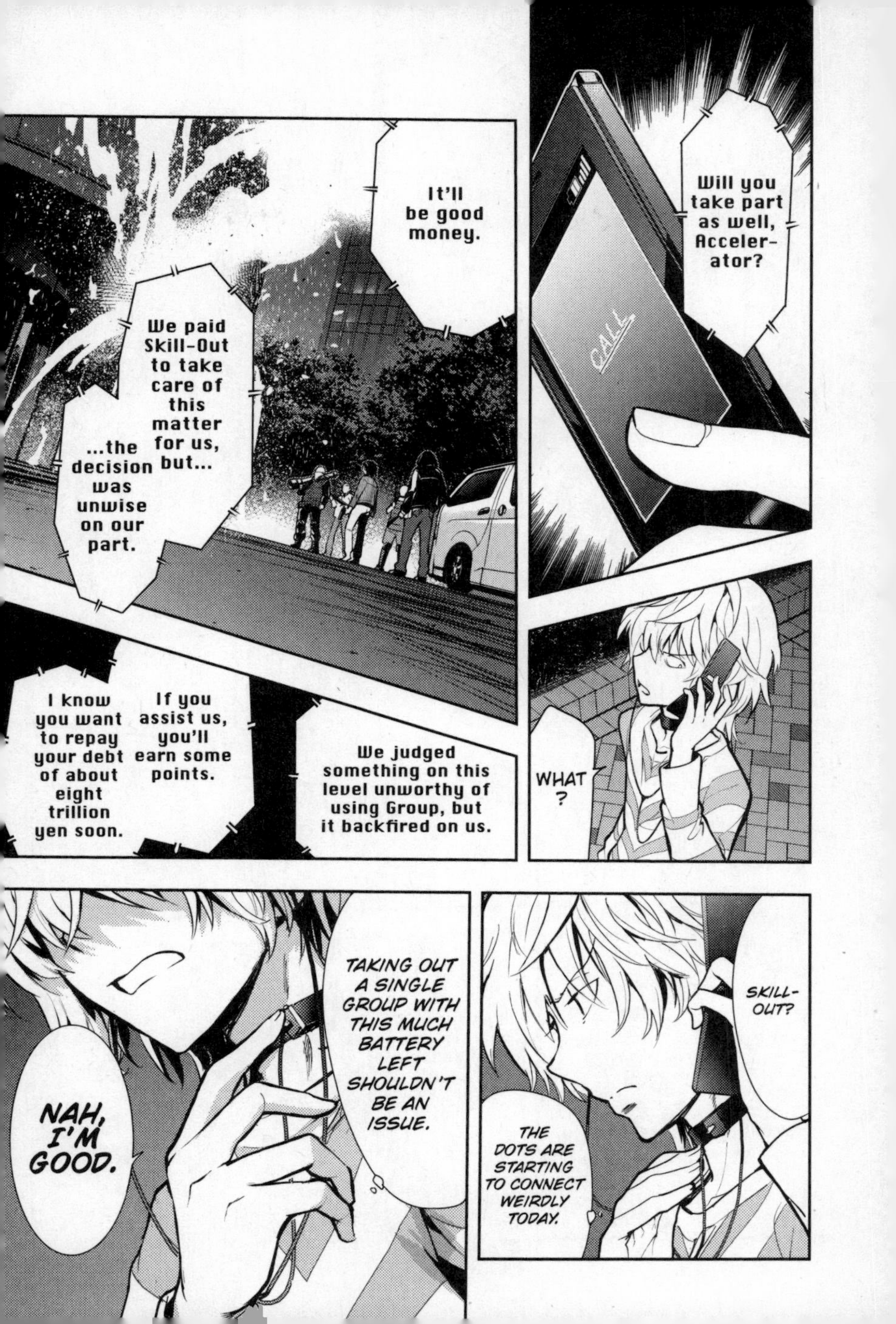
Will you take part as well, Accelerator?
It'll be good money.
We paid Skill-Out to take care of this matter for us, but...
...the decision was unwise on our part.
WHAT?
We judged something on this level unworthy of using Group, but it backfired on us.
If you assist us, you'll earn some points.
I know you want to repay your debt of about eight trillion yen soon.
SKILL-OUT?
THE DOTS ARE STARTING TO CONNECT WEIRDLY TODAY.
TAKING OUT A SINGLE GROUP WITH THIS MUCH BATTERY LEFT SHOULDN'T BE AN ISSUE.
NAH, I'M GOOD.

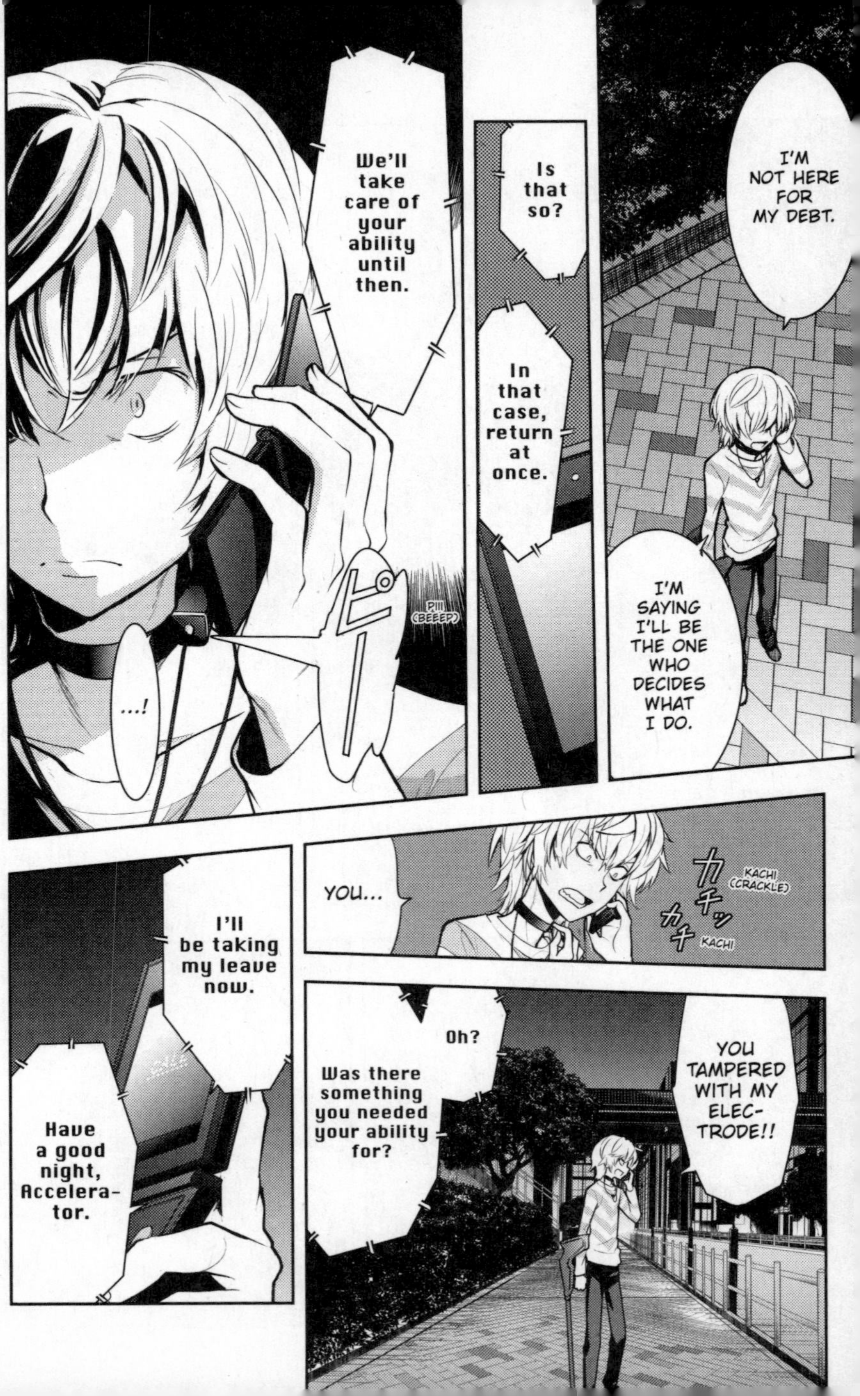
I'M NOT HERE FOR MY DEBT.
I'M SAYING I'LL BE THE ONE WHO DECIDES WHAT I DO.
Is that so?
In that case, return at once.
We'll take care of your ability until then.
PIII (BEEEP)
...!
YOU...
KACHI (CRACKLE)
KACHI
YOU TAMPERED WITH MY ELEC-TRODE!!
Oh?
Was there something you needed your ability for?
I'll be taking my leave now.
Have a good night, Accelera-tor.

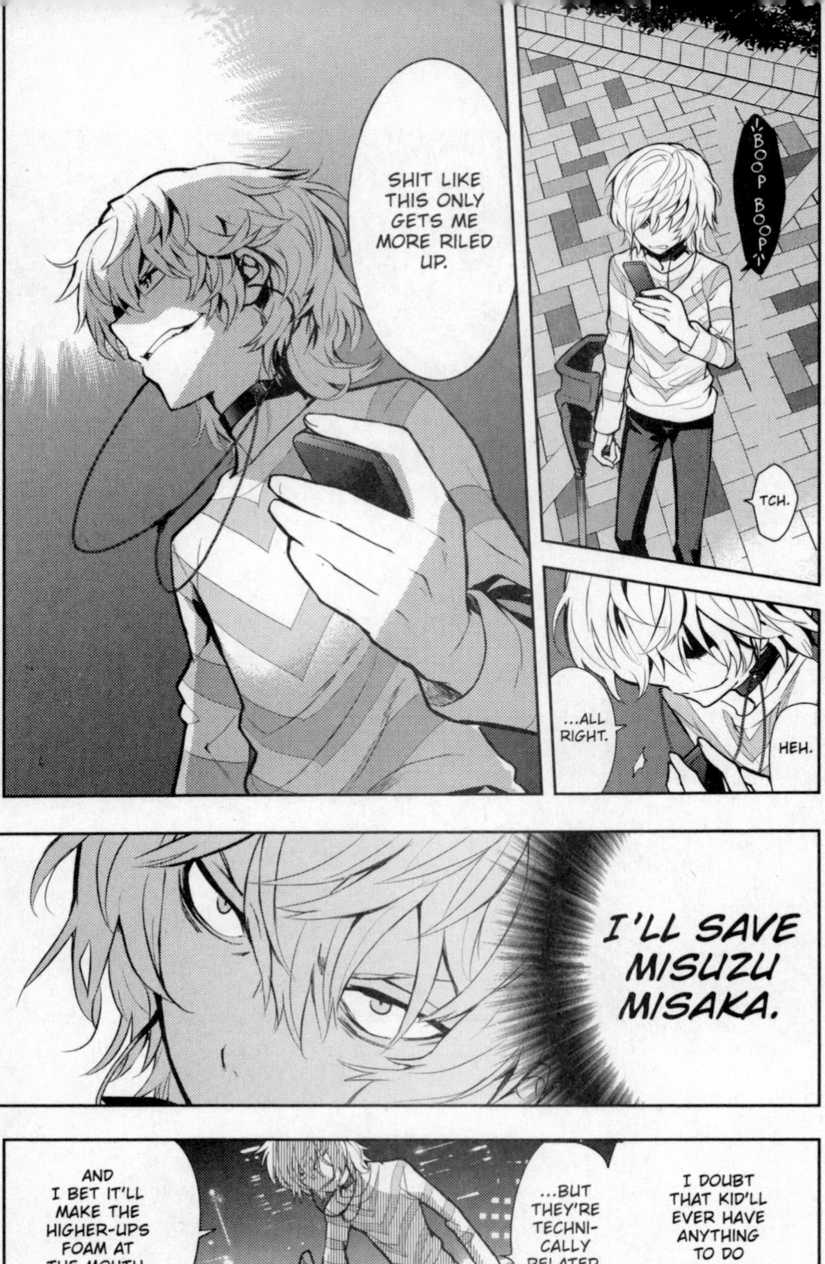
BOOP BOOP
TCH.
HEH.
...ALL RIGHT.
SHIT LIKE THIS ONLY GETS ME MORE RILED UP.
I'LL SAVE MISUZU MISAKA.
I DOUBT THAT KID'LL EVER HAVE ANYTHING TO DO WITH HER...
...BUT THEY'RE TECHNICALLY RELATED.
AND I BET IT'LL MAKE THE HIGHER-UPS FOAM AT THE MOUTH.

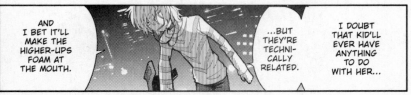

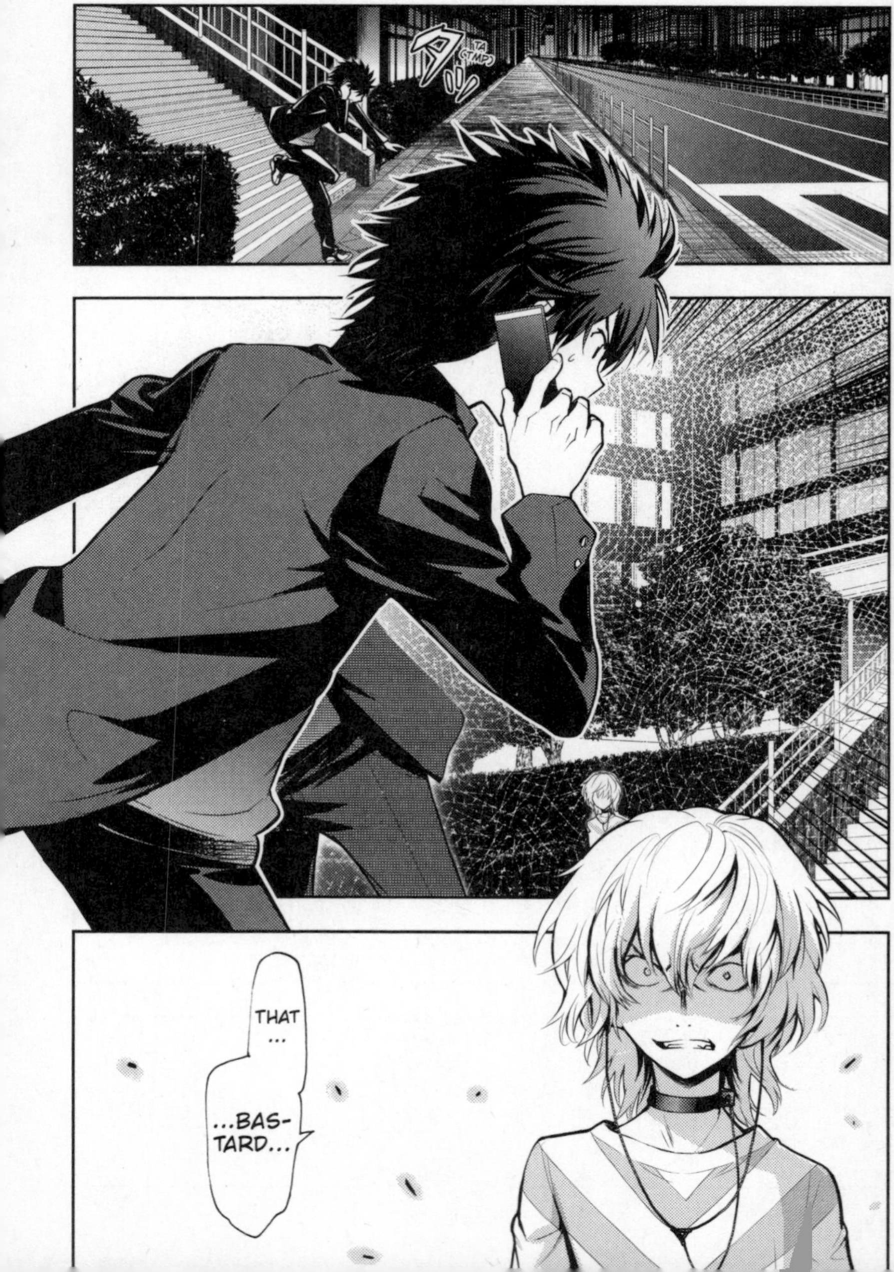

TA (STMP)
THAT ...
...BAS-TARD...

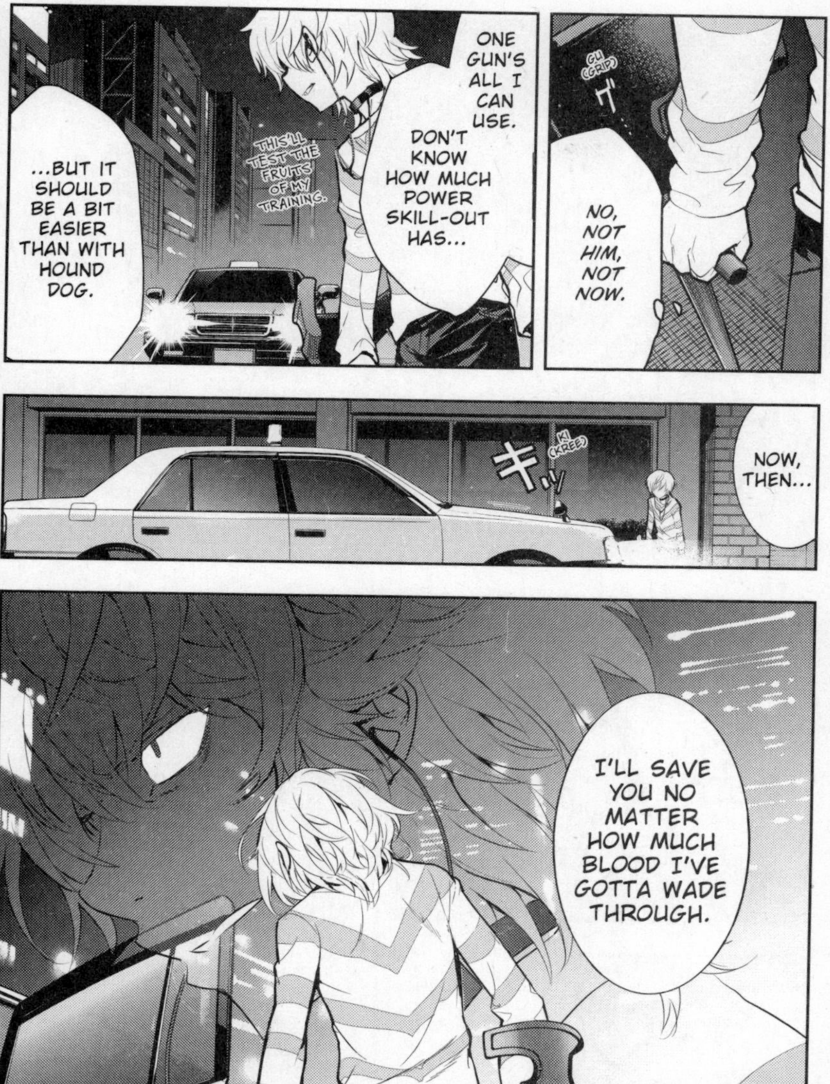
GU (GRIP)
NO, NOT HIM, NOT NOW.
ONE GUN'S ALL I CAN USE.
DON'T KNOW HOW MUCH POWER SKILL-OUT HAS...
THIS'LL TEST THE FRUITS OF MY TRAINING.
...BUT IT SHOULD BE A BIT EASIER THAN WITH HOUND DOG.
NOW, THEN...
KI (KREE)
I'LL SAVE YOU NO MATTER HOW MUCH BLOOD I'VE GOTTA WADE THROUGH.

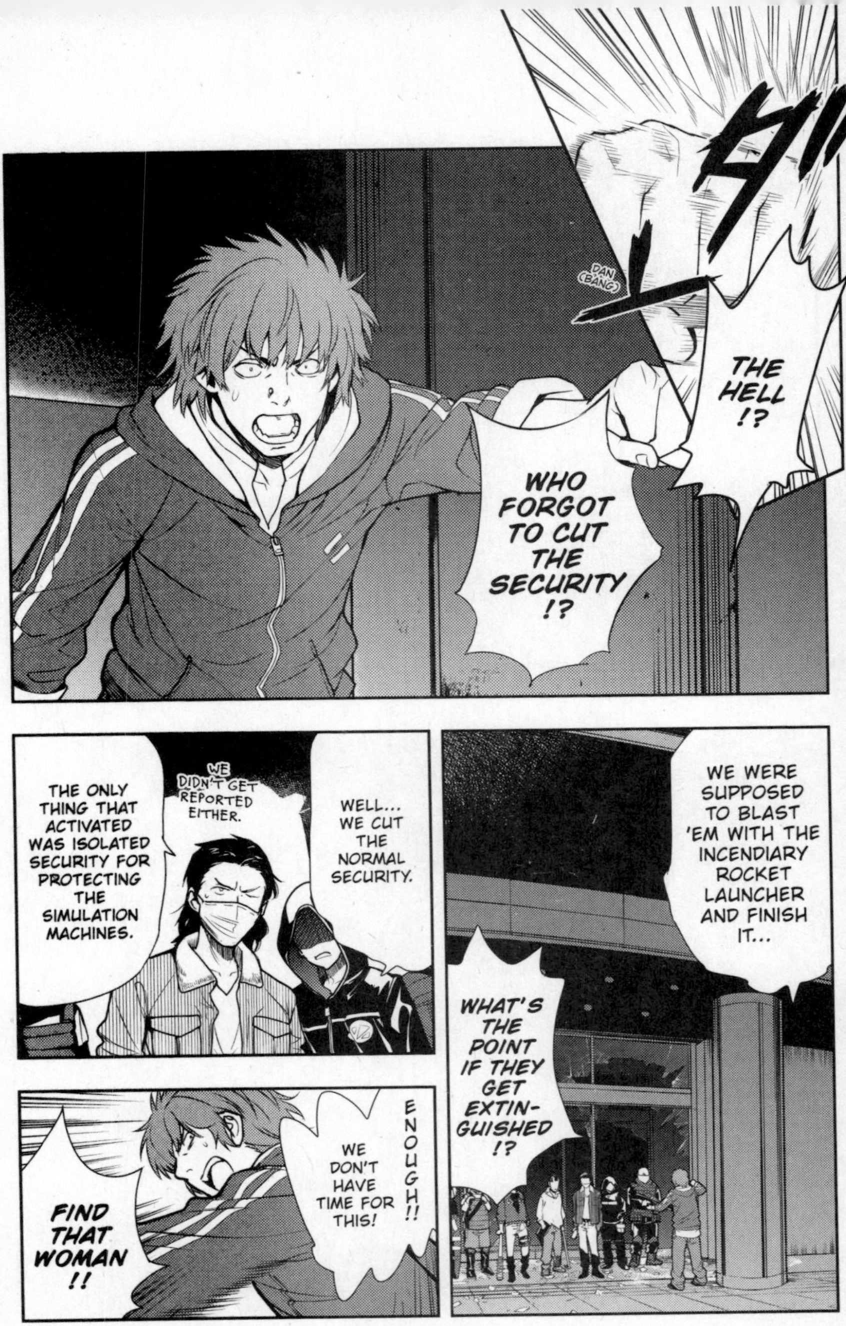
DAN (BANG)
THE HELL !?
WHO FORGOT TO CUT THE SECURITY !?
WE WERE SUPPOSED TO BLAST 'EM WITH THE INCENDIARY ROCKET LAUNCHER AND FINISH IT...
WHAT'S THE POINT IF THEY GET EXTIN-GUISHED !?
WELL... WE CUT THE NORMAL SECURITY.
WE DIDN'T GET REPORTED EITHER.
THE ONLY THING THAT ACTIVATED WAS ISOLATED SECURITY FOR PROTECTING THE SIMULATION MACHINES.
ENOUGH!!
WE DON'T HAVE TIME FOR THIS!
FIND THAT WOMAN !!

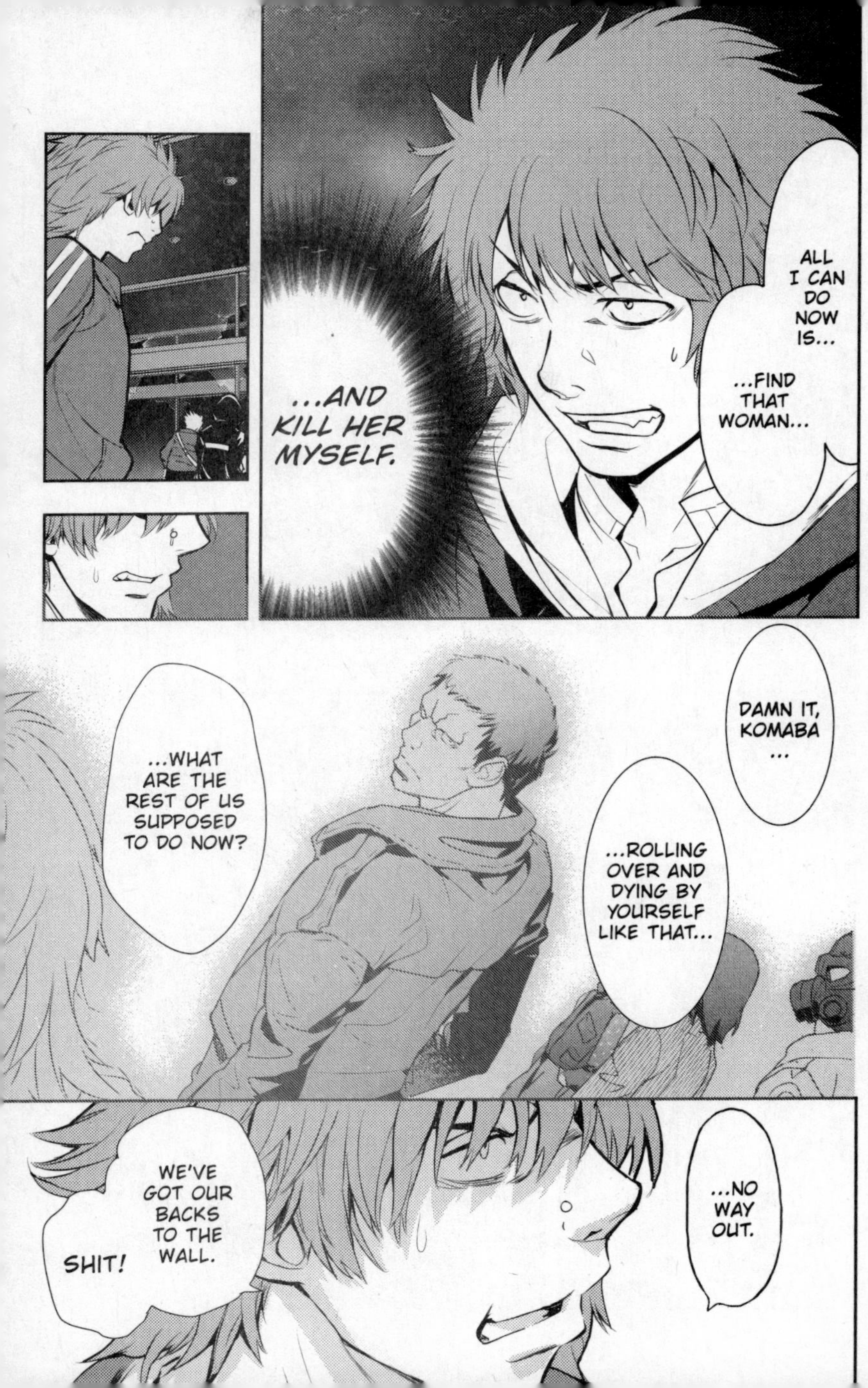
ALL I CAN DO NOW IS...
...FIND THAT WOMAN...
...AND KILL HER MYSELF.
DAMN IT, KOMABA ...
...ROLLING OVER AND DYING BY YOURSELF LIKE THAT...
...WHAT ARE THE REST OF US SUPPOSED TO DO NOW?
...NO WAY OUT.
WE'VE GOT OUR BACKS TO THE WALL.
SHIT!

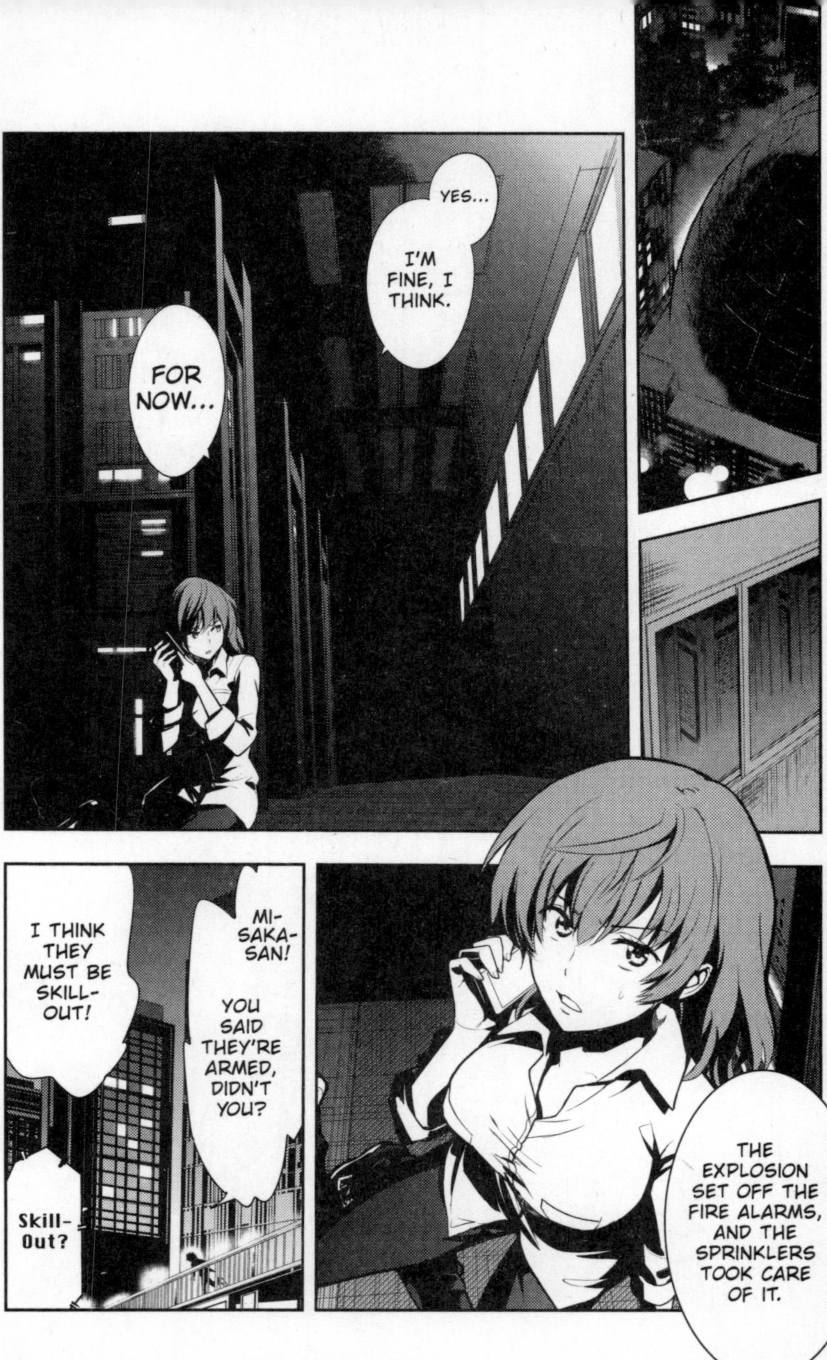
YES...
I'M FINE, I THINK.
FOR NOW...
THE EXPLOSION SET OFF THE FIRE ALARMS, AND THE SPRINKLERS TOOK CARE OF IT.
MI-SAKA-SAN!
YOU SAID THEY'RE ARMED, DIDN'T YOU?
I THINK THEY MUST BE SKILL-OUT!
Skill-Out?

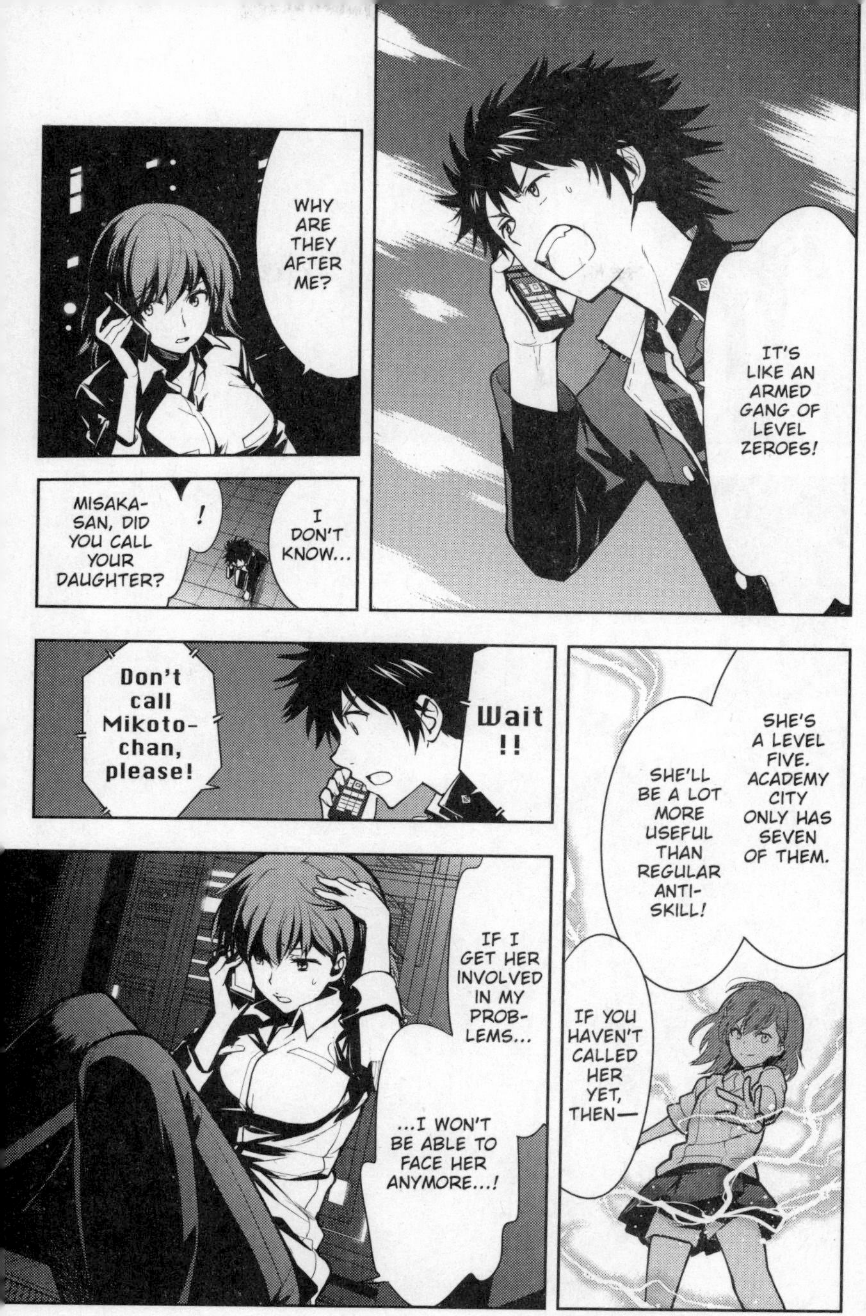
IT'S LIKE AN ARMED GANG OF LEVEL ZEROES!
WHY ARE THEY AFTER ME?
I DON'T KNOW...
!
MISAKA-SAN, DID YOU CALL YOUR DAUGHTER?
SHE'S A LEVEL FIVE. ACADEMY CITY ONLY HAS SEVEN OF THEM.
SHE'LL BE A LOT MORE USEFUL THAN REGULAR ANTI-SKILL!
IF YOU HAVEN'T CALLED HER YET, THEN—
Wait!!
Don't call Mikoto-chan, please!
IF I GET HER INVOLVED IN MY PROB-LEMS...
...I WON'T BE ABLE TO FACE HER ANYMORE...!

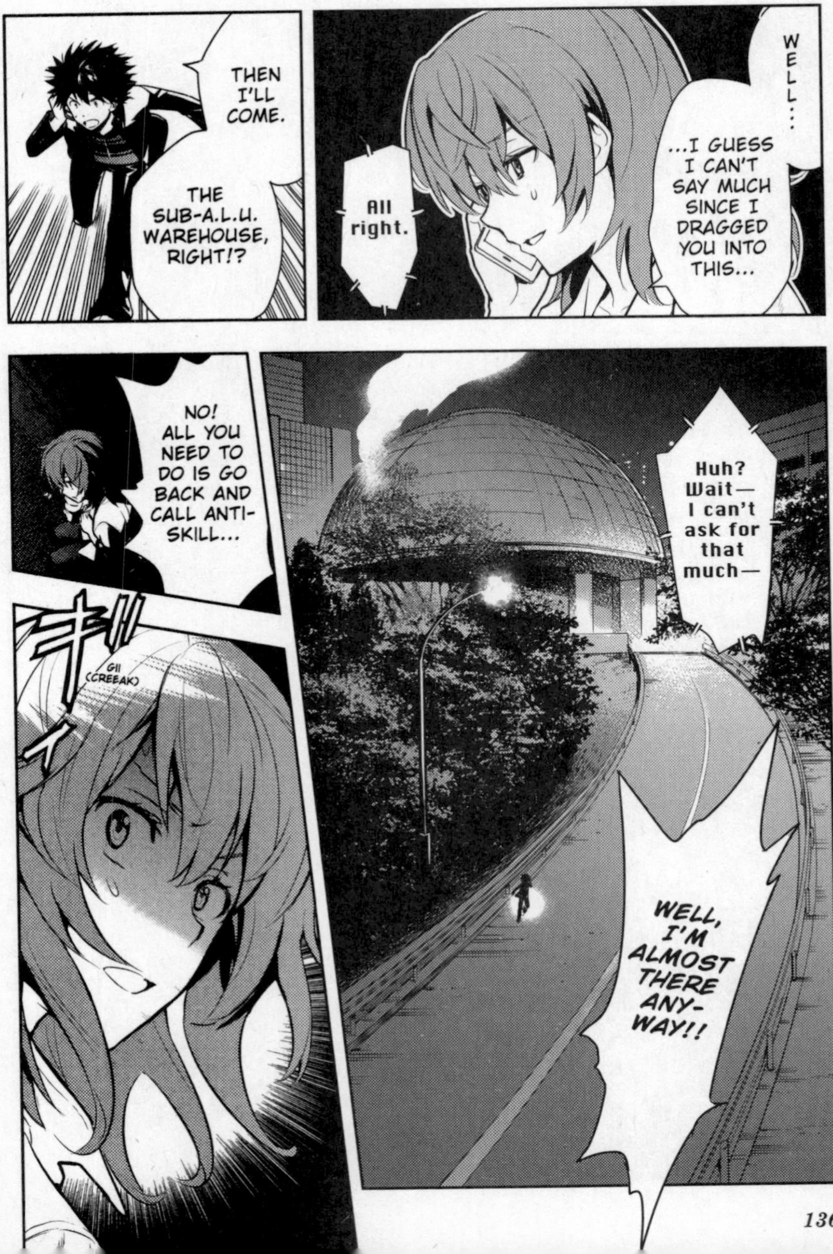
WELL...
...I GUESS I CAN'T SAY MUCH SINCE I DRAGGED YOU INTO THIS...
All right.
THEN I'LL COME.
THE SUB-A.L.U. WAREHOUSE, RIGHT!?
Huh? Wait— I can't ask for that much—
WELL, I'M ALMOST THERE ANY-WAY!!
NO! ALL YOU NEED TO DO IS GO BACK AND CALL ANTI-SKILL...
GII (CREAK)

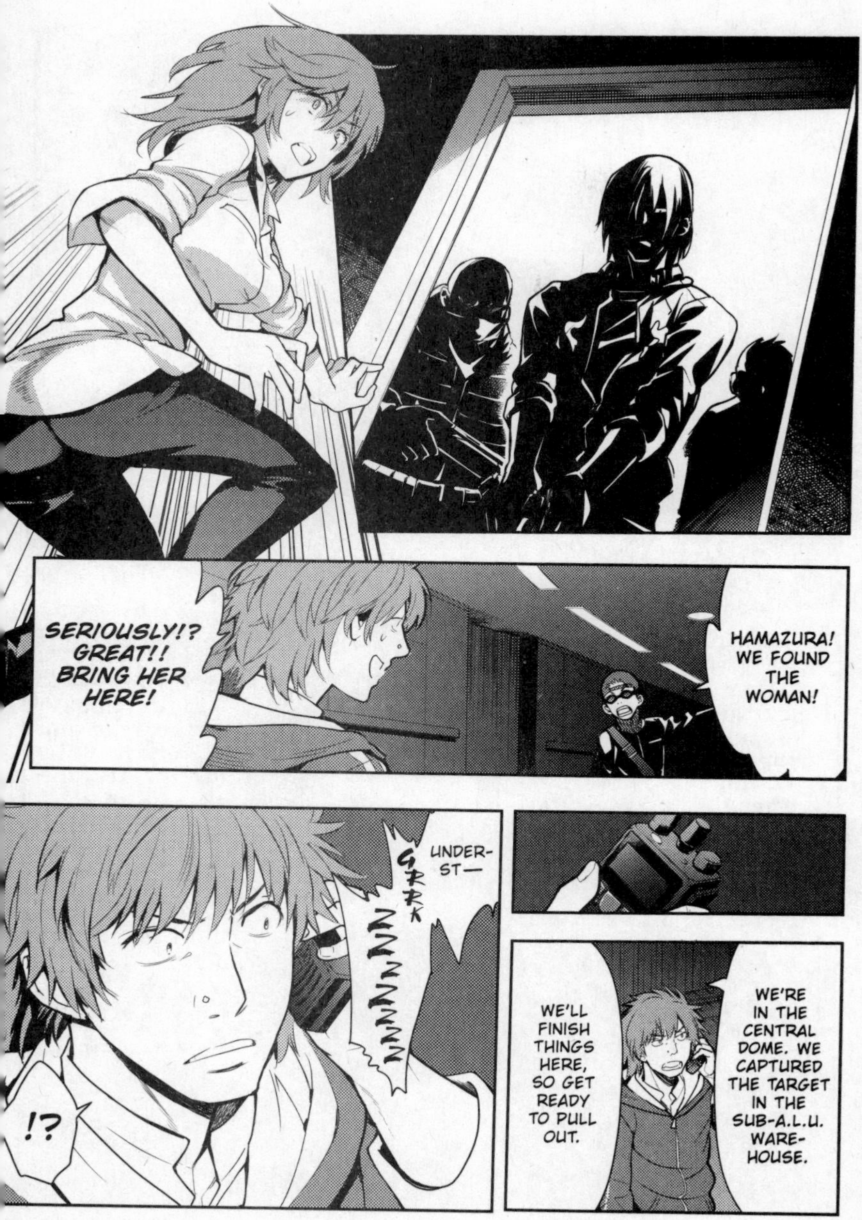
HAMAZURA! WE FOUND THE WOMAN!
SERIOUSLY!? GREAT!! BRING HER HERE!
WE'RE IN THE CENTRAL DOME. WE CAPTURED THE TARGET IN THE SUB-A.L.U. WAREHOUSE.
WE'LL FINISH THINGS HERE, SO GET READY TO PULL OUT.
UNDERST—
GRRK
ZZZZZZZZ
!?

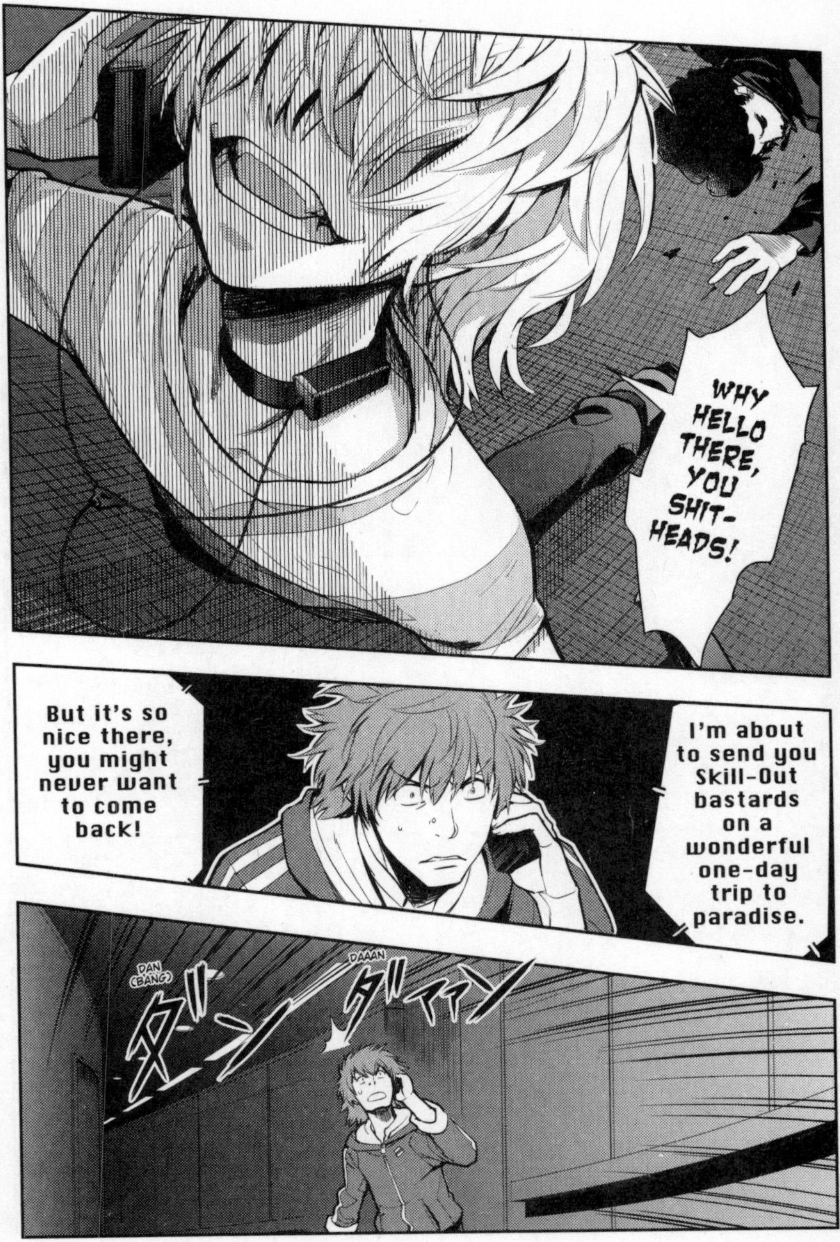
WHY HELLO THERE, YOU SHIT-HEADS!
I'm about to send you Skill-Out bastards on a wonderful one-day trip to paradise.
But it's so nice there, you might never want to come back!
DAAN
DAN (BANG)

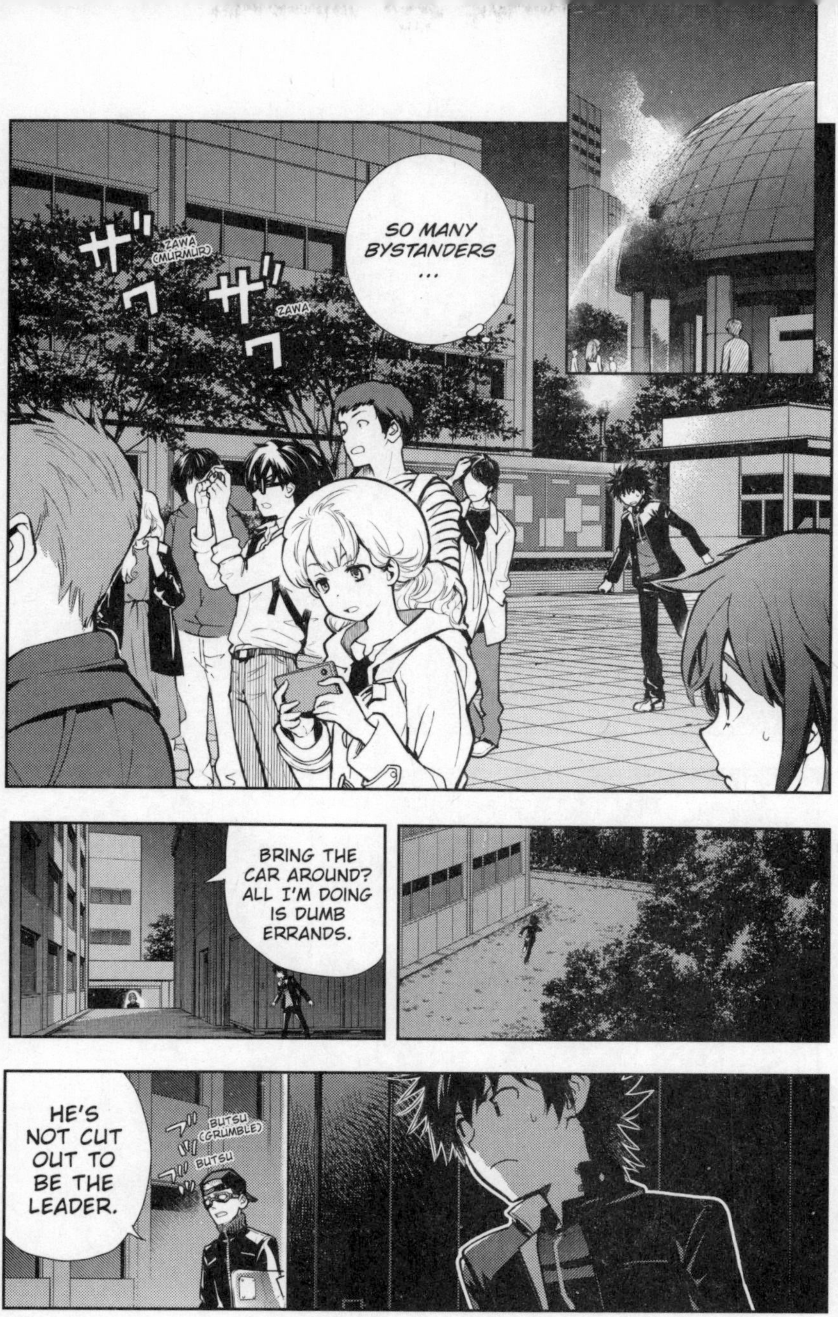
SO MANY BYSTANDERS ...
ZAWA
ZAWA (MURMUR)
BRING THE CAR AROUND? ALL I'M DOING IS DUMB ERRANDS.
BUTSU (GRUMBLE)
BUTSU
HE'S NOT CUT OUT TO BE THE LEADER.

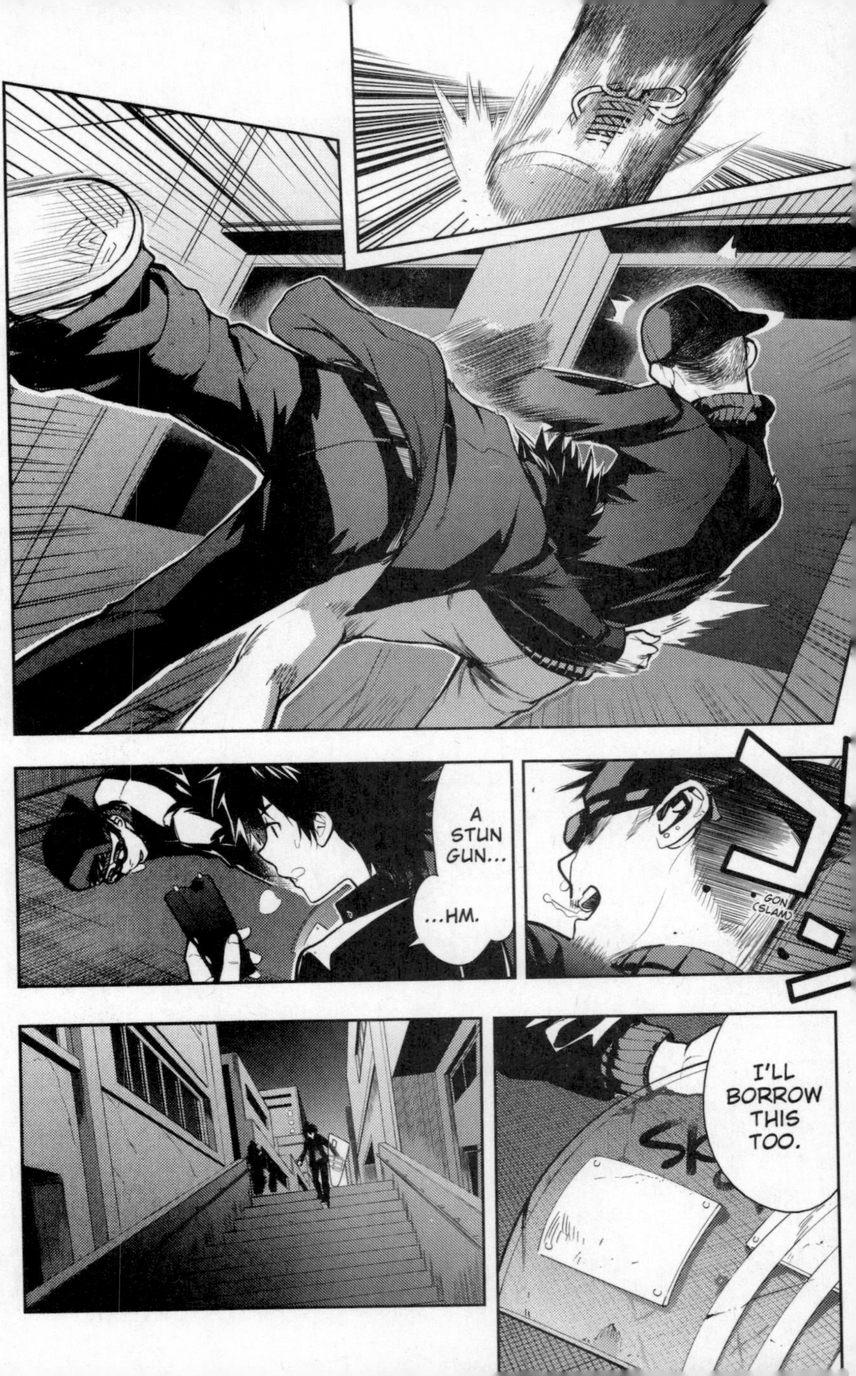
GON (SLAM)
A STUN GUN...
...HM.
I'LL BORROW THIS TOO.

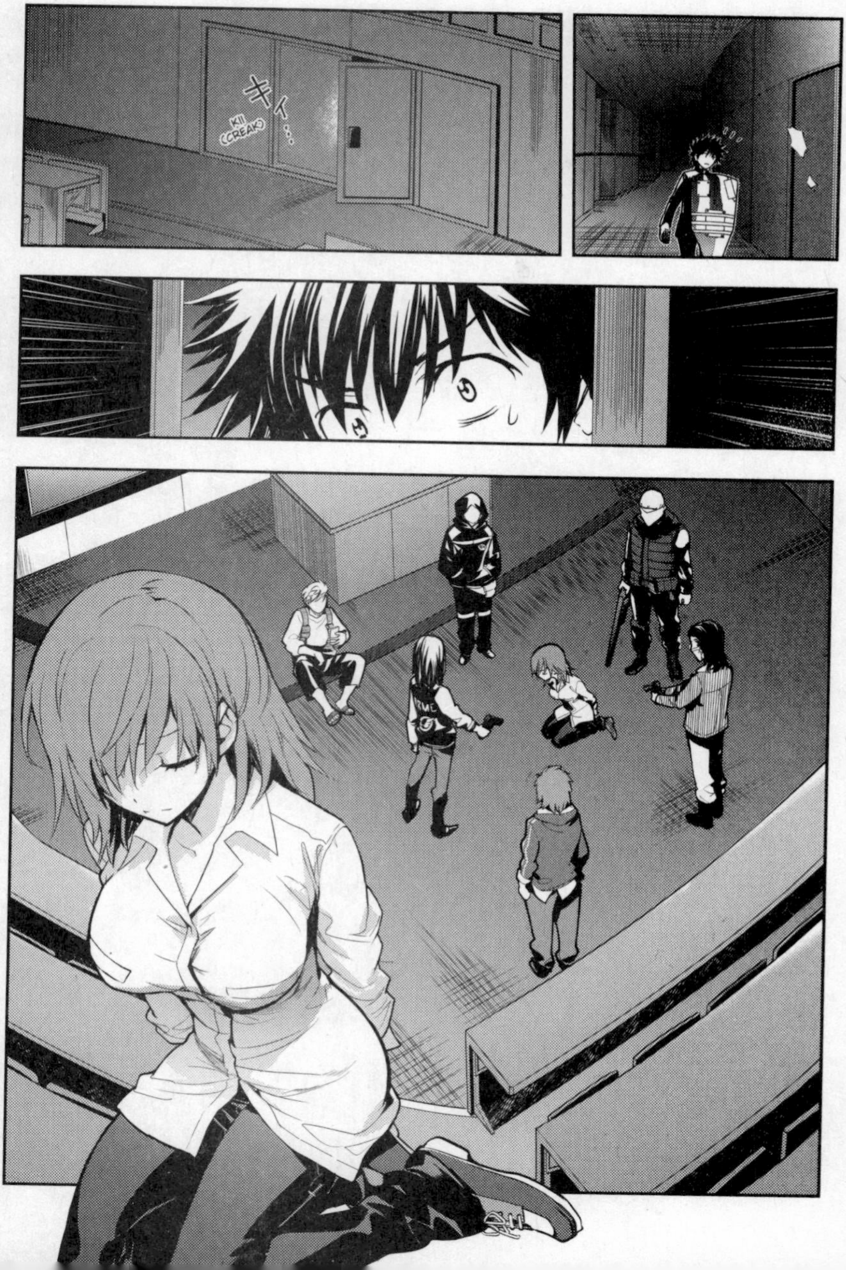
キイ…
KII (CREAK)

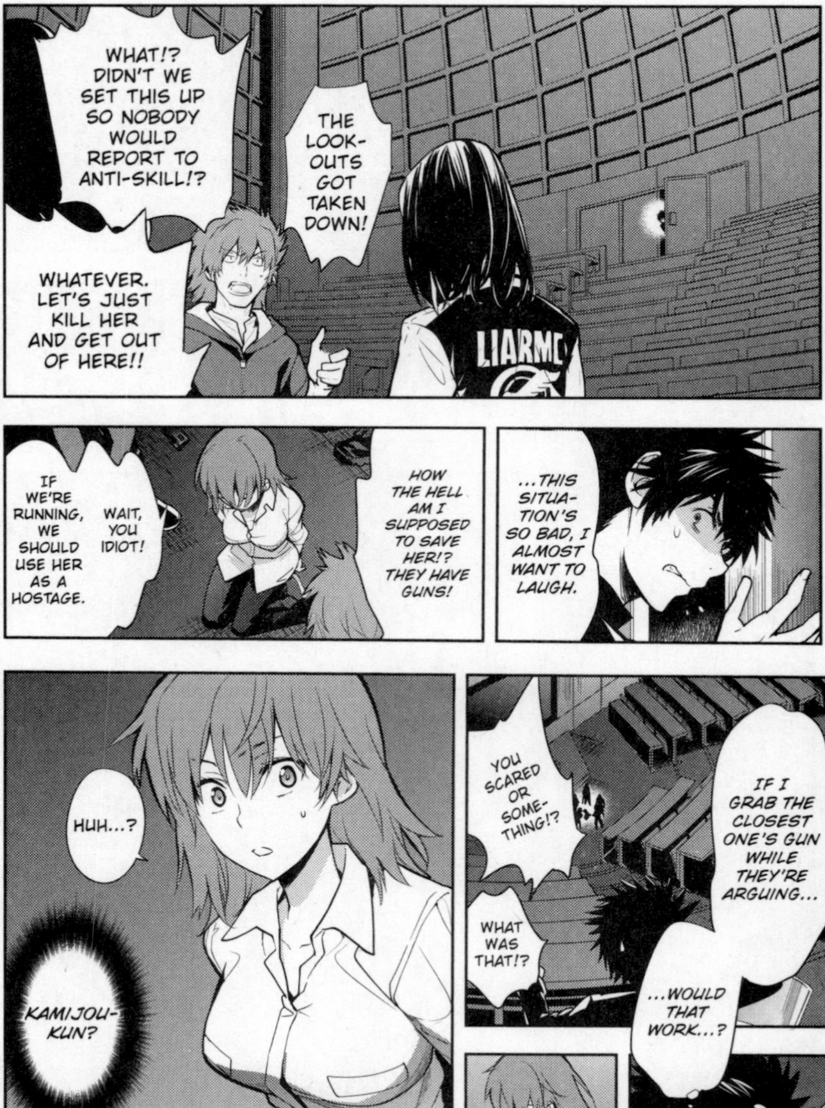
THE LOOK-OUTS GOT TAKEN DOWN!
WHAT!? DIDN'T WE SET THIS UP SO NOBODY WOULD REPORT TO ANTI-SKILL!?
WHATEVER. LET'S JUST KILL HER AND GET OUT OF HERE!!
...THIS SITUATION'S SO BAD, I ALMOST WANT TO LAUGH.
HOW THE HELL AM I SUPPOSED TO SAVE HER!? THEY HAVE GUNS!
WAIT, YOU IDIOT!
IF WE'RE RUNNING, WE SHOULD USE HER AS A HOSTAGE.
IF I GRAB THE CLOSEST ONE'S GUN WHILE THEY'RE ARGUING...
YOU SCARED OR SOMETHING!?
WHAT WAS THAT!?
...WOULD THAT WORK...?
HUH...?
KAMIJOU-KUN?

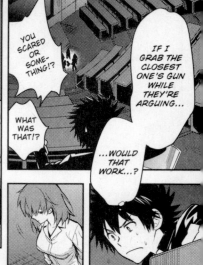

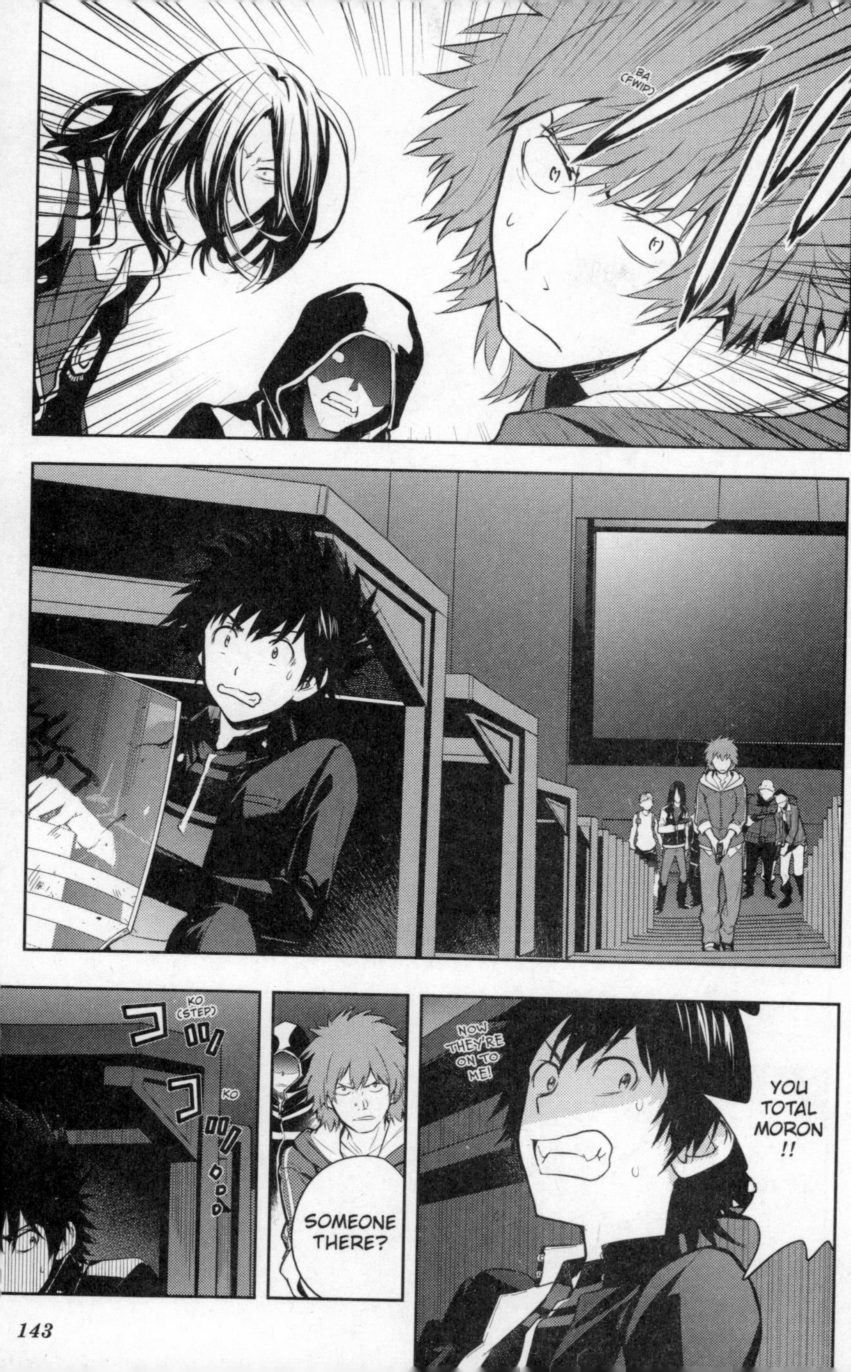
BA (FWIP)
YOU TOTAL MORON !!
NOW THEY'RE ON TO ME!
SOMEONE THERE?
KO (STEP)
KO

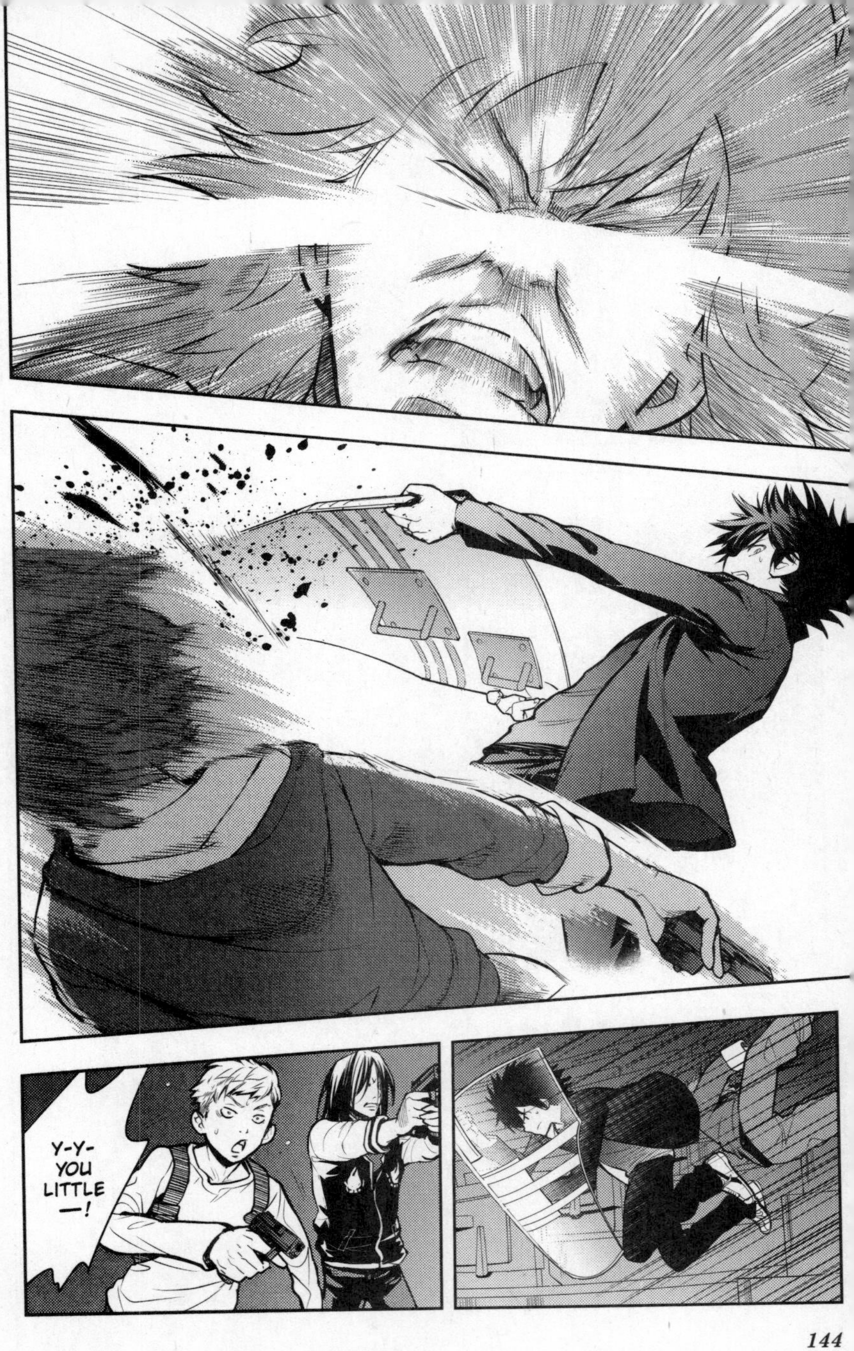
Y-Y-
YOU
LITTLE
—!

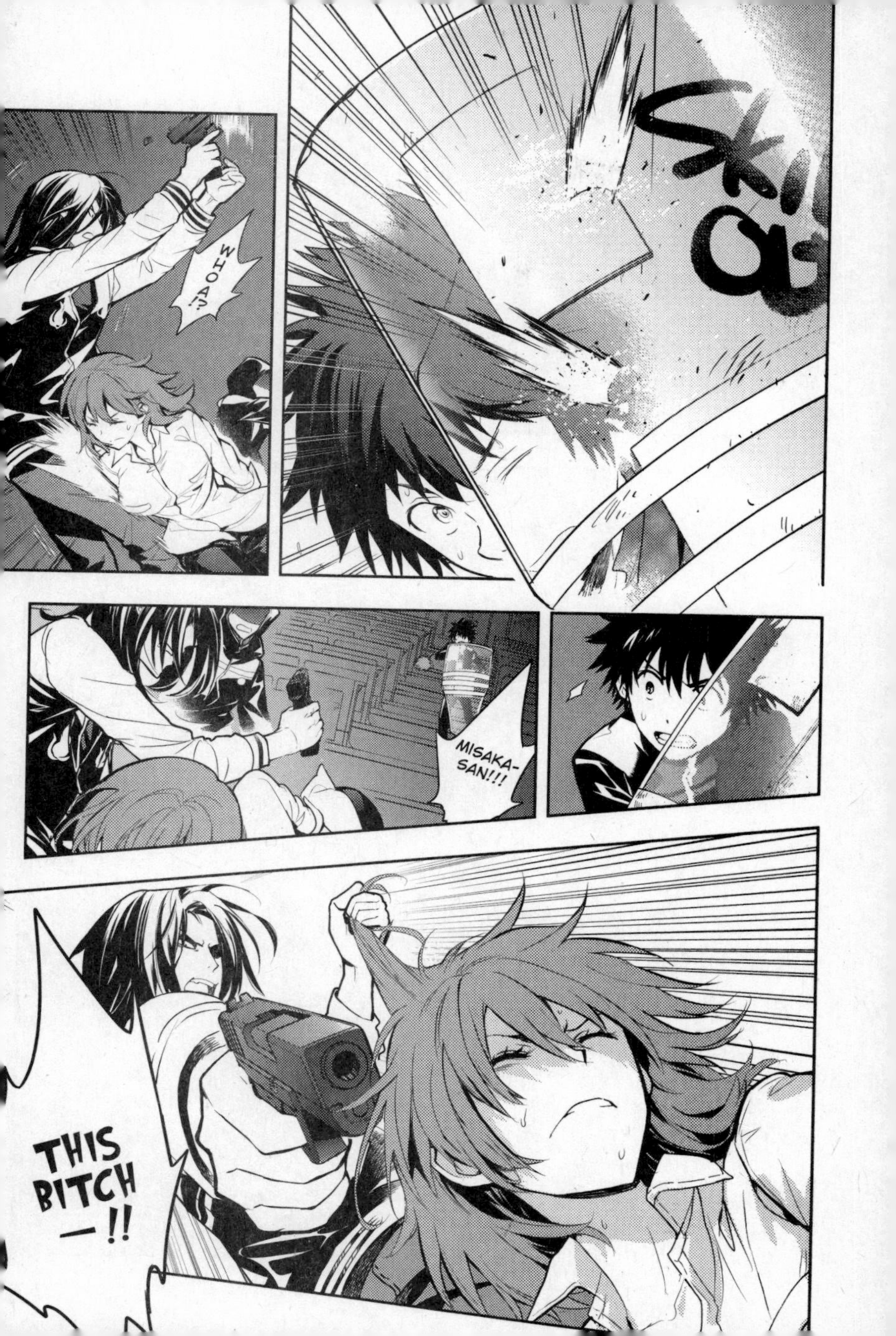
WHOA!?
MISAKA-SAN!!!
THIS BITCH—!!

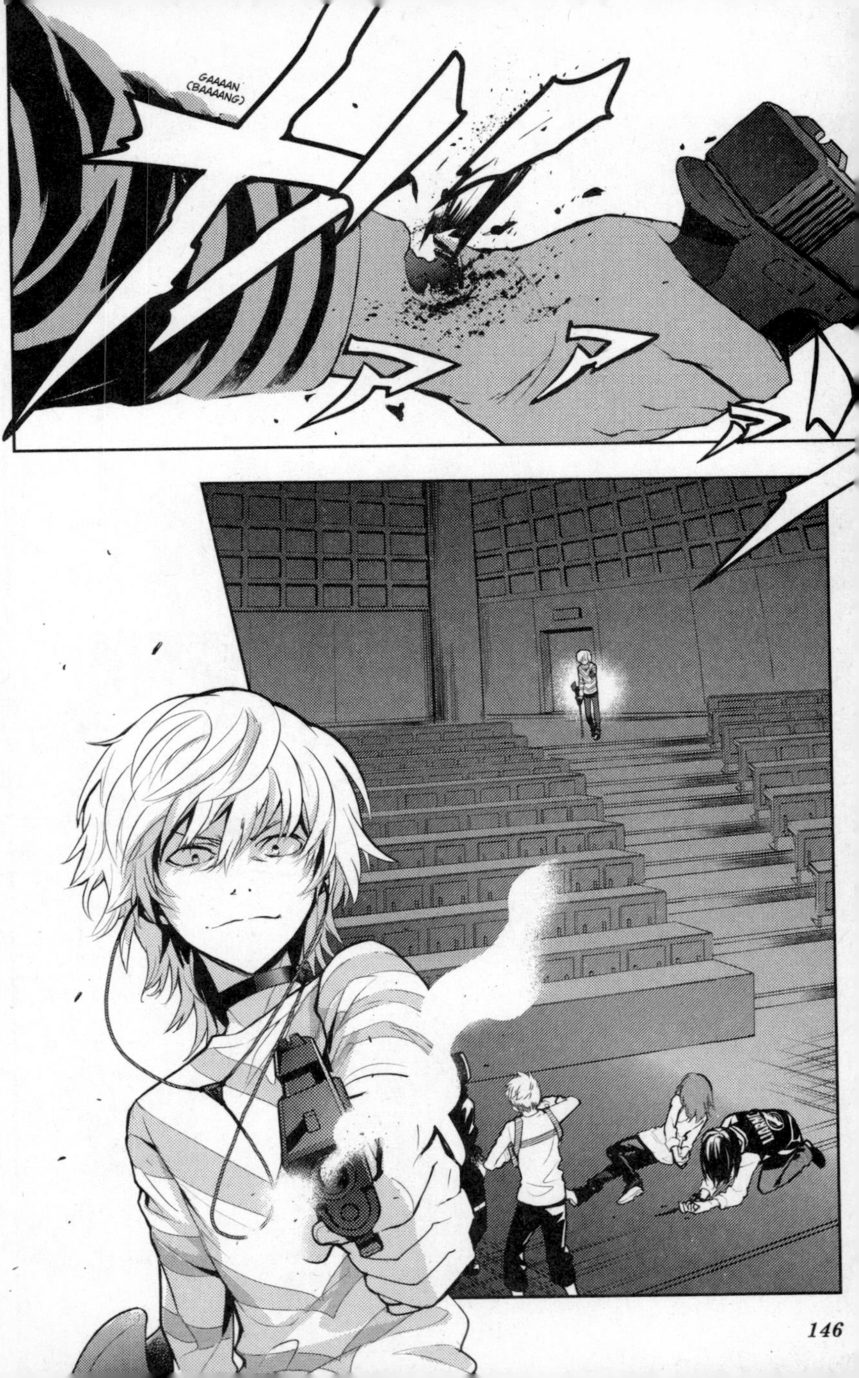
GAAAAN
(BAAAANG)

A Certain Magical Index

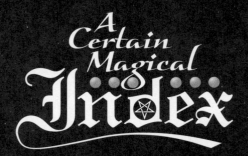

A Certain Magical Index

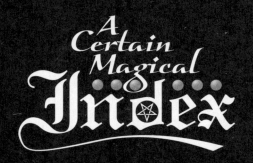

#122 MISUZU MISAKA ③

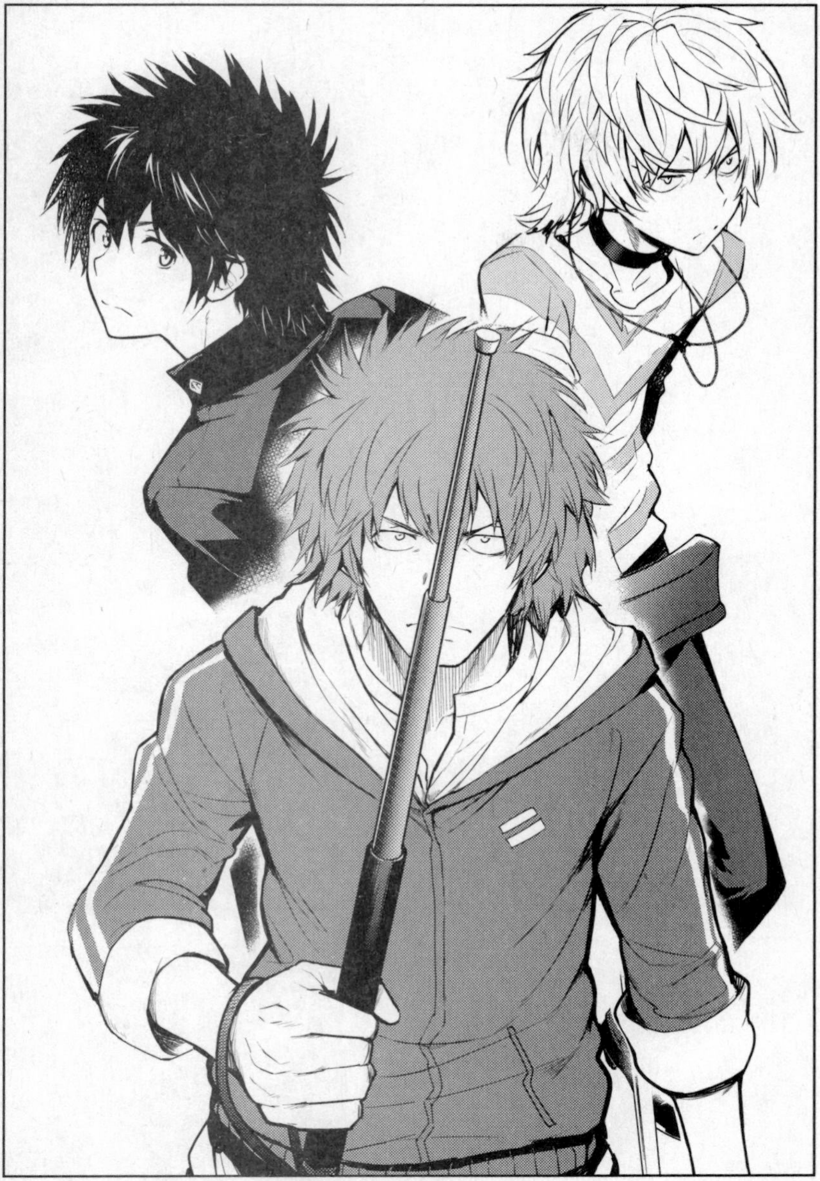

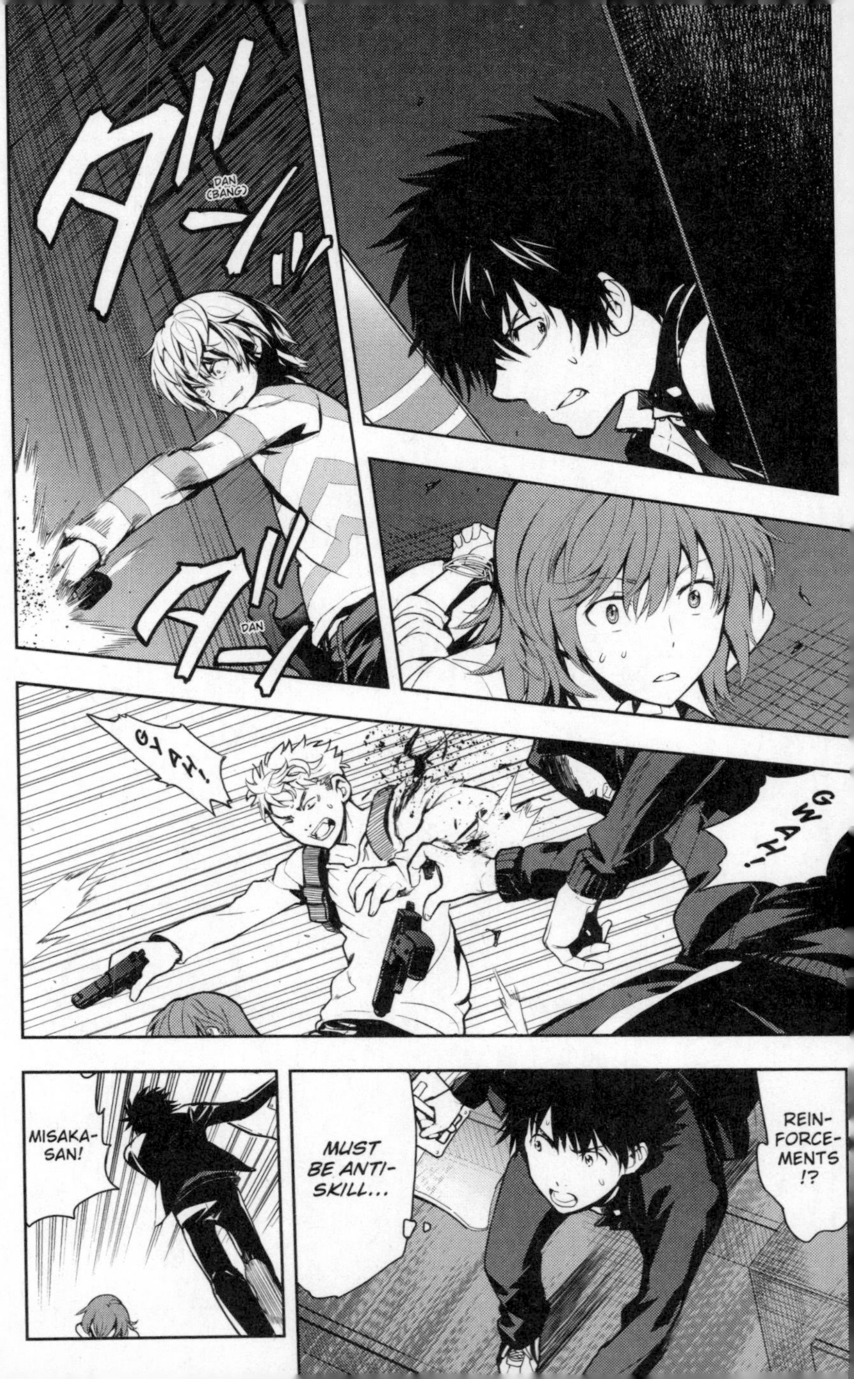
DAN (BANG)
DAN
GWAH!
GYAH!
REIN-FORCE-MENTS!?
MUST BE ANTI-SKILL...
MISAKA-SAN!

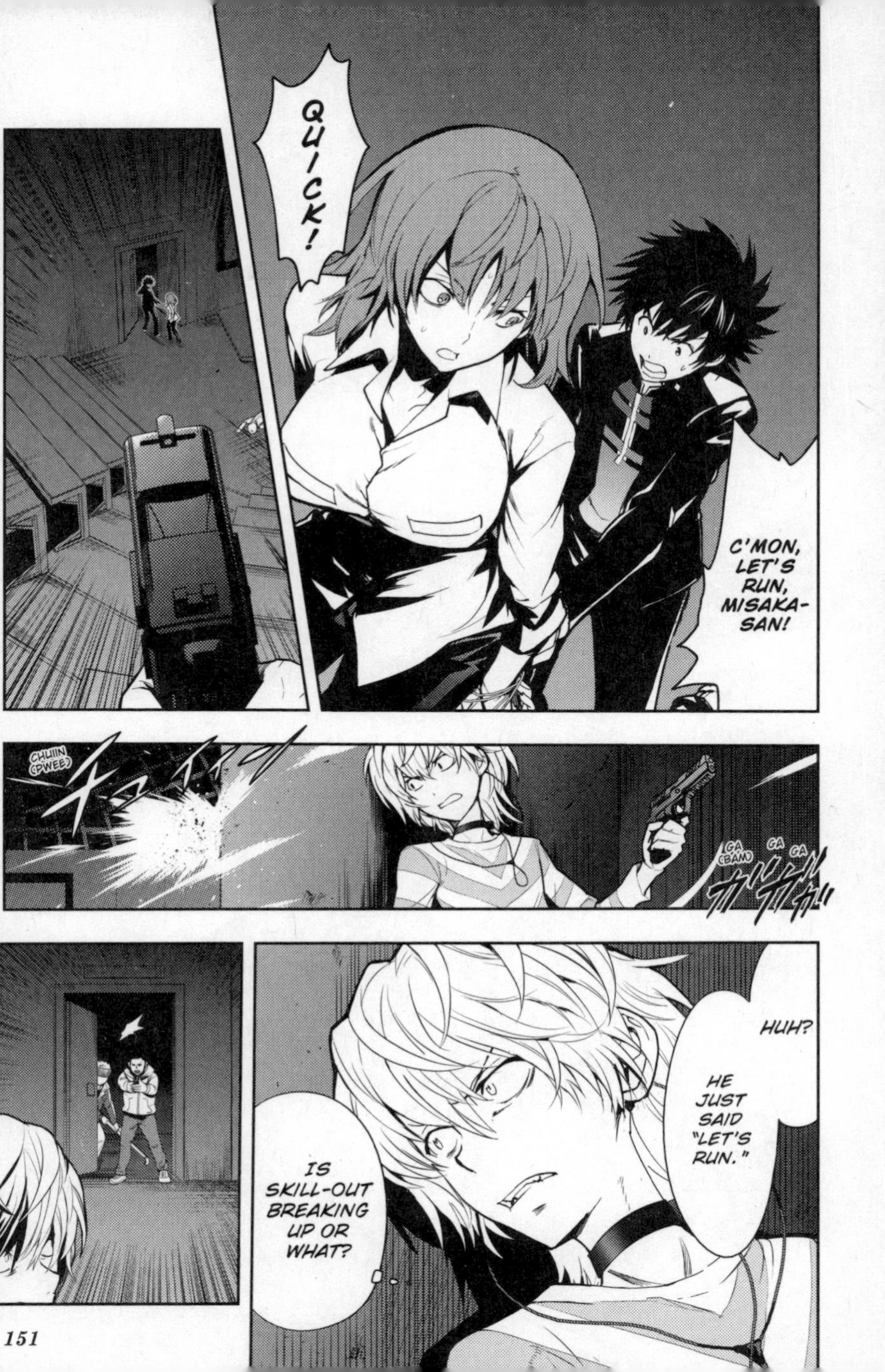
QUICK!
C'MON, LET'S RUN, MISAKA-SAN!
GA (BAM) GA GA
CHUIIN (PWEE)
HUH?
HE JUST SAID "LET'S RUN."
IS SKILL-OUT BREAKING UP OR WHAT?

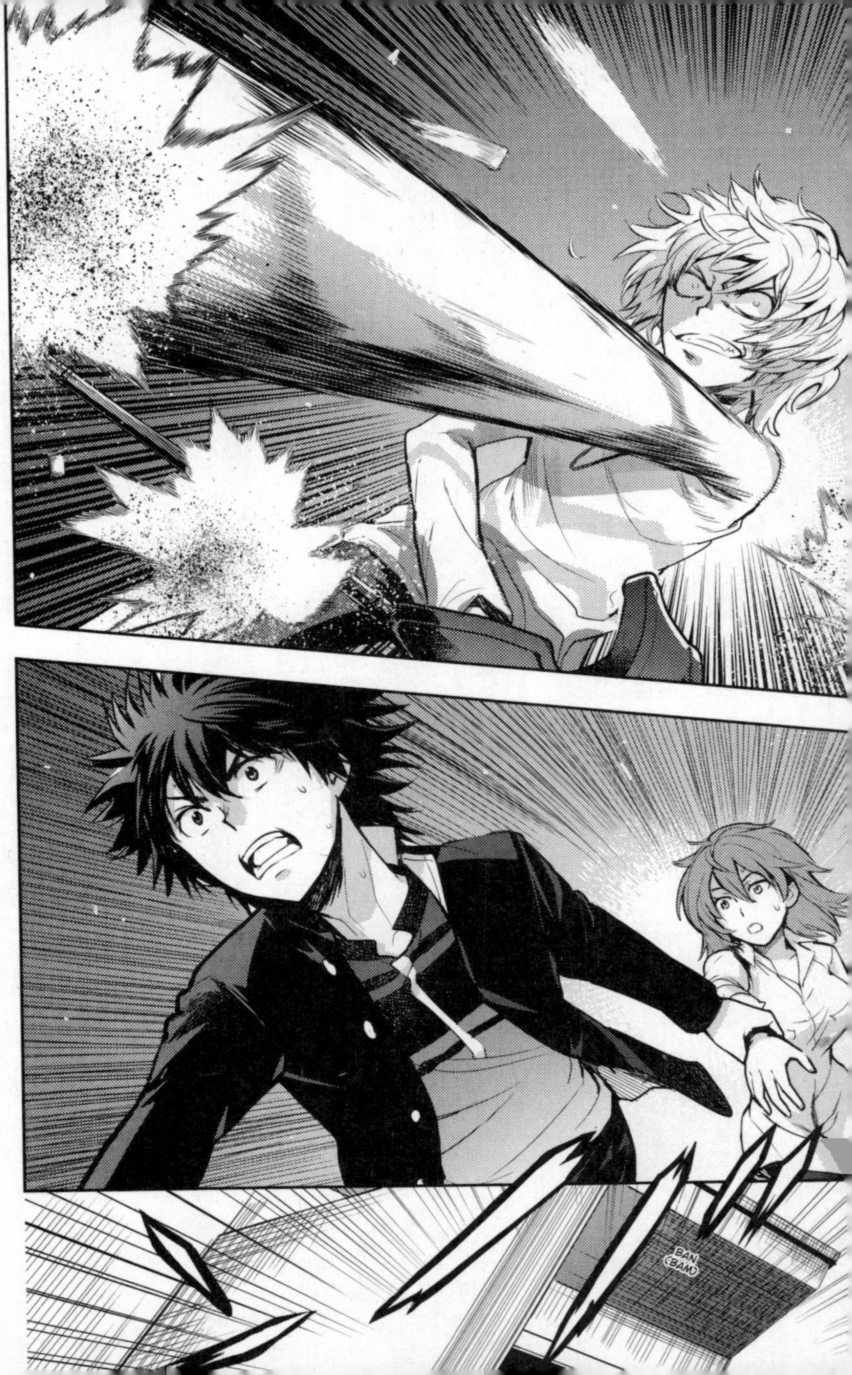
BAN
BAM

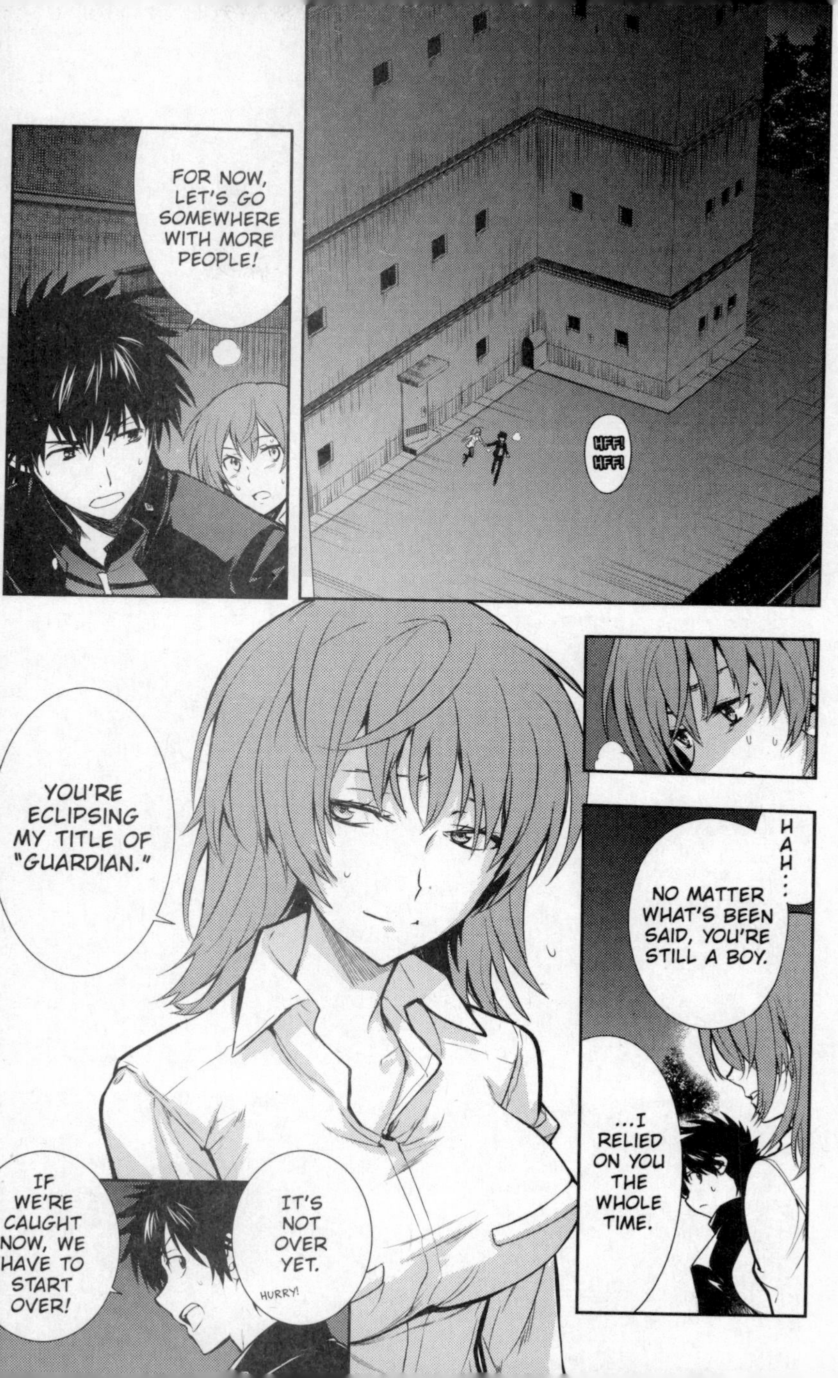
HFF! HFF!
FOR NOW, LET'S GO SOMEWHERE WITH MORE PEOPLE!
HAH...
NO MATTER WHAT'S BEEN SAID, YOU'RE STILL A BOY.
...I RELIED ON YOU THE WHOLE TIME.
YOU'RE ECLIPSING MY TITLE OF "GUARDIAN."
IT'S NOT OVER YET.
HURRY!
IF WE'RE CAUGHT NOW, WE HAVE TO START OVER!

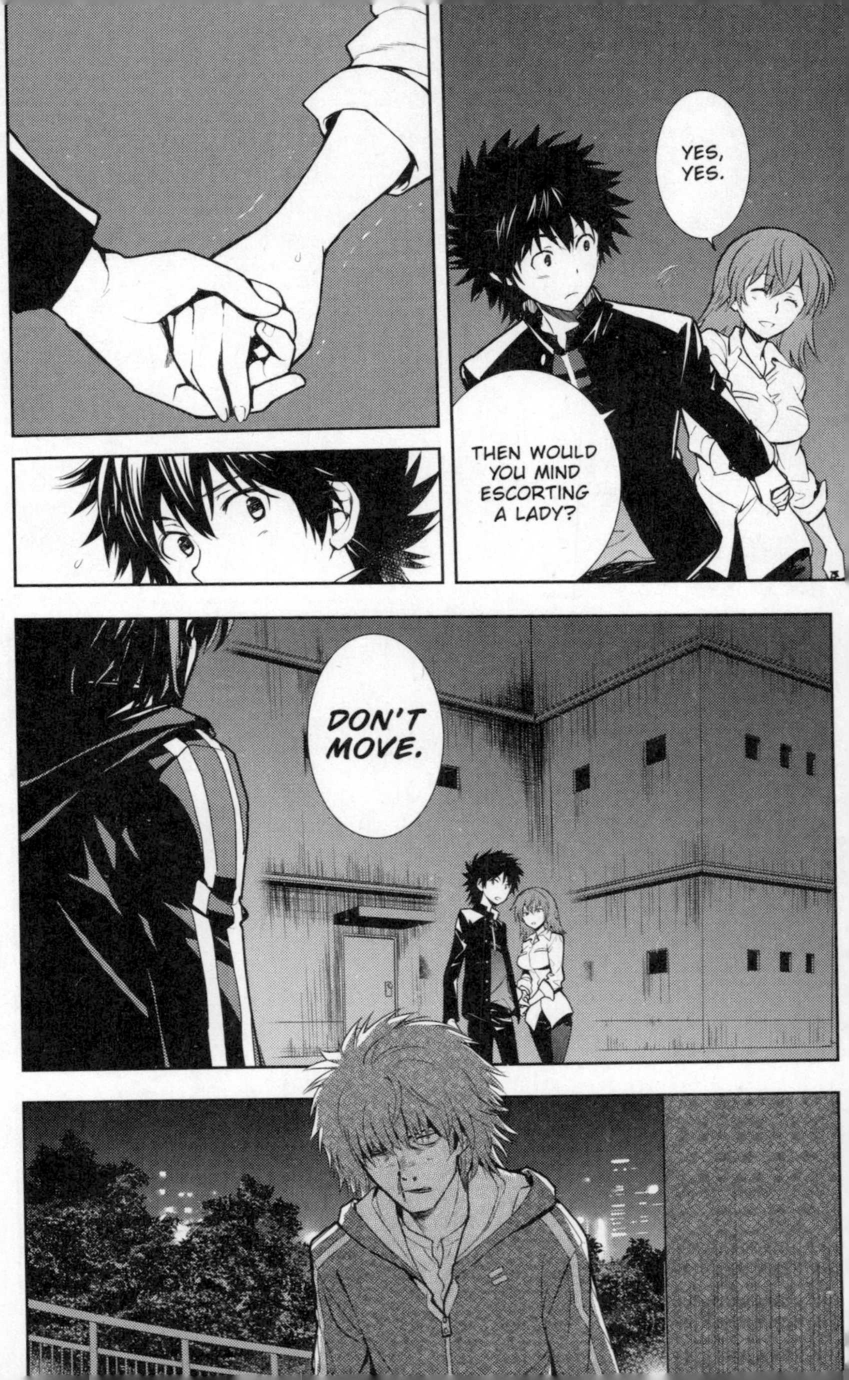
YES, YES.
THEN WOULD YOU MIND ESCORTING A LADY?
DON'T MOVE.

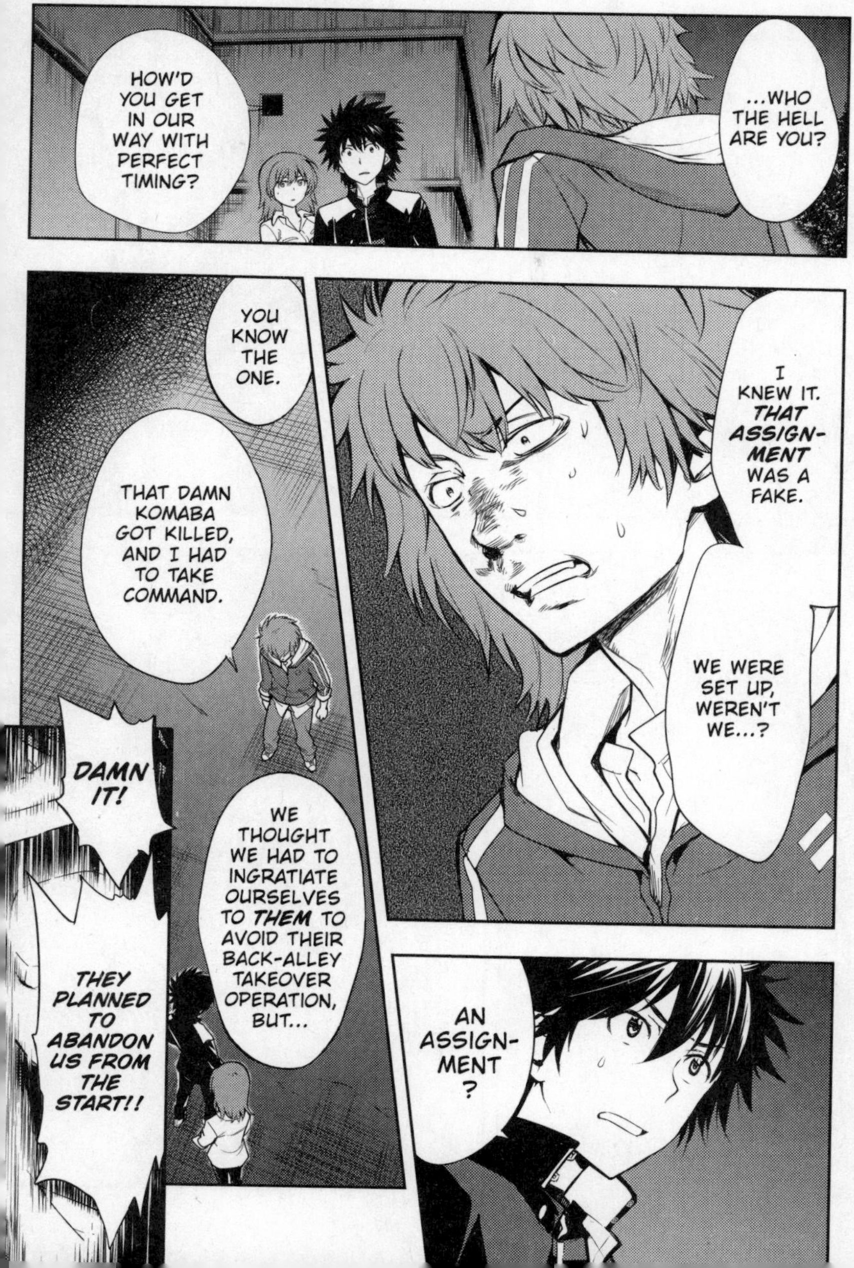
...WHO THE HELL ARE YOU?
HOW'D YOU GET IN OUR WAY WITH PERFECT TIMING?
I KNEW IT. *THAT ASSIGNMENT* WAS A FAKE.
WE WERE SET UP, WEREN'T WE...?
AN ASSIGNMENT?
YOU KNOW THE ONE.
THAT DAMN KOMABA GOT KILLED, AND I HAD TO TAKE COMMAND.
WE THOUGHT WE HAD TO INGRATIATE OURSELVES TO *THEM* TO AVOID THEIR BACK-ALLEY TAKEOVER OPERATION, BUT...
DAMN IT!
THEY PLANNED TO ABANDON US FROM THE START!!

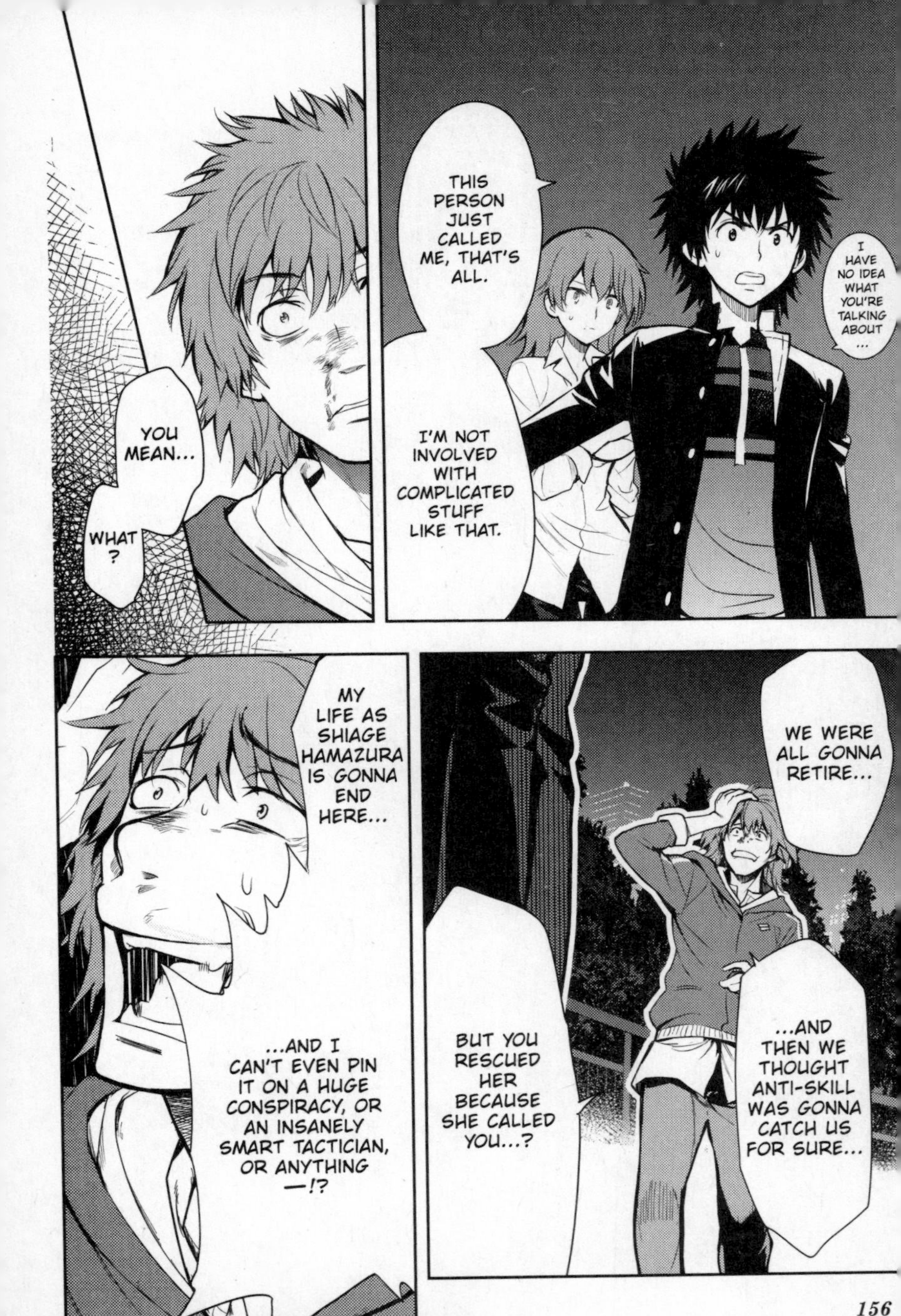
I HAVE NO IDEA WHAT YOU'RE TALKING ABOUT...
THIS PERSON JUST CALLED ME, THAT'S ALL.
I'M NOT INVOLVED WITH COMPLICATED STUFF LIKE THAT.
YOU MEAN...
WHAT?
WE WERE ALL GONNA RETIRE...
...AND THEN WE THOUGHT ANTI-SKILL WAS GONNA CATCH US FOR SURE...
BUT YOU RESCUED HER BECAUSE SHE CALLED YOU...?
MY LIFE AS SHIAGE HAMAZURA IS GONNA END HERE...
...AND I CAN'T EVEN PIN IT ON A HUGE CONSPIRACY, OR AN INSANELY SMART TACTICIAN, OR ANYTHING—!?

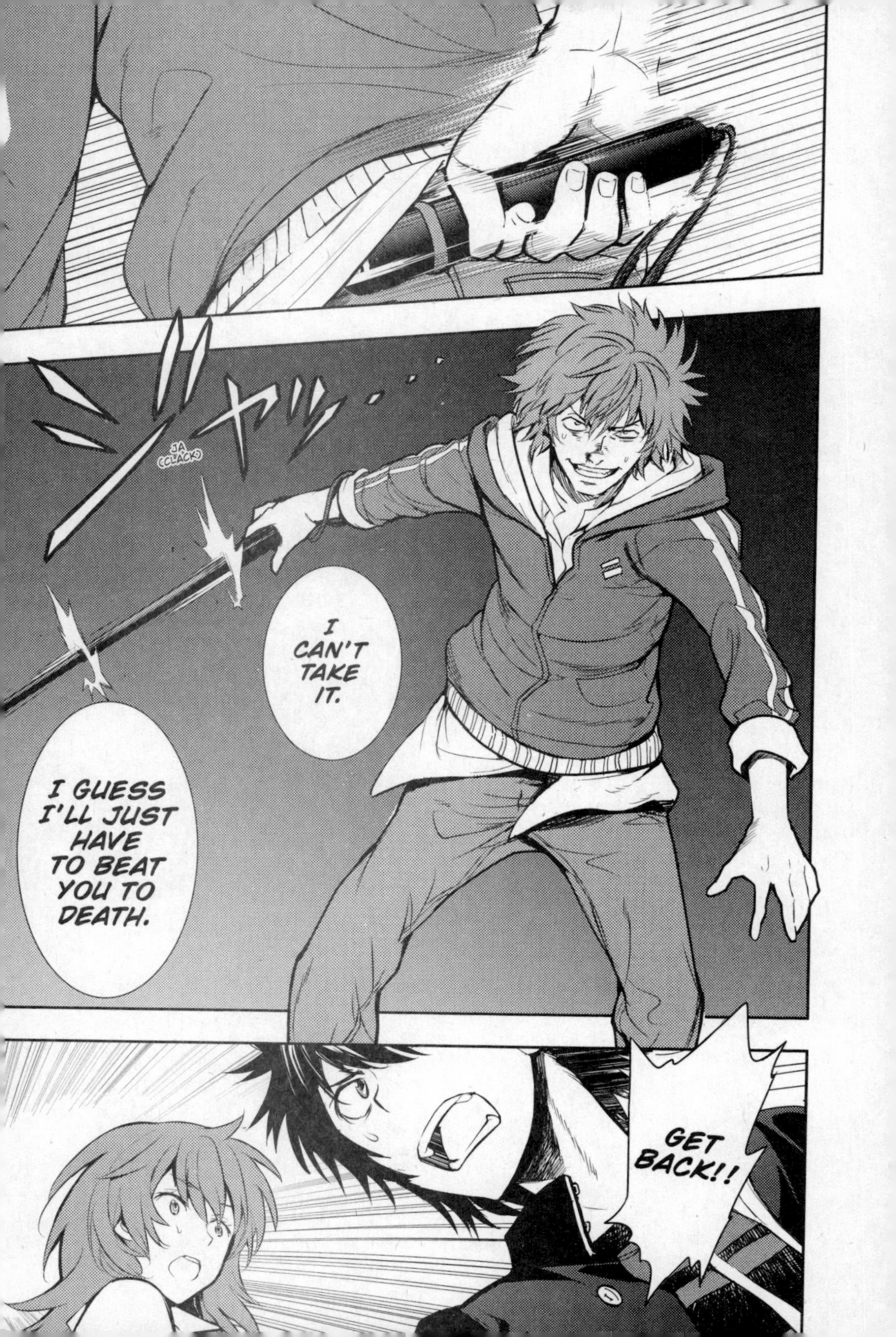
JA (CLACK)
I CAN'T TAKE IT.
I GUESS I'LL JUST HAVE TO BEAT YOU TO DEATH.
GET BACK!!

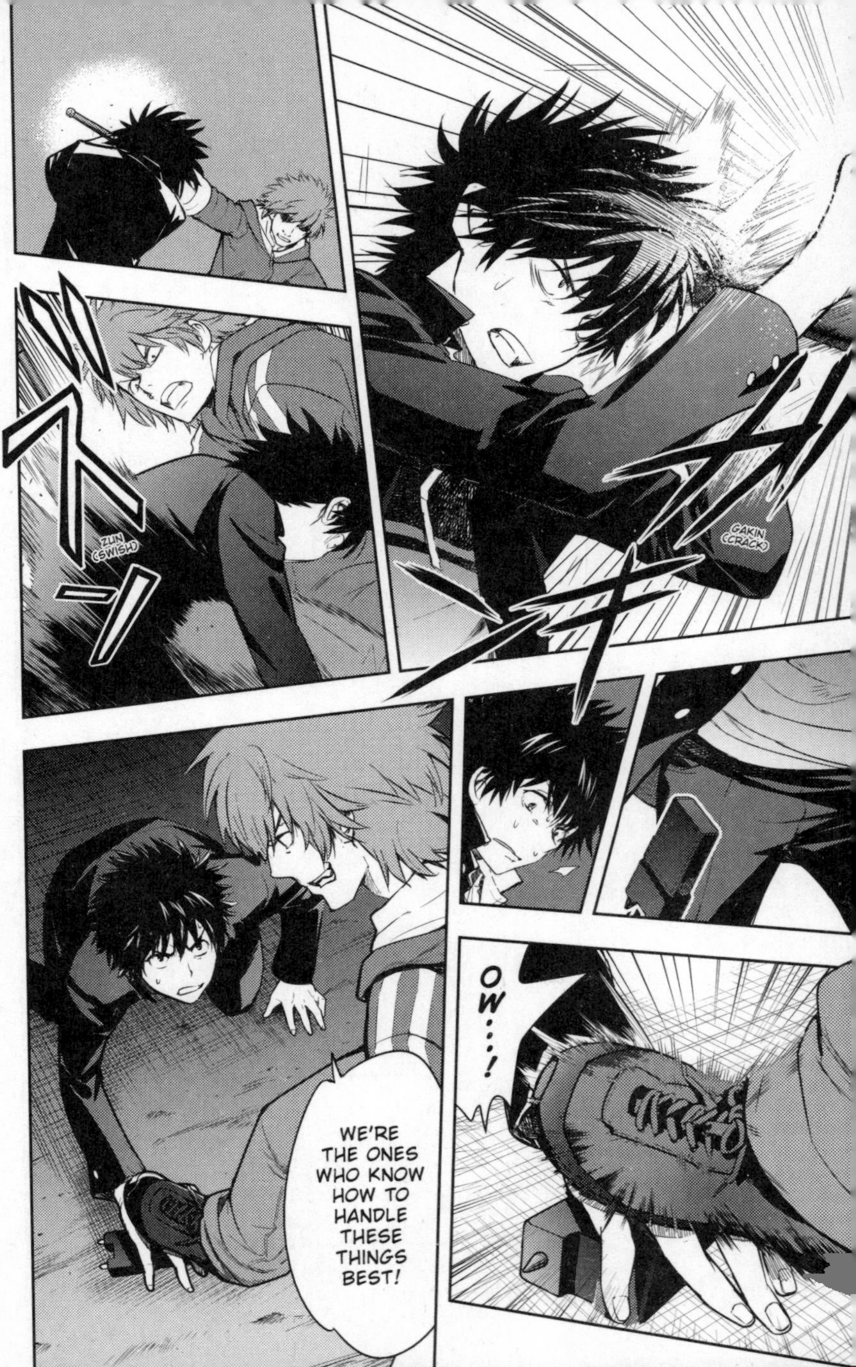
GAKIN (CRACK)
ZUN (SWISH)
OW...!
WE'RE THE ONES WHO KNOW HOW TO HANDLE THESE THINGS BEST!

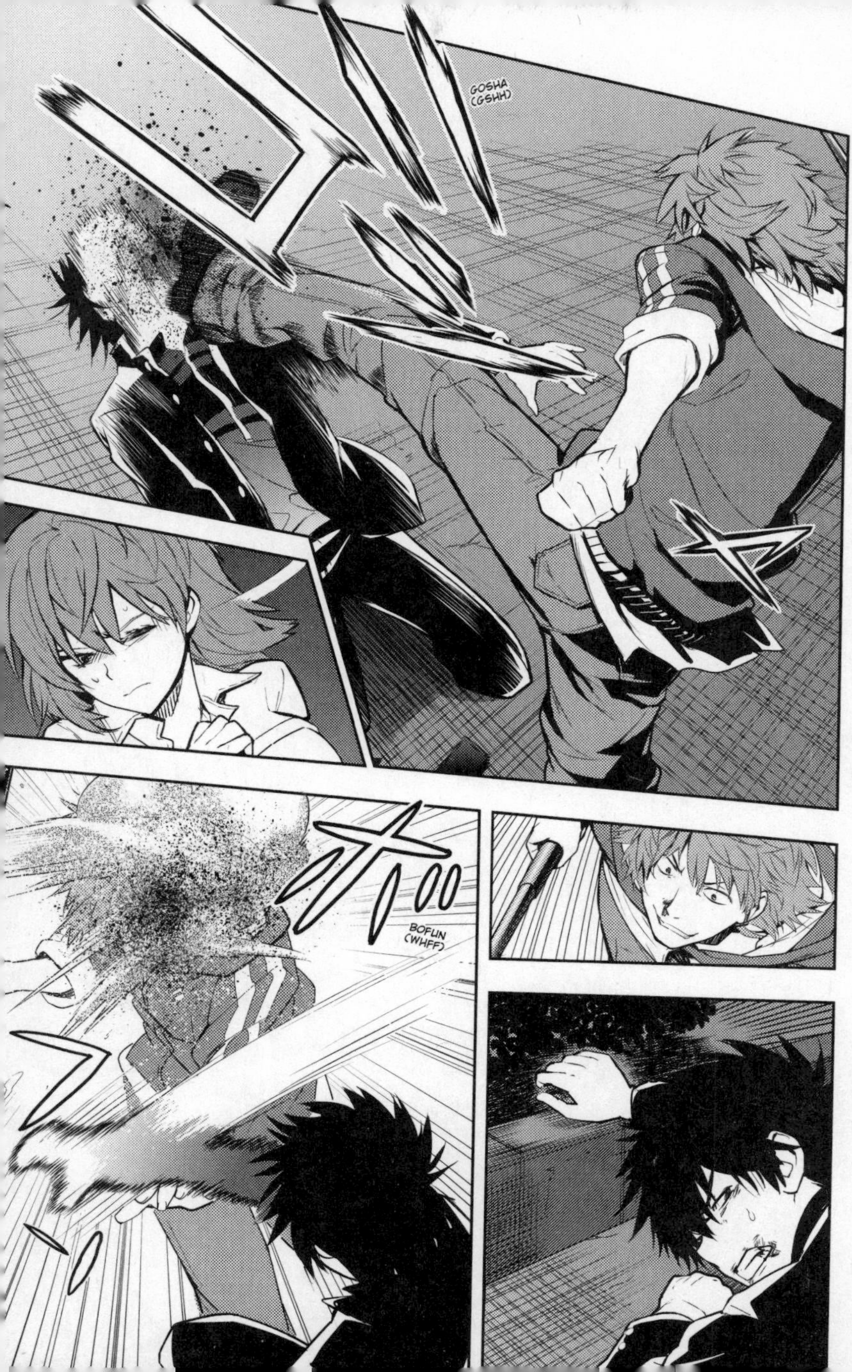
GOSHA (GSHH)
BOFUN (WHFF)

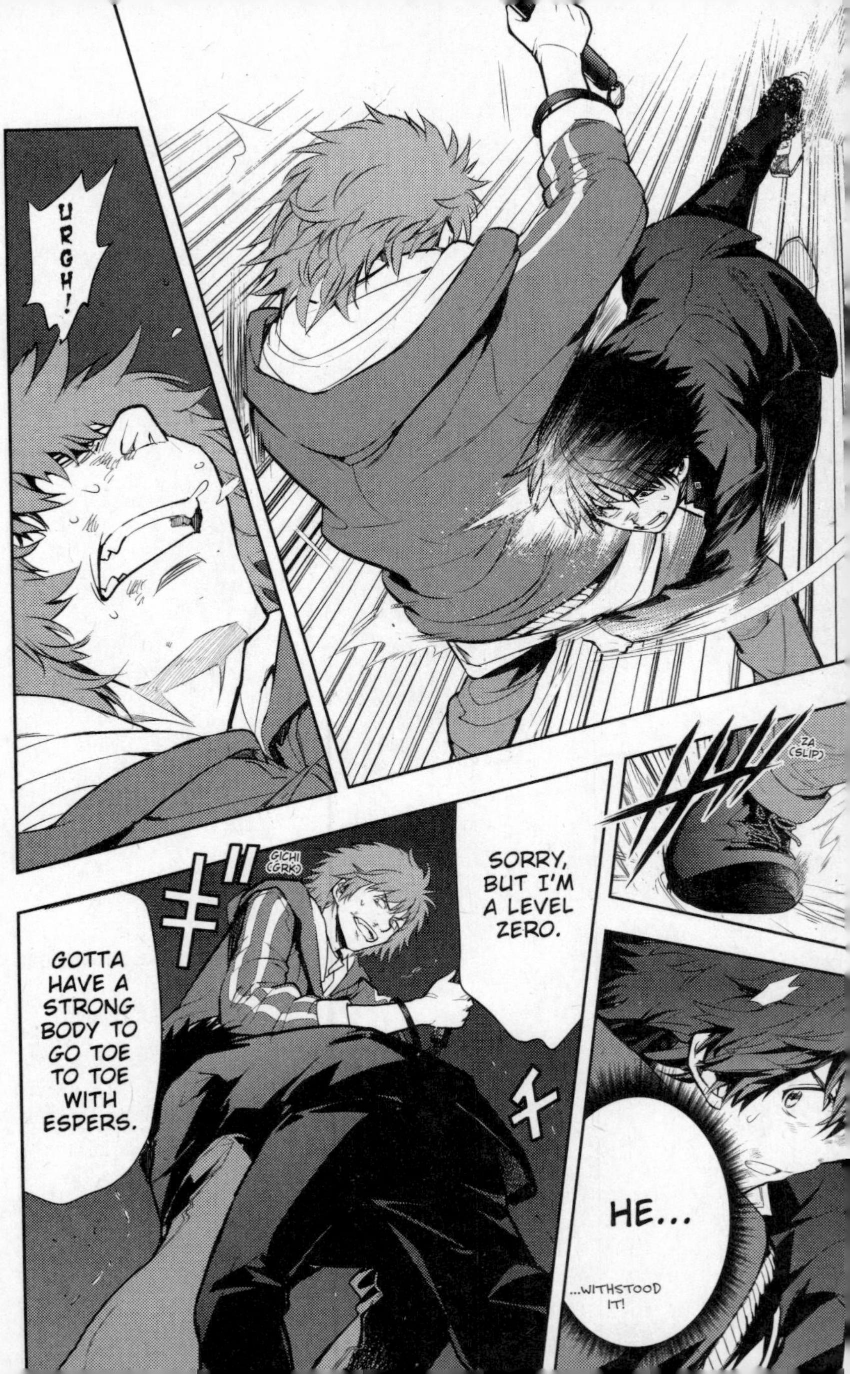
URGH!
ZA (SLIP)
HE...
...WITHSTOOD IT!
GICHI (GRK)
SORRY, BUT I'M A LEVEL ZERO.
GOTTA HAVE A STRONG BODY TO GO TOE TO TOE WITH ESPERS.

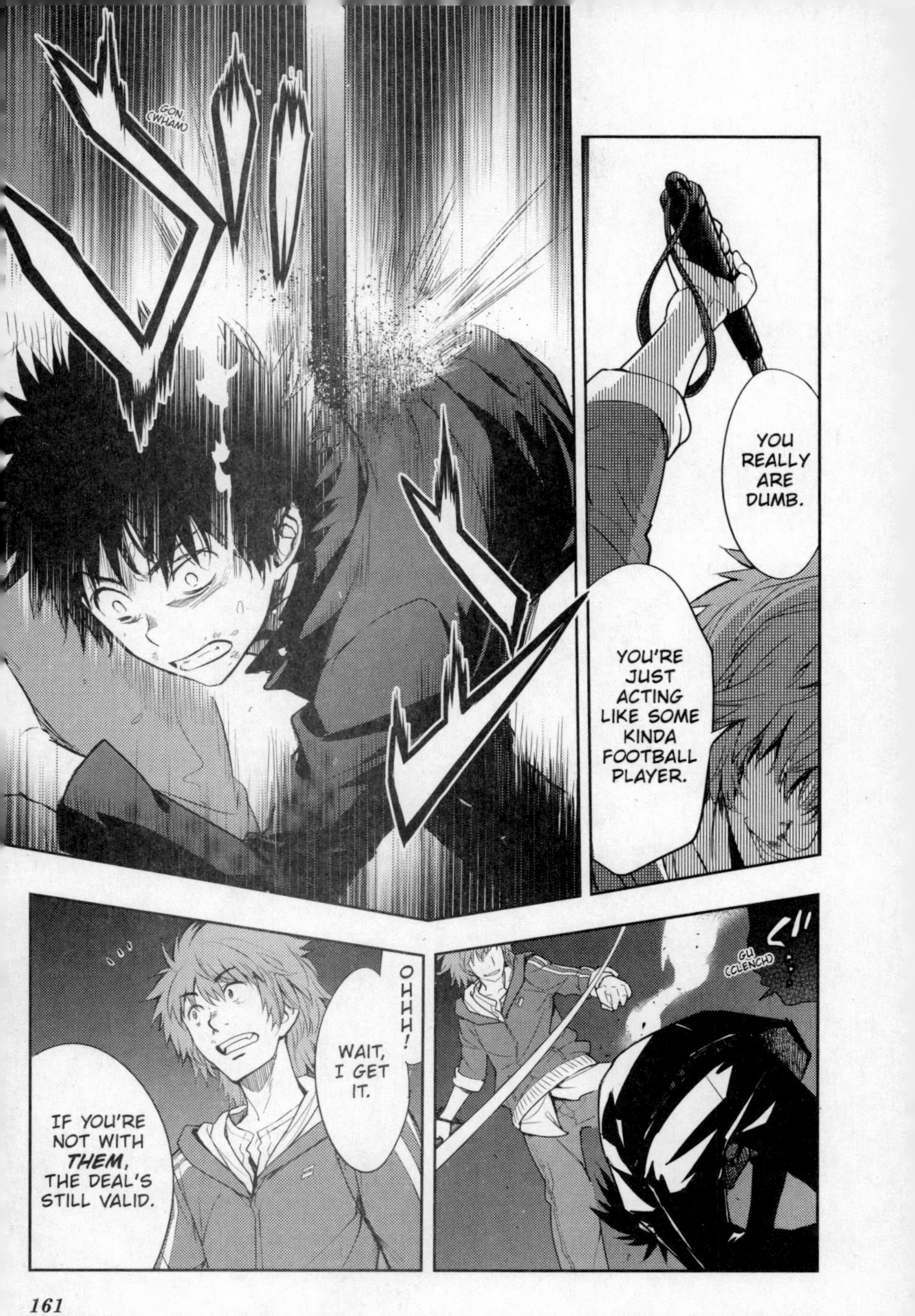
YOU REALLY ARE DUMB.
YOU'RE JUST ACTING LIKE SOME KINDA FOOTBALL PLAYER.
GON (WHAM)
GU (CLENCH)
OHHH!
WAIT, I GET IT.
IF YOU'RE NOT WITH *THEM*, THE DEAL'S STILL VALID.

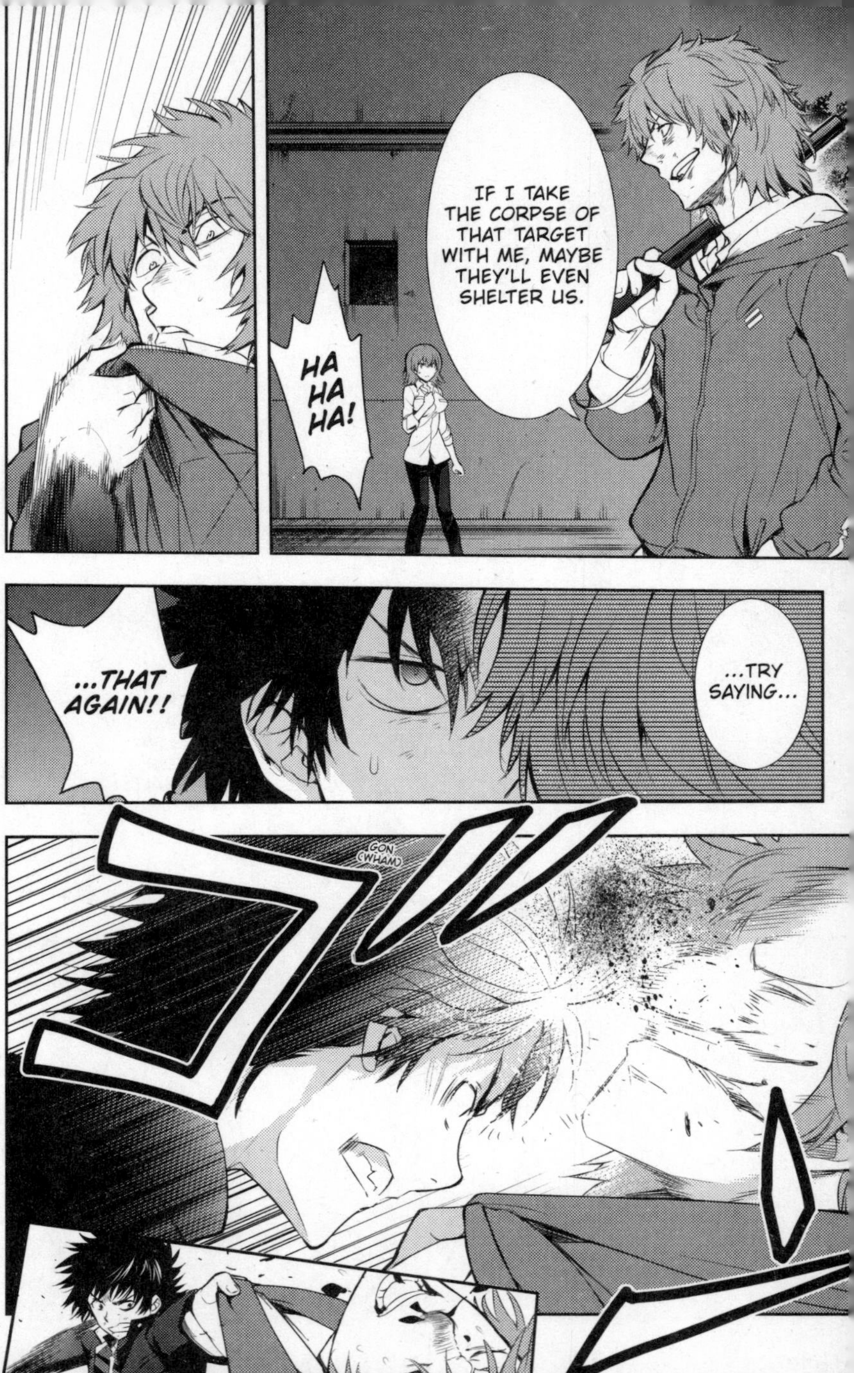
IF I TAKE THE CORPSE OF THAT TARGET WITH ME, MAYBE THEY'LL EVEN SHELTER US.
HA HA HA!
...TRY SAYING...
...THAT AGAIN!!
GON (WHAM)

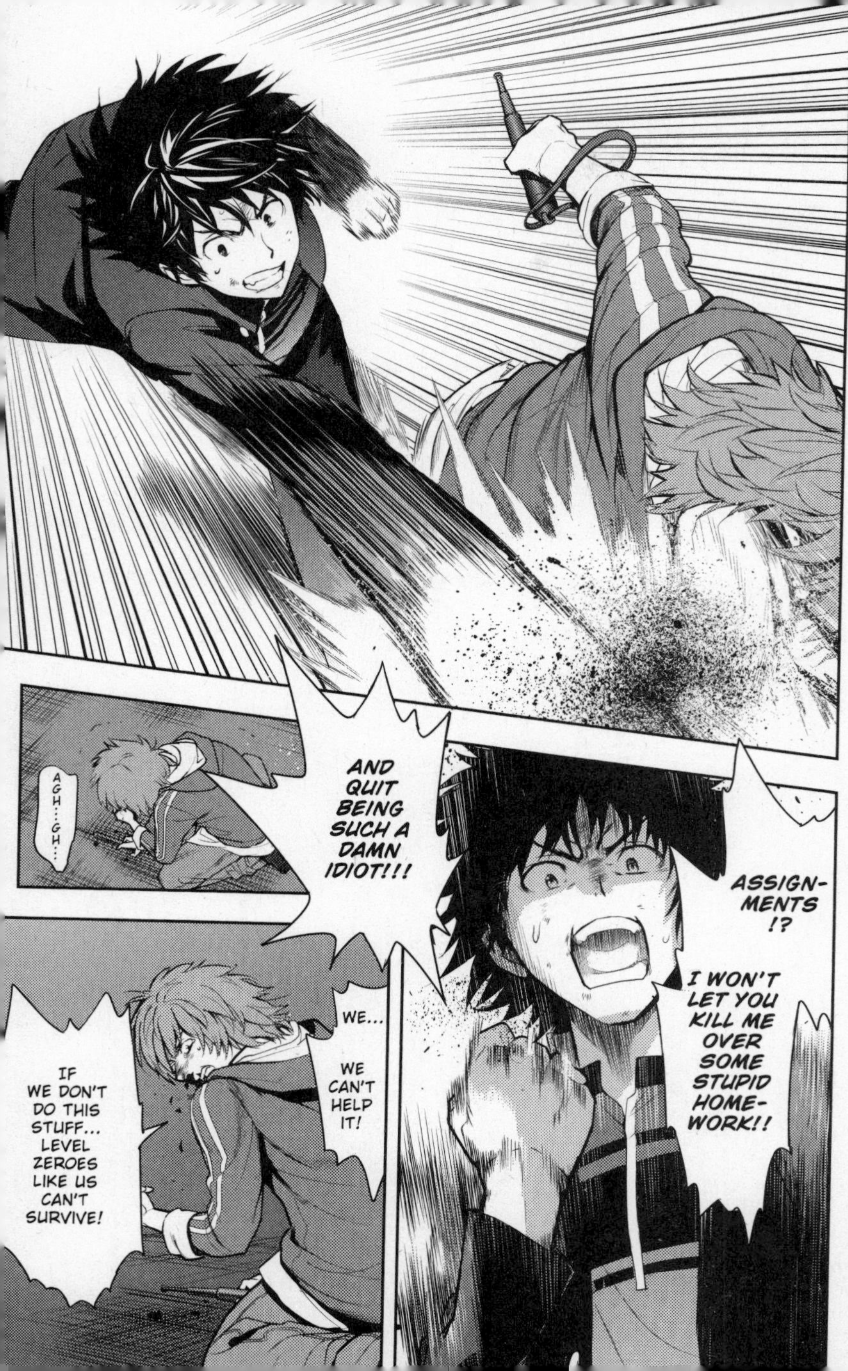
AND QUIT BEING SUCH A DAMN IDIOT!!!
ASSIGNMENTS!?
I WON'T LET YOU KILL ME OVER SOME STUPID HOMEWORK!!
AGH...GH...
WE...
WE CAN'T HELP IT!
IF WE DON'T DO THIS STUFF... LEVEL ZEROES LIKE US CAN'T SURVIVE!

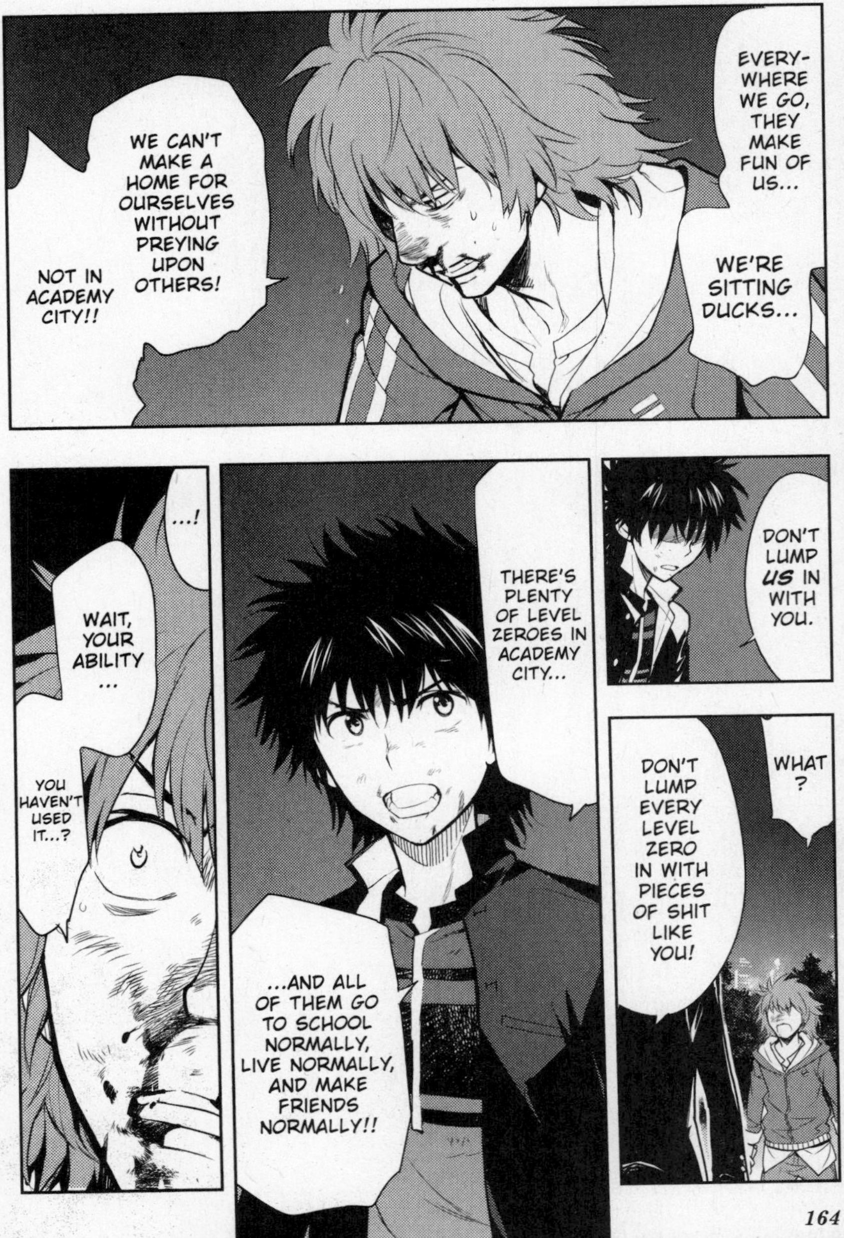
EVERY-WHERE WE GO, THEY MAKE FUN OF US...
WE'RE SITTING DUCKS...
WE CAN'T MAKE A HOME FOR OURSELVES WITHOUT PREYING UPON OTHERS!
NOT IN ACADEMY CITY!!
DON'T LUMP *US* IN WITH YOU.
WHAT?
DON'T LUMP EVERY LEVEL ZERO IN WITH PIECES OF SHIT LIKE YOU!
THERE'S PLENTY OF LEVEL ZEROES IN ACADEMY CITY...
...AND ALL OF THEM GO TO SCHOOL NORMALLY, LIVE NORMALLY, AND MAKE FRIENDS NORMALLY!!
...!
WAIT, YOUR ABILITY...
YOU HAVEN'T USED IT...?

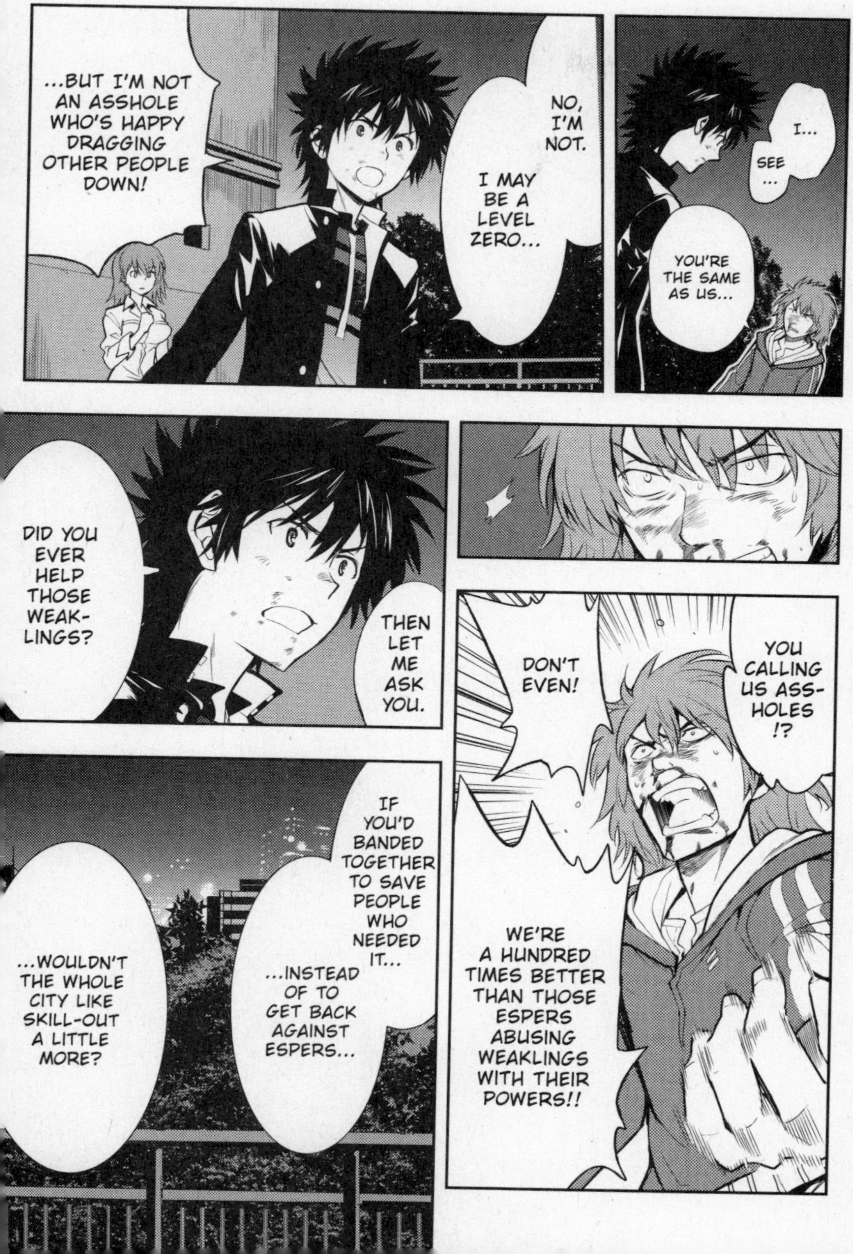
I...
SEE...
YOU'RE THE SAME AS US...
NO, I'M NOT.
I MAY BE A LEVEL ZERO...
...BUT I'M NOT AN ASSHOLE WHO'S HAPPY DRAGGING OTHER PEOPLE DOWN!
YOU CALLING US ASSHOLES!?
DON'T EVEN!
WE'RE A HUNDRED TIMES BETTER THAN THOSE ESPERS ABUSING WEAKLINGS WITH THEIR POWERS!!
THEN LET ME ASK YOU.
DID YOU EVER HELP THOSE WEAKLINGS?
IF YOU'D BANDED TOGETHER TO SAVE PEOPLE WHO NEEDED IT...
...INSTEAD OF TO GET BACK AGAINST ESPERS...
...WOULDN'T THE WHOLE CITY LIKE SKILL-OUT A LITTLE MORE?

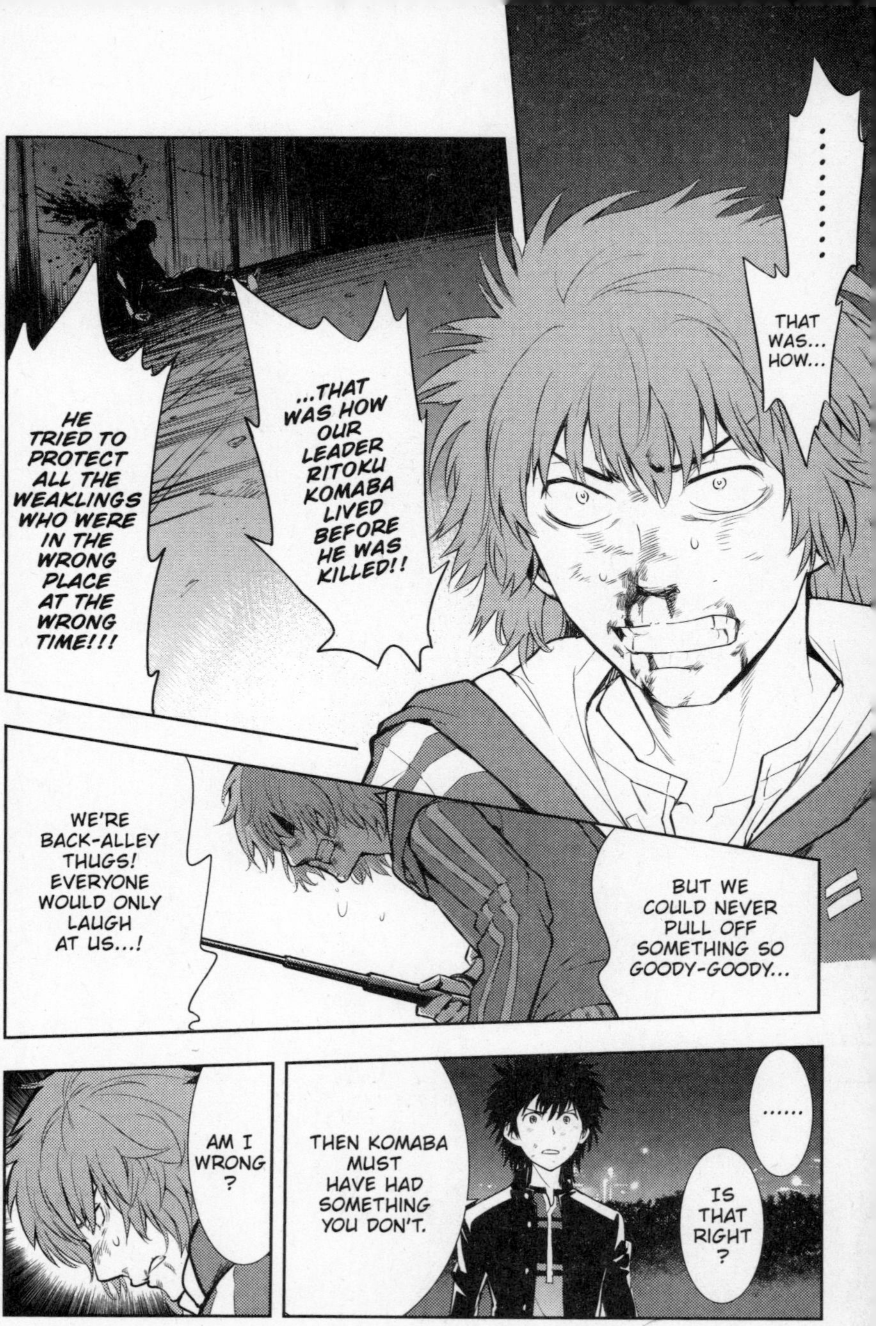

......
THAT WAS... HOW...
...THAT WAS HOW OUR LEADER RITOKU KOMABA LIVED BEFORE HE WAS KILLED!!
HE TRIED TO PROTECT ALL THE WEAKLINGS WHO WERE IN THE WRONG PLACE AT THE WRONG TIME!!!
BUT WE COULD NEVER PULL OFF SOMETHING SO GOODY-GOODY...
WE'RE BACK-ALLEY THUGS! EVERYONE WOULD ONLY LAUGH AT US...!
......
IS THAT RIGHT?
THEN KOMABA MUST HAVE HAD SOMETHING YOU DON'T.
AM I WRONG?

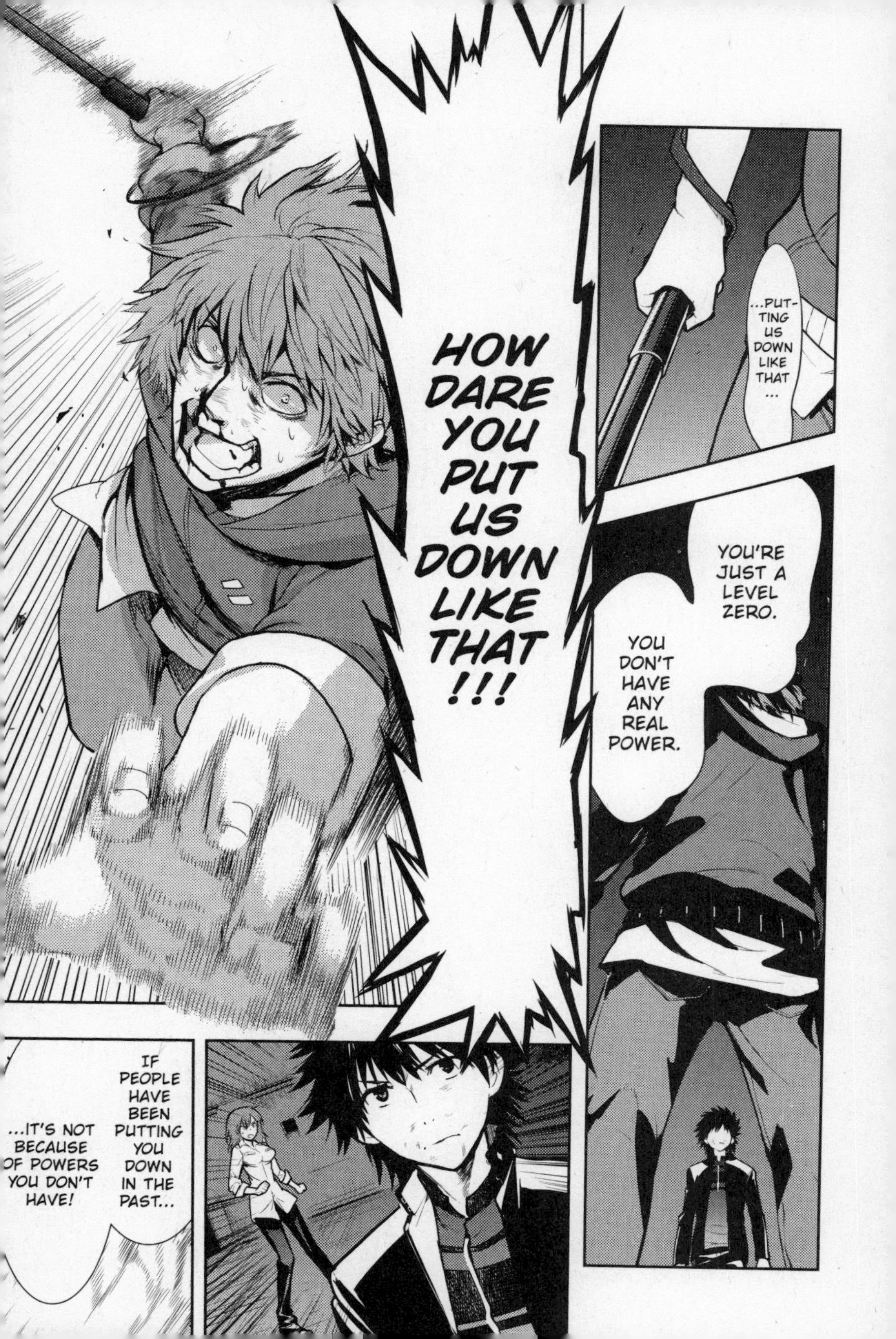
...PUTTING US DOWN LIKE THAT...
YOU'RE JUST A LEVEL ZERO.
YOU DON'T HAVE ANY REAL POWER.
HOW DARE YOU PUT US DOWN LIKE THAT!!!
IF PEOPLE HAVE BEEN PUTTING YOU DOWN IN THE PAST...
...IT'S NOT BECAUSE OF POWERS YOU DON'T HAVE!

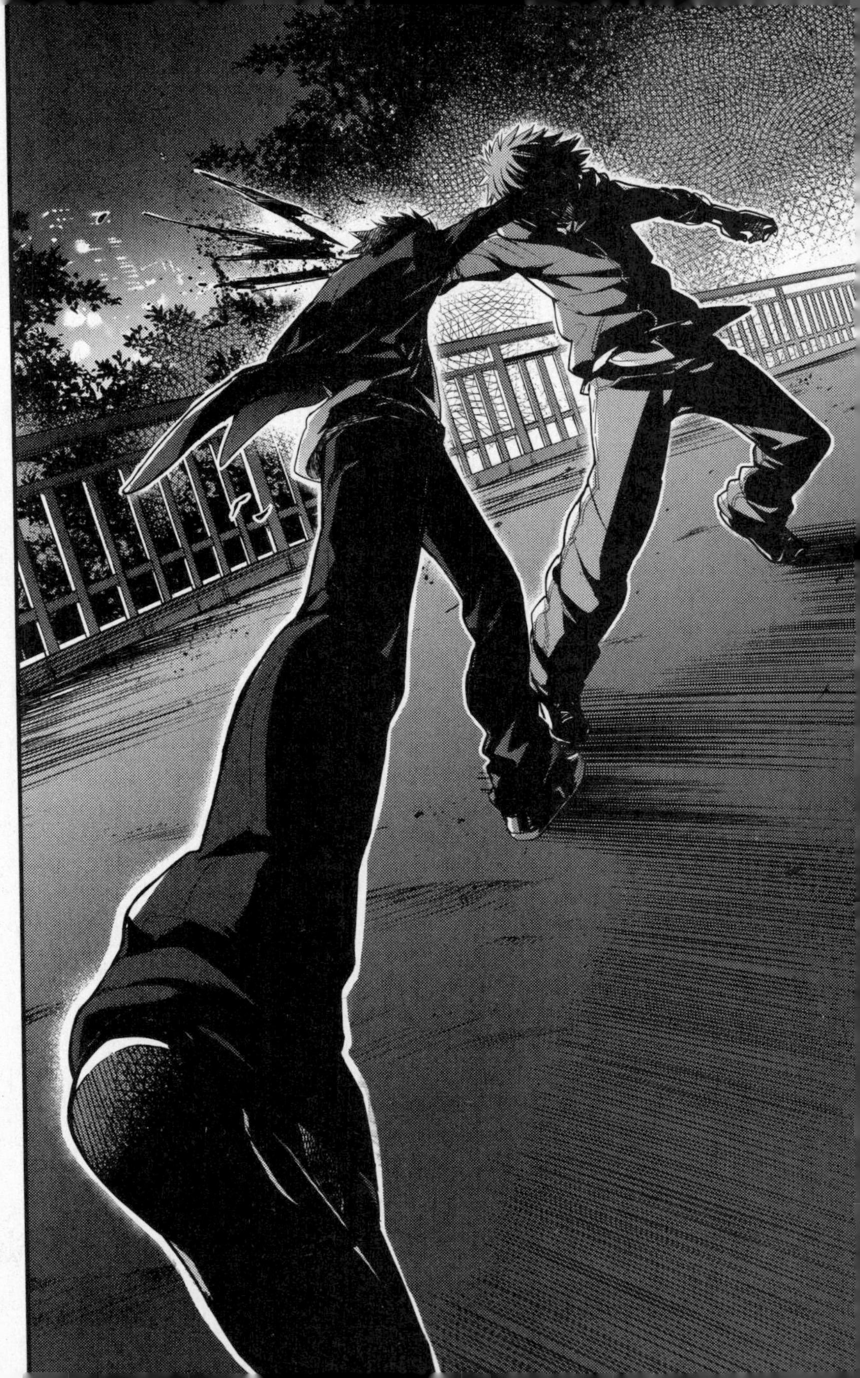

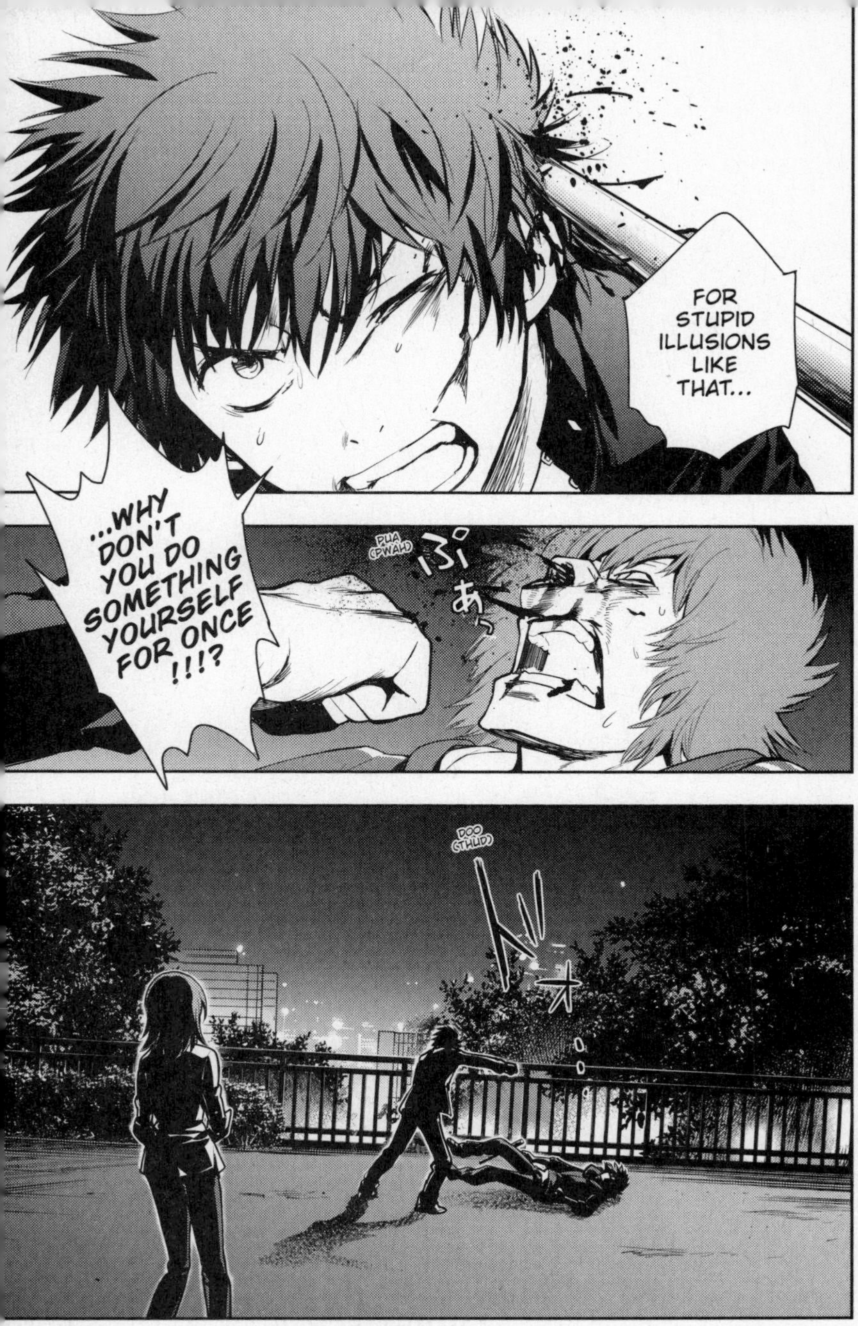
FOR STUPID ILLUSIONS LIKE THAT...
...WHY DON'T YOU DO SOMETHING YOURSELF FOR ONCE !!!?
PUA (PWAH)
ぷあっ
DOO (THUD)
ドォ

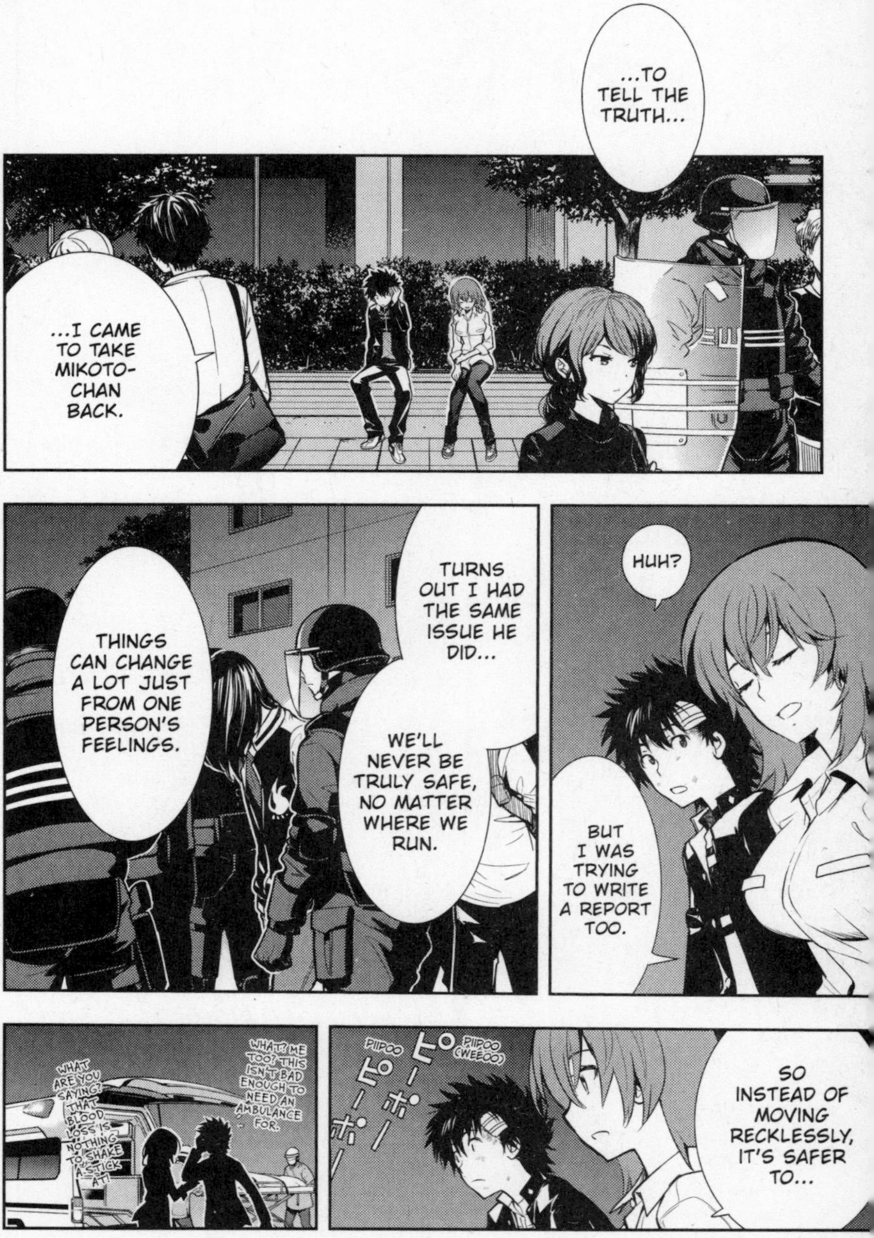
...TO TELL THE TRUTH...
...I CAME TO TAKE MIKOTO-CHAN BACK.
HUH?
BUT I WAS TRYING TO WRITE A REPORT TOO.
TURNS OUT I HAD THE SAME ISSUE HE DID...
WE'LL NEVER BE TRULY SAFE, NO MATTER WHERE WE RUN.
THINGS CAN CHANGE A LOT JUST FROM ONE PERSON'S FEELINGS.
SO INSTEAD OF MOVING RECKLESSLY, IT'S SAFER TO...
ピーポー
PIIPOO (WEEOO)
ピーポー
PIIPOO
WHAT? ME TOO? THIS ISN'T BAD ENOUGH TO NEED AN AMBULANCE FOR.
WHAT ARE YOU SAYING? THAT BLOOD LOSS IS NOTHING TO SHAKE A STICK AT!

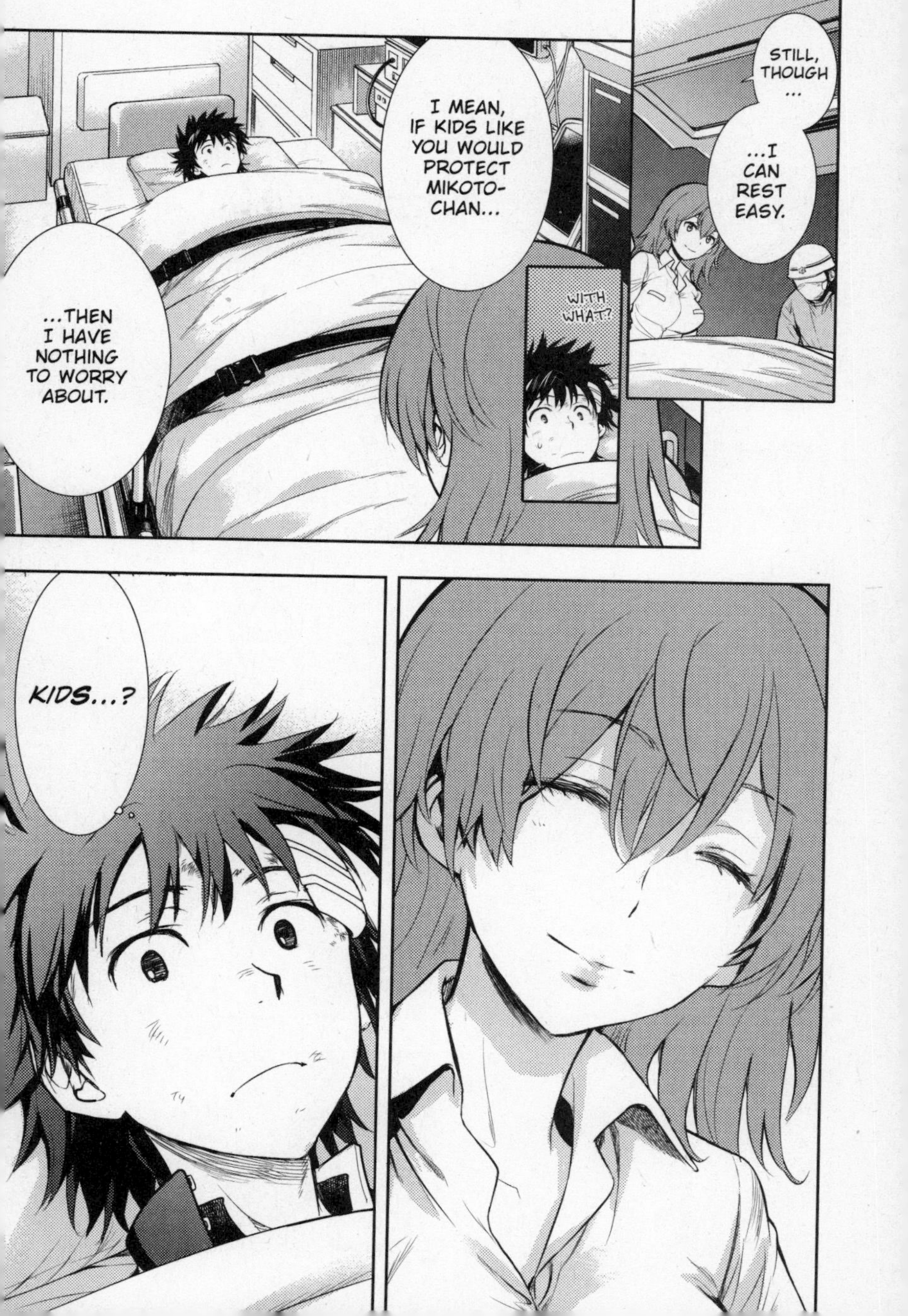
STILL, THOUGH...
...I CAN REST EASY.
WITH WHAT?
I MEAN, IF KIDS LIKE YOU WOULD PROTECT MIKOTO-CHAN...
...THEN I HAVE NOTHING TO WORRY ABOUT.
KIDS...?

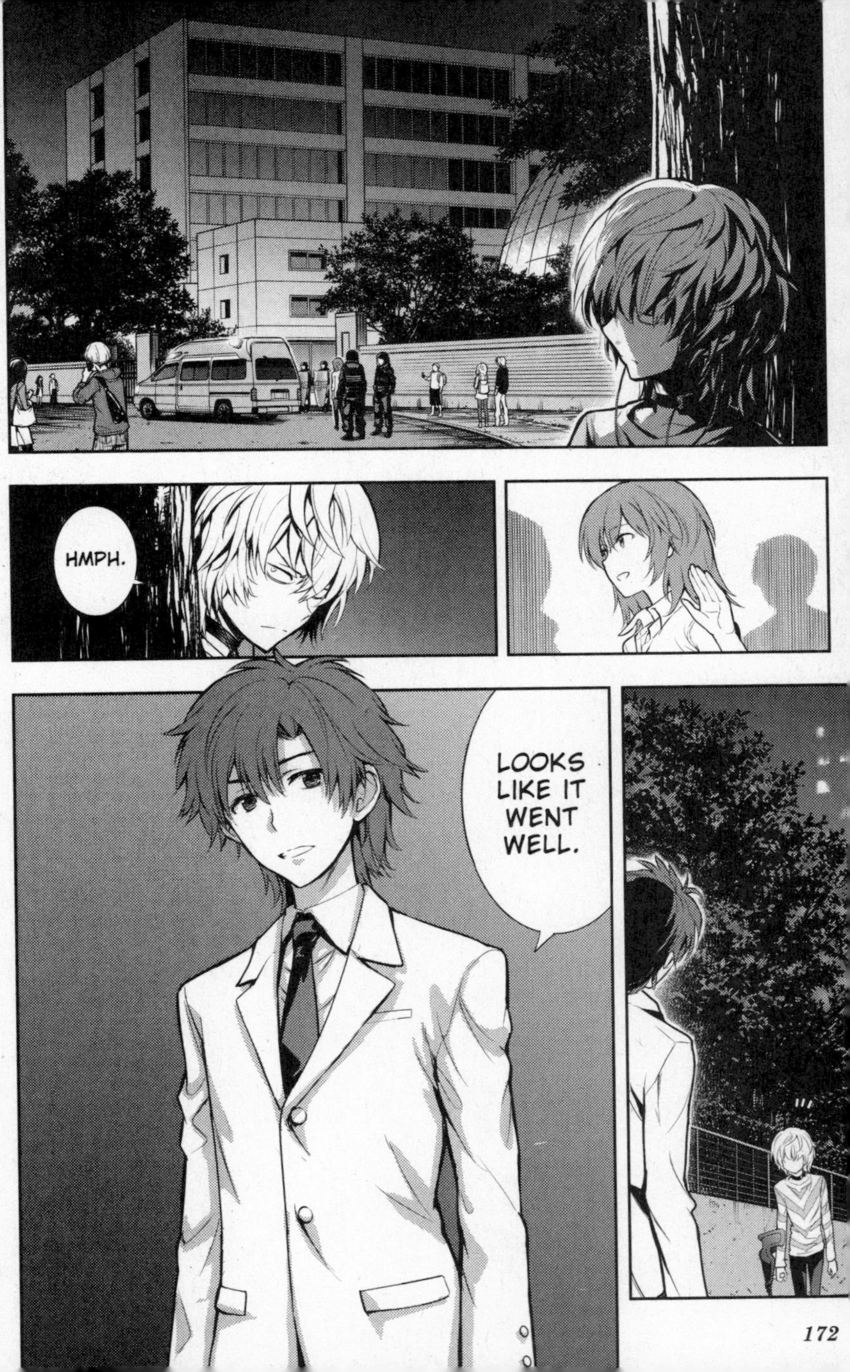
HMPH.
LOOKS LIKE IT WENT WELL.

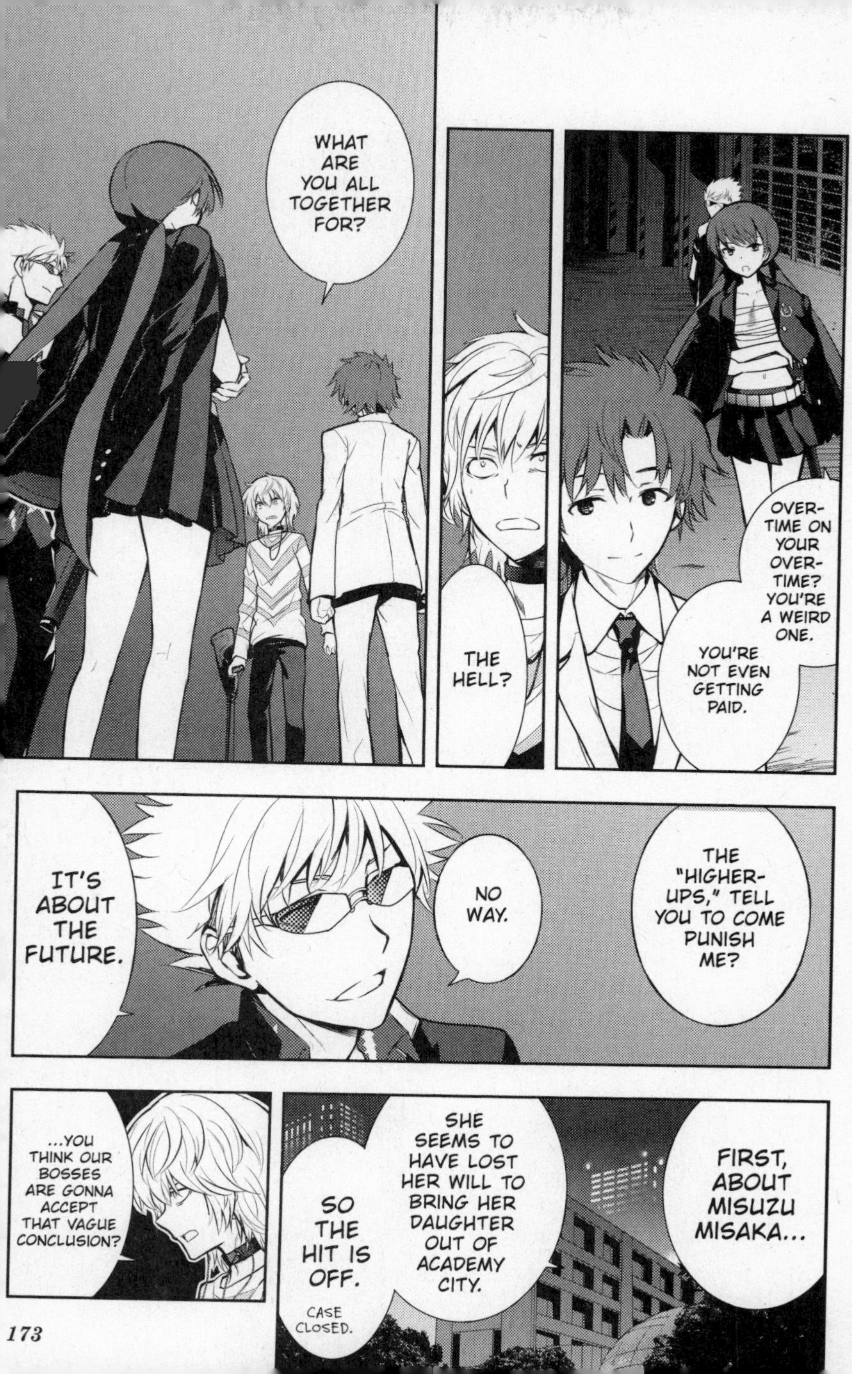
OVER-TIME ON YOUR OVER-TIME? YOU'RE A WEIRD ONE.
YOU'RE NOT EVEN GETTING PAID.
THE HELL?
WHAT ARE YOU ALL TOGETHER FOR?
THE "HIGHER-UPS," TELL YOU TO COME PUNISH ME?
NO WAY.
IT'S ABOUT THE FUTURE.
FIRST, ABOUT MISUZU MISAKA...
SHE SEEMS TO HAVE LOST HER WILL TO BRING HER DAUGHTER OUT OF ACADEMY CITY.
SO THE HIT IS OFF.
CASE CLOSED.
...YOU THINK OUR BOSSES ARE GONNA ACCEPT THAT VAGUE CONCLUSION?

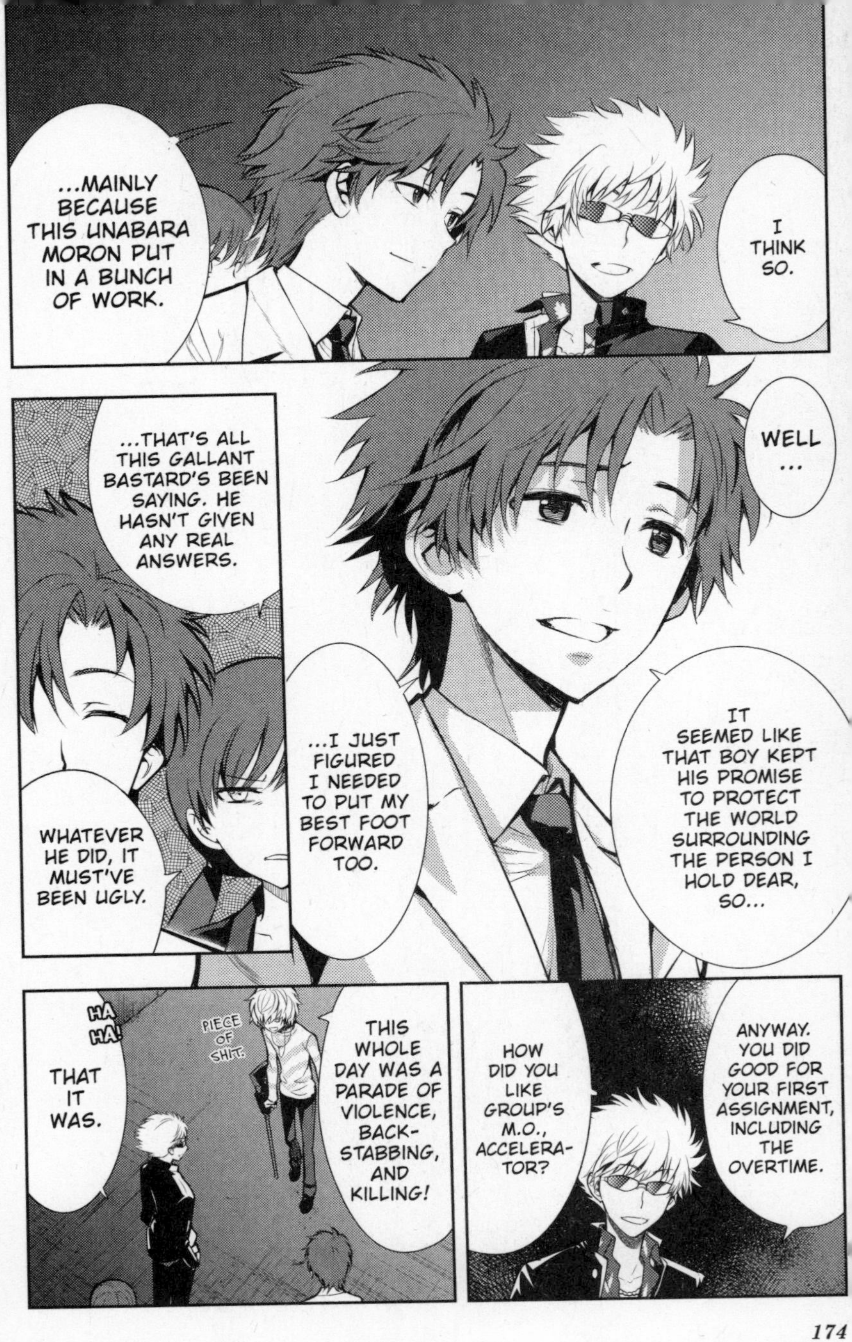
I THINK SO.
...MAINLY BECAUSE THIS UNABARA MORON PUT IN A BUNCH OF WORK.
WELL ...
IT SEEMED LIKE THAT BOY KEPT HIS PROMISE TO PROTECT THE WORLD SURROUNDING THE PERSON I HOLD DEAR, SO...
...I JUST FIGURED I NEEDED TO PUT MY BEST FOOT FORWARD TOO.
...THAT'S ALL THIS GALLANT BASTARD'S BEEN SAYING. HE HASN'T GIVEN ANY REAL ANSWERS.
WHATEVER HE DID, IT MUST'VE BEEN UGLY.
ANYWAY. YOU DID GOOD FOR YOUR FIRST ASSIGNMENT, INCLUDING THE OVERTIME.
HOW DID YOU LIKE GROUP'S M.O., ACCELERATOR?
THIS WHOLE DAY WAS A PARADE OF VIOLENCE, BACK-STABBING, AND KILLING!
PIECE OF SHIT.
HA HA!
THAT IT WAS.

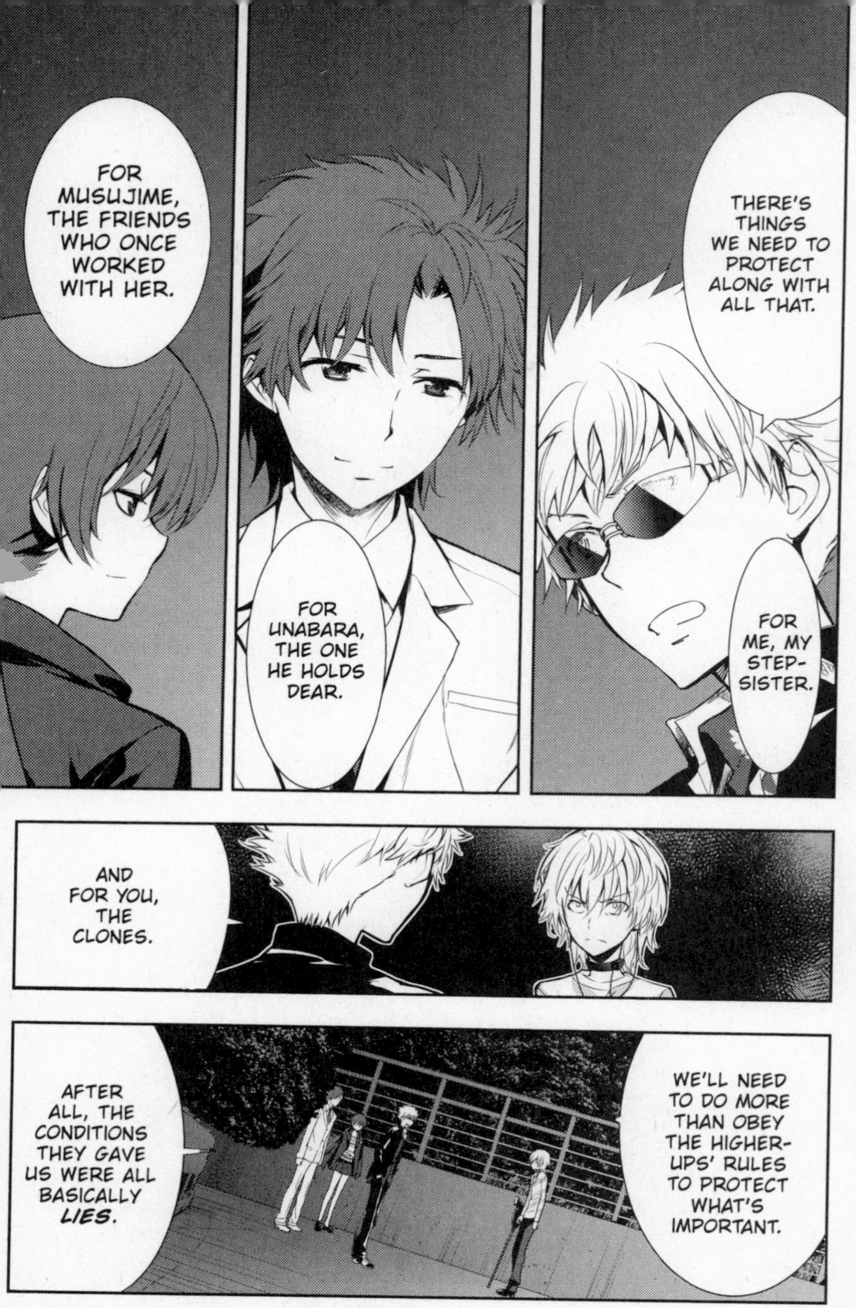
THERE'S THINGS WE NEED TO PROTECT ALONG WITH ALL THAT.
FOR ME, MY STEP-SISTER.
FOR UNABARA, THE ONE HE HOLDS DEAR.
FOR MUSUJIME, THE FRIENDS WHO ONCE WORKED WITH HER.
AND FOR YOU, THE CLONES.
WE'LL NEED TO DO MORE THAN OBEY THE HIGHER-UPS' RULES TO PROTECT WHAT'S IMPORTANT.
AFTER ALL, THE CONDITIONS THEY GAVE US WERE ALL BASICALLY ***LIES***.

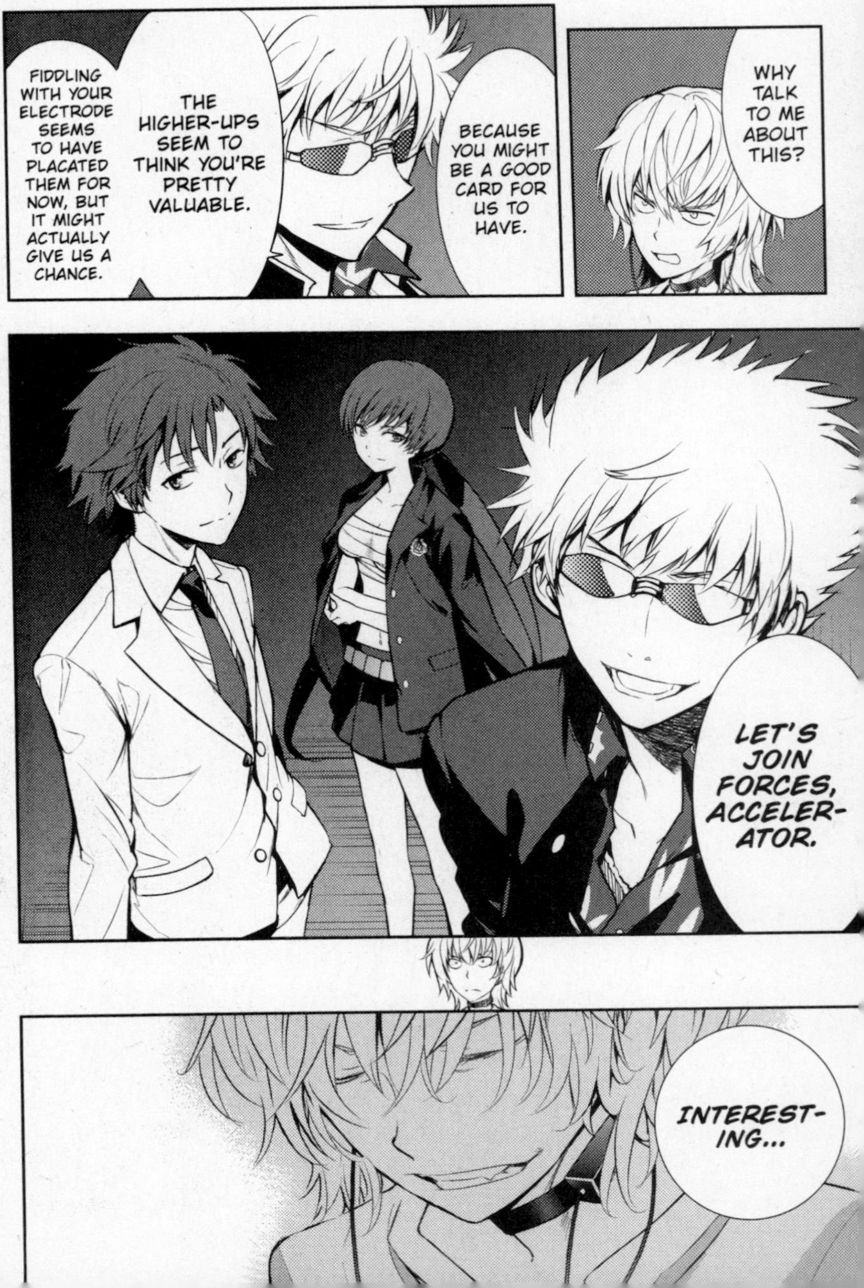
WHY TALK TO ME ABOUT THIS?
BECAUSE YOU MIGHT BE A GOOD CARD FOR US TO HAVE.
THE HIGHER-UPS SEEM TO THINK YOU'RE PRETTY VALUABLE.
FIDDLING WITH YOUR ELECTRODE SEEMS TO HAVE PLACATED THEM FOR NOW, BUT IT MIGHT ACTUALLY GIVE US A CHANCE.
LET'S JOIN FORCES, ACCELER-ATOR.
INTEREST-ING...

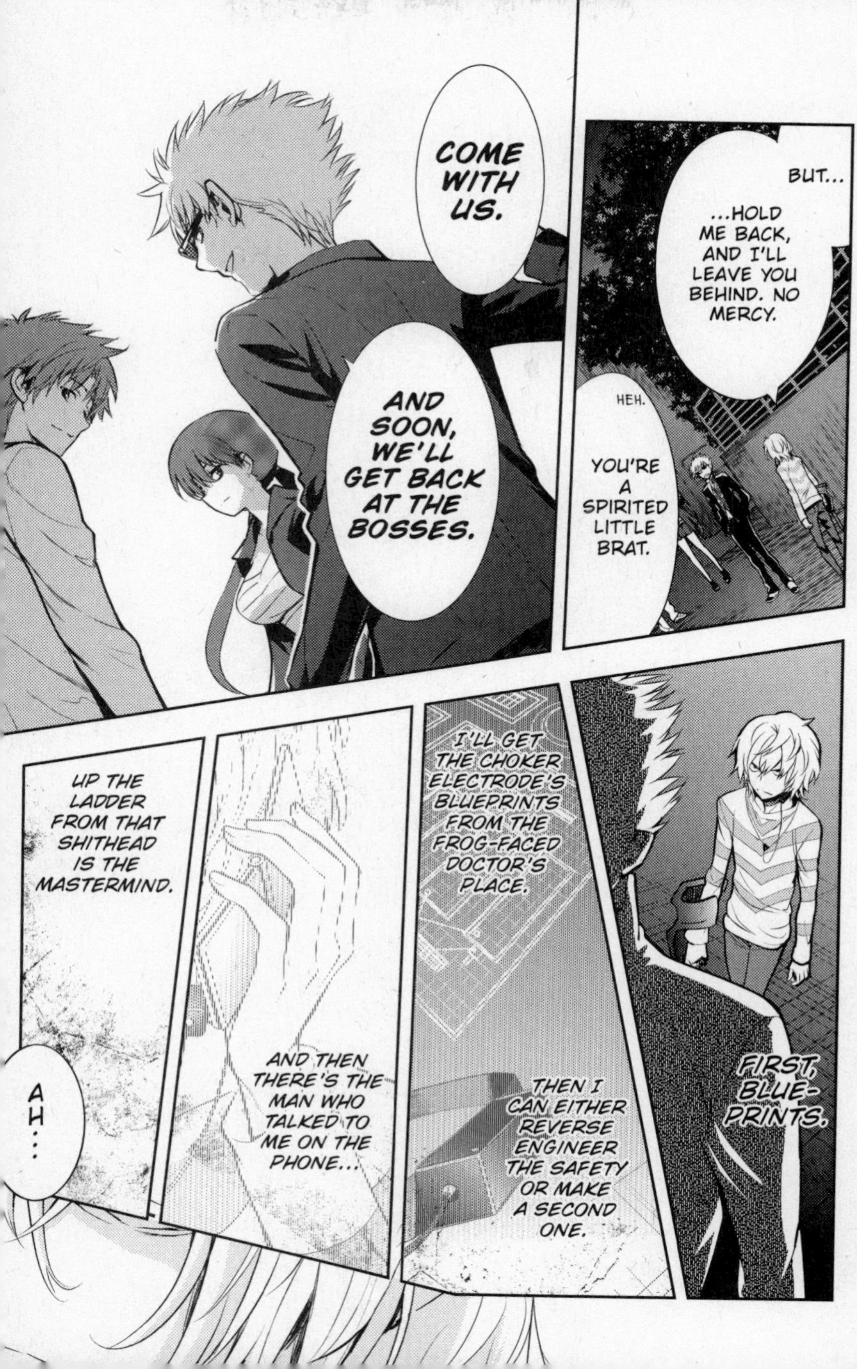
BUT...
...HOLD ME BACK, AND I'LL LEAVE YOU BEHIND. NO MERCY.
HEH.
YOU'RE A SPIRITED LITTLE BRAT.
COME WITH US.
AND SOON, WE'LL GET BACK AT THE BOSSES.
FIRST, BLUE-PRINTS.
I'LL GET THE CHOKER ELECTRODE'S BLUEPRINTS FROM THE FROG-FACED DOCTOR'S PLACE.
THEN I CAN EITHER REVERSE ENGINEER THE SAFETY OR MAKE A SECOND ONE.
AND THEN THERE'S THE MAN WHO TALKED TO ME ON THE PHONE...
UP THE LADDER FROM THAT SHITHEAD IS THE MASTERMIND.
AH...

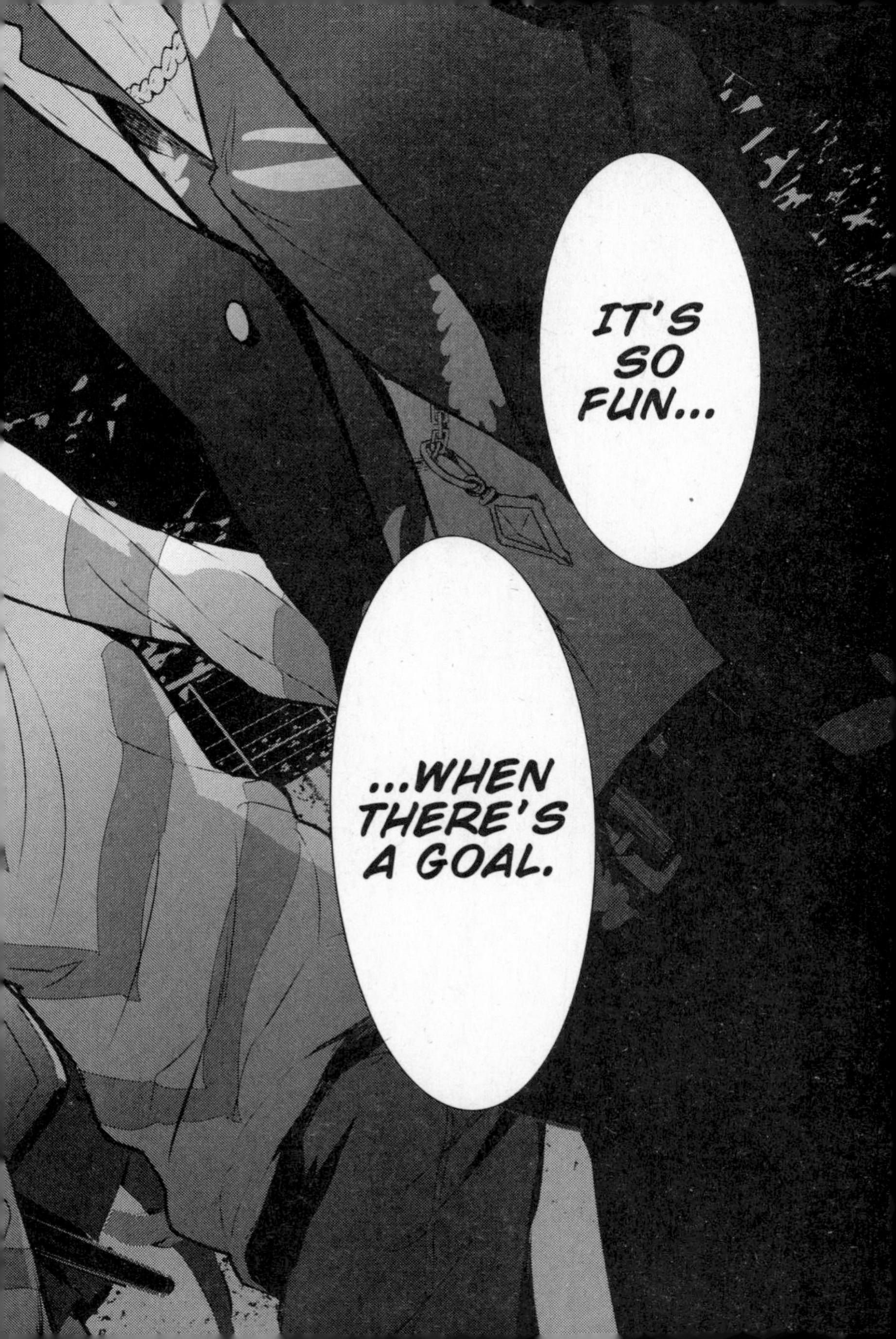
IT'S SO FUN...
...WHEN THERE'S A GOAL.

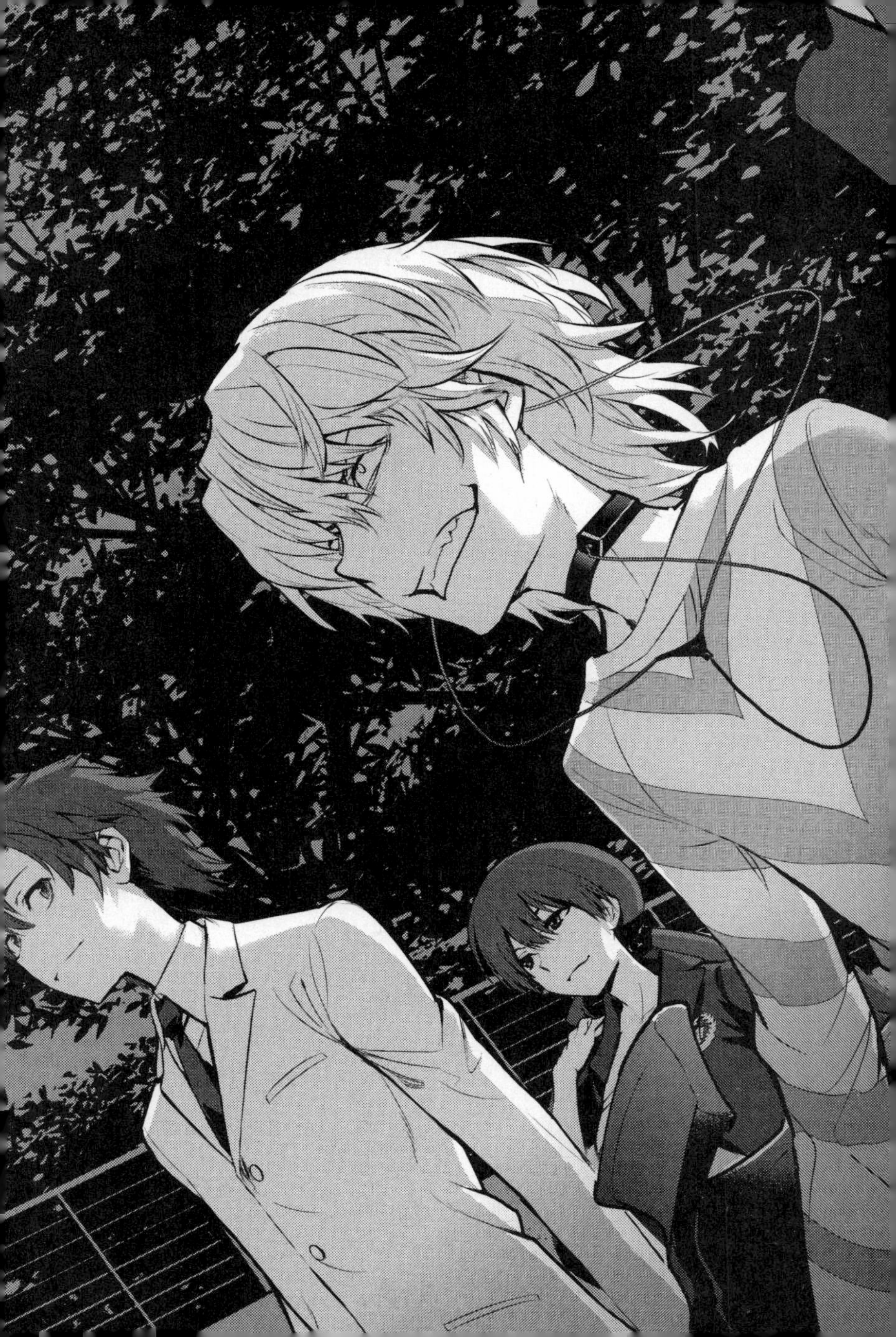

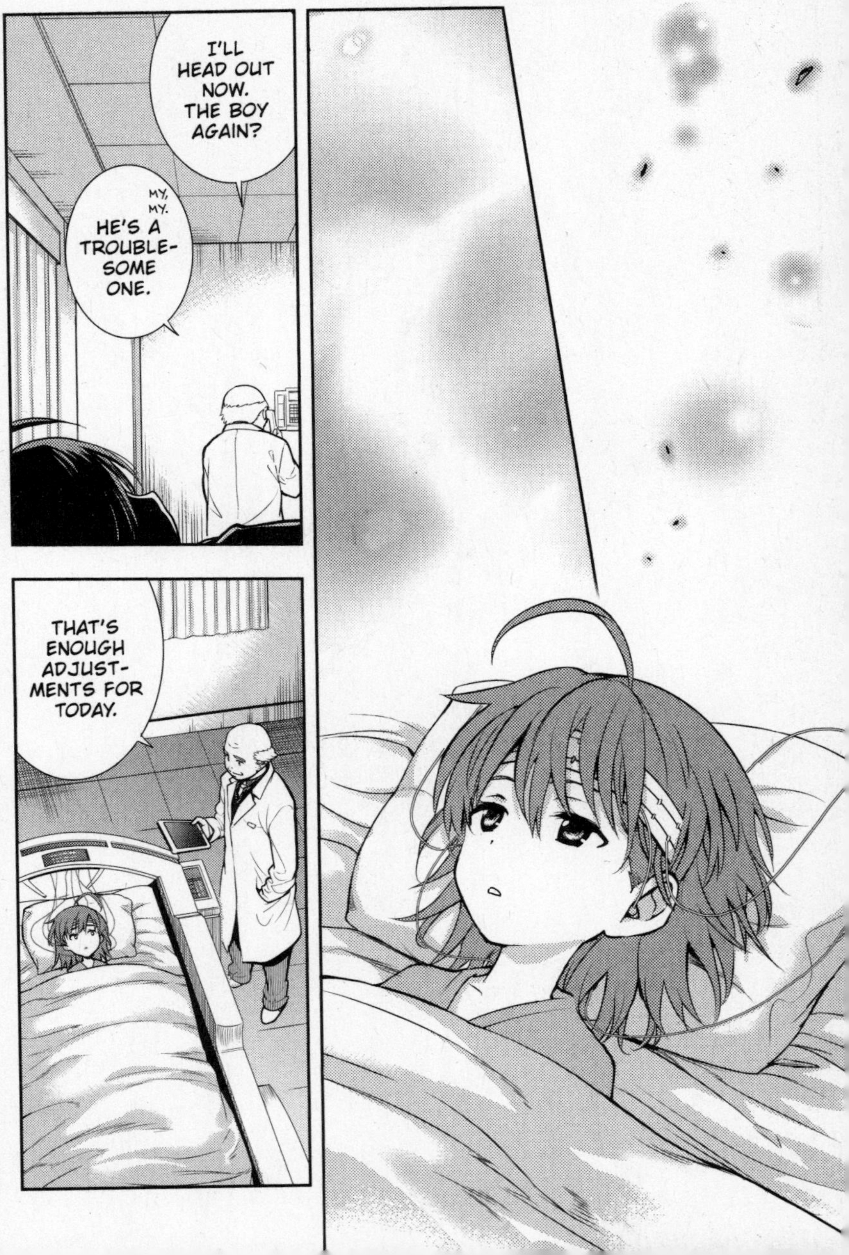
I'LL HEAD OUT NOW. THE BOY AGAIN?
MY, MY.
HE'S A TROUBLE-SOME ONE.
THAT'S ENOUGH ADJUST-MENTS FOR TODAY.

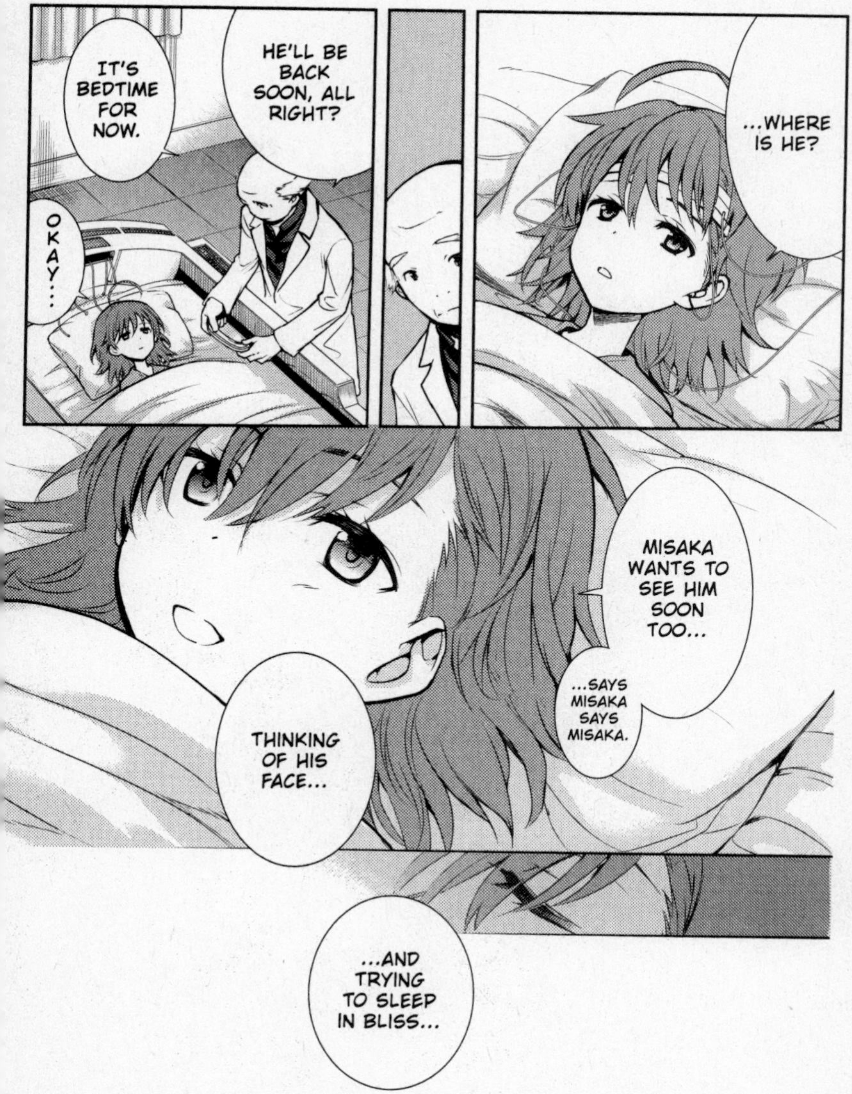
...WHERE IS HE?
HE'LL BE BACK SOON, ALL RIGHT?
IT'S BEDTIME FOR NOW.
OKAY...
MISAKA WANTS TO SEE HIM SOON TOO...
...SAYS MISAKA SAYS MISAKA.
THINKING OF HIS FACE...
...AND TRYING TO SLEEP IN BLISS...

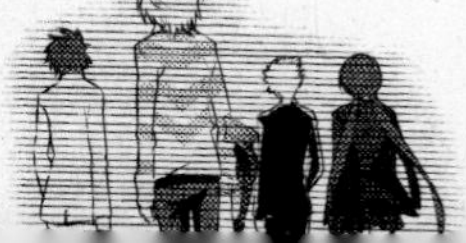

A CERTAIN MAGICAL INDEX 20 END

A Certain Magical Index

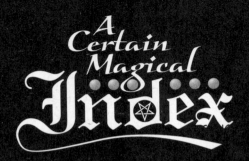

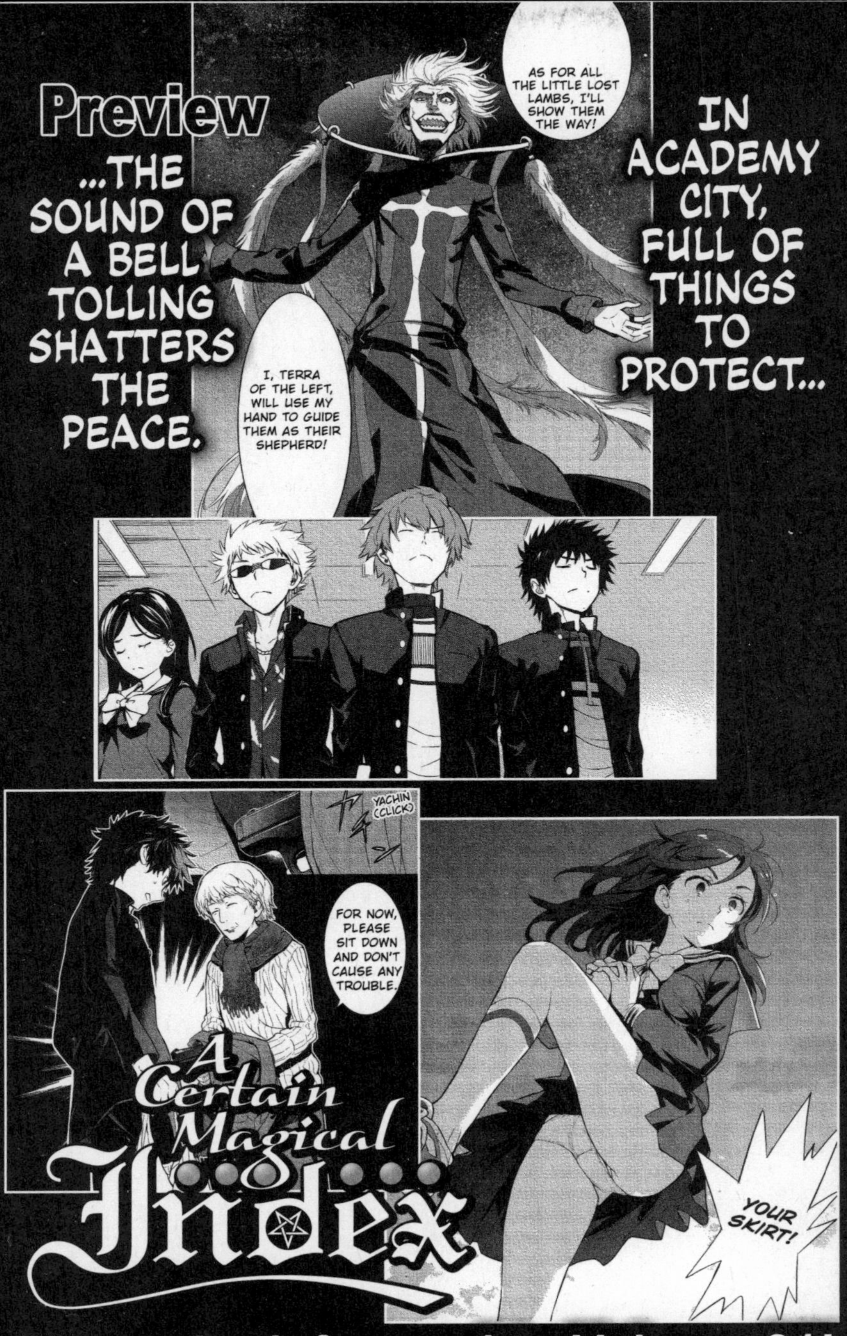
Preview
IN ACADEMY CITY, FULL OF THINGS TO PROTECT...
AS FOR ALL THE LITTLE LOST LAMBS, I'LL SHOW THEM THE WAY!
I, TERRA OF THE LEFT, WILL USE MY HAND TO GUIDE THEM AS THEIR SHEPHERD!
...THE SOUND OF A BELL TOLLING SHATTERS THE PEACE.
YOUR SKIRT!
YACHIN (CLICK)
FOR NOW, PLEASE SIT DOWN AND DON'T CAUSE ANY TROUBLE.
A Certain Magical Index

Please look forward to Volume 21!

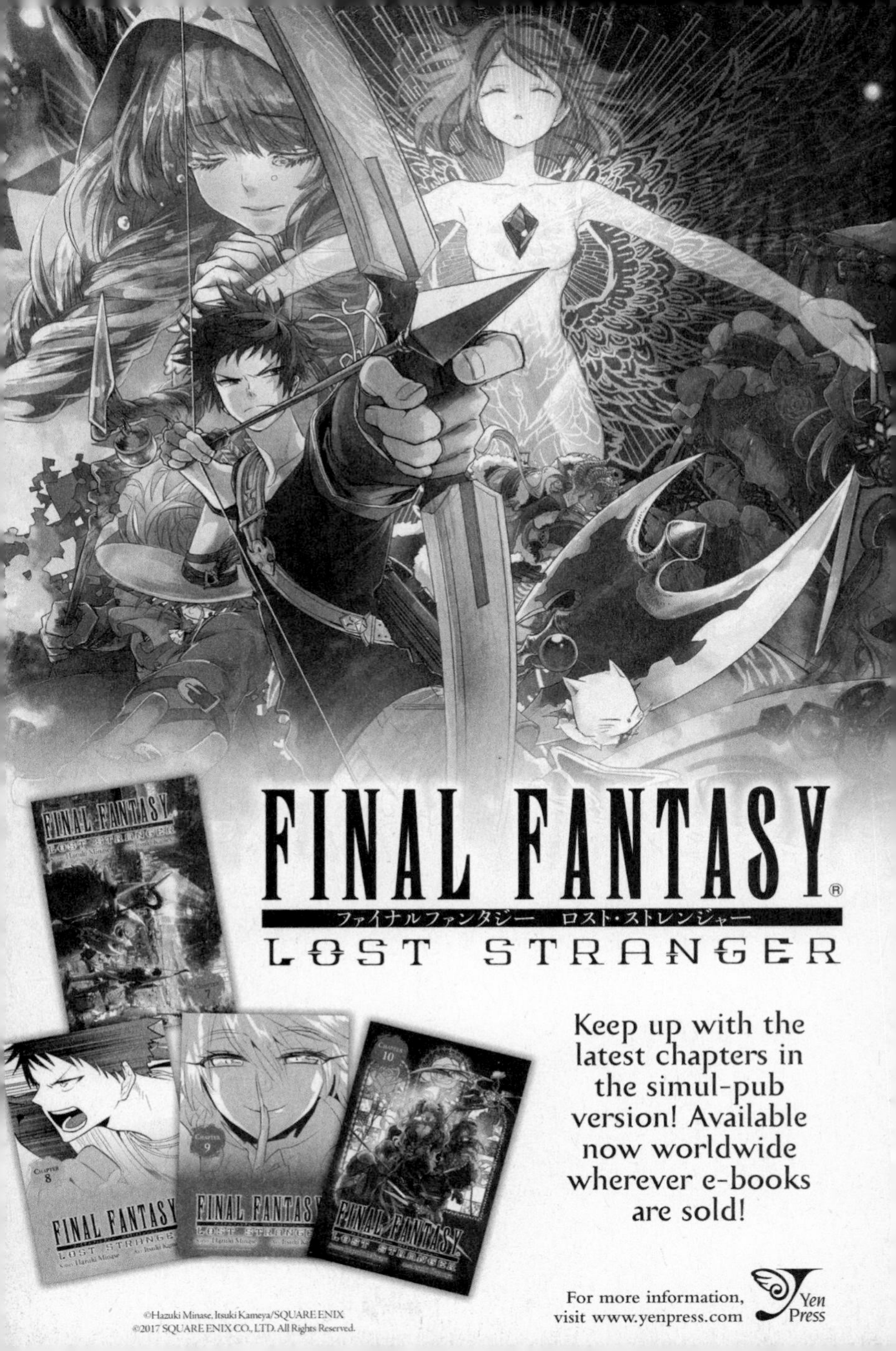
FINAL FANTASY®
ファイナルファンタジー　ロスト・ストレンジャー
LOST STRANGER
Keep up with the latest chapters in the simul-pub version! Available now worldwide wherever e-books are sold!
For more information, visit www.yenpress.com
Yen Press
©Hazuki Minase, Itsuki Kameya/SQUARE ENIX
©2017 SQUARE ENIX CO., LTD. All Rights Reserved.

IN THIS FANTASY WORLD, EVERYTHING'S A GAME—AND THESE SIBLINGS PLAY TO WIN!

A genius but socially inept brother and sister duo is offered the chance to compete in a fantasy world where games decide everything. Sora and Shiro will take on the world and, while they're at it, create a harem of nonhuman companions!

No Game No Life ©Yuu Kamiya 2012 Illustration: Yuu Kamiya
KADOKAWA CORPORATION

No Game No Life, Please! © Kazuya Yuizaki 2016 © Yuu Kamiya 2016
KADOKAWA CORPORATION

LIGHT NOVELS 1–8 AVAILABLE NOW

LIKE THE NOVELS?

Check out the spin-off manga for even more out-of-control adventures with the Werebeast girl, Izuna!

ENJOY EVERYTHING.

YOU SHOULD COME PLAY WITH YOTSUBA TOO!

Join Yotsuba as she delights in the
things many of us take for granted in
this Eisner-nominated series.

VOLUMES 1-12
AVAILABLE NOW!

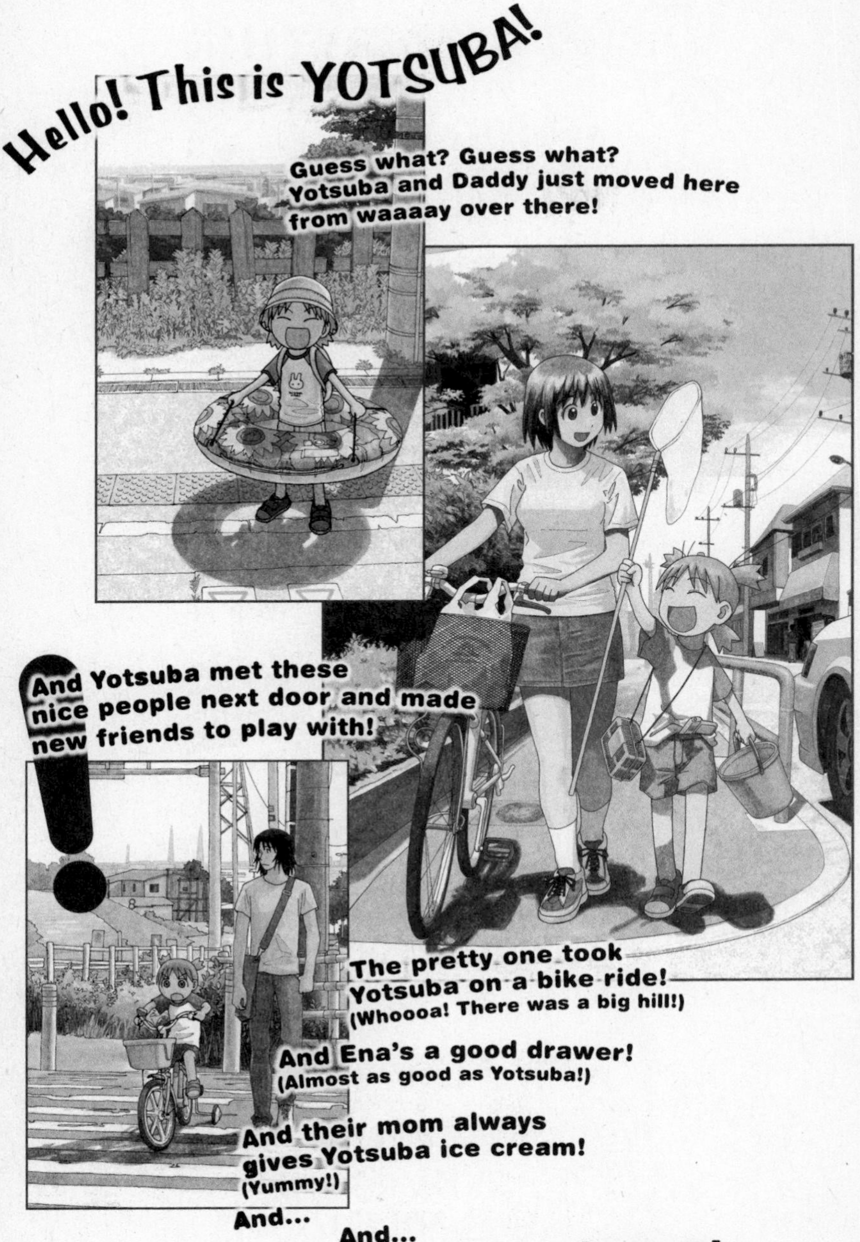
Hello! This is YOTSUBA!
Guess what? Guess what? Yotsuba and Daddy just moved here from waaaay over there!
And Yotsuba met these nice people next door and made new friends to play with!
The pretty one took Yotsuba on a bike ride! (Whoooa! There was a big hill!)
And Ena's a good drawer! (Almost as good as Yotsuba!)
And their mom always gives Yotsuba ice cream! (Yummy!)
And...
And...
OHHHH!

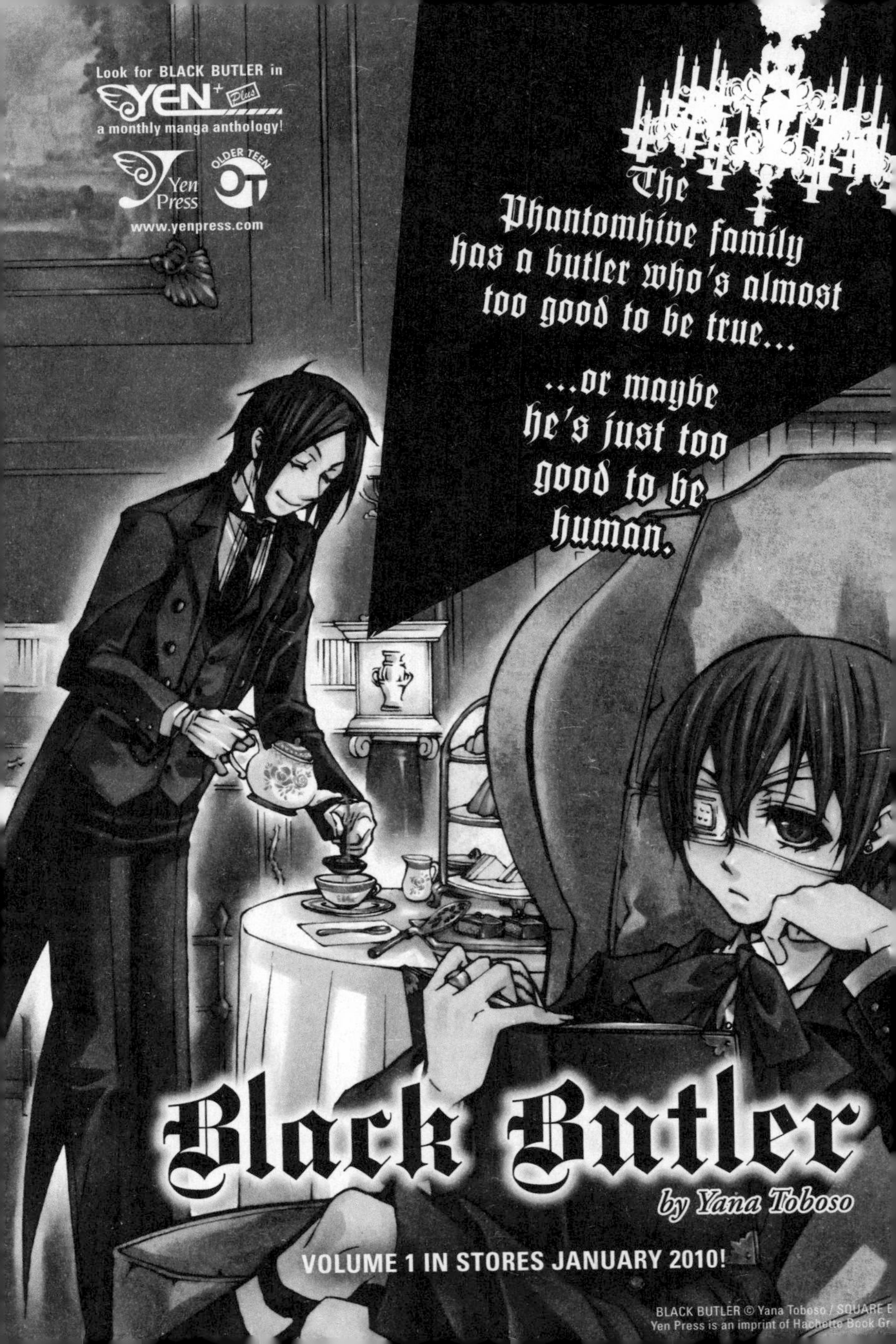

Look for BLACK BUTLER in
YEN+ Plus
a monthly manga anthology!
Yen Press
OLDER TEEN OT
www.yenpress.com
The Phantomhive family has a butler who's almost too good to be true...
...or maybe he's just too good to be human.
Black Butler
by Yana Toboso
VOLUME 1 IN STORES JANUARY 2010!
BLACK BUTLER © Yana Toboso / SQUARE E
Yen Press is an imprint of Hachette Book Gr

PRESENTING THE LATEST SERIES FROM

JUN MOCHIZUKI

THE CASE STUDY OF VANITAS

JUN MOCHIZUKI
THE CASE STUDY OF
VANITAS

**READ THE CHAPTERS AT
THE SAME TIME AS JAPAN!**

**AVAILABLE NOW WORLDWIDE
WHEREVER E-BOOKS ARE SOLD!**

www.yenpress.com

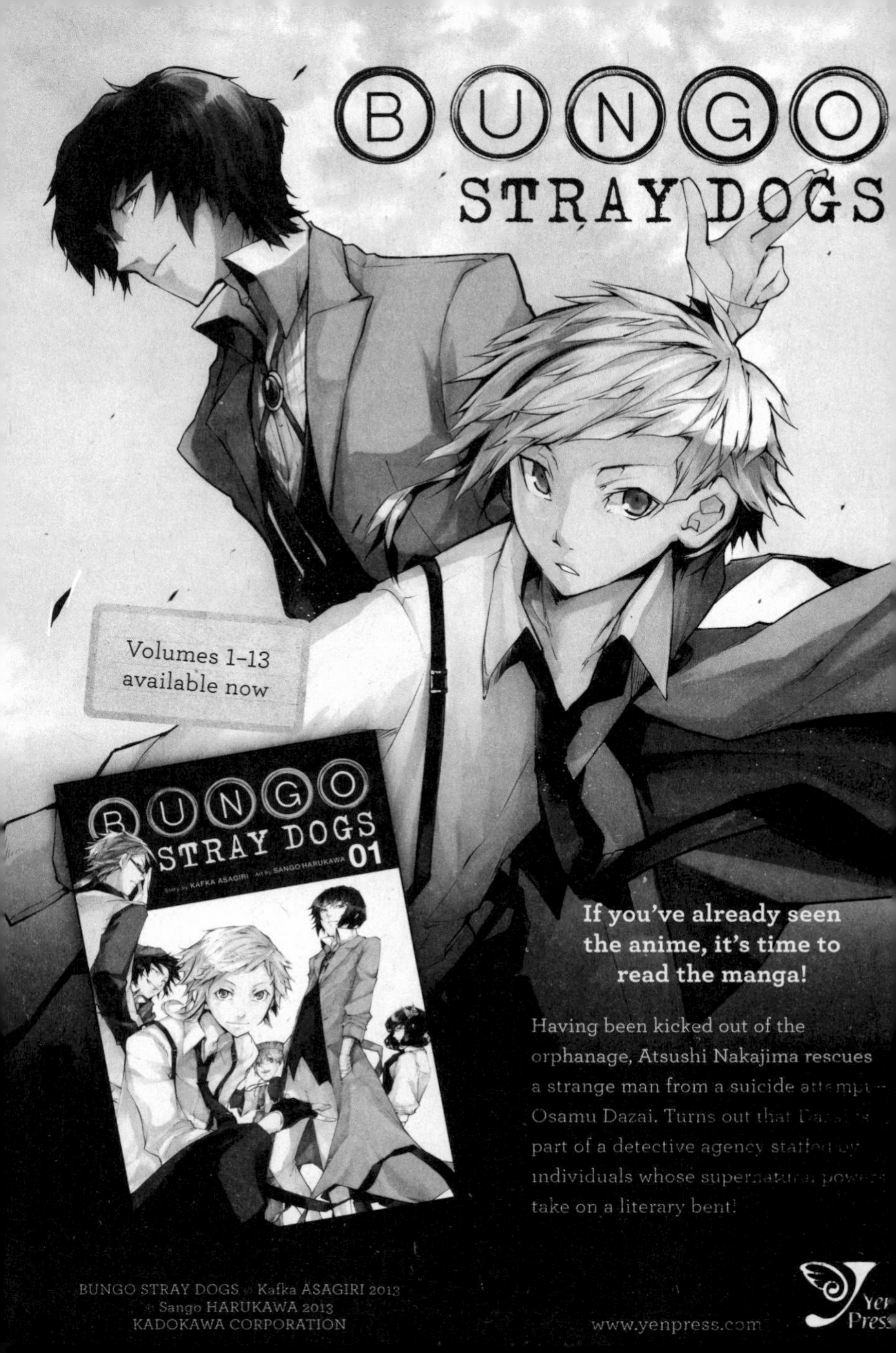
BUNGO
STRAY DOGS
Volumes 1–13
available now
BUNGO
STRAY DOGS
01
Story by KAFKA ASAGIRI Art by SANGO HARUKAWA
If you've already seen
the anime, it's time to
read the manga!
Having been kicked out of the orphanage, Atsushi Nakajima rescues a strange man from a suicide attempt— Osamu Dazai. Turns out that Dazai is part of a detective agency staffed by individuals whose supernatural powers take on a literary bent!
BUNGO STRAY DOGS © Kafka ASAGIRI 2013
© Sango HARUKAWA 2013
KADOKAWA CORPORATION
www.yenpress.com
Yen Press

AL INDEX ⓴

Kazuma Kamachi
Kiyotaka Haimura
Chuya Kogino

Translation: Andrew Prowse

Lettering: Phil Christie

This book is a work of fiction. Names, characters, places, and incidents are the product of the author's imagination or are used fictitiously. Any resemblance to actual events, locales, or persons, living or dead, is coincidental.

TOARU MAJYUTSU NO INDEX Vol. 20
© 2018 Kazuma Kamachi
© 2018 Chuya Kogino / SQUARE ENIX CO., LTD.
Licensed by KADOKAWA CORPORATION ASCII MEDIA WORKS
First published in Japan in 2017 by SQUARE ENIX CO., LTD.
English translation rights arranged with SQUARE ENIX CO., LTD.
and Yen Press, LLC through Tuttle-Mori Agency, Inc.

English translation © 2020 by SQUARE ENIX CO., LTD.

Yen Press
150 West 30th Street, 19th Floor
New York, NY 10001

Visit us at yenpress.com
facebook.com/yenpress
twitter.com/yenpress
yenpress.tumblr.com
instagram.com/yenpress

First Yen Press Edition: January 2020

Yen Press is an imprint of Yen Press, LLC.
The Yen Press name and logo are trademarks of Yen Press, LLC.

The publisher is not responsible for websites (or their content) that are not owned by the publisher.

Library of Congress Control Number: 2015373809

ISBN: 978-1-9753-3197-9 (paperback)

10 9 8 7 6 5 4 3 2 1

WOR

Printed in the United States of America